CAMBRIDGESHIRE RECORDS SOCIETY

(formerly Cambridge Antiquarian Records Society)

VOLUME 19

CAMBRIDGE AT WAR

THE DIARY OF JACK OVERHILL
1939-1945

Edited by
Peter Searby

CAMBRIDGE 2010

Jack Overhill, c. 1946, aged 43.
Ramsey and Muspratt.

CAMBRIDGE AT WAR

THE DIARY OF JACK OVERHILL
1939-1945

Edited by
Peter Searby

Cambridgeshire Records Society

Volume 19

2010

Published by the Cambridgeshire Records Society

County Record Office, Shire Hall, Cambridge CB3 0AP

Diary text © Estate of the diarist Jack Overhill 2010

Introduction and editorial matter
© Cambridgeshire Records Society 2010

British Library Cataloguing in Publication Data

A catalogue record for this book
is available from the British Library

ISBN 978-0-904323-21-4

Printed in Great Britain by the MPG Books Group,
Bodmin and King's Lynn

To the memory of my father

Arthur Searby 1905–1951

Contents

List of illustrations — xii
List of maps — xiii

Foreword — xv

Introduction — xvii
  The Cambridge of Jack Overhill's youth:
    a Tale of Two Cities — xviii
    Jack Overhill's early life — xxiii
    Jack Overhill: author — xxx
    Jack Overhill: swimmer — xxxix
    Pacifism and political objections to the anti-Nazi war — xli
    Editorial principles — xlvii
    A note on the British currency and monetary values — xlvii

The diary
  1939 — 1
  1940 — 21
  1941 — 69
  1942 — 137
  1943 — 201
  1944 — 253
  1945 — 295

Epilogue — 331

Index — 333

List of Illustrations

Jack Overhill, *c.* 1946, aged 43 (Ramsey & Muspratt)   *frontispiece*

	page
E.T.O. with his grandchildren, Jack and Jess, and Collie and Floss, 1928	xxix
Jack, Jess, and their children, Jack and Jess, with Collie and Floss, Grantchester, 1932	xxix
Saxon Street. (Cambridgeshire Collection B.Saxo. K3. 31117)	xxxvi
The men's swimming place on the Cam (Cambridgeshire Collection K.P. K4. 28715)	xxxvi
Evacuees arriving at Cambridge from London in late August 1939 (Cambridgeshire Collection S.1939 20144)	2
Children receiving gas mask instruction in Ramsden Square, August 1939 (Cambridgeshire Collection S.199 11463)	2
Poster recruiting for National Service, 1939 (Cambridge University Library: War posters)	11
Poster recruiting for the Territorial Army, 1939 (Cambridge University Library: War posters)	19
Cambridge Police headquarters in St Andrew's Street protected by sandbags, late 1939 (Cambridgeshire Collection, S.1939 44281, photographer A. L. Brunney of A. M. R. Photographers)	20
One of the entrances to Cambridge's Public Air Raid Shelter no. 1 (Cambridgeshire Collection S.1939 11690)	20
Local Defence Volunteers drilling on Cambridge Town Football Club ground, 1940 (Cambridgeshire Collection T.G. K40 21814)	20
Jack junior diving from the top of a tree, 21 July 1943	39
Children at Milton Road Junior School with pots and pans collected for scrap metal (Cambridgeshire Collection S.1940 21816, *Cambridge Daily News*, 11 July 1940)	68
Railings at Emmanuel College being removed for scrap metal (Cambridgeshire Collection S.1940 21815. *Cambridge Daily News*, 9 July 1940)	68
Houses in Great Eastern Street damaged in an air-raid on 28 August 1941 (Cambridgeshire Collection S.1941 28194)	79

Hurricane crash at Bene't Place, 27 September 1941
 (Cambridgeshire Collection S.1941 43390, *Cambridge
 Daily News*, 27 September 1941) 136
Tea to celebrate VE day in Hobart Road, May 1945
 (Cambridgeshire Collection S.1945 7620) 307
Children gathered outside St Andrew's church hall,
 Chesterton, to celebrate VJ day, August 1945
 (Cambridgeshire Collection S.1945 45061) 307
Jess Overhill and her daugher Jess, January 1946 330

The society acknowledges with gratitude the help of Chris Jakes in supplying the illustrations from the Cambridgeshire Collection which are listed here. It is also grateful to the Syndics of Cambridge Universith Library for permission to reproduce the images of the war posters on pages 11 and 19. Images not otherwise credited were kindly supplied by the Overhill family.

List of Maps

Newtown, the commons and the river Cam, *c*. 1900   l
Central Cambridge *c*.1940   li
 Both maps were drawn by Ian Agnew.

Foreword

Few books can be completed without the help of friends, and Jack Overhill's diary would not have reached publication without the support which others have given me. In February 2005 Chris Jakes, the Librarian of the Cambridgeshire Collection at the County Library, drew my attention to the 25 typescript volumes of Jack Overhill's diary, extending from 1932 when he was 29 until shortly before his death in 1989, aged 86. In my editing of the diary's war years, 1939-45, Chris has been a constant guide and help—easing access to the typescript and answering queries about that remote world, Cambridge during the Second World War.

The editor's task was complicated by the closure for reconstruction of the main library, including its reference section and the Cambridgeshire Collection, in February 2007—its reopening then being expected in the spring of 2008; at the time of writing (August 2009) it is predicted to occur in October 2009. A reference library should not be closed for thirty months, whatever the economic imperatives; it has been a surprising action by a library service normally very concerned to meet the wishes of Cambridge readers. During the closure a partial replacement for the Cambridgeshire Collection was set up in Milton Road library, and I should like to thank the staff there warmly for their help during the constricted service; they greatly eased the editor's task.

The diarist's son, Jack junior, welcomed the proposal for this edition and allowed me to include the material I chose; such generosity is very rare in like circumstances. He also lent me his copy of the diarist's unpublished autobiography. In our frequent conversations he and his wife Jill freely discussed with me the manifold and sometimes refractory character of Jack senior, and added depth and subtlety to the impression of his personality that I had gained from his writing. They helped me to understand him a little more. Jack and Jill Overhill were looking forward eagerly to the publication of this volume, and the prospect cheered Jack in his declining years.

Sadly, he died in January 2008 aged 80, one of the last of the persons mentioned in his father's war diary. Tony Cowley, a close friend of the diarist, gave me a recording of *A Regular Snob*, a lasting remembrance, in Jack Overhill's measured and deliberate bass voice, of life and endurance in a long-vanished Cambridge, where as a child he trapped sparrows to add nourishment to the household's diet.

The committee of the Cambridge Records Society welcomed my proposal for this volume and have encouraged me during the editorial task. That is especially true of the editors Rosemary Horrox and Elisabeth Leedham-Green. They showed patience over my revisions of the Introduction following second thoughts some months after its initial submission, and their labours turning the discs into print are responsible in large measure for the quality of this edition. I take this opportunity to thank them warmly.

At an early stage in the editorial process I discussed my plans with my old friend John Pickles. He read many drafts, commented on the scope and nature of the text being constructed, and offered advice on using the on-line version of the 1901 census—for example discovering that among the many mistakes in transcription 'Overhill' appears as 'Overall' and 'Saxon Street' as 'Savon Street'. His counsel is responsible for much that is of value in the following pages.

Not least am I grateful to my wife Norma for our detailed discussion of the work in progress and the elusive character of Jack Overhill the diarist. She has welcomed his intrusion on our hearth in the last four years, but I think she will hope that this publication will persuade him to depart.

Peter Searby, August 2009

Introduction:

Jack Overhill, his life, his diary, and his ideas

In 1932 Jack Overhill (1903-89), a lifelong resident of Cambridge and successively a bookmaker and a shoe-repairer, began to keep a diary; it was only one of the many pieces of writing to which he devoted much of his leisure. As always with his compositions there was no manuscript stage; an expert typist, he typed the diary at speed, making many fewer alterations than he did in some of his novels. He kept copies of his other works, but not of his diary pages though he valued them perhaps above all others.[1]

Jack continued his diary until shortly before his death in 1989 at the age of 86. With some omissions of days and months the diary is a continuous and unique record, in twenty-five volumes, of fifty-seven years in the life of an active and eccentric member of the Cambridge working class. At over 3,000,000 words it is probably the longest diary ever written in the city — certainly outside the university and maybe even including it. Its contents are very varied in incident and sentiment, detailing (at all events during 1939–45) Jack's working and family life, his political opinions as a conscientious objector, his ceaseless writing, his intensive study for a London External degree, his swimming and dog-walking; and also the wartime scene in Cambridge—shortages and rationing, the many air-raids, the presence of many soldiers and their intrusive and sometimes ribald conduct. Such passages attest to Jack's acute reporting skills, while other entries strikingly reflect a contrasting side of Jack's personality, his meditativeness, so much at variance with his daily outpouring of energy: a tree or a tune will at times remind him of events twenty or thirty years previously, and he is lost in sad and pleasing reminiscence.

---

[1] After Jack's death his son, also called Jack, gave his father's diary and other writings to the Cambridgeshire Collection in the County Library in Cambridge.

The Cambridge of Jack Overhill's youth: a Tale of Two Cities

In 1907 *Cambridge* was published by Adam and Charles Black in their Twenty Shilling series containing many volumes on towns appealing to tourists; its author was Mildred Tuker, a graduate of Newnham.[2] The most striking and attractive feature of *Cambridge* was its reproduction of seventy-seven watercolours by William Matthison, a professional artist from Oxford. All except two of the plates (Grantchester mill and Madingley windmill) are scenes of colleges, or places prominent in graduates' memories or reminding them that the university was nearby; thus in the painting of the old Addenbrooke's Hospital a don in cap and gown walks across an empty and leafy Trumpington Street, while two infants splash in a puddle. The volume, a triumph of colour printing to be unequalled until advances in technology in the 1960s, emphasises in its romantic and roseate illustrations the beauties of university Cambridge. Matthison, declared the *Cambridge Daily News*, 'selected the daintiest spots in a town famous for its architectural beauty …'. He ignored the cramped, insanitary and poverty-stricken courts to be found huddled within the ancient town, like for example Falcon Yard off Petty Cury; he ignored too the substantial middle-class property constructed near the colleges in Victorian times, for instance in Jesus Lane. He gave readers an image of Cambridge as an essentially pre-modern city, perhaps even a medieval one: the image of Cambridge which many possess still.

But another Cambridge was built in Victorian times on the erstwhile open fields of the parish of St Andrew the Less which were enclosed in the early nineteenth century: land stretching from the river north of Newmarket Road to Trumpington Road in the south was built upon, apart from Parker's Piece, Midsummer Common and the thirty-eight acres of the new Botanic Garden. Bricks and mortar marched steadily along Hills Road to just beyond the railway (which reached Cambridge in 1845), while Mill Road was developed from the

---

[2] For what follows I have drawn upon, besides Mildred Tuker's volume itself, the essays in Mike Petty, Sarah Woodall and Colin Inman (eds), *Cambridge: Memories of Times Past* (2007).

corner of Parker's Piece to Romsey Town one mile away;[3] in a small terraced house in Romsey Town Jack Overhill was born in 1903. By then the 'new Cambridge' comprised houses, most modest and a few grand, for gradations within the working and middle classes.

Among the first land to be built on after enclosure was near the western end of what is now Lensfield Road, at the junction with Trumpington Street; here that inveterate sportsman Henry Gunning of Christ's College went shooting for snipe on marshy terrain in the 1780s, and a few decades later this was the area of working-class housing known as New Town.[4] After moving in 1908 Jack spent much of his life there in Gothic and Saxon Streets. The enumerator's book in the 1901 census for St Paul's parish tells us the social composition of the two streets a few years before the Overhills' residence: occupations listed include engine-driver, carpenter, painter, cab-driver, coachman, bootmaker, shop assistant, laundress, dressmaker, gardener and labourer; university servants ranging from bedmaker to 'carver in college hall' formed a large group—reminding us that Old Cambridge was present in theNew.[5] The occupants of these streets were typical of much in the eastern growth of Cambridge in their hard lives and frequent poverty: one of Eglantyne Jebb's purposes in the perceptive study she composed as Matthison was painting a verdant Cambridge was to confute the popular belief that there was 'a large leisured class in Cambridge and comparatively little poverty'.[6]

Middle-class properties in the 'new Cambridge' were in the minority; the most striking were large houses of four or five storeys in Brookside, paradoxically, a few yards away from

[3] Peter Bryan, *Cambridge: The Shaping of the City* (2nd edn, Cambridge, 2008) pp. 102–20.

[4] Peter Bryan and Nick Wise, 'Cambridge New Town: a Victorian microcosm', *Proceedings of the Cambridge Antiquarian Society*, 94 (2005), 199-276. The name is now often spelled Newtown.

[5] T[he] N[ational] A[rchives]: Enumerator's Book, 1901 Census, Cambridge, St Paul's Parish: RG. 13/1531, pp. 12, 13, 19, 20, 21.

[6] Eglantyne Jebb, *Cambridge: A Brief Study in Social Questions* (1906), p. 31. Jebb went on to found the Save the Children Fund; she was the niece of the Regius Professor of Greek, Sir Richard Jebb.

the Overhills and their neighbours. Brookside, where stately trees stood next to Hobson's Brook, was in Edwardian times one of the very few places in the eastern extension of the city where a dainty scene might have been painted. Tenants listed in Brookside in the 1901 census included Francis Jenkinson the University Librarian, a fellow of Gonville and Caius, two Anglican clergymen and two solicitors; in addition there were a farmer, an insurance agent, a grocer and a miniaturist, and also nine widows and single women, three under sixty and six over that age, 'living on their own means'. Two Brooksiders had one resident servant each, but most had two or three.[7]

Between the inhabitants of Brookside and their neighbours in Gothic Street — and their like in other parts of the city — a gulf was fixed, in social class, income, education and above all in what they expected from life. We may put matters succinctly by stating that the people of Gothic Street belonged to the servant classes and Brooksiders to the servant-employing class. For example, in 16 Gothic Street lived the painter Harry Constable and his wife Kate and their son and two daughters, who with Harry's brother and a boarder were crammed into two rooms downstairs and two bedrooms: while in 7 Brookside, a much larger house which happened to be Holy Trinity vicarage, lived the Revd Charles Proctor and his wife, three female servants and a footman.

A gulf yawned between working-class families and members of the university — both undergraduates and senior members. In Edwardian England members of the university were drawn markedly from the prosperous middle and professional classes, most of whom had attended independent schools like the Perse in Cambridge, or 'public' boarding schools of which the best-known was Eton. There was only a handful of undergraduates from backgrounds like Jack Overhill's: schools like the Perse offered scholarships, but they were very few, and elementary schools rarely offered the tuition needed to win them. The university offered scholarships too, but again they were few, and pupils competing for them had to stay at

---

[7] TNA: RG. 13/1531, pp. 22, 23, 24, 25. In 1913 there were in Brookside eight college fellows and other senior members of the university: W. P. Spalding, *Street and General Directory of Cambridge* (1913), p. 69.

school until eighteen. Young men aspiring to Cambridge thus had to be supported for four or five years after the leaving age in elementary schools—an unthinkable burden for most working-class families. By the Second World War the path to Cambridge was made easier by the setting up of hundreds of State grammar-schools with free tuition and excellent sixth forms—a process that had been called 'the Silent Social Revolution' (the title of a book by G. A. N. Lowndes).[8] The local State grammar-school, the Cambridgeshire High School for Boys, was founded in 1900; the diary tells us of one pupil, a friend of the Overhills, who won a scholarship to Trinity in 1941. Forty years before, such an achievement was rare indeed, and for boys like Jack Overhill Cambridge University was not a destination they could aspire to: it was beyond their imagination, and—as 'No Mother Love', Jack's autobiography, shows—its undergraduates were aliens to be taunted from a safe distance.

In the Victorian age Cambridge was in some ways a typical English market town. It was academically distinctive, but it had also for centuries been a commercial centre for the surrounding countryside, particularly its agriculture; the cattle market, traditionally held in the Market Place, was moved to Pound Hill (on the Chesterton side of the river) in 1842, and in 1885 to a much larger location at the junction of Hills Road and Cherry Hinton Road, near the railway station and convenient for the transport of cattle. The line from London reached Cambridge in 1845, and was an agent of rapid change, stimulating the growth of building in the eastern extension and ending the customary use of the river as a means of transport. It stimulated the growth of industry, and immigration to the city too by families (like the Overhills) wishing to grasp its economic opportunities.

Eglantyne Jebb, writing in 1906, stressed that Cambridge was a much more industrial town than it was often considered: there was the large printing works of Cambridge Uni-

---

[8] The themes which follow are touched on in two volumes in *A History of the University of Cambridge*, vol. 3, 1750–1870, Peter Searby (Cambridge, 1997), pp. 74–6; and vol. 4, 1870–1990, Christopher Brooke, (Cambridge, 1993), pp. 240–52.

versity Press, and also cement works, flour mills, gasworks, an electric power station and steam laundries, and establishments, large and small, making everything from bricks to sausages; many were located in the 'new Cambridge' to the east, which experienced most of the increase in population between 1801 and 1901, from 9,000 to 38,000.[9] The outlying district of Chesterton had also been urbanised, and when it and some other areas were included in the borough in 1912 Cambridge's population was 55,000. It was a modern town with modern problems.

As in many other towns, Victorian growth aggravated problems which had been ignored for centuries, notably the existence of a main sewer outfall into the Cam. A college squib of 1860 suggested that undergraduates might as a Long Vacation diversion 'through a rank sewer drive a frail canoe'. In 1895 the Town Council carried through a wide-ranging sewrage scheme which ended the nuisance.[10] The city was large enough to warrant public transport, and in 1880 a horse tramway system was opened; one line went from the northern end of St Andrew's Street to the railway station, and another from the Senate House to the far end of East Road. Trundling along, the trams were easily outpaced by the bicycles, ideal transport for Cambridge, which were seen in numbers after the invention of the safety bicycle and the pneumatic tyre in the 1880s. The horse trams were also of course much slower than motor buses, introduced in the city in 1907; the tramway ended in February 1914.[11]

In the quarter century from 1914 to the beginning of the Second World War the city expanded further with the inclusion within its boundaries in 1935 of Newnham, Cherry Hinton and Trumpington, and villages to the north such as Girton and Fen Ditton; while the built-up area grew also on the northern, eastern and southern sides. This growth consisted, besides

---

[9] Jebb, *Cambridge: A Brief Study*, pp. 45–6.
[10] *The Victoria History of Cambridgeshire and the Isle of Ely*, III, The City and University of Cambridge (1959), p. 105, including the quotation.
[11] Mike Petty, 'Cambridge 1907', in *Cambridge: Memories of Times Past*, pp. 4-5; J. A. Charles, *One Man's Cambridge: The Life and Times of J. H. V. Charles* (2006), pp. 50–1, 66–7.

some council houses for rent, largely of semi-detached houses which were bought by members of the lower-middle class.[12] That is where a sociologist would have placed Jack Overhill (though Jack would have indignantly described himself as 'a worker') when in 1931 he moved with his young family to a semi-detached house in Trumpington.

Jack Overhill's early life

Jack Overhill's parents, Ellington and Eliza, came from Haverhill (Suffolk), as had their immediate ancestors. In 1895, when Ellington (often called E.T.O.) was 32 and Eliza 28, they moved to Cambridge.[13] In the course of the next twelve years they occupied a succession of modest houses in East Road and Romsey Town. Perhaps debt explains their moves. Life was certainly hard. They had thirteen children, two of whom died in infancy; Jack, the third youngest, was born in 1903 in a four-roomed house in Thoday Street, near the south-eastern end of Mill Road. Moves quickly followed to two houses nearby, and then in 1908 to another in Gothic Street, dating from the 1830s, more than a mile away from Thoday Street, between Panton Street and the Trumpington Road, in Newtown (or 'New Town'). Executive housing now occupies the area, an irony that would not have been lost on Jack Overhill.

At about the same time as the move to Gothic Street — that is, when Jack was five — his father and mother separated in bitterness. E.T.O. accused his wife of giving birth to another man's child: an absurd paranoid fantasy, we were told by the diarist's son, typical of the many he muttered throughout life. The parents were never reconciled. Four boys, including Jack, went to live with their father, and the girls with their mother.[14] The split distressed Jack permanently; his autobiography is entitled 'No Mother Love'. Jack was torn between his two parents and felt guilty about it; though strictly forbidden to visit his mother he did so, in secret, and while still an infant

---

[12] Bryan, *Cambridge: The Shaping of the City*, pp. 126–31.

[13] Most details of Jack Overhill's life are taken from his typescript autobiography, 'No Mother Love' [NML]. There is a copy in the Cambridgeshire Collection.

[14] There was a fifth boy, Tom, born in 1889; he lived elsewhere.

stole out to live with her for five or six weeks, only to return to Gothic Street again because he missed his father.

Jack's father was usually aloof and unclubbable and often truculent, though he was capable of many acts of kindness too. Highly respectable, he abjured debt, gambling, dirt and the pawnshop, and he angrily refused charity; he was a member of the Oddfellows' Society, that touchstone of Victorian rectitude, and its payments of 10s a week tided him over times of slack work.[15] A radical, he hated the royal family, clergymen and the boy scouts movement, which he thought was a scheme to recruit soldiers. Set apart from others by being illiterate, he was a considerate though sometimes a perverse father; in character Jack owed something to him, while drawing from a wide gene-pool and possessing much that was uniquely his and made him sharply different from his siblings. He was more talented than they were, and when he was seven was given the task of bringing his father's knowledge of the world up to date by reading *Reynolds News* to him every Sunday.[16] Unlike his easygoing brothers and sisters Jack throughout life was exceptionally combative and driven by powerful ambition. He disliked his male kin's fondness for beer and was always a teetotaller, and knowing that smoking damaged one's wind and was harmful to swimmers he kept away from tobacco.

Jack's father was an outworker, in the army of marginal labour ground down by their struggle with the machine. We tend to think of such men and women as handloom weavers in South Lancashire during the reign of George IV. Nevertheless, in Cambridge during the reign of Edward VII E.T.O. made boots in his workshop at home for Bretts, a high-class shop in Trinity Street, being paid 5s 9d for a pair of men's boots and 5s 3d for women's. An expert craftsman—using waxed thread he could make sixteen stitches to the inch in

---

[15] For the converson of pre-decimal coinage see the note at the end of the Introduction.

[16] *Reynolds Weekly Newspaper* was founded in 1850 and appeared on Sundays. It had several changes of title and when it closed in 1967 was known as the *Sunday Citizen*. It appealed to a mass readership, combining political radicalism and sensationalist news coverage.

leather[17] — he was finding it ever harder to make a living as he battled the machines of Northampton, especially as he slowed down in his 40s. Able to make a pair of boots each day as a young man — say six a week — he could only manage three or four a week when in Gothic Street, and in 1914 he lost his cherished status as a bootmaker when the bankruptcy of his employers forced him to become a mere boot-repairer. From a gross income of 15s or £1 a week, he paid 5s for rent and coals. Meagre amounts of meat provided two cooked meals a week, while young Jack trapped sparrows to thicken gravy, among the trees by Hobson's Brook, near the grand houses of Brookside where dons resided. Most meals consisted of bread and butter and a small piece of American cheese costing 8*d* a pound in the Home and Colonial Stores in Petty Cury.

The house in Gothic Street was crowded; father and sons shared the two bedrooms, and the bootmaker's workshop was the kitchen. In about 1913 the family was given notice to quit (E.T.O. did not know why) and they moved to a larger house of the 1830s a few yards away from Gothic Street — 7 Saxon Street, whose rent was rather more, at 5*s* 6*d* a week. One way and another the house in Saxon Street was occupied by the Overhill family for over forty years, and they were the last to inhabit it before its replacement with much grander property after the Second World War. It stood a few feet away from the Spread Eagle and Cross Keys public houses, which still stand. The revelry of soldiers and camp followers within the pubs is often angrily mentioned in Jack's wartime diary.

Jack was a pupil at elementary schools in Russell Street and, after his father's inevitable quarrel with the headmaster, in East Road. His ability stood out. In 1914 he won a place (his fees were remitted) at the Higher Grade School, which offered more advanced studies than the run of elementary schools. It was in a state of the art building in Melbourne Place, and its pupils were expected to leave at fifteen, one year later than

---

[17] So I was informed by Jack Overhill junior.

the minimum at other Cambridge elementary schools.[18] (The building now houses Parkside Community College.) His father, both envious and resentful of such opportunities, agreed to Jack's attending the Higher Grade School, but declared that Jack would leave earlier than fifteen. 'Fourteen's long enough. … I can take you away at fourteen if I like, there's nothing to stop me.'[19] So Jack left the Higher Grade School in 1917 two days before his fourteenth birthday, and began to work with his father as a shoe-repairer. He became adept, though he found that he had no liking for the trade.[20]

Jack became one of the many young men and women in Victorian times and later—indeed at least until the changes following the 1944 Education Act—who realised that their schooling had not gone far enough for what they wanted to do in life; through formal instruction and self-education too they laboured to gain knowledge. Jack's immediate ambition was to get an office job, knowing that he had the ability needed, and he began at Russell Street night school to learn shorthand, book-keeping, and commercial English and arithmetic. After he did get an office job, in 1920 when he was seventeen, his struggle continued. He learned French from a Hugo's primer, practising on 'sexy' (his word) French novels bought on Cambridge market stalls. French shorthand followed, and Spanish and Portuguese also. In words which remind us just how Victorian he was and which few people would now utter, Jack recalled in 'No Mother Love' the need to check his libido by studying intensively and, he wrote, 'to counterbalance what I thought were slightly unnatural leanings to and lustings for the opposite sex', I 'took up the study of company law'.[21]

As for so many people before the coming of electronic pleasures reading was always enticing for Jack. As a schoolboy he was fascinated by school stories in *The Magnet* and *The*

---

[18] By an act of Parliament in 1899 the leaving age for elementary schools was set at 12, but like many other places Cambridge had a local bye-law setting it at 14 for its own schools.

[19] NML, p. 66.

[20] By 1918 Jack lived alone with his father. His brother Percy had died, and Fred and Henry ('Nap') had left Saxon Street.

[21] NML, p. 142.

Gem. 'I not only read about life at Greyfriars and St Jim's. I thought about it, dreamed about it. I knew by heart all the leading and most of the lesser lights at both schools.'[22] Across Trumpington Road from Saxon Street was the Leys School, but Jack did not believe it was a real public school because it was not like Greyfriars. Boys' magazines retained their allure for Jack throughout his life, even though they conjured up a world very remote from his ideal. His intellectual progress suggests the limitations of George Orwell's contention, in his essay 'Boys' weeklies', that school stories were designed to inhibit the growth of radical attitudes among their readers. The extracts from *Pickwick Papers* that Jack studied in commercial English at Russell Street led him to the entire novel, and to others by Dickens, and then to many other writers. His favourite was Jack London, whose tales of the South Seas gladdened Jack's deep-seated desire to escape Saxon Street for an hour or two, and whose plausible dystopia, *The Iron Heel*, about the growth of Fascism within capitalist America, matched the vision that Jack came to as a young man. To write Jack London's biography became an unfulfilled ambition.

To assist in the transformation of society was a strong motive for many of these self-educators, and it was for Jack; the annals of the Labour Party and the trade unions are filled with their intellectual struggles, while Jack's hopes were more revolutionary. The growth of his consciousness during Jack Overhill's early manhood coincided with the hopes following the Russian Revolution and the end of the First World War. In some pregnant words in his autobiography Jack wrote that

> I had a feeling of expectancy about national events. A political and social upheaval was impending. Soon, the workers would come into their own.... At the end of September [1919] there was a general railway strike. I welcomed it as a sign of the change in the social order that I thought was imminent. I believed in working-class unity, hoped other trade unions would strike and that there would be a bloody revolution. I was ready to fight in it. When I saw workers helping to break the strike I looked on them as enemies of their own kind. Ignorance was the reason for their actions — it couldn't be anything else. That was another

[22] NML, pp. 90–1.

incentive to learn. I'd got to learn; only by doing so would I be wideawake to the guile and cunning of those in control of the country. They were the men with money, not the politicians whom they danced on strings. I was disappointed when the strike petered out in less than a fortnight. I thought the workers had more guts.[23]

He soon ceased to expect an imminent revolution but hoped for many years that British society would be transformed, although Jack—very preoccupied with his writing—took few active steps to bring that about. His hostility to the structure of British society lay behind his attitude to the Second World War.

Jack's motives for his educational progress were not as straightforward as these quoted paragraphs imply; as for so many others in his generation, he had a disinterested desire for enlightenment as well as ambitions for material advancement and political change. His candidacy for a London External B.Sc. (Econ.) in the 1930s, while undertaken partly for the increased earning power a degree would confer, for the most part reflected a wish to study for its own sake, while the dogged repetition of his entry, time after time following failures, was above all the result of a determination to win at all costs, despite the feelings of depression and anxiety that often assailed him. Following yet another failure, he wrote with typical courage in his diary in August 1945 'I shall sit again next year and for as many years as it is necessary to pass'.

When he was seventeen, in 1920, Jack got a job with the Cambridge bookmaker W. P. Hollis. The move was a success, and Jack's competence and value to the firm enabled him to lever many rises, so that his pay increased from 15s to 30s a week in one year. Jack stuck with Hollis, though according to his son the pleasures of bookmaking were merely arithmetical. Even so Hollis increased his pay again, and by 1923, when he was twenty, Jack could afford to marry Jess Toates from Histon, if they lived in Saxon Street. His father sanctioned Jess's moving in, though he ominously made clear that he disliked all other women but Jess.

[23] NML, p. 131.

E.T.O. with his grandchildren, Jack and Jess, and Collie and Floss, 1928.

Jack, Jess, and their children, Jack and Jess, with Collie and Floss, Grantchester, 1932

The imposition of a betting tax in 1926 made bookmakers fear for their future. W. P. Hollis gave Jack notice in 1927. Jack decided to take the plunge and set up as a bookmaker on his own account, in Saxon Street, but to live elsewhere; Jack and his wife feared friction with E.T.O. when their second child was born—Jack junior was to arrive in 1927. So Jack bought a semi-detached house in Trumpington—99 Shelford Road— and the young family moved there in November 1927. Jack bought 7 Saxon Street too and used an office in it while E.T.O. continued to live there. Jack and his family lived in Trumpington until the outbreak of war in 1939, while Jack travelled the four miles to Saxon Street to pursue his bookmaking business. In the 1930s the Overhill family enjoyed modest well-being, although Jack lacked the capital needed to cushion them during the bad patches in his calling. But when racing closed down on the outbreak of war the Trumpington house was rented out and the family moved back to the rickety dwelling in Saxon Street, which was already scheduled for eventual slum-clearance. Jack took up boot-repairing again, renting a shop in Castle Hill. These changes are detailed in the first entries relating to the wartime years in Jack's diary.

Jack Overhill: author

Jack began to attempt writing for publication soon after he left school in 1917. 'Intent on becoming an author I made a practice of going upstairs into the front-room to write in the early morning before breakfast. I wrote a number of short stories and sent them to editors, who sent them back.'[24] Failure to persuade an editor rarely discouraged Jack, a man of indefatigable energy, and he began to contribute to amateur magazines, run off on hand printing presses or duplicating machines for the many sharing Jack's desperate desire to get into print, and eager for serious intellectual friendship too. They asked each other questions, to be answered by post, such as 'What is your opinion of the relative merits and demerits of Capitalism and Communism?' which involved Jack and others in 'mugging up the subject before answering the letter'. 'I

---

[24] NML, p. 118.

liked best,' wrote Jack, 'the pass-round magazines. There was only one copy made up of the original works of the authors, poets and artists, but because it saved the producers the trouble of printing and duplicating they were always larger, had more variety and were not spoiled by reproduction like the printed and duplicated copies.'[25]

Commercial success came about in 1930, when the *Cambridgeshire Weekly News* paid Jack one guinea for a short story, and he had a couple of other small successes. In 1932 he took the initial step in what became a major part of his endeavour as an author, the writing of novels. The first concerned 'a group of Cambridge undergraduates', a theme which surprises us since Jack shows dislike for them as a class in the little he wrote about them in 'No Mother Love'; and he had only a slight acquaintance with the university itself. In 'No Mother Love' Jack describes the hectic technique he adopted for this first novel, and for many of his later ones too; his words show why some readers find them hard to read. 'I started just before Christmas — without notes and ready to let the story shape itself round the main ideas. I found writing a novel a good opportunity of saying what I wanted. I dragged into the story religion, politics, pacifism, unemployment — anything and everything I agreed and disagreed with. I sometimes said it through my characters and sometimes straight out myself.'[26] Jack wrote 140,000 words in 127 days. After trimming 20,000 words from the script he found a home for the novel with the Mitre Press, which published it as *Romantic Youth* (1933) in return for a payment of £86 5s, a premium often then being demanded by certain publishers from untried novelists. It received favourable notices in the Cambridge newspapers, but sold fewer than 300 copies, producing royalties of about £7 — much less than the premium.[27]

In *Romantic Youth* Jack wrote that the Cambridge colleges formed a 'giant octopus [which] continues to grow, stretch-

---

[25] NML, pp. 144–5. 'Pass-around magazines' are discussed in Christopher Hilliard, *To Exercise our Talents: The Democratization of Writing in Britain* (Harvard, 2006), pp. 36–7, 62–3.
[26] NML, p. 223.
[27] NML, pp. 224–7.

ing long tentacles over the town in search of prey'.[28] Undergraduates were ignorant of the toil of the working people they depended on. Meanwhile they neglected their studies, while these were in any case mostly useless for earning a living: the slump of the 1930s cast many shadows over the novel. Jack introduced summarily, and without enough characterisation, the eight or so undergraduates he focused on. They are hard for the reader to disentangle—a fault Jack was to be guilty of again. Their courses of study are not described. They have picaresque adventures in Cambridge, Cottenham and Cornwall, for which Jack drew upon his own pursuits and dreams: swimming and boating in the Cam, betting, bookmaking and horseracing, and boxing (Jack had a lifelong fascination with it, despite his pacifism). At the heart of the novel is an undergraduate, Jerry, and his love affair with Peggy. When a dog eats a crucial letter the courtship goes wrong, but it is righted by the end; Jerry leaves the 'rusty, obsolete' university for real life with Peggy. This conclusion reminds us, like the diary, that Jack's attitude to everyday life was far more conventional than his absolutist political views suggest. But the novel does not convey a sense of real life. Jack did not repeat the experiment of a university novel.

All but one of the twenty-five novels he wrote in the next half-century concerned working-class life in twentieth-century Cambridge,[29] the exception being an historical novel, *The Miller of Trumpington*, described below. They were composed at great speed, Jack typing at times for as much as ten hours a day and often late into the evening; for a decade he was also studying for his London external degree—a hurdle he found hard to surmount, since not to our surprise his aspirations outran his energy. During the war he was also repairing perhaps a hundred pairs of shoes a week. Jack frequently altered the text he had composed, particularly in his later scripts, but he did not allow himself time to reflect on his writing before he revised it: his hyperactivity left him feeling that he had lit-

[28] *Romantic Youth*, p. 7.
[29] 'The Money Bug' is in two parts, both written in 1944, and counted as one novel here.

tle time to spare. This was a tragedy for his literary ambitions, since his creative powers lagged behind his verbal fluency.

He might be compared with Flora Thompson [Laura Timms], a near-contemporary from a similar background who had had merely elementary schooling; she edged her way to authorship, pondering on and revising her sketches before at last producing her masterpiece, *Lark Rise*, in 1939.[30] Jack had need of forthright friends, as men and women in like circumstances found in the associations of part-time authors which were such a distinctive feature of the literary scene between the wars.[31] There was most probably one within reach of Jack Overhill, but he was not a member of any such group, despite his earlier involvement with duplicated and pass-round magazines. One surmises that his discovery of what he thought of as his authentic creative voice may have exaggerated his self-belief – though we may also perceive that his confidence was brittle.

But he did have one helpful friend who was a professional writer. The popular novelist Neil Bell offered in one of his books to advise aspiring authors.[32] Jack wrote to him in March 1938. So began a long and close epistolary friendship, which was helped by their similar quasi-Communist opinions and their belief that 'democracy' was a sham; fortunately, though they were both neurotic and liable to depression (Neil was to commit suicide in 1964)[33] and both men were contentious, their friendship was strong enough to keep them from ever quarrel-

---

[30] Gillian Lindsay, *Flora Thompson: The Story of the* Lark Rise *writer* (1990), pp. 134–40.

[31] Hilliard, *To Exercise our Talents,* pp. 34–55, *et seq.* Hilliard makes some pertinent comments on Jack's writing.

[32] Neil Bell (1887–1964) was born Stephen Critten in Southwold, the son of a boat-builder whose lack of talent for business led to the firm's closure. After unhappy years as an elementary school teacher Stephen began to support himself through writing in 1927, changing his name to Southwold, the name adopted by his children. After writing under it for some years he began to write under the name Neil Bell, by which Jack knew him.

[33] Neil Bell was a hypochondriac. During the war he imagined that he had a duodenal ulcer; that explains his request for Ryvita (recorded in the diary), which Jack tried to satisfy. In 1964 he imagined that he had cancer; he had also lost his gift for writing, and his pleasure in reading. Suicide followed.

ling with each other. On receiving news of Neil's suicide Jack wrote 'He was my mental twin and his going left a gap in my life that has never been filled and never will'.[34] An indomitable archivist, Jack bound up and kept all Bell's 538 letters, written mostly with a fountain pen filled with green ink.

Blessed with a creative fecundity which pleased the public taste, Neil Bell published seventy-five novels, tales for children and collections of short stories in the twenty-seven years from 1927 to 1954, earning over £35,000 in the process.[35] He was in an ideal position to advise Jack on how he should attempt the art of writing, and a memoir prepared by Neil's daughter sketches their relationship during the many years they were corresponding.[36] If the tone of letters becomes more informal and intimate, Neil's attitude on technical matters was always ambivalent. In an early letter he wrote 'it may be that your narrative gift is so weak as to be almost lacking', and a few days later 'another trying habit of yours is to lead the reader up the garden enticing him on with the promise of something happening and then nothing does happen. In a novel something must happen every time the reader expects it. ... Do try and stop your characters clacking on and on. They get so prosy.'[37] These words are persuasive, but some months later Neil undermined them by confessing his doubts whether 'one man ought ever to advise another ... once I began to take advice on how my books should be written all self-confidence (cocksureness if you like) goes by the board'. In May 1940 Neil counselled Jack to make 'a careful synopsis of each chapter *before you begin to write* the story'[38] — and then, shortly

[34] Stephanie Southwold, 'The Lonely Road', p. 356. See note 36 below.
[35] Neil Bell, *My Writing Life* (1955), p. 254. Before his suicide in 1964 over twenty further books by Neil Bell appeared.
[36] Late in his life Jack lent Neil's letters to Neil's daughter, Stephanie Southwold, and she prepared a memoir, 'The Lonely Road: The Story of Neil Bell' (no date) which was not published. There is a typescript copy in the Cambridgeshire Collection, and much of the following account of the two men's relationship is based on it. Neil's letters to Jack are now (February 2010) in the Cambridgeshire Collection.
[37] 'The Lonely Road', p. 195, and p. 196 for the next quotation.
[38] 'The Lonely Road', p. 200, and p. 202 for the next quotation.

afterwards, he admitted that he might be alone in criticising some of Jack's paragraphs as 'irrelevancies'; others might not think of them like that. 'I'm the last man to dogmatise and the worst model you could take.'

There are further examples of Neil's inconsistency. Behind it lie the fluctuating moods of both men and Neil's desire to comfort Jack when he was depressed: 'You're talking bunkum … quite unworthy of your real everyday self. … You know you are not a failure.'[39] But as late as 1960 — over twenty years after Neil had received the request for guidance and Jack had completed 'Queen Street' — Neil was making fundamental criticisms of that novel, perhaps because he was aware that the same flaws still existed in Jack's writing, and that he was reluctant to accept advice.

> It is axiomatic that a novel should introduce to the reader within a page or two the central character or characters (not more than three or four) and get the reader interested in them. In the first twelve or so pages of *QS* there are dozens of people mentioned by name and little else told about them. … one is confused, attention flags, and bang goes your novel. I think that is a fatal flaw in *QS*. You'll think this is a captious letter … .[40]

In fact, Jack came near to publication with his novel 'Queen Street', a thinly disguised and truthful documentary, with some fictitious additions, about life in Gothic Street.

> I felt in the shoes of all my characters, men, women and children, the whole two hundred of them; and as the setting of the story was the neighbourhood I had lived and worked in for thirty years, I was quite at home in it. The story, starting in 1910 and ending in 1938, was written in three books and as it was unplanned and I did not write from notes — I was never more than two pages ahead — it almost wrote itself. … I resurrected men, women and children long since in their graves; boys I'd gone to school with, and killed in the 1914–18 war, came to life; others that had gone away and were almost forgotten returned to their old haunts.[41]

In the Cambridgeshire Collection there is a key to the true identity of the characters in the novel. 'Queen Street' was sent

---

[39] 'The Lonely Road', p. 214. The letter dates from 1942.
[40] 'The Lonely Road', p. 332.
[41] NML, p. 261, and pp. 262-7 for what follows.

Saxon Street. The Cross Keys, seen on the left, was no. 9; no. 7, Jack Overhill's house, is just visible beyond the triangle of sunlight on the road. Gothic Street goes off on the right.

The men's swimming place and changing rooms on the river Cam.

to Michael Sadleir at Constable's in March 1939, as the Germans marched into Czechoslovakia. Sadleir was attracted to the novel, but sent Jack a 'questionnaire relating to subjects and incidents in the book that might lead to libel'. After Jack's candid replies the typescript was sent to Harrap. They turned it down. 'And they added the cutting observation: "There is too much sex in the book ... the author seems obsessed with sex." When I was a boy [Jack wrote] there was nine bastards in Gothic Street; I wasn't responsible for any of them. Neither was I responsible for the sexy atmosphere of 'Queen Street'.'

Only one of his many proletarian novels was published, *The Snob* (1947), which is based on events in Jack's life and that of his brother Fred.[42] Lacking a plot or a story, it is a series of vignettes—a shoe-repairing workshop, the Western Front, stealing fowls from a poultry farm—which might be called 'Scenes from proletarian life'; they recall the essays of James Greenwood and Henry Mayhew from earlier generations. The novel lacks the human personality, whose exploration is salient in most novels; many people who are less than shadows flit across its pages, and even the protagonist, Jim, does a lot but has little substance. It is almost as though the writer is inside the society he is referring to, and assumes that the reader is too and so has no need to have the people in it described. The book appeared under the imprint of the Pilot Press, a venture of Charles Madge; he is better known for his work with Mass-Observation, and later in life as Professor of Sociology at Birmingham. He may have discerned an underlying virtue in the novel, as did Pamela Hansford Johnson, herself a novelist of note, in her review in *John O'London's Weekly*. She wrote that 'it is not really a novel—it is far too formless for that; but it is a first-rate documentary',[43] putting her finger on the strength of Jack Overhill's writing, and also its flaw—his weakness at creating strong narratives. A sentence in Neil Bell's autobiography makes a similar point: success would come to Jack 'when he lights upon a percipient publisher, for these novels are first-rate sociological studies

---

[42] The novel was earlier titled 'Jim Baxter–Snob'. A snob was a maker or repairer of boots or shoes.

[43] Quoted in NML, p. 384. Many other laudatory reviews are also cited.

and will I imagine be a happy hunting ground for students of sociology in a hundred years' time'.[44]

Jack's third published novel, *The Miller of Trumpington* (Staples Press, 1953) contrasts with his two earlier publications and his unpublished working-class novels. *The Miller* offers a series of picaresque adventures in Georgian England; they begin in the Cambridgeshire village of Trumpington (Jack's village in the 1930s and after the war) and finish in Grantchester, less than a mile away, after travels to London and elsewhere.[45] It blends the historical knowledge Jack had absorbed for his degree and the conventions of much popular fiction, showing the influence of Neil Bell's writing and also Jack's lifelong fascination with boys' comics. Tom Brian, the miller, is a revolutionary of prodigious strength and energy in whom it is easy to see Jack's fantasy self-image; he plots to assassinate George III and William Pitt, and becomes a champion prize-fighter. Livelier than *The Snob*, it lacks its deeper purpose and sociological appeal but possesses a stronger narrative which carries the reader along. It is certainly the most readable of Jack's published novels, and perhaps it is the best. But Jack wrote no other novels like it.

Fifteen of Jack's scripts form a series, the 'Cash chronicles',[46] composed in 1942 and 1943, and, after a gap of twenty-one years, between 1964 and 1977. The first is 'Whims of the Father' and the last 'Whence? Why? Whither?', written when Jack was seventy-four. They are a fictionalised version of the Overhill family's fortunes, from the early years of the twentieth century to the 1970s, taking in the two world wars, times of poverty, and Jack's relationship with publishers and the BBC. The series is a gigantic *roman à clef*, and, as there is for 'Queen Street', an index in the Cambridgeshire Collection gives the real names of its characters, including, besides many

[44] Bell, *My Writing Life*, p. 235.
[45] An earlier miller of Trumpington is a protagonist in Chaucer's 'The Reeve's Tale'.
[46] Jack was apt to confuse readers: he had a close friend called Cash, but he also gave that name to the fictionalised version of the Overhills. Similarly, his own forename was given to his son, and his wife's to their daughter. In the diary he has sometimes to distinguish them as 'Big Jess' and 'Little Jess'.

Overhills and their friends, the editor of the *Cambridge Daily News*, several BBC producers and Sir Angus Wilson, who appears as Ian Argyle. The vast effort the series entailed met with no success with publishers. In an attempt to improve his utterance Jack altered the typescript of all fifteen volumes in ink, feverishly scrawling on page after page and rendering them almost illegible.[47] One cannot contemplate the shelves of unpublished Overhill novels without feelings of sadness at energy wasted in the pursuit of a fruitless obsession.

But he did have literary success elsewhere.[48] He excelled at reportage, most evidently in the text of the diary published here. Jack guarded his diary — pressed for time, he made no copy — taking it with him into the air raid shelter while leaving his money in the house. He seems to have been unconscious of the artistry with which he composed it, and to have regarded the diary as a validation of his past — as a proof of his existence and a guarantee of his survival — rather than as a fruit of creative talent. There is an irony here: his diary will be read and valued while his novels for good reason continue to be ignored. Jack created one other piece which demonstrated his talent supremely — his talk 'A Regular Snob' which he gave on the Third Programme in January 1967. It is described in the Epilogue, where its timing places it.

Jack Overhill: swimmer

Saxon Street was only a few hundred yards from the river Cam, and at seven or eight Jack learned to swim without formal instruction. 'For a time I swam with one foot on the bottom; then I pushed off from a ladder and got my legs working together. Once I could swim I was in and out of the water all day long.'[49] Another enthusiasm soon joined it: 'best of all I like to read in the shade of a tree beside the river on a sum-

---

[47] At least that is so with the copies lodged with the Cambridgeshire Collection.

[48] An excerpt of 4,500 words from 'Back Street Boy' was published in Angus Wilson, editor, *Writers of East Anglia* (1977); the excerpt recounts the fortunes on the Western Front of Jockey Saggers, a Cambridge postman who had joined the army.

[49] NML, p. 36, and pp. 92–3 for the next quotation.

mer day' — doubtless during intervals between sessions in the water.

One day in the early 1920s, standing on a bridge over the river Jack 'saw a man swimming a stroke like the trudgeon, but 'he thrashed his legs up and down instead of doing a scissor kick'.[50] He was moving very fast, and Jack was intrigued. He read about the Australian invention, the crawl, in *Harmsworth's Universal Encyclopedia* (Jack was subscribing to the parts) and in an Amateur Swimming Association pamphlet. He mastered the new stroke by prodigious effort. 'I literally lived the crawlstroke. I thought about it, read about it, dreamed about it. I practised over chairs, boxes, tables and desks.'[51] At length he could synchronise his limb movements, and was soon swimming in the Cam all year round — a spartan practice often mentioned in the diary. His two children, Jess and Jack, learnt to swim as infants, with help but no forceful cajoling from their father; Pathé made a short film of young Jack in the water. At eight (1935) Jack was schoolboy swimming champion of Cambridge. His father wrote an article for *Health and Strength* about his exploits.

> Swimming was only a pastime. ... But what a pastime! I spent golden hours on and in the water with my family during the summer. Sometimes, on Sundays, we hired a punt in Cambridge and picnicking at favourite spots along the bank, leisurely made our way upstream to Grantchester. We passed the University bathing sheds on the way and encouraged by Jack [his son] I learned to do handstand dives and back somersaults from the sixteen feet high dive — an excellent example of bringing up father.[52]

Jack, described by his son as 'willing to help anybody who wanted him', formed with two other enthusiasts the Granta Swimming Club to teach many unemployed and impoverished men in 1930s Cambridge to swim; it attracted 300 members. He also examined for the Royal Life Saving Society,

---

[50] NML p. 140. A trudgeon or trudgen: 'a swimming stroke in which each hand alternately is raised above the surface, thrust forward, and pulled back through the water', *Chambers' Dictionary*.
[51] NML, p. 151.
[52] NML, p. 222.

which in due course honoured him with a medal after twenty-one tireless years.[53]

Pacifism and political objections to the anti-Nazi war

Jack Overhill was a conscientious objector during the Second World War, among many thousands of men (and fewer women, upon whom the obligation to enlist pressed less heavily) who refused to join the armed forces.[54] They were moved by a variety of impulses, which might be termed 'political' and 'moral'. The moral case, derived from religious and other ethical traditions, was that killing was an unjustifiable evil. It was strongly put by the Peace Pledge Union, founded by the Reverend Dick Sheppard in 1934—though it is necessary to record that after Britain was forced into war it was justified on religious or moral grounds by most Christians and very many members of the PPU.[55] The different objections to the abomination of war overlapped, and many pacifists advanced both groups of them, Jack Overhill being one, though for him much the stronger case was the political—which was a logical extension of the left-wing beliefs he had held since his youth, that democracy was a sham. Real power was in the hands of the few, and any war was intended to serve their interests, not those of the many.[56] It was stimulated by arms manufacturers and others with selfish desires to provoke conflict.

Pacifist sentiment was widespread within the university in the 1930s, drawing strength from memories of the horrors of the Western Front in the First World War, from guilt at the alleged injustices of the Treaty of Versailles, and from suspicion of armaments manufacturers and their allies pressing for rearmament.[57] Jack Overhill wrote in 'No Mother Love':

[53] NML, p. 229.

[54] 'Conscientious objector' and 'pacifist' are not exact synonyms, but they were so regarded at the time, as they will be here.

[55] For example, two prominent members of the PPU who resigned when in 1939 they perceived the need to defeat Hitler by force were the Nonconformist preacher Maude Royden and the historian G. D. H. Cole.

[56] Jack outlined his political beliefs in his autobiography, and the passage in question is quoted on pp. xxvii–xxviii.

[57] T. E. B. Howarth, *Cambridge between the Wars* (1978), pp. 218–20; NML, pp. 231–2 for the following quotation.

> Concerned about the way affairs were shaping in Europe [in 1933] I attended meetings, first as chairman and then as secretary of the individual members section of the Cambridge Anti-War Council. Maurice Dobb was the prime mover of the Council. The meetings bored me. I came away from them with a feeling of time wasted. My wife and I took part in a torchlight procession to register a protest against the drift to war and I helped at the Council's exhibition that showed the horrors of modern warfare. ... I was delegated by the Council to the Cambridge Peace Council, which was made up of bodies of all shades of opinion. I went to one meeting. That was enough.

These words tell us a lot about Jack. He confided his strong opinions to the diary, and talked about them to swimmers he met on the bank of the Cam. But he was reluctant to join any political party, and he did not have the patience to take part for long in the routine of meetings and administration that lie behind political advance; it is obvious in the diary that he preferred the sound of his own voice to anybody else's. He was not a true political *activist*.

In the summer of 1940, after the conquest of Holland, Belgium and France, the British people feared that a German invasion would probably be attempted. The rapid collapse of Holland was thought by many, including the Dutch royal family in its British refuge, to be largely the work of Germans residing in Holland who were manipulated by the Nazis. Fears of a similar 'fifth column' in Britain were widespread, and whipped up by the *Daily Mail* and the *Daily Express*.[58] There was no 'fifth column', but the authorities panicked at the thought of the enemy within, arresting '750 officials, active members, and other supposed sympathizers' of the British Union of Fascists, including 'some very small fry'.[59] Following Churchill's

---

[58] Richard Thurlow, 'The evolution of the mythical British fifth column 1939-46', *Twentieth Century British History*, vol. 10.4 (1999), pp. 477–98, esp. pp. 484–9. Markings on telegraph poles by boy scouts and girl guides were suspected to be messages in code made by British fascists to aid invading Germans.

[59] A. W. B. Simpson, *In the Highest Degree Odious: Detention without Trial in Wartime Britain* (Oxford, 1992), pp. 196–9, 203. Thurlow, 'The mythical British fifth column', pp. 489–91, points out that most members of the BUF were British patriots certain not to aid German invaders. But the authorities can hardly be blamed for taking no chances with them dur-

command to 'collar the lot', German and Austrian residents were rounded up and interned, including many refugees from Naziism, Jews and gentiles, some of them working in British war factories.[60] At the same time Jack was predicting Britain's defeat in his diary without a note of regret, while in April 1941 he wrote that perhaps Germany's conquests were justified and to Europe's benefit; with her abilities she might succeed in making Europe an economic unit.

Jack's underlying objections to the war were shared with the Soviet Union and the Communist Party of Great Britain [CPGB], the organisation closest to being Jack's spiritual home, although with typical independence of spirit he refused to join it. After the Nazi-Soviet pact of August 1939, he and the CPGB regarded Britain and Nazi Germany as similar capitalist societies. Right-thinking people should not support the war between them, and the Soviet Union was more equitable and righteous than either. The British State was suspicious of the CP's intentions, and Special Branch and MI5 watched it carefully. But the security services reported that in the factories the patriotic British workforce were suspicious of the CP's propaganda, 'although they articulated real grievances'. So 'the Home Office was determined that it should do nothing to increase sympathy for CPGB activities', and let sleeping dogs lie.[61]

When Germany attacked the Soviet Union in June 1941 Jack did not conceal from the diary his support for the Red Army's struggle, while continuing to abstain from any activity which

---

ing the crisis of 1940. The internment of German refugees was a different matter.

[60] The most authoritative account is François Lafitte, *The Internment of Aliens,* originally written at speed and published as a Penguin Special in November 1940; one of the most substantial volumes in that series, it was republished by Libris in 1988 with a new introduction by the author. Lafitte was a research officer of the Miners' International Federation before working for Political and Economic Planning from 1938 to 1943; he then became social affairs correspondent of *The Times,* and subsequently Professor of Social Policy in the University of Birmingham. See also Peter and Leni Gilman, *'Collar the Lot': How Britain Interned and Expelled its Wartime Refugees* (1980), pp. 1–46.

[61] Thurlow, 'The mythical British fifth column', pp. 494–5. The suppression of the *Daily Worker* in January 1941 was a departure from the policy of tolerating the CP: on this incident see below, p. 75.

might aid the British cause: logically a difficult stance to maintain since Britain and the Soviet Union were now allies, and the CPGB supported the Churchill coalition and the war effort of the Western Powers, proclaiming, as Richard Thurlow writes, 'greater enthusiasm for the war than Churchill'.[62] Jack and those of the same mind might be called 'pacificists', as A. J. P. Taylor termed them—men who did not regard war as wrong in all circumstances; it was sometimes right, or necessary.

Jack was fortunate; in 1941 he was told that shoe-repairing was a reserved occupation at his age (he was then 38), and when in April 1944 he did go before a tribunal it decided to continue his exemption while he remained in his occupation. As the historian of pacifism states, 'the C.O. movement of 1939-45' was shown '"great respect and kindness" throughout the war (except for the panic in the summer of 1940)'.[63] Conscientious objectors still had to undertake firewatching duties, and the diary makes clear that Jack suffered anguish over whether it was right to obey. To be *compelled* by the State to undertake certain tasks was repugnant to pacifists of inflexible principle,[64] while what was termed a non-combatant unit (like the RAMC) they regarded as in fact military in nature because it was essential for the prosecution of the war; it was for this reason that Jack declared before the tribunal in April 1944 his reluctance to serve in the RAMC though many pacifists did. On the other hand he suffered from acute claustrophobia, and prison might be almost a death sentence, while if he agreed to firewatch locally other people would watch his shop on Castle Hill; ironclad conscience might result in his

---

[62] Andrew Thorpe, *The British Communist Party and Moscow 1920–1943* (2000), p. 267; Thurlow, 'The mythical British fifth column', p. 496.

[63] Martin Ceadel, *Pacifism in Britain 1914–1945: The Defining of a Faith* (Oxford, 1980), p. 303. The interpolated quotation is from the *Christian Pacifist* for August 1939.

[64] Thus Eddie Hooley of Liverpool stood upon his pacifist faith and did not admit that he suffered from disseminated sclerosis, which would have brought automatic exemption. He was imprisoned until informed medical authorities insisted on his release: Pat Starkey, *'I Will Not Fight': Conscientious Objectors and Pacifists in the North West during the Second World War* (1992) p. 13.

having to guard it himself every night. So he decided to serve in his neighbourhood. But for Jack normal labour relations applied: he went 'on strike' if conditions were not right at the firewatched premises. Jack Overhill's quibblings add to the fascination of a paradoxical document. It arouses admiration for the energy and endurance of its composer.

Jack's personality was unique, but how far were his views shared by others: in particular, how common was his attitude to the war and to combat? At first the State was unwilling to accept political objections, and though it gradually relaxed this attitude Jack did not admit to his tribunal that his objections were *political* (the boundaries were in any case blurred), no doubt fearing an unsympathetic response.[65] The sources do not attempt to assess the number of such objectors, although one declares that 'of those applying for unconditional exemption, a considerable proportion were known as political objectors, mostly socialists or communists who did not object to war as such but who objected to a capitalist war, although the entry of Russia into the war in 1941 confused the issue'.[66]

The total of those provisionally registered as conscientious objectors under the National Service Acts from June 1939 to June 1941 (that is, claiming CO status when registering for national service) was 61,170.[67] Meanwhile, it seems likely that Moscow's and the CPGB's decision in September 1939 led to an increase in party membership from 17,000 to 20,000, despite some prominent dissentients; Communists were by nature loyal to the party and to the Soviet Union, the only state working to create a socialist society, and in any case there were signs during the 'phoney war' of 1939–40 that the British Gov-

---

[65] Tribunals gradually accepted that political objections fell within the National Service Acts 'if it could be said that the objection was so deeply held that it became a matter of inner conviction as to right and wrong and not merely an opinion': Denis Hayes, *Challenge of Conscience: The Story of the Conscientious Oobjectors of 1939–1949* (1949), p. 64.

[66] Rachel Barker, *Conscience, Government and War: Conscientious Objection in Great Britain 1939-45* (1982), p. 20.

[67] I have reached this number by aggregating the totals in Hayes, *Challenge of Conscience*, pp. 13, 362. Over 1,000 of the 61,170 were women.

ernment was half-hearted in the struggle.[68] A membership of 20,000 suggests the order of magnitude of the British population opposed to the war for political reasons, though some allowance may have to be made for those outside the party, like Jack, who agreed with it. The total of young male registrants claiming exemption because of conscientious objections political in nature will have been far smaller than 20,000 (since the CPGB included many women, and men too old to fight) — though it would be fruitless to try to assess their numbers.

It is certain, however, that after June 1941 there were very few people who like Jack were 'pacificist' — refusing to assist the British war effort while praising the Red Army. He was in a tiny minority — and he would have been quietly proud of it. We may see in Jack Overhill's diary his exceptional attitude over other wartime concerns: for example his hatred of Churchill as a leading member of the British ruling class has to be set against Angus Calder's perception that in 1940 and 1941 Churchill's defiant words — 'we shall never surrender' — 'did express something inarticulate, perhaps dormant but perhaps not, in the hearts and minds of his countrymen … all classes were clear that there nowhere was, nor ever had been, anyone quite like this man they were cheering … it was profoundly reassuring to suppose that Britain was led at this moment by a great man.'[69]

---

[68] Noreen Branson, *History of the Communist Party of Great Britain 1927–1941* (1985), pp. 275–6; Juliet Gardiner, *Wartime Britain 1939–1945* (2004), pp. 251–2.

[69] Angus Calder, *The people's war: Britain 1939–1945* (1971 paperback edn), pp. 111–13. Between July 1940 and May 1945 never less than 78 per cent of those questioned by opinion pollsters approved of Churchill's prime ministership.

Editorial principles

As with most copious diaries there is much repetition in Jack Overhill's. I have omitted about forty per cent of his original writing on the war years, 1939–45—a great deal of domestic detail, including the diarist's activities with his dogs and in the river—while endeavouring to retain the flavour of what Jack wrote on such matters. Omissions have been shown in the usual way: three dots (…) reveal phrases omitted within sentences; where necessary, the place of a previous or following punctuation mark is shown thus … ; . More substantial excisions of entire sentences or entries are also indicated by three dots, thus … . A complication here is that Jack himself typed three dots as shorthand for 'There is no more to be said'. To distinguish these from editorial dots I have transcribed them thus: - - - .

The typescript is clean and legible, despite the now yellowing character of the poor quality paper which was available, or that Jack could afford. Sometimes his typing is best read under a strong light, since Jack, most likely owing to economy, used his ribbons until they were pale and almost inkless. But there are remarkably few crossings out or second thoughts, and very few mistakes in spelling or syntax either. These have been silently corrected. More might have been expected, in view of the late hour in which Jack did much of his typing. Perhaps nothing better indicates the excellence of his schooling, and the value of Jack's strivings for self-education.

A note on the British currency and monetary values

Before decimalisation in Febuary 1971 there were 240 pennies in each pound sterling; there were twenty shillings in each pound and twelve pennies in each shilling. In the decimal structure each pound contained 100 pennies, each worth 2.4 times an 'old' penny. Thus the twelve 'old' pennies constituting a shilling were replaced by five new pennies, and the shilling as a unit of currency disappeared, as did the florin (a tenth of a pound), the half crown (an eighth of a pound) and the ten shilling note (ten 'bob'—50 new pence).

Before decimalisation it was customary for sums of money to be expressed by the formula £ s d, or pounds, shillings and pence. Thus three pounds and five shillings would be expressed as £3 5s 0d (or simply £3 5s); after February 1971 it would be expressed as £3.25. In the following text of the diary Jack Overhill's frequent references to money are allowed to stand in the old formula and not converted to the decimal structure. Nor is any attempt made to convert the money of the 1930s and 1940s to what purports to be its purchasing power at the time of publication. The pre-1939 pound sterling is often deemed to be now 'worth' around sixty times its face value then. But such a formula is misleading, since some items were far less expensive in real terms seventy years ago and some far more; in the 1930s a substantial semi-detached house might be bought for £500, while at the time of writing [2009] it would cost not £30,000 but £150,000 at least. On the other hand, many items of food cost more in real terms in the 1930s than they do seventy years later. It is therefore difficult to compare relative living standards, and doubly difficult when we reflect that many articles were not available at all in the 1930s—for example the array of electronic machines and gadgets that most households now possess—while others were far more available and affordable for some people than now—for example domestic servants. For the type of rich people that Jack Overhill fulminates against it was customary in the 1930s to employ one or two full-time servants, while now they would generally be deemed unaffordable, and have in any case largely been replaced by the inexpensive domestic appliances that have taken much of the drudgery out of housework.

There is another reason why I have chosen not to update Jack Overhill's figures. It is my hope that his diary may still be read in a century, and later, by those eager to discover what life was like in Cambridge in that remote epoch, the Second World War. For those readers, our children's children and succeeding generations, a comparison of a distant era with another scarcely nearer would be more mystifying than enlightening.

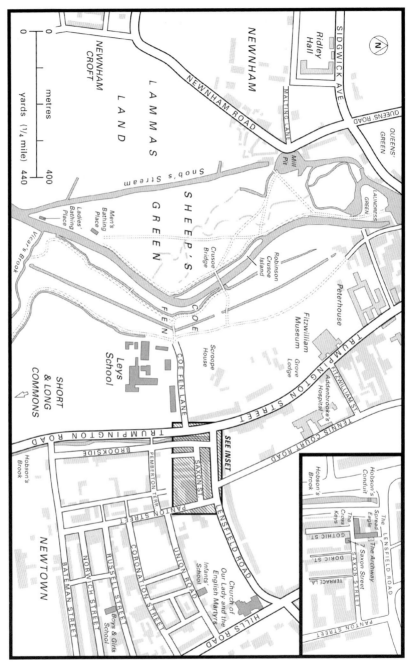

Newtown, the commons and the river Cam c.1900

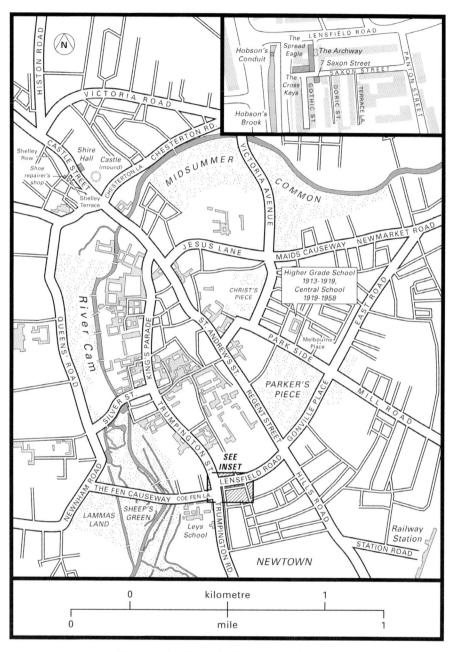

Central Cambridge, c. 1940

From the diary of Jack Overhill:

I wish all I had to do was write novels for a living. What a dream!   *17 October 1941*

Don't forget too, that first and last in my life — and it takes precedence over everything — writing, reading, sex and the rest of it I'm a swimmer, right to the marrow of my bones; … I can think of no greater pleasure than swimming along in a green-banked stream with the sun shining down … then soaking the sun into my body on the bank.   *16 August 1942*

Have I recorded that when there's a raid on it's my diary I always collar. We have money in the house, but take the diary! But it's part of us. I can earn some more money, but that's not replaceable.…   *11 October 1942*

The Diary

1939

September 1939

Sunday 3 September: Yesterday was another day of crisis. I packed up all studying and work on the book and began to build a trench in the garden. ... We stayed up to hear the news at 12 o'clock [at midnight, 2 September]. It was very gloomy: if Hitler did not reply to the British note war would be declared today as existing between the two countries. ... [At 11 a.m.] Here is the news. War exists between Britain and Germany. ...

This afternoon we went to Grantchester. ... On the way I saw Jack and a little crowd of boys and girls—evacuees—round the telephone box in the village. Jack was ringing up a number in Muswell Hill as one of them wanted to phone home: she'd been crying ever since she arrived. I talked to her and persuaded her to spend the shilling instead, not to worry her parents. One boy said it was no use crying, they couldn't hear her. They asked all sorts of questions: were they near Buckley as that was in Buckinghamshire! Were they close to Wales? Had the Germans yet raided E. Finchley? How could one girl get in touch with her boy friend (she was about 13) as she didn't know to which town he was sent? ... It was quiet and peaceful at the Meadows: we were all rather gloomy: none of us went in the water. I said they would try to take the Siegfried Line and they'd find it wasn't a row of tin cans. ...

Monday 4 September: The siren had us out of bed about 3 o'clock this morning. It was an eerie wail, seeming to identify itself with the raiders. Jess jumped out of bed and said 'Oh, Jack, here they come.' I got out of bed, went to the children's rooms, and tried to encourage them all. We came down in our gas masks, I got the dogs in, filled up the bowl with water in case of a burst main, and then we stood in the passage of the house. ... The 'All clear' sounded in about half an hour.

Evacuees arriving at Cambridge from London in late August 1939.

Children receiving gas-mask instruction in Ramsden Square, August 1939

We never slept any more. My heart thumped as I lay in bed: nervous reaction or the cup of tea I had … . I also went to get some wood and corrugated iron for a shelter with Bert Cash[1] in his car. It looked like 1914 again on East Road — the soldiers marching and whistling. …

Tuesday 5 September: … [*Jack went to see a man called Morris about employment.*] He is a laboratory worker, running, I think, an experimental farm near Cottenham. A queer little fellow, getting on for 50, he listened to what I said with his head on one side, rather birdlike and took a long time to thaw. Yet he was sympathetic for all his strange manner. … He also said they ought to build some of the farm roads up instead of building battleships. If he could find me a job he said he would, but doubted if I could bike the ten miles night and morning to his farm under present conditions and do a day's work. …I wrote to Neil Bell and thanked him for *The Abbot's Heel* … . …

Wednesday 6 September: There was another air-raid warning this morning; when the 'All Clear' sounded Young Jess went to the Meadows to look for her bathing costume which she had left there the previous night. She'd been gone about five minutes when the siren went off again — another warning. … As it happened she was taken in a shelter in a big house round there by an air-raid warden. It was gas-proof, lit by electric light. With about a dozen others she had tea and sang songs until the 'All Clear' was sounded. We were concerned during her absence. …

I then went and straightened out my account with a local bookmaker. There were several there. … When I left one of them said I had put the wind up him — I had made a short political and economic survey of things as best I could — and he wished I had kept away. There seems to be no hatred in anyone. All the glory has gone out of war.

Shelford Road looked a shambles this morning when the sirens went: traffic stopping, men tumbling out of lorries, people standing about looking puzzled, worried, scared … . When we arrived here we heard an imitation siren from the

---

[1] This woodwork teacher at Bottisham Village College was a close friend of Jack.

bathroom; then there came a voice shouting 'All Clear', 'All Clear'. Jack had gone to the lavatory and was practising he said in case the siren failed! ...

One man told me a few days ago that a country worth living in was worth fighting for; that his son who was nearly 18 would fight for it as he had done. He was very keyed up .... I let him alone. At a time like this people must make their own decisions.

Friday 8 September: ... I thought I would go and live at Saxon Street. After all, I own the place. Bert came over with his car this morning and we started shifting things from Shelford Road; mostly books, as I intend to let the house furnished.

Sunday 10 September: I went to Saxon Street this morning and took the copper out in order to have a gas cooker fitted in its place. ...

Tuesday 12 September: ... Shifted the piano. It was a job: had to take the window out at Saxon Street, but I mean the children to keep on with their music studies if possible. Two more journeys to Shelford Road ...as we are now at Saxon Street. What a shant to take any woman to. Poor old Jess has some work to do. And that's how my dreams of giving her the first £100 on the book have ended. I could cry with sheer frustration at times, but it's no good. I must carry on. I looked round the house as I left and said 'Let's hope we come back'. Then I said 'We will come back'. And so we will, even if our prospects are pretty poor .

Wednesday 13 September. I started work this morning at Smithy Fen, the other side of Cottenham. A farm job: one the man Morris has given me ... .The distance from here is about ten miles, the last two miles terribly rough farm roads. ... I took her [i.e. Jess, his wife] a cup of tea up and started out just after 6.00 ... and I got to the farm at 7 o'clock. I knocked at a cottage door and an old man put his head out of the window and after enquiring who I was told me to make myself at home with the comment that I was an early bird. ...

I had a bit of breakfast and a cup of tea in an old shed. ... I met the foreman and two other workmen—three men and a boy— at 7.20 when they came into the farm-yard with the horses (three of them) ... One of the men, Cyril Burkitt, reminded me very much of Neanderthal man as he's pictured in the *Outline of History*.[2]... In the morning I helped to cart wheat, then beans. I put fresh straw in the pigsties in the afternoon. ...I got a puncture coming home; and it rained. Jess was upset because I didn't go upstairs to see what a good job she had made of the ceiling (she's busy whitewashing and paper-hanging). ... Talk about 'Heartbreak House'. Well, this is it.

Thursday 14 September: Pitched beans all day. Was in the 'stage hole' when stacking. The work is hard, but the monotony is worse. My shoes soon let in water and I was wetfooted all day. Another puncture coming home. I had a letter from Bell. He told me to drop calling him 'Mr' and he would do the same. Said write to him when I liked. The house is such a shant, Jess so down in the mouth that it's difficult to keep one's spirits up. Fancy coming back to oil lamps! ...

Friday 15 September: Spent the day pitching beans and mucking out the yard ... There was talk at dockie time about fruit at Cottenham selling at 12*lbs* for a penny.

I've been wetfooted again all day. I get like that trying to catch the horses in a meadow ... they seem half-starved and uncared for to me. Their eyes are all matter, and all they get to eat besides grass is chaff and a few (such a few) oats and a bit of chopped swede. ... What a farm it is. Harness, woodwork, everything rotten and falling to bits. I had a bit of an argument with the foreman. He deliberately provoked me and I couldn't stand that. Said men who wouldn't fight were 'yellow-bellies'. I asked him why the hell he didn't volunteer. ... [He] was nonplussed (piqued, perhaps) by my answer. ...

Saturday 16 September: ... I'm trying to cut down expenses. Scrounging round the butcher's after two pennorth of pieces for the dogs is one way of doing it. ...

Monday 18 September: They were making revelry in the pub across the street [i.e. the Spread Eagle] last night. Jess and I could hear them as we lay in bed. It was an impossible attempt to catch the fevered war atmosphere of 1914 by reviving all

---

[2] An illustrated history of the world written by H. G. Wells and published in twenty-four fortnightly parts and then in two volumes in 1920. A remarkable venture of popularisation.

the old songs. ... All that brought back memories of Jess and I lying in bed listening to them singing 'Golden dreamboat' in 1923, during the first months of our marriage. Golden, golden days --- ...

Tuesday 19 September: ... It was a wet morning and my new tyre burst. I went to Jess's sister's in Histon and repaired it with string. Luckily it held and saw me to work and back. ... How I eat. Sometimes a half-quartern [i.e. 2*lb*] loaf at dockie, then a big dinner when I come home. ... My mind is as flat as a pancake.

Thursday 21 September: I carted muck all day today all day up and down rutted roads. Every now and again I took off my gumboots and wrung my socks: and normally I've got dry feet. I counted the telegraph poles to while away the time: thought of Napoleon and his travels in a coach along bad roads. I don't know why. ... There's no talk of sex on the farm; none at all.

Friday 22 September: I got the sack today. It was a relief. The foreman was offensive in manner when he paid me off; due, I think, to our verbal exchanges which have been going on all week. I haven't spared him. ...

Monday 25 September: I'm still helping to get the house shipshape. East Road looked a bit militarified when I passed today; nothing like 1914 though. ...

Tuesday 26 September: I went to the Labour Exchange for work this morning as I have had no reply for a benchman's (boot repairing) job I wrote for. I didn't get work as they only had clerical jobs under the military, which I don't want. I went to Shelford Road this afternoon; called on the village schoolmaster to pay the clothing club. ...

Wednesday 27 September: Been sending out 'accounts rendered' to get some money in [i.e. for his bookmaking business]. (What a hope!) running errands, writing letters. I'm trying to get a lock-up shop. Am going back to shoe repairing. ...

Thursday 28 September: There's lots of stories going around about the evacuees: one of them about how the children preferred beer and doughnuts for breakfast at one house instead of eggs and bacon. The expectant mothers are a fruity source of scandal.

Friday 29 September: I filled in our National Register forms today.³ A government passport to our persons. Sent to the Guildhall about our coal rations. ... Sugar has gone up to 4½d a *lb*. Government price. No profiteering! ...

About [C. B.] Meyer [a German refugee] again. He said what about the German idea of ruling the world: it was being instilled in the schoolchildren. I said what about 'Rule Britannia'; we'd been doing that for years. ... I said Jack London used to think the Anglo-Saxon race the best. He asked did I. I said I might have done years ago; not now. Reading a lot of biology had cured all that. ...

October 1939

Sunday 1 October: I put up some shelves in the children's bedroom and made a coat hanger. ...Jack and I had a ride round this afternoon. I bought two fireside chairs for five bob in a lane at the back of Burleigh Street; and the seller, an old man, delivered them within an hour on a handcart. Our identity cards were brought round this morning.

Monday 2 October: ... Went to Fred and bought some leather. Jack lost his right football boot and found a left one. I turned this, making it a right one, which was like making a boot. Ha, ha, I'm a bootmaker! ...

Tuesday 3 October: I went to the Labour Exchange again. They told me I wasn't entitled to unemployment pay as I only had two stamps on my card. I said what about the seven years before I went into business on my own. They said it didn't count. ...

Naturally, I made no application for public assistance.

I went to a Communist meeting with Bert Cash. At the endof

---

³ On National Registration Day (29 September) each householder had to list on a form provided everybody living in the house. From this information identity cards were compiled, and issued to the persons named. The information was used by food offices to fill in names and addresses on ration books.

the meeting I addressed the speaker and said the Communist Party were making a mistake in supporting the war. The answer was that members of the Party would better serve the party in the army than in prison; they were not so far removed from the people. I said they were not so far removed from the people when they were in the army than when they were dead (people in the audience clapped and stamped then). Continuing, I said that talking about going in the army and fraternising was sheer nonsense. In the army one did as he was told; it was kill or be killed. Things in this country were not like they were in Russia in 1917. ... I said that if the Communist Party had been wise they would have followed Russia's lead and opposed the war. ... Maybe Germany and Russia were drawing closer because there were fewer ideological differences now: Germany may be going Communist as they were liquidating many of the capitalists. Further, I said that the men who fought the last war were disciplined for it from boyhood (I mentioned the severity of national school discipline and the discipline ... after school days when working boys were under their employer's thumb so much in their jobs); .... All this from me; and I'm a Liberal: or shall I say a Radical?

Saturday 7 October: They are putting notices up about giving away vital secrets ...

Sunday 8 October: ... Listened to a Communist speaker on Midsummer Common this afternoon. He knew his stuff and I helped to keep the crowd in order. ... A lot of the crowd wanted to crush fascism and they wanted to crush the speaker as well! ...

Monday 9 October: Rained all day. Got a lock-up shop up Castle End. ...

Tuesday 10 October: ... I read a bit in the evening: Olaf Stapledon's *Last and First Men*.[4] Then a stray dog came in the house. We didn't know what to do with it. Jim and Jock want no interlopers and to turn it out during the black-out seemed a bit hard. It was a black terrier bitch, about six months old. Luckily Jess thought she'd seen a notice in the local paper the

---

[4] Olaf Stapledon's fiction about mankind's possible future was published in 1930, and in Pelican Books in 1937.

previous evening about a lost dog … [and so] I was able to take Judy home to her people in St Barnabas Road.

Wednesday 11 October … However this war develops, certain it is that things are different from the beginning of the last war. There was the great retreat from Mons then in less than three weeks. I don't believe there's been 500 casualties on the Western Front at present … . …

Thursday 12 October. I wouldn't like to make a list of all I have done today. Just a lot of running about; I totalled up that I'd been to 26 places; all to do with the shop, [and] the house at Shelford Road with a mixture of miscellaneous shopping to buy things to put this place a bit ship-shape (Saxon Street). It looks as if we have now let the house at Shelford Road.

My nephews, Henry and Albert Overhill, came to see me tonight: aged 20 and 16. I advised Henry about being a conscientious objector to the best of my ability as he is in the next age-group, due to register in nine days.

Friday 13 October … Bought bloaters for dinner coming home — 3½d each. The price of them nearly broke Jess's heart. …They [i.e. the Communist Party] say their manifesto of September 2nd was a mistake … .On October 7th they declared this was an imperialist war and urged peace (so I beat them to it). …

Saturday 14 October. We've sunk some U-boats: the Germans have sunk the *Royal Oak*.[5] The newspapers are boosting up how we levelled up the scores. I can see nothing to delight in or gloat over. Good lives lost on both sides — and for what?
It rained hard today. I finished making the bench and stool at the shop. … The place doesn't look so bad: I've been generous with the paint brush. Took my first job in: a pair of heeling. I did them for nothing just for luck. …

Sunday 15 October. The old man [i.e. Jack's father] gave me a lot of rivets this morning and some of his old tools. I took them over to the shop with Jack. …

---

[5] On the night of 13-14 October a U-boat penetrated the supposedly impregnable defences of Scapa Flow (in Orkney) and sank the *Royal Oak* with the loss of 833 lives.

Monday 16 October. I made a start at the shop this morning: walked there with the dogs. They had several dust-ups in the shop and soon made themselves at home. ...

Edwards came over this afternoon with his wife ... and he was so struck at the sight of me at work that he took a photo of me. ... Jack came round and after the Edwardses and Jess had left I helped him with his English homework (clauses). He stayed on until I left—6 o'clock—when we went to the free library for some addresses for the circulars [to publicise the shop]. They shut the public library now at black-out time, so we didn't stay long. I managed to scribble down seventy-odd addresses. I did some algebra, economic history and constitutional law during the day and managed to keep busy although I did so little repairing. ...

I heard from the food rationing office today. I can start tomorrow. I shan't though. I've made a start at shoe repairing and I'll stick to it. I think I can make it go.

I applied for the food rationing job at the County Hall, the first week of the war. The distribution of food I considered a peaceful occupation, not helping on the war, and one I was justly entitled to work at, as I would help in a more equitable distribution in times of peace, let alone in times of war. ...

Tuesday 17 October. I worked hard today, yet I only repaired four pairs of ladies' soles and heels. Years ago, when I was about fifteen I did as many as eight pairs of sole and heeling in a morning. ... Shoes are more of the 'fancy' type nowadays—wooden heels, suede covering etc—and they make a novice like me rather nervous in case I damage them.

Jess and I quarrelled tonight. One thing led to another until finally she pointed to a couple of black marks on a towel and accused me of making them through not washing my hands properly when I came home. Exasperated I immediately burned the towel, stuffing it on the fire. A stupid thing to do, of course, but I felt depressed and miserable. ... Happily, it's all over now, as we made it up today. We'd have a job to get on without each other now. (I've written this bit on Wednesday).

Recruitment poster for National Service, 1939.
The matrix of the poster was printed centrally, with the local details added by stamp.

Wednesday 18 October. There was a substitute Cambridgeshire, run in two classes, today. ... I won £3 7s, which was very acceptable. The contrasted manner of my earnings, shoe repairing and bookmaking, was very noticeable today. ...I did a bit of Algebra today, [and] some Economic History and wrote a lot of letters clearing up odd items. I don't seem to be able to get started on the writing, but I will do. War news: generally quiet. Stalemate and more peace offerings, which will eventually be accepted, I think.

Thursday 19 October. What have women done that they should have high heels inflicted on them? The poor, misguided creatures. It rained hard today and the leaves are falling fast: 'Brown autumn sheds its store'. The Backs are still golden though. The end of summer passed unnoticed this year owing to the war. ...

Friday 20 October ...I was slack this morning and sat moodily weighing up things ... as I read some economic history in the shop, when Jock came up to be made a fuss of, then Jim, which ended in their usual dust-up. Somehow, dogs seem to sense when one is troubled. ...I felt envious of all the 'big bugs' living up Huntingdon Road and Madingley Road as I wrote out addresses [for circulars] today. Many reverend gentlemen and other pushers among them, I noticed: all riding on the back of the workers.

Saturday 21 October ... Jess and I went over to see the tenants at Shelford Road ... We thought they were going to pay the first week's rent, but the husband asked me if I would allow it to stand over until next week as he'd had a lot of expenses. I agreed, but it made me feel rather dubious. ... Money is tight and I'm hoping they're regular payers to help us along a bit.

Monday 23 October. No work at the shop. I fixed up a programme how to spend my days. ... I study constitutional law to and from work in the mornings, when I walk to the shop with the dogs. I go in the river [to swim] coming home to dinner. I cycle to the shop in the afternoon, having a look in the library to see the newspapers on the way. Not that one gets much out of them.

Thursday 26 October. I've come back to my boyish haunts and consequently think a lot about things that happened twenty or more years ago. The period between the ages 14 and 17 was very fruitful. I learned shoe-repairing then; and shorthand, typewriting, bookkeeping. I also tried to write. …I get a bit fretful at times and Jess is often in the dumps. She is much thinner.

Saturday 28 October. Jack was at the shop with me all day. He made things with leather. It rained hard, but we kept cheerful with sweets and apples. Tonight I went to Shelford Road to collect the rent, but never got it. I called on a client of mine on the way back who owed me a little money. I got what he owed me. The last time I saw him he was a Labour man, dead against war. He'd changed to a Tory and was all for this war or any other. Simply bubbling over with enthusiasm about our chances. …

Monday 30 October … I heard some undergraduates talking about a German invasion at the back end of the summer. One of them said there would be no Oxford and Cambridge then. Wonder that I never shouted out an insult.

Lately I've thought a lot about the wandering Jew and living for ever. There's plenty to find out about the universe so one could keep busy a long time if not for ever. I don't even know the names of common flowers. …

November 1939

Wednesday 1 November. Work is still slow. I am studying regularly again now for the Inter B.Sc. Part 2.[6] Sent a short letter to the local paper about hairdressers shutting early. Went to a mock tribunal for COs the other night. …

Sunday 19 November. I tried for a teacher's job last week: one of the evacuated schools here. Work at the shop is scarce … . At the interview (I saw an elderly French woman) I was told the teacher was required to teach shorthand, typewriting and commercial English to girls, some French, mostly English, about 16 years of age, many of whom had matriculated or

[6] Jack began to study for a London External B.Sc (Econ) degree in 1935.

passed the school certificate examination, on three afternoons and one morning. The fee was one guinea [£1 1s] a week. I pushed it up to 25s and was told I would hear shortly: the appointment had to be confirmed in London. Beggars can't be choosers, but I hope I don't get it or that sufficient work comes in at the shop to justify me turning it down. What a wage! It isn't the hours, but the split system that makes the remuneration so small. …

I saw and heard Churchill broadcast a bit of propaganda at the Victoria Cinema the other night (on the films). He looked a nasty bit of work: his speech was a nasty bit of work. He referred to the Germans as Huns! I said to Jess that it was disgusting (so did Lord Haw Haw broadcasting from Germany): that if I were a German and heard that I'd probably lose my pacific tendencies. …

Neil Bell sent me his latest novel *Not a Sparrow Falls* a fortnight ago. Yesterday I received a book of short stories from him. Both are good. In my early twenties I had two ambitions. One, to write Jack London's biography. Two, to have a five-minute chat with H. G. Wells, whom I regard as a sort of spiritual (for want of a better word) father and to whom I attribute almost every bit of knowledge I have. Jack London's biography has been done—and done well, (*Sailor on Horseback*: I forget the writer's name) [7] and as for the chat with Wells—I'm not so optimistic as I was! …

The war seems to be petering out. …stalemate on land, sea and air. … Stock exchange betting is seven to one that there is peace by Christmas. …After the Queen's speech on the 'News' at the Vic [the Victoria Cinema] last week there wasn't a solitary clap or voice raised at all.

December 1939.

Sunday 17 December. A long lapse since I last wrote anything in here considering it's wartime: but, at present, there's little to write about every day … . … This morning I walked to Shelford Road with Edwards to get the agreement signed

---

[7] The author of *Sailor on Horseback* was Irving Stone.

with the tenant there (afterwards he went in the river with me: he thought it was cold) and I said I believed in the Marxist theory that this social system breeds wars, but I thought they would patch this one up before it gets out of hand to boost the existing economic order up a little longer. The reservation is whether Germany is going 'Communist': if so, this war may develop into the inevitable war between capitalism and communism instead of the inevitable struggle being delayed.

Lately, the news has centred round Finland and Russia.[8] The latter are, in my opinion, trying to consolidate themselves against the imperialist powers both in the Balkans and the Baltic. Naturally, this country is slinging mud at her; ... They have also resurrected the League of Nations and expelled Russia from it (the first member to be expelled — the only communist one), which is totally absurd. ... Heaven help the British Empire if we (France and Great Britain) provoke her too much. ...There is to be a drive not to increase but to lower wages and to urge the workers to cut down consumption according to Reynolds's 'Secret History' [i.e. *Reynolds' News*] out today.

The papers are all full of a sea fight between the German pocket battleship *Graf Spee* and three of our cruisers.[9]...

Eric came down a fortnight ago. ... [We talked about] the fight the *Rawalpindi* had put up at sea.[10] He said he had been on that and it was lunacy on the part of the captain to make

---

[8] In October Russia pressed Finland to cede territory, to strengthen Russia's frontier in the North. Upon her refusal Russia invaded on 30 November. Finland won some surprising victories, but made peace in March 1940 and ceded territory, since lacking substantial foreign help she could not in the long term defeat the much stronger Russian forces.

[9] The German 'pocket battleship' *Graf Spee,* searching for British merchantmen in the south Atlantic, was on 13 December engaged by three British cruisers, whose armament was collectively inferior to the *Graf Spee's* 11" guns. All four ships were damaged. The *Graf Spee* attempted refuge in Montevideo. Mistakenly believing in the imminent arrival of a much stronger British force Captain Langsdorf scuttled his ship and committed suicide.

[10] The *Rawalpindi*, an armed merchantman, was sunk by the German battleships *Scharnhorst* and *Gneisenau* between the Faeroes and Iceland on 23 November. The liner *Athenia* was sunk without warning by a U-boat on the first day of the war, being thought to be armed.

a fight of it, her decks (top-hampers, I think he called them) being so much out of the water the Germans couldn't miss her. They didn't at five and half miles! He also said that down the London Docks there was talk of why the *Athenia* was torpedoed: she was carrying gold bullion. He said that he saw a Canadian newspaper that censured the efforts to save the gold instead of the people. Why so many lifeboats were sunk was because they were full—of gold.

This is poor paper I'm typing on, but it's the best I can afford: 1s 2d a ream. The other I used before this was 4s. Can't afford that now. We're very hard up. Work at the shop is disappointingly slow. This reminds me that Charlie Craske, a chap I went to school with … came in and said there was a job going for a male shorthand-typist and clerk at the place where he is now working. I inquired further: the job was about £4 a week (a lot of money to me now), but the firm he is working for are doing a contract job for the Air Ministry … and that was enough for me. I work on no war jobs. The other day my brother Fred said he could put me in line for an army contract for repairing boots. He grinned when he said it, although I think he was in earnest. He knew my answer. …

E.T.O.'s [Jack's father] been causing a lot of rumpus recently. Talk about turning us grey. I had to tell him at last that he would have to go. … I got him a nice cottage and a flat (off the Council). He turned them both down and I had to be firm, so I went to a firm of solicitors and explained matters, when they sent him a letter saying he would have to get fresh accommodation. Still he wouldn't go until the end, but he cleared out yesterday morning, leaving his furniture here. We think he's gone to Haverhill. I can't have him here again. It isn't a question of putting him into the gutter; he gets 10s a week old age pension and 5s a week from his club besides having £60 or £70 in ready money, and if he wants any financial help I'm ready to provide it somehow. We just can't put up with his overbearing ways. To enumerate them—and his insults—would fill a book. I said I would stand by him when I was a kid. I will if he lets me, but it must be at a distance. Life here during the last three months has been intolerable. …

Fred's boy [Fred jnr] lost a lady customer a pair of shoes. She asked him [Fred snr] if his boy had had no education. He said he'd had the same as him: 'Noah's Ark, Alfred and the Cakes, and God Save the King'. I went to the CO tribunal here the other day. It was a quite informal affair. Both applicants I heard were registered unconditionally, and I thought the judges pretty fair, but the *Peace News* said it's a class affair, favouring undergraduates. Probably, they're right. ...

Edwards is scared of razors: he's a barber: I'm scared of shoemakers' knives. I can't afford a phobia nowadays, however.

About COs again. A thought of mine the other day: the 16,000 conscientious objectors of the last war did more good ethically than the 10,000,000 killed. At a Cambridge meeting of various sects a week or two back a resolution was passed against Cambridge being made a training ground for Air Force officers after being made a centre for evacuees. It was sent to the local paper, but wasn't published. ...

When Russia first attacked Finland it was suggested in some of the Tory Press that we drop the war with Germany, line up with them and go for Russia as she was the real menace. All this indecision makes the progress of this war more difficult for those who are waging it. ...The Emergency Powers Act, passed a short time ago had a rough reception and had to be toned down.[11] I don't wonder. Its powers were so far-reaching there were left precious few 'rights of the individual' that I read about such a lot in the constitutional law I am studying for my examination next month ...

I had a friendly letter from Neil Bell the other day; told him I thought H. G. Wells the greatest man for dusting away cobwebs that had ever lived in my reply to him; adding that though not giving to lionising people I would consider it an honour to sole and heel H. G. W.'s boots—just once—in return for all he'd done for me. I think having a master subjugates one; destroys original thought. I hope I can keep working on my own account. ... I would like to make a pilgrimage to Jack London's grave in the Valley of the Moon in California. I saw

---

[11] The Emergency Powers (Defence) Act was passed on 24 August, ten days before war was declared. It gave the government power to make regulations necessary to protect and defend Britain and to prosecute the war.

a chap the other day when I was going to work with whom I went to school. It made me wonder where the thirty odd boys were who were in my class. What a subject for a novel. It would need a series of novels, like those that Zola wrote to do it well. I could do it. Doesn't H. G. Wells think a lot of Voltaire? I must try some of his stuff.

Sunday 24 December... Saw the *Son of Tarzan* which was pretty good, and a lot of wartime propaganda that made us long for a little Christmas atmosphere on the screen. ... I had a letter from Neil Bell last week. He seemed struck by my suggestion of a novel about the lives of the scholars in a classroom, so I wrote saying perhaps he would do it. ... Anyway it would give him plenty of scope. He suggests that I write a book about a shoemaker, with my brother Fred as the central character. I'm writing one about a shoemaker now — my grandfather. Still, I don't mind doing another, so today I started a fresh novel. Shall call it 'Jim Baxter – Snob' ... Today I did about 2,500 words of this new novel. ... I noticed they had *Romantic Youth* on sale in Boot's yesterday.[12] I wasn't thrilled a bit. This novel-writing game has become a grim business. It makes me wonder if Fudge the publisher owes me anything in royalties. Even a few shillings would be very acceptable just now. Jess [his wife] has been working hard decorating the front room. She was anxious to get it done for Christmas now that E.T.O. isn't here. ... I hope the old man is sensible and keeps out of mischief and takes the first house he's offered. But he won't.

[12] *Romantic Youth* was the first of Jack's novels to be published, in 1933. Its sale was not large, and royalties were much less than the premium which Jack had had to pay the publisher, the Mitre Press.

1939

Young Men
YOU HAVE BEEN WARNED
BY EVENTS

COME FORWARD NOW

and by JOINING the

Territorial Army

show that you are prepared, if needs be, to

DEFEND YOUR HOMES

and the cause of Freedom and Justice

Better NOW than too late

Ask your Employer to help you to Defend your Country

FOISTER & JAGG, ST. ANDREW'S HILL, CAMBRIDGE

Poster recruiting for the Territorial Army, 1939 Printed by Foister & Jagg, St Andrew's Hill, Cambridge.

One of the entrances to Cambridge's Public Air Raid Shelter no. 1. It was adapted from wine cellars in Peas Hilll.

The Cambridge Police Headquarters in St Andrew's Street protected by sandbags. A photograph taken in late 1939.

Local Defence Volunteers recruited in summer 1940 against the threat of German invasion, photographed drilling with broomsticks on Cambridge Town Football Club ground; rifles were not yet available. The LDV were soon renamed 'the Home Guard'.

1940

The 1940 entries in the manuscript are occasional until the end of May, but occur on most days thereafter.

January 1940

Sunday 21 January. I've been busy revising work for the Inter B.Sc. (Part 2) again lately (as well as writing the book about the snob [bootmaker] which Neil Bell suggested). Work at the shop has been slack. The weather has been very wintry since Christmas, frost and snow. I've been in the water nearly every day. The river was frozen today and all I could do was go down the ladder and duck. ... Snow fell all morning and spoiled the surface. It has snowed intermittently all day.

Last Friday I went to London for the exam. It was a frosty morning. There were little setbacks in travelling, the most noticeable [being that] the subway at South Kensington was blocked up as an air-raid shelter. I saw the barrage balloons over London for the first time. The examination building was a queer place. No lobby downstairs, piled up with sandbags. I had to take my gas-mask: that was a compulsory order. I went to Victoria and took the electric train to Streatham Hill where I met Eric after I came out of the examination room.[1] ... We went to a place called George's and had some grub, ... We then came back to Tottenham Court Road, made inquiries at the London Central YMCA when I was sent to 35, Gower Street: bed and breakfast 5s. Eric and I went in Lyons [café] for a short time (turning out time 8 o'clock) then I went to my lodgings and went to bed after a good bit of revision work. It was a comfortable doss but [for] the noises from the other rooms and the house generally. It was a lodging house and sounded like one. I thought some of my neighbours were pigs. I did well I thought at the examination, but had better

---

[1] Eric Goldsmith and Jack Overhill had met as pupils in the Cambridge Higher Grade School in 1913; they had remained close friends.

wait and see. I'm too wary now to be cocksure about passing exams.

Today I made a start on the book again and did over 2,000 words. I would like to keep that rate up. ...

February 1940

Friday 9 February. ... Work at the shop is shockingly slack. I shall have to get out there soon unless something happens or we shall starve. [Frank] Edwards and his wife came to tea last Sunday. A lot of talk about the war and the chances of his age-group being called up; he's 32.

A week or ten days ago it snowed heavily: now it's cleared and rains have added to the floods, as the river is over the banks on the Green. The cold spell started a few days before Xmas. Frost and snow for weeks made getting about terrible; especially in the black-out. ... The journeys [round Cambridge] were terrible: snow, frost-bound, piled up high beside the roads, thick on the pavements, slippery, where it had thawed a little and frozen again. I can never remember weather like it; not for so long a period. ...

I'm 37 tomorrow. The years still roll by, can't expect them not to, but they're going damned quick; too quick. ... I'm working hard at the book 'Jim Baxter – Snob'. To date I've written 80,000 words and am at it morning, noon and night. Some nights I have to go to the Greyhound [Coldham's Lane] to get Fred to talk, especially when I want material to write about. He mellows a bit about the fourth pint. ...

March 1940

Sunday 17 March. I passed the Inter B.Sc. Part 2 examination and have entered for the final. Been too busy writing 'Jim Baxter – Snob' to have time to write any notes. It's been rather harassing—I've carted the typewriter backwards and forwards to the shop every day to get on with the story in between times—but I'm now writing the last chapter. It's very long and been a lot of hard work; that's all I'll permit myself to say about it.

Jack's not done very well this term at school: 19th in exam, 22nd in term. He came in my bedroom and cried about it the other morning. I told him not to dwell on failure; brush it aside and start again. …

The war between Russia and Finland is over. Another defeat for us. Diplomatically, we are being beaten all along the line. My nephew Bill Overhill was struck off the register of conscientious objectors the other day. I thought he would be; he presented a case that was clearly not one of conscience.

The Cambridge Borough Council are on my track about this house (7 Saxon Street). I wrote them bluntly yesterday: they THREATENED arbitration proceedings which MIGHT cost me money. Told them I wanted no third party to tell me when I'm robbed whether by Cambridge Borough Council or a thief in the street: that compensation primarily centres upon my livelihood: that rather than accept £22 (their offer) for this house and business I'll accept nothing. They can go to hell. They mean to have the place, the law is on their side, they will: let them. But I'm not being deluded into the belief that I'm being paid by accepting a sum like that. Emphatically no.[2] …

The war drags on. I hope for peace; it's possible, although Humphreys said to me yesterday that he thinks it will drag on for years until we've captured all the German trade—if we can. …

May 1940

Friday 31 May. Great things have been happening lately. After the Finnish war there was a little lull, then war broke out in Norway, followed by Germany attacking Holland and Belgium. She also marched into Denmark a few weeks ago without any fighting. Since then, everything has gone catastrophically for the Allies, …; the Germans came through the Maginot Line (technically not so, according to the newspapers, but through the place where it ends!) and have reached the coast of northern France. We are now living under the threat of invasion, which seems very real, as there are guards at all strategic and important places (the local General Post Office, for example) and all signposts have been taken down. A few days ago, Belgium capitulated on the orders of their king (who the

---

[2] Saxon Street had been condemned as unfit for human habitation.

Daily Mirror are trying to prove IS not their king, but somebody impersonating him: a German: the real Leopold being killed with his wife in an accident several years ago!) and we are evacuating the remnant of our army from north France. Our losses must have been terrible — the newspaper 'leaders' are saying the nation must prepare itself for tragic facts — and it looks as if the British Empire has collapsed in about a fortnight. Well, it had got to end one day ... All that 'Zilliacus' said in his book *Why we are Losing the Peace* (or *Between Two Wars*) has and is coming true.[3]

People keep saying we have huge resources; maybe; but they take time to marshal. We shall never be allowed time to do it, I'm sure. It seems that our men were inadequately equipped to meet Germany's eighty-ton tanks, [and] that little preparation has been going on these last 18 months. There's been treachery, too, as the French premier hinted when he spoke of vital bridges not being blown up to stay the German advance.

Other items are: Chamberlain has been turned out of office; Churchill has taken his place. New Zealand has brought in conscription. Canada has offered to take all the children from this country under 12 as evacuees. Fifteen French generals were relieved of their command last weekend. Fear of parachutists has led to a new home defence corps (Bert Cash has joined).[4]

We all seemed wide of the mark in estimating Germany's strength. The Maginot Line seems to be the biggest white elephant in history. ...Cripps has gone to Moscow: trade talks![5]

---

[3] Konni Zilliacus (1894–1967) was of American and Finnish parentage and became a British subject in 1918. A left-wing activist in the Labour party from 1919 until his death; MP for Gateshead 1945–50. A strong Communist sympathiser, and forceful critic of Ernest Bevin's foreign policy; he was expelled from the Labour Party in 1949 and readmitted in 1952.

[4] The Local Defence Volunteers, later the Home Guard.

[5] Stafford Cripps, a brilliant patrician barrister of very left-wing opinions, was sent by Churchill as ambassador to the USSR in May 1940, in the hope that his influence would draw Stalin from the Nazi camp where he had been from August 1939 onwards. But until the German invasion Cripps was held at arm's length by the distrustful Russians, though after the invasion he helped to effect the Anglo-Soviet alliance. He returned to Britain in January 1942: Peter Clarke, *The Cripps Version*, 2002, pp. 183–241.

What a load of baloney. There'll be no British Empire to trade with by the time agreement is reached. But, it is admitted his mission is also a diplomatic one! Stalin and his men must be smiling at the *volte face*. Before recognising him they have insisted he be accredited with full ambassadorial powers. They have been granted — on the way! Three months ago it was being estimated in this country that one Finnish soldier was equal to a regiment of Russians, as feeling was bitter against Russia over Finland. In the pictures the other night the people was clapping Stalin again. The turncoats!

… I went for a walk to Ditton with Fred on Whit Monday. That evening I went to a local deaf-mutes' club with Frank Edwards. They were a genial crowd. I know the deaf and dumb alphabet, which is very simple. I cycled to Saffron Walden for a swim with Jack a few Saturdays ago. The bath water was dirty and full of chlorine. My eyes smarted for a week. The custodian told me that about 150 soldiers went in it every day from Debden aerodrome, about three miles away.

I'm having a job to pay my bills. Am negotiating with the Prudential about my insurance now. …

I'm learning Italian for the final B.Sc. What an optimist! … I finished writing 'Jim Baxter – Snob' on 24th March; finished revising it on the 14th May, when I sent it to Neil Bell. He said it was the best I'd done so far. … Chances of publication are thin owing to the paper shortage (now acute), but he said there is a chance and [to] send it to Constable's. I'm tinkering about on a fresh one now. No good being idle if chances of publication these days are slight. …

June 1940

Monday 3 June. … [On the Cam at Grantchester] Jack punted into the bank coming back where the stump of a tree jutted out into the river. He couldn't get under it and a fast stream swept the boat on, so he had to grasp the tree stump and hold on in an attempt for us to get back to him. We couldn't manage it in time, the stump was too big for him to get a grip, and after dangling a few seconds, his feet just skimming the water he let go and dropped into the river. The ducking didn't hurt him much, anyway, although he had his clothes on. He was a funny sight while he held on kicking. ...

The regulations are tightening up and one has to be careful what they say, especially regarding impeding the war effort. ...

I received 'Jim Baxter – Snob' back from Bell today. He kept it so that his wife could read it. Her opinion didn't seem as good as his, ... I don't know I am sure if she's any judge. Of one thing I feel certain: it won't get published now by Constable's, ...What a game this writing is. Sometimes I think, I think I'm just a bit silly to keep trying. Be a lot easier just to laze about than flog myself repeatedly like I do.   ... I've got an idea for another book.

Jack tells me they're making machine-gun nests on Hills Road bridge ...

From now until the summer of 1941 there were air-raid warnings in Cambridge almost every night, as bombers were detected approaching southern England. Not every warning was followed by bombers flying over the city, and bombs were dropped on fewer occasions still; in his diary for 16 September 1945 Jack, quoting the official figures, writes that there were '424 Alerts and a few false alarms during the war'; among them there were about 20 raids in which bombs were dropped on Cambridge.

Wednesday 19 June. France has packed in.[6] Churchill has determined that England shall fight on alone. This attitude, according to the press, is ridiculed in Germany. I should think so, too. Now we must wait and see — if we get the chance.

We keep getting air-raids. The week before last there was one on the Thursday night and two on the Friday night. Last night the siren went off at about 11.30. About 12.30 I was awakened by a terrific crash. I called the children down into our bedroom, They got in the bed with Jess. I dressed and lay on the couch that is in our bedroom. Then we heard gunfire. The crash turned out to be a bomb (I heard at the bathing sheds tonight that there were two bombs, as they had discovered two craters)

---

[6] France surrendered after her humiliation by the German *blitzkrieg* of May 1940. Her coastline and northern France were occupied by German troops.

on some houses in Vicarage Terrace, killing nine people and injuring a lot more. (My brother Tom lived there years ago.) The gunfire was from a Spitfire that went up from Duxford and brought down the machine that dropped the bombs. Lots of people say they saw it brought down. I wasn't one of them. Jess and I went and had a look at the damage done this morning. Nine houses were just a pile of rubble. They were digging for the bodies. The houses in the next street were stripped of their chimney pots and damaged so that the people had to get out of them (I was told this while we were looking on). I heard from my brother Fred that later in the day the parson was there praying over the rubble. ... This is all we've got to look forward to now. I think public opinion is growing against the futility of the war, however, so it might be over sooner than is generally expected. I feel certain that Churchill realises above all people the hopelessness of HIS cause. ...

Racing has stopped again from today. This puts me in a precarious position financially as I'm still not getting a living at the shop. Work is so spasmodic. Any little crisis upsets it.

Dunlop Kidman is posted as missing, believed killed. ... He was a Spitfire pilot and I'm afraid there's little chance of him turning up. Age-groups are rapidly being called up. I am still wondering why, as I feel Germany will never allow this country the time to recover from the shattering blows it has lately received in the war. ...

A chap who works at the local infirmary [Addenbrooke's Hospital] told me the staff there, numbering 150, have no proper gas-masks. It is a county infirmary in the borough; and that causes the trouble.[7] Each says the other should provide them. Of course, the military authorities stand aloof, deeming themselves not responsible. This is a good example of the way this country does things. ...

---

[7] Addenbrooke's Hospital was begun in 1766. Until the setting up of the National Health Service in 1948 it was controlled by subscribers and others, and supported by subscriptions and gifts. Inhabitants of the borough and county received treatment by virtue of the subscriptions paid on behalf of their localities.

A CO chairman asked an applicant the other day if he would chase a parachutist with a poker if he saw one. Morals aren't the only thing that slide during a war. Common sense seems to slide as well. Hysteria everywhere. ...

Cobber Kain, a famous air ace has been killed. He seemed to be out to make his 'bag' of enemy planes a record. He was about 22. ... once when his plane was damaged he parachuted, lost consciousness a bit, came to passing through some clouds and remembered saying he must be in heaven. My comment at the time was to the effect that he was conceited, thinking he was in heaven after killing other people (he'd just brought down an enemy plane in flames), but all that seems trivial now he's gone, poor fellow. How youth is perverted and destroyed nowadays. It's very, very sad.

I'd like to start on another book, but it hardly seems worthwhile.

Sunday 23 June. There was another air-raid on Friday night. The children came down and got into the bed with Jess for a time while I lay on the couch in the bedroom and swore. ... about our leaders of the last few years, not Jerry. We'll have to get up though. A bomb falling anywhere near this house and it will collapse.

They're calling up men now more rapidly. As if that will help when all they can do is to train them with broomsticks. There's no equipment for them and unless I'm mistaken this country will not be given the chance to provide any. The efforts of millions of soldiers will not mend all the cracks made by the National Government since 1931. It's annihilation, starvation and capitulation now, I'm thinking.

I'm slack at the shop and am wondering how I shall manage to carry on much longer. ... I'd like to start another book and get on with some examination work, but the tenseness of the times makes me feel inclined to sit on the fence and go easy. As Frank Edwards said the other day a lot more study won't make me any better corpse. That's a true estimate of public feeling now, I reckon. ... Say what they like about getting under way. Germany has unlimited supplies and a big advantage over us now with France, according to the treaty terms with Germany, having converted into another enemy country; for that's what it amounts to. ...

They're building blockhouses about here now. There's one on Coe Fen, where Dale's garden used to be. What a wicked waste of energy it all is. There's enough to fight in this world without fighting one another. There's a lot of national slogans about like 'Go to it' … and 'Arms for Everybody' … . How people love slogans, catchwords, dressing up in uniforms and similar nonsense. …

Tuesday 25 June. Another raid last night, lasting from 12.00 till 4.00 a.m.. People round here were excited when the siren went off, those in the cottages going into the bigger houses in Lensfield Road. Some of them went into the shelters and there were arguments between them and an ARP warden who told them they were going to the shelters at their own risk. … One woman, short and fat (Mrs C....) bawled out crossly that … they would be staying in their own homes at their own risk; they would all fall down. Then there seemed a general exodus from Gothic Street. Really, it is the sensible thing to do. These houses wouldn't take much shaking down.

We soon heard the 'ump, ump' of the enemy plane (or planes), as we know their sound now. A light appeared in the sky as I looked out of the window (a silly thing to do though tempting); whether it was a flare I don't know, but then I saw the plane blotting out the stars. It went Duxford way. Later we heard either gunfire or the explosion of bombs. One cannot establish any fact in these matters the next day, everything is so severely censored. … Jim and Jock [the dogs] take no notice of the siren: a hell of a row it is. …

We are assured that there is plenty of food in the country. Not so very assuring when we remember other assurances stated by our leaders: the impregnability of the Maginot Line, for example; or the strength of our air force.

I'm solely depending on the work at the shop now. What a precarious existence. Tonight I was offered another job — at a local aerodrome. I turned it down; and it didn't need much thinking about either. … The Backs of the colleges round about King's is chockful of army lorries. How everything goes by the board during a war …

Wednesday 26 June. Another air-raid last night. I lay awake expecting the siren to go off and it did. We got up, brought Jess and Jack's beds downstairs, made them up in the front room and went back to bed again. The 'All Clear' sounded about 3 o'clock, but I never slept until 4.00 and then only fitfully. Two ARP wardens acted the part of chattermags outside under the archway and the lorries rushing about put the finishing touch to it all. …

Young Jess is working hard for the School Certificate. What a cheerful time for studying. … I'm reading Neil Bell's *Son of Richard Carden*. Tried it years ago, but never finished it. It's only patchily good. They're making up the beds in preparation for an air-raid, so I'd better chuck it and lend a hand.

July 1940

Sunday 7 July. This last few days we've been setting about the French fleet.[8] … Billy Webb, a man of about 50 and a friend of Frank Edwards, was threatened the other night by a Local Defence Volunteer with a rifle because the latter heard him say 'When the hell are they going to stop all this?', referring to the tank trap built on the bridge. … Life is cheap at the moment in England. LDVs and soldiers shoot quickly if people don't pull up when challenged. And we've still got to get used to being challenged. Bed seems the best place after dark. But is it, for then there's the raiders? I saw two members of the CUOTC [Cambridge University Officers' Training Corps] come out of the Pickerel Inn yard the other Saturday night, one of them letting off his revolver.

The siren is not sounded now unless there is a massed raid. The moral[e] of the people was getting low through constantly being got up at nights, that's why. … Jock the newspaperman living near here said 'We're on our oon mook heap now, Jack' to me the other day. He wasn't very enthusiastic either. …

Jack won the diving for boys under 13 at his school sports the other afternoon (Friday). He was second in the 30 yards for boys under 14, just pipped by Eric Ford, a big, heavily built

---

[8] Britain wished to deny the French fleet to Germany, and on 3 July a British naval force destroyed two battleships and a battle-cruiser at Oran, in French Algeria.

boy of 14½. ... It was a very hot afternoon. Jess minded the shop while I went to have a look. I took three photos quickly and hope they come out. ...

Neil Bell has sent me his latest (and he says probably his last) book, *So Perish the Roses*. I haven't read it yet. It's about Charles Lamb, whom Bell thinks a lot of. Bell's very pessimistic about the war. Thinks it will be over by September (I do, too), and that it will end in devastation. I'm wondering, as an alternative, if Germany will starve us out. Am laying in provisions against a siege. There'll probably be a famine after the war, in any case.

Now racing has collapsed, the book 'Jim Baxter – Snob' has been rejected and I'm slack at the shop; the outlook is pretty arid, for Constables sent back the novel. Said they would have taken a chance and published it but for the present difficult times. It didn't help people to forget the war; its very qualities were against it. Told me to put it away for the present. Thought I wouldn't do any more writing [studying?] until after the war (can't afford the books to study) but have started another book.

Sunday 21 July. ... Barbusse thought war was racial suicide; so do I.[9] Everything I've read about the British constitution – and I took it as a subject for a degree – has buttered it, except Ramsay Muir. Fundamentally our government is similar to the German government. Cabinet dictatorship has its failings – and plenty.

The other day Young Jess asked me what 'Fifth Column' meant (the papers are full of 'Fifth Column' talk nowadays) and after explaining Franco's description an easy explanation suddenly came to me and I said 'the enemy within the gates'. ...

Another row in Gothic Street the other night. A married couple left their children, four of them under seven, one eighteen months, alone all night after a row. Jock the newspaper chap took them in his house and had a good row with the mother about it. Said a lot about what would have happened if the siren had gone off, adding he took the baby into bed with him

---

[9] Henri Barbusse's novel *Le Feu* (1916) described the horrors of trench warfare, in which Barbusse had taken part.

and the missus; an odd touch that, as 'the missus' is the woman he lives with and he doesn't like it to be known they sleep together. He gave the show away (if it wanted giving away) in his excitement.

A man was sent to prison the other day for talking against the war. The man who gave evidence against him said he told the man he was a traitor and didn't deserve to live in a free country! ... Frank Edwards registered as a CO yesterday week with the thirty-twos. Jack broke the front room window yesterday. Beating the bombers, perhaps.

August 1940

Friday 2 August. Yesterday I had a day out with Jack—a very enjoyable one, spent beside the river at Grantchester. It was a glorious morning and we walked there with Jock and Jim by way of the road through Newnham. The day was delightfully drowsy and as we walked along Barton Road I said to Jack: no wonder children remember their summer holidays! I told him about the sexual relationship between men and women as we walked along the road to Grantchester and found I was still talking about it when we reached the Meadows. ... I think I made a pretty sound job of it [the talk]. I remember reading Wells on the subject; he thought it better, simpler and easier for teachers to tell children all about sex at school; they could do it more objectively than a child's own parents. I think he's right, for I'm a free and easy sort and if I felt the subject a bit awkward, what must some feel like. We had lots of swims and did plenty of sunbathing. I was broke, but luckily found sixpence in the meadows so we were able to buy some chocolate in the village. After dinner we went to the 'Pool' [Byron's Pool] and had a swim there. The Cashes and the Jesses (they minded the shop—didn't it want some looking after—one pair of women's heeled!) came up later in a punt and canoe respectively.

The siren went off as a test at one o'clock and Jock barked at it. Blessed if it didn't go off again—that night when we were abed. I thought as it was stated they wouldn't be sounding it unless there was a serious likelihood of serious bombing that it was advisable for us to go to a shelter. We went to one in Trumpington Street: the wine-cellar of a big house. But it wasn't for long. The 'All Clear' sounded and home we came to bed. I was surprised. Just before the siren sounded I heard bombs dropped in the distance (confirmed next day as at Linton) and really expected shrapnel to be falling in the streets on the way to the shelter. There was bit of muddle before starting out, Jess being unable to find her shoes and having to take her hair grips out! It was a case of getting slacker in habits as there's been a spell without the siren going off. ... I wrote Bell about his book *So Perish the Roses.* It was good. I'm studying Italian and desultorily writing another book.

Tuesday 6 August. I knocked off work Saturday dinnertime and started again this morning: a long week-end as, unofficially, it was Bank Holiday. Funny I should get a Bank Holiday after not getting one for 20 years when most other people are working (Government orders!) The time has been spent beside the river at Grantchester and as the weather has been a treat, it's been great. Yesterday was Jack's birthday; he's 13 and getting a big chap. I gave him five bob, as much as I could spring, on Saturday. He bought a catapult (2*s* 3*d*) and potato gun (1*s*) that I know of …

London University sent me my intermediate certificate last week. I'm reading Michael Sadleir's *Fanny by Gaslight* [1940].[10] It's very good. …

I saw a letter in the paper from the Rev. Bernard Marshall of the Catholic Rectory on Saturday evening. People have been complaining about the church clock chiming at night. He said he wants to be a good neighbour, [and] will other people write him about the clock chiming, whether they like it or not. I wrote. Told him I like it as much now as I did 32 years ago when the sound of its chiming came into the infants' school in Union Road (now a bookbinder's), which I was then attending. I also said it was part of the neighbourhood like the rooks on Brookside. So it is. Church bells can't be rung now (they're to be rung in the case of an invasion), but church clocks can still chime. I bar church, but not their clocks.

---

[10] Michael Sadleir (1888–1957) was a director of Constable, the publishers, and as Jack's main contact there recurs frequently in the diaries. He was the author of several novels and works of literary criticism and history.

Friday 16 August. I am typing this at the shop in Shelley Terrace as the air-raid siren sounding the 'All Clear' is dying away. Not a long raid, under half an hour, and the first in daylight. I went down the cellar with Mrs Williams who lives over the shop and her two babies. ... I was expecting this, as they'll be sure to be hunting for the aerodromes about here. ...

I wrote to Neil Bell last week and suggested he wrote a biography of D. H. Lawrence. I think the latter is his meat and said so. I'm reading Lamb's letters. And carrying on with another book that I've provisionally called 'Tormented Flesh'. Have done about 35,000 words at present. The tempo of the air war is increasing. Doesn't look as if the war will finish with the year from its beginning now as I thought it probably would a few weeks ago. ... I'm making fair progress with Italian. ...

Report of Frank Edwards's appearance before the Cambridge Tribunal for Conscientious Objectors: 20 August 1940.

The Proceedings opened with Frank Edwards reading the oath. The Clerk of the Court then read a copy of his statement objecting to military service.

Judge Lawson Campbell:[11]	You are a hairdresser. Is it your own shop?
Edwards:	Yes.
L.C.	Any men working for you?
E.	Not now; two before the war.
L.C.	You are on your own now then, are you?
E.	Yes.
L.C.	How long have you held these views?
E.	Since a child.
L.C.	How old were you then?

---

[11] William Lawson Campbell (1890–1970): Harrow and Magdalen College, Oxford; barrister, 1914; County Court judge 1937–1962; chairman of various Cambridgeshire quarter-sessions 1941–65. He lived in Great Shelford, a village just outside Cambridge.

E.	About ten when I first had these views, and started taking notice of the horrors of war.
Professor Clapham.[12]	Yes, yes, we have done all that. How would you have dealt with the international situation last September?
E.	That's a difficult question to answer. I am not a professional politician.
C.	You must have formed some opinion.
E.	Certainly. I've thought for last few years that the affairs of the world were not conducted properly. Statesmen haven't got together as they should have done.
C.	What if one country has an armed force and another has not?
E.	That doesn't affect my conscience.
Judge Lawson Campbell.	You must answer the question.
Professor Clapham.	In a world, some armed and others not, what is your view?
E.	I still stand for disarmament.
C.	I see. Surely, you've heard of Denmark. Do you agree with them?
E.	I think that better than armed resistance.
C.	You think the bullies of the world should take what they like?
E.	I've met a few bullies and never had to resort to force. I've always managed to get along by argument.
C.	That is not the question. The international bully should have his way; that is your view?

---

[12] John Clapham (1873–1946): Fellow of King's College, Professor of Economic History at Cambridge, 1928–38.

E.	I've always got on all right with people.
C	You would have no police.
E.	Not an armed police. I believe in civil body to use persuasion.
C.	Any friends in the police?
E.	A number of customers.
C.	Haven't they told you they have to use force?
E.	I've never discussed their duties with them.
C.	I infer from your statement that your views are not religious, but humanitarian.
E.	Yes.

Judge Lawson Campbell read aloud the seven names on a short statement submitted by Edwards as proof that he had held his pacifist beliefs for years.

Judge Lawson Campbell.	Who are these people on your pacifist list? Are they pacifists?
E.	No. Some of them have served in the army. I could have got many more; 100 names if necessary.
L.C.	I see by your statement that you are only willing to do work of real service. What do you consider to be such work?
E.	I think my present work is.
L.C.	So you think you should go on barbering in Mill Road?
E.	I see nothing dishonourable in that.
L.C.	No, no.
E.	I believe, I think, I am performing a useful service. People often wait an hour for my services.
Professor Clapham.	Ladies think a lot of time spent on their hair is well spent. That doesn't prove that the time is well spent.
E.	I don't say I spend a lot of time on a customer's hair. There is a difference in ladies' and gentlemen's hairdressing.

The Inquiry closed.

Wednesday 21 August. Last Sunday as I was walking along the river bank on the way to Grantchester Meadows where we spent most of the day, I suddenly saw a black cloud of smoke rising in the distance. … it turned out to be smoke rising from the crash of two Blenheim bombers. … all the occupants of the two machines were killed. …

The siren went off this morning as I was going to work just after 9 o'clock. … [The family] went into Mrs Ludman's across the street. Her son's in the RAF as an instructor and every noise she heard she kept saying 'that's right, bring 'em down', meaning our man bring down the German planes. At the same time she was kissing her servant because she was scared. … the destructive and protective instincts working together. …

Frank Edwards went before the tribunal for COs yesterday. He was removed from the register. The inquiry into his conscience was a farce. I took a shorthand note of the proceedings … . I'm buying a sewing machine for stitching work at the shop. Price £2. And I can't afford even that. …

Monday 26 August. A lot of bombs were dropped on Cambridge last night. The siren was not sounded. At about 2.30 I was awakened by the sound of a distant explosion and said to Jess that it was a bomb. We heard an aeroplane approaching and recognised it as one of Jerry's by the drone of the engine. Almost immediately there was a tearing sound and a violent explosion that shook the house and almost sent the windows in (it cracked three); there was the loud patter of falling debris on the roof, which at the time I thought was shrapnel. I got out of bed and there was a whistling noise; sign of another bomb falling. I couldn't remember if a whistle denoted a bomb falling in the distance (it does), but to avoid flying glass crouched at the foot of the bed. There was no explosion. Later we heard that this bomb had fallen in Brooklands Avenue and had not gone off.

I spoke to Jess as she was climbing over the foot of the bed and took hold of her to buck her up; she suddenly went limp; she had fainted. … It was still dark as I couldn't light up, the bedroom not being blacked out. I called to the children downstairs (I take their beds up and down stairs night and morning) and they were all right (they take things pretty lightly), and Jess soon pulling round we went round to Pemberton Terrace to see what damage had been done by the bomb that shook us up. ... The bomb had fallen on a tree, knocking it down and also part of a garden wall. All the windows and some of the doors were blown out in the immediate vicinity, but there were no casualties. ...

Tuesday 27 August. There was another raid yesterday afternoon. Jack and I were painting 'Boot Repairs' on the shop window and when the siren sounded we went down the cellar. ... They're all up the river, so I'll leave off and go and have a swim.

Thursday 29 August. I've just heard it said that about 100 incendiary bombs were dropped on Cherry Hinton last night; and a high explosive bomb. The bomber was brought down by a Spitfire, or so it is rumoured, but it isn't much good taking notice of stray news nowadays. We had a restless night. We didn't get up, but could hear the German planes. There was a lot of people running about the streets, too. Hearing the purple was showing (the colour before the siren goes off, indicating raiders in the vicinity) they just hung about as they often do, thinking it is not worth while going to bed.[13] The siren didn't go off last night and the raiders were over the town, so how they muck things about I don't know. ...

I had a dip (the second today) and at Paradise Corner Jack dived from the top of a willow tree. ... it's the first time I've seen him. Bert Cash and I roughly measured up the height of the dive; it was nearly 30 feet. ...

Aeroplanes are droning past as I type ... And it's a queer sight to see tanks and armoured cars punting round the streets and dugouts and sandbags at the sides of the roads with block

---

[13] Air raids: warnings of the approach of bombers were sent by telephone to command posts, which would then sound the siren. The message called 'the purple' immediately preceded the sounding of the siren to advise places exempt from the blackout (such as war factories) that lighting should be extinguished immediately because of the imminent approach of bombers. Jack's words suggest that these messages may sometimes have resulted in coloured lights being shown briefly out of doors: T. H. O'Brien, *Civil Defence* (1955), pp. 89–90 *et seq.*

Jack junior diving into the Cam from the top of
a tree, 21 July 1943.
This picture appeared in the local press.

houses on the fields and commons surrounded with barbed wire. We finished off the day by going to the Victoria and seeing *Mice and Men* [from John Steinbeck's novel *Of Mice and Men* (1937)]. …

Friday 30 August. It's nearly 10 o'clock at night and as I type I can hear the loud 'oomp, oomp' of the German aeroplane engines in the south. They're over every night now. This afternoon just before 5.00 the siren sounded. I had just finished work at the shop and was settling down to do some writing on the novel I am doing. Down the cellar I went, nursing Mrs Williams's baby son Ronnie for some of the time … . The 'All Clear' hadn't sounded when I left off just before 6.00. As I cycled home the town seemed dead. Traffic was at a standstill, but there were a number of people about, at their doors and windows, and soldiers and air-force men were standing about staring upwards in the direction of droning planes. I noticed one warden was carrying his rattle (for use in case of gas). The 'All Clear' sounded soon after I got home. ...

Saturday 31 August. The siren didn't go off in the night as I expected but it did this morning just after 8 o'clock as we were getting up. We went across the road to Mrs Ludman's, whose house is the basement type. The room was full of her lodgers and people of the neighbourhood. As I walked along the street the enemy planes were roaring right overhead and an ARP warden told me to take cover. A bomb exploded in the distance with a terrific rumble as I walked into Mrs Ludman's kitchen. I sat on a step and did a bit of Italian and then got tired of waiting and came back home. ... The siren went about two minutes before the enemy planes went over. Parker's Piece is the nearest place on which public shelters have been built around here (those we went to in St Peter's Terrace — or near there in Trumpington Street — are really private, only being open to the public at certain hours) and the 'Piece' is a good five minutes walk from here.

... There's plenty of planes buzzing around all the while and the way the troops are on the move in tanks and armoured cars and lorries indicates ... the possibility of invasion within a day or two; or at least that our leaders think so. ...

September 1940

Tuesday 3 September. ... A number of German aeroplanes passed over about an hour after we had got to bed and a few minutes later we heard distant explosions. We could hear these planes for a long time and either they were going very slow or the stillness of the night intensified the sound of their engines. There's no raid warning at nights. They just let us take pot luck.

I can hear Jock the newspaper chap talking outside. ... The other night when he was half tipsy he was shouting in the street that Jerry bombs were no good; they never exploded! ... If it were true, all I can say is: a good job, too.

Evening. The family spent most of the day beside the river. The weather has been beautiful. ...

Wednesday 4 September. ... I walked to Paradise where the family were with the Cash's at midday.[14] It was terrifically hot, the sky a clear blue, and the journey being about two miles, I was glad of a swim. I had dinner there and then another quick dip before going back to work. The shop in the afternoon was as hot as a bakehouse. ...

Monday 9 September. ... Yesterday morning I found a little baby girl, so young she couldn't talk, near a bridge over the brook [Hobson's Brook, at Brookside]. I took her home and thought what b.s some parents are. ...

... London is getting an awful pasting from enemy aircraft and I don't think ... that it can last at the rate things are going. I can hardly believe Germany will give this country a chance to get production under way during another winter. ...

Tuesday 10 September. The church bells were rung at many places over the weekend — [an] indication of invasion. The papers say it an accident they rang, but Jess was told today that an attempted invasion on a small scale was actually tried. ... This may be a rumour; they are legion nowadays. Last night incendiary bombs were dropped on Marshall's aerodrome in the town; flares as well. This was told us by the brother of a man at work there who helped put them out, so I expect it is true. ...

The custodian at the bathing sheds told me a swimmer named A. C. Leigh (a member of the Granta Swimming Club, aged about 20, whom I know very well) was down there yesterday, rubbing his hands with glee because next Monday he is being 'given' a Spitfire. He's been in the RAF just over a year. ... Bert Cash joined the Home Guard, but resigned because they wouldn't give him a gun. He thinks he didn't get a gun because he has left-wing views. There's several Home Guard members round here; rather boozy chaps who wouldn't stand much chance against trained men of any sort. ...

---

[14] Paradise is an area of Newnham on the west bank of the Cam, and often a place for swimmers and picnickers.

... How I long for peace and normal conditions, even as they existed before the war. Times like the present make people think they didn't know when they were well off if they were not satisfied with their lot say a couple of years ago.

Friday 13 September. I had the day off yesterday. ... [The diarist and his son Jack] biked to Haverhill, picking a few blackberries on the way and stopping near Horseheath to have some grub. ... We bought some fruit and sweets and then cycled to Saffron Walden. The journey was made a bit difficult through the signposts being down because of the war. There was also a fair amount of wind, the day being dull, and it rained most of the afternoon. We had a swim at Saffron Walden and arrived home just before 7.00, when we took the dogs for a short walk and got ourselves a chip supper, ... Our day's ride was about 47 miles. I was very tired when I went to bed between 9.00 and 10.00, but I hadn't been there long when the siren sounded ... . The warning was of short duration and reminded us like the tanks, lorries, guns and soldiers we saw about the roads, fields and woods during the way that there was a war on. I thought we should be stopped and asked for our identity cards. We were not. And people never hesitated in directing us for all the warnings to be on guard against strangers in case they are German parachutists. One old man toddled down a garden and asked us if we were from London. He said he was, he had been bombed out of it.

Saturday 14 September. Early afternoon. Racing resumed today, but there is very little doing. That was hardly to be expected with the intensity of the air-raids and (according to Churchill's broadcast a couple of days ago) invasion imminent. There's a fleet of boats ready the other side of the Channel all along the French coast to bring Jerry over according to all accounts. ...

We went to the Edwards' last night and had supper there. When Frank and I were fetching the fish and chips we could see anti-aircraft shells bursting in the sky like rockets London way. Had a letter from Eric yesterday (it took three days to come from London) and he said it's been ghastly there.[15]

---

[15] Eric Goldsmith, a London friend of the diarist: see note 1, p. 21.

All steam and electric trains stopped and shell craters 40 feet wide. He said the war can't last long. ...

Tuesday 17 September. The siren sounded last night just after 1.00. Jess had a bad head and felt too ill to get up, so I went to a shelter with the children and then came back home. It was bright moonlight night with big, big clouds to help the raiders. I made Jess a cup of tea and had one myself and in between times mooched up the street, dropping in on Bill Hiner's (Bill Adams in 'Queen Street') to see how he and his wife were getting on, as he's bedridden and on his last legs. The poor old fellow looked pretty bad and was sitting up in bed. He muttered something about a raid being on in London and that's all, apparently dazed, while his old lady — they are both well over 70 — said tearfully how dreadful it all was. ... The 'All Clear' sounded at about 2.30 when I went to meet the children coming out of the shelter. I dozed fitfully for about two hours and then the siren went again ... There was another warning at about 9.30. The children had gone to school ... and as I'd been to Langford's [Fitzroy St.] to get some leather it delayed me and I happened to be at home when it went off. I was glad of that as Jess, although up, had a bad head still and was unable to go to a shelter. ... the 'All Clear' went about 10.15 and off I went to work with the dogs. ...

Eric came down on Saturday after all, ... He put up with Frank Edwards and over the weekend the three of us had a number of walks, going to King's College Chapel on Sunday morning to try to go up on the roof, but that's not permitted now the war is on. We went beside the river up Paradise in the afternoon where the family was with the Cash's and Mrs Edwards and two boys whom Young Jess is friendly with ... . They had a fire in a copse and were baking potatoes as well as having a ukelele and mouth organ on the go. ...

Sunday 22 September. Last night after I had finished writing, just after 9 o'clock, I had a walk round the town. Lorries full of soldiers off somewhere — I thought I heard a policeman on point duty calling out to some of them that the purple light was on and at the risk of arrest hung round him to find out exactly what he was saying, but couldn't: I have no doubt they would soon arrest a suspicious character these days on the chance that he was a Fifth Columnist—extra specials were on duty, soldiers, crowds of them, walking about fully armed, the blackout and distant flashes, probably gunfire or high explosives in London, reminded me there was a war on. I felt there would be a raid warning during the night and when I got to bed had the itch—literally—and couldn't get to sleep until between 1.00 and 2.00. About 4.00 I was in a deep sleep and then the siren sounded and up we had to get and go to a shelter. It was short warning and I heard this morning the enemy planes were over and gone long before the siren sounded. It was a beautiful night, moon shining bright in a sky patchy with big white clouds.

I heard a doctor of medicine say at the river the other day that God was kind to us when somebody had the brains and initiative to invent Spitfires to beat back the German attacks! I wondered at his state of mind and what God, who was kind enough to give the Jerries their bombers and Messerschmidt fighters, thought about it.

Evacuees, men, women and children are crowding into the town from London. It's hot as hell there. And now they are repairing the houses round here to shelter some of them. It matters no longer that the stairs are dark and winding and that there is no air space ... .

... The afternoon turned out wet and reading the newspaper and dozing the last thing I expected was to hear the siren, but it sounded and we went to a shelter. ... Talk about gas is creeping into the papers, as if that's expected before long in the new attempt at frightfulness. Racing was expected to have started again last week, but three meetings were abandoned owing to the tense conditions that have arisen in the country through the imminence of invasion, and at present attempts to start it again during the back-end [autumn] are a washout. A good thing too, in a way, although goodness knows, I'd be glad to win a little cash.

Monday 23 September. The siren sounded again last night at 8.30 and we were in the shelter till 11.30. ... I keep trying to write, but it's do a paragraph and then go to a shelter. ...

Tuesday 24 September. A hell of a night. There was a warning just before 9.00 and we were in a shelter till midnight. As soon as we got to bed the siren went again, but as the children had had so little sleep we thought we would keep abed. We wished we hadn't. The 'All Clear' went at 2.00; there had been plenty of planes over and we heard several explosions. I dozed off, although it might have been a deep sleep; I don't know, for I've heard there was another warning before the next one I heard at about 4 o'clock. For the next hour there was the nerve-racking noise of a German bomber cruising over the town. At last he loosed his bombs. There was a whistle and I said to Jess 'Hold tight, here they come'. There were three crashes, each followed by a bright flash, the windows rattled, the house shook. Jess nearly went off again and young Jess was shaken up when I got downstairs. I popped down to see old Bill Hiner and his missus and Jack made some tea. At 6.00 we went to look at the damage in Tenison Road where one of the bombs had fallen. There was an enormous crater, doors were off, houses damaged and glass all over the place, but nobody was hurt. It was in a garden opposite to Mr Chandler's house (my old headmaster), which was badly knocked about. Jack and I got by the wardens for a close view and I called at the house to find that he and his daughters were quite all right. He shook hands with me through the window, literally smashed out with the door, and was smilingly unruffled, which I thought was good at his age as he's over 80. Another bomb fell on Fenner's; [as for] the third there seems to be some doubt where it fell, but there were no casualties. ...

Thursday 26 September. ... I pictured the bombs [on 24 September] as falling two or three yards apart—could almost see them!—but actually they were 200 or 300 yards apart, such is the speed of the bombers. Last night (Wednesday) the siren sounded about 9.00 and we were in the shelter till 11.00: nothing happened. There was a lot of East-enders there and I tried to make a couple of children comfortable beds on chairs with Jack's and my coat. I tried to read Wells' *Fate of Homo Sapiens* [1939] there (very appropriately), but there was too much noise and I didn't get through a dozen pages during the two hours, although I read about 150 pages during the day. The Germans say they bombed Cambridge on Tuesday night because we bombed Heidelberg (university town). ... People have put Union Jacks out and scribbled defiance of Hitler on their windows near where the bombs fell in Tenison Avenue. ... I'm very slack at the shop. Don't know whether all the raid warnings are the cause. It's depressing and hardly gives me courage to write.

Friday 27 September. ... We heard this morning that bombs were dropped round Harston and Haslingfield; perhaps Newton or Fowlmere, rumour is varied; anyway, that direction. ... *Peace News* says there are ten COs in prison, and a number detained waiting for them to submit voluntarily to the medical examination (three of these have been released). What a change from the last war. I know a man who was in prison with over 1,000.

Sunday 29 September. ... I feel that this war cannot go on much longer. Bayonets will have to be introduced into the lives of the people if it is. ... Soon this country will have to reorganise its financial system; it will be done, I think, on German lines. What complications will then arise with America, about our only rather dubious ally, who will remain linked to gold? ... What a muddle the mismanagement of our leaders has made for us as well as themselves. All to protect a monied class who hang on to the old order like grim death. Great Britain lost this war and her Empire when we sabotaged the cause of the Spanish workers.

I am reading Tressell's *The Ragged Trousered Philanthropists* [1914]. Wells's *Fate of Homo Sapiens* was patchily good. I thought it rather wordy and a lot of it rather ambiguous in presentation. His old crispness and direct method of presentation seemed to be lacking. Or was it me? Anyway, I had to sit and puzzle pretty often about what he meant. Bags of what he said was just destructive criticism; nothing constructive about it at all. ... That's no good. He dislikes Russia and Communism, yet admits when pulling it to pieces that changes for the better have taken place in Russia. He can't have it both ways and seems to be tinkering with a bolstered-up system of capitalism still. Frankly, I think he's all in the air; up the pole now. As his silly article in a Sunday newspaper a fortnight ago showed. He then just ranted against Germany. Wonder he didn't say exterminate them all. ...

October 1940

Wednesday 2 October. ... We don't dislike hearing the siren now ('Wailing Winnie' as the newspapers are calling it) as we are glad to get below ground. That's preferable to lying abed and hearing enemy planes continually droning overhead looking for somewhere to let loose their load. ... They're billeting evacuees in the town again.

I'm still trying to write that novel. Some days I do 1,000 or 1,500 words, but it's a job. At present I've written about 60,000 words. ...

Saturday 5 October. The siren sounded last night just after 12.00. I saw the family to a shelter and then came back to Gothic Street to see how old Bill Hiner and his missus were faring. Enemy bombers were roaring overhead all the while. Everything seemed a bit nightmarish in old Bill's. He on his deathbed and his frail little wife beside with the heavy roar of the bombers as a perpetual menace to the peace of old age. My thoughts went back 30 years when we lived next door to them, to a Christmas night when my brother Perce and I sat over the fire, lonely as the Old Man and Nap were out, listening to Bill and his family having a sing-song. 'When the fields are white with daisies' was one of the songs they sang and I always think of that night whenever I hear it sung now. Bill was strong and fit and well then, not much older than I am now, which is a pointer to old age, and it seemed strange that the gap that had brought me to manhood had almost killed him off. And life seemed a good deal of a dream altogether as I sat there: the memory was a dream and I seemed to be living in one; a very nasty one because of the noise of the engines overhead. ...

Sunday 6 October. Another warning last night (it's called the 'Alert' now) lasting from 12.00 to 3.00. ... It's not much use going to bed until after turning-out time. The soldiers row and squabble in the archway under our bedroom windows for a long time after coming out of the pub 20 minutes to half-an-hour after licensing hours; the regulations are so slack. Most of them are Scotchmen and seem to talk a foreign language. There's high jinks and revelry in the Spread Eagle every evening. The popular war song seems to be 'Over the Rainbow', which is tuneful and catchy. ... 'Roll out the Barrel' is the modern 'Tipperary'. ...

...We're getting two ounces of butter now and four ounces of sugar each a week — while it lasts. I'm busier at the shop because of the influx of evacuees of both sexes and all ages, but my earnings still leave a lot to be desired. Money is still important, yet not so important as it seemed time back. Everything dwindles in view of the major catastrophe of the war and its events.

Tuesday 8 October. ... There was a warning last night between 10.00 and 11.00; another between 1.00 and 4.00. We went to a shelter both times and all felt washed out this morning. It was a cold night and cold down there. When we came back just after 4.00 we had a cup of 'Bovril' each and then went to bed just before 5.00. It is almost impossible to get on with the novel I'm writing. I leave off at 6.00, come home, have a wash, eat my tea, read the evening paper, take the dogs for a little walk, feed them ... bring the children's beds downstairs and blackout (Jess often does her whack in these little jobs — I mustn't forget that). Then I sit down to write a paragraph or two and the siren sounds and off we go to a shelter. ...

Wednesday 9 October. ... Every night there's lone enemy planes cruising round; these seem a menace and they are as they generally let something go before clearing off. Yet when these are over there is never a warning sounded.

Thursday 10 October. The siren sounded early last night ... about 8 o'clock ... [The family went to the shelter and] returned home just before the 'All Clear' at 11.15. There were no more warnings during the night, but at 3.00 in the morning I heard nearly a dozen heavy explosions in the distance, ...

Bevin the Labour leader is working hard for HIS cause: going round shaking hands with the workers saying 'I'm Bevin'... .

He was bought by the Old Gang ages ago. This system's resiliency is largely due to its absorption of the workers' leaders …

Friday 11 October. There was a warning last night just after 10.00. We'd only been in bed a few minutes and off we had to go to the shelter. … There were some very little children there, upset and irritable through being disturbed in their night's sleep and I helped to make them comfortable too. We got home about 12.30 and was [thus] awakened at 1.00 by two heavy explosions that made the windows rattle hard. We heard today they fell at Potton, but rumours are not very reliable, although bombs are falling all over the place round here like rain, only more damaging. … It has just struck 8.00 and we've had our first warning of the evening. … The warning lasted about half an hour … . Work is brisker at the shop, but very broken and it hangs out the day. …

Monday 14 October. Everything was quiet on Saturday night: we had a good night's rest. At night there was a short warning between 12.00 and 1.00. We got up and went to a shelter although Jess at first hung fire. I pointed out that we must be consistent … There were no planes about during the warning, … but after we returned bombers as usual started cruising about and just before 4.00 I was awakened by a heavy explosion. … I heard today the explosion was near Meldreth; … More often than not the bombers turn up after the 'All Clear'. …

   After I wrote the above round about 7.30 I started on the novel. Straightaway the siren sounded and off to a shelter. I did some writing down there and some Italian then came and had a look at Bill Hiner and his wife and dropped in [at] home to do some typing, but I heard Jerry over and went back to the shelter for a time, returning a short while ago to carry on with the typing. It's now about 11 o'clock and the 'All Clear' has just sounded so the family will be here soon, pretty cold, too, I expect. … The night is glorious; there is almost a full moon.

Wednesday 16 October. Jack and I took the dogs for a walk last night and just as we got home at about 7.30, there was the sound of a plane and I went out the back and listened. Jack called out from the front room, asking if it were a German and I said I wasn't sure. Just then there were flashes in the sky and a whistle and I darted into the house knowing it was a falling bomb. Instinctively, I wanted to avoid flying shrapnel, but there was the thought that perhaps I was getting out of the frying pan into the fire, as the likelihood of the house collapsing has always to be considered. In the kitchen I crouched slightly with hunched shoulders, as if I were about to take the whole weight of the house on them: I told the children to get under the table, shouting out … . There was a terrific explosion and I hurried along the passage to see Jim [the dog] go under the table first, followed by Jack and Jess with Jock [the other dog] bringing up the rear, only partly able to get under, his tail and rump sticking out. … we had to laugh, serious as it was, at our actions, especially at the dogs taking cover as well. … We went to the shelter till just after 10.00 when the 'All Clear' sounded and then came home to bed … . There was another warning at midnight and up we got and went to the shelter again, this time till 4 o'clock … [but] Big Jess wouldn't come because of a woman down there who bosses about a bit. I tried to stampede her into going, coming home to see how she was getting on (she was downstairs and had been under the table!) and urging her not to be so silly, but it was no good, … I shall stay with her in future if she doesn't go …

We felt tired today and I had a twenty-minute nap on the floor of the shop, being woken up by an old woman who is always coming into the shop. She wanted to know the time—it was 4.15 … Sometimes she comes to ask me to go and push her window up, to sharpen her knives, open tinned fish, knock nails in her shoes, to repair her shoes, give her a pair of shoes … and the other day she wanted me to pull a back tooth out for her, but I declined that job. …

Thursday 17 October. … Rumours are terrible. There were all sorts of tales about the bomb that dropped on Tuesday night, which burst in Barrow Road, killing a man and bringing his house down, …

Sunday 20 October. Morning—about 11 o'clock, the sun shining brightly. I'm upstairs in the room that was my office before the war and which is now full of my stuff. I come here sometimes to get out of the way and work. … [It contains] a few little things we've stored in case of siege and starvation. We've had three quiet nights. Enemy planes have been over and the windows have shaken as a sign of bombs, but we've been able to keep abed. ...

We're quibbling still over the new Soviet states, Lithuania, Latvia and Esthonia [thus], refusing to recognise them and a few paltry millions involved in the changeover. Only Russia can stop Germany's march into Asia so we'd better look out. Heard Lord Haw-Haw broadcasting the other night.[16] He's Germany's pet announcer, caricatured here a lot, but not so silly as this country would like people to believe. He referred to Duff Cooper as 'Dud' Cooper and our hypocrisy instead of democracy. ...

Jack rubbed my head the other morning and said 'Hullo, you curly-headed booby', grinning broadly at the same time. A take-off for the song 'Ma curly-headed baby' which Paul Robeson sings so beautifully. ...

Monday 21 October. It was a glorious afternoon yesterday—St Martin's Summer—and Jess and I biked to Ditton to see some houses demolished in a recent raid. One of them had been reduced to a mass of heavy cement blocks each weighing more than half a hundredweight [about 25 kilos], yet the people got away with their lives. ... The siren sounded at 7.45 ... . The warning was the longest we have had so far, lasting till about 2.15 ... . There were more bombs falling than I'd heard before all round the town; once a stick was loosed and we counted ten explosions. I mooned about outside until about 1.00 when I went to bed. After the 'All Clear' I heard two more exploding bombs and two more bombers overhead. It was a restless, uneasy night. ...

Tuesday 22 October. ... Jess tells me the shops were denuded of stocks today in the town. ... The East-end children round here have made the neighbourhood the same as it was before the last war. Plenty of noise and plenty of litter.

---

[16] The nickname Lord Haw-Haw was originally given to Norman Baillie Stewart, who broadcast Nazi propaganda in a braying upper-class voice. By 1940 the name was transferred to William Joyce, of American and Irish parentage, whose broadcasts of Nazi views were widely listened to in Britain: M. A. Doherty, *Nazi Wireless Propaganda: Lord Haw-Haw and British Public Opinion in the Second World War* (Edinburgh, 2000).

Wednesday 23 October. Frank Edwards and I were off to the weekly meeting of the local pacifist group tonight. The search-lights were up and down Trumpington Street, outside Pembroke College there were suddenly some flashes. We were wondering what they were when from the direction of Newmarket Road and Ditton there were three terrific crashes. Almost immediately a bomber sounded overhead and we took cover for a few seconds in the doorway of the Little Rose. I was on the way to the shelter, … when there were some more flashes and another stick of bombs fell, this time in the direction of Duxford. …

… Germany wants the French fleet, or what remains of it, and there seems a likelihood of France declaring war on us. Obviously, this war cannot go on. This country's leaders are outmanoeuvred in every way and it will be years before our army is ready to give battle. London and the other towns that are being so heavily bombed will never be able to hold out that length of time. … There's going to be an official enquiry into the knocking about of the conscientious objectors. So there should be.

Friday 25 October. A warning this morning at 6.0 a.m.. We went to a shelter. Moonlight and very cold. Lasted only a few minutes. Never went back to bed. Read Neil Bell's *Lord of life* over the fire while Jess got breakfast. … In the town yesterday we passed some RAF men on the march. They're stiff and doll-like in their movements, stamping their feet and exaggerating the swing of their arms. Jack said they looked as if they wanted oiling. Apt, I thought.

Saturday 26 October. A bright morning and as I type I can hear bagpipes. The Cameronians stationed here are on their way to church, marching down Trumpington Road. I saw them last Sunday; only the pipers and one officer wore kilts. What barbarous music. …

The other night some of the people in Gothic Street thought they heard a bomb fall. It was nothing of the sort; merely an army lorry banging into the wall of the house at the bottom of the street. Soldiers were paying a visit to their lady-loves in the street—other men's wives. I heard Mrs [A. J.] Green, wife of the licensee of the Cross Keys at the top of the street, relate her experiences following the noise of the apparent explosion … to Mrs C. …, the little, fat, short newspaperwoman who lives with Jock, the newspaperman. Mrs C. … replied in a loud voice that it wasn't any bloody bombs: it was them at numbers 17 and 19, that's what it was, carrying on when their husbands were away, she'd report it, wouldn't have that in the street, … --- and a lot more, shouted rather than spoken at those living at numbers 17 and 19, not to Mrs Green a yard or so away. …

Monday 28 October. I went to see mother yesterday afternoon, taking the dogs for a walk. On the way home the siren sounded. The warning lasted about three quarters of an hour—from 4.45 p.m. to 5.30 p.m. the 'All Clear' sounding as we were having tea.

Neil Bell's book *Lord of Life* was about a terrestrial catastrophe, leaving nineteen men and one woman on earth. Very good. It reminded me that I have not read Jack London's *Scarlet Plague* [1915], which I believe is about the last man and woman left on earth … . I tried hard to get this book years ago and failed. …

There was racing today. I took a few bets and lost nearly a quid [£1]. That's a fortune nowadays. … Have written 70,000 words of 'Tormented flesh'. Going very slowly through lack of time.

Tuesday 29 October. … Jerry bombers were over nearly all last night although the siren never went. It gets on our nerves and is so unsettling that sleep is very patchy.

Wednesday 30 October. As I was locking the door last night before going to bed a couple of bombs dropped in the distance. A few minutes later two more dropped. As usual we went to bed uneasy. Enemy planes were over most of the night. A plane dived as if to bomb, but nothing happened, thank goodness. …

Thursday 31 October. … Last night the siren went at 7.30. … I went to the shelter with the children until 9.00 when Jess turned up and we came home. The 'All Clear' hadn't gone but we were hungry. I went to the shop to get some fish and chips. In Panton Street there were distant flashes and I waited for the crashes. They soon came; somebody was getting it.

There were more flashes, more crashes—Duxford way—followed by the sound of an enemy plane approaching. I stood close to the wall of the Girls' Perse School and waited till it had passed over. It was pitch dark, couldn't see the proverbial inch in front of me. I carried on and there were more crashes as I walked up Russell Street. I got the fish and chips and as a woman was frightened at the fish shop door, walked to the end of the street with her. She had a torch and flashed it. I told her it was illegal while a raid was on. She didn't know. We had supper and the children went to bed as usual on the floor while Jess and I sat over the fire till the 'All Clear' sounded at 10.30, when we went to bed. …

… [There were several raids in the day.] We heard bombs falling today just after 1.00 [p.m.], followed by what sounded like gunfire. Heard down the shelter that bombs fell during the afternoon raid as well, but I never heard them. …

November 1940

Friday 1 November. I took my typewriter to work this morning as I was slack (I took it nearly every morning when writing 'Jim Baxter', carrying it over a period more than 250 miles, much of the distance being rough going, there being frozen snow on the ground for weeks, which I slumped over in gumboots during that very hard winter last year that I shall always remember), but several jobs came in and I only typed a few lines. Then Mrs [Joan] Edwards brought Frank's blackout canvas sheets to repair, the wind having torn them at the corners last night. I knew that would be a long job; it took all the afternoon.

As I was cycling back to work at 2.30 there was a warning which lasted half an hour. I had to go to Fred's just before 6.00 to get him to punch some eyelets in the canvas sheets … then I rode with them to Frank Edwards', getting there right on 6.01 p.m. right on blackout time so that he could carry on work. … here I am at 8 o'clock, just going to have tea. Then I shall try to write 1,000 words … the siren will probably sound again soon. So the days pass, mostly in frustration. …

Sunday 3 November. Just been delivering a few letters instead of posting them to save money, … . I met a man who was once a bookmaker on the journey. The same man I mentioned in this diary some years ago after meeting him one winter's evening …: he said then if I remember rightly that Englishmen were better than other men among a lot of other absurdities I catalogued. He had changed his tune today. Thought we were in a hell of tangle in this country, that the most we can hope for is to keep Hitler out, that there could be no victory, that it was all lies to say not much damage had been done in London and elsewhere and that there had been bad leadership politically the last ten years. I quote all this as an indication of the change in public opinion, even among die-hard Tories.

Reading a book called *Physiology of Sex* [Kenneth Walker, Pelican, 1940] and as it may be helpful for the book I'm writing I have suspended work on the latter for a couple of days. …

Monday 4 November. There was a warning for just over half an hour between 5.00 and 6.00. Jack was at the pictures — a Sunday jaunt now since they've started opening on Sundays in Cambridge recently … . Had an evening on my own reading copies of the *Encyclopedia of Modern Knowledge*,[17] which I bought several years ago. … I'm still rather loosely learning Italian. Work and writing takes up a lot of time, leaving little for anything else. However, I'm improving.

Sunday 10 November. There's been no warning for several days, but we've had a series of mild shocks. When I was putting pennies in the gas meter down the cellar at the shop on Friday morning there was a loud explosion. I heard later it was a time-bomb that went off at Coton. Can't say whether it was true or not. That evening at 9 o'clock heavy explosions shook the windows. Sounded close, but probably a good way off.

Last night as we sat having tea between 5.00 and 6.00 there were more heavy explosions; and later in the evening there were some more. Frank Edwards, his wife and Molly were having tea. I had a walk round the town with him; it was black, wet and depressing. Jerry went over as we were in Trumpington Street and we nipped into Fitzwilliam Street as

---

[17] The encyclopedia was published in 1936–7 in five volumes.

it was narrow for cover in case he let something go. In the early hours of the morning I was awakened by an enemy bomber approaching: he passed over and almost immediately there were explosions. Even though a plane can go a mile in about 12 seconds he couldn't have been far off as it was no more than half a minute between the time he passed over and the bombs dropping. The windows rattled but the bombs didn't sound heavies. The pilot must have been well aware of his target or he let them go indiscriminately, as there was no hanging around looking for it. ...

Hundreds of tons of bombs must have been dropped around here in the search for the numerous aerodromes that encircle the town. ... Have done about 80,000 words of the book. A good fortnight.

Tuesday 12 November. ... Jack goes to the 'Band of Hope'. I went and listened outside the door of the institute where it's held and was in time to hear the service: hymns and prayers and a bible story. The parson also offered up a word or two to God; it was all about the joy in the heart put there by heaven... . Sounded like the ravings of a loony to me. Wondered how I could beget a son that could listen to it! To add insult to injury when I told him he'd better pull his socks up, coming 20th in class, he told me to shut up. Whatever made me follow the advice of some of these psychologists like A. S. Neill and let my kids say and do as they like?[18] ...

The shops are getting empty. No cheese now; few sweets; no chocolate. And eggs are to be short, livestock food is to be rationed --- and so on and so on. ... James [rightly Joseph] Kennedy who was ambassador here from [the] USA until recently has been reported as saying Great Britain is not fighting for Democracy but for self-preservation .... The *Daily Herald* replies by saying we ought to make our war aims clear ...

---

[18] Alexander Sutherland Neill (1883–1973): educational prophet, the child of teachers who gave him a strict Scottish Calvinist upbringing stressing rigid order and discipline, against which he reacted. He was influenced by the ideas of Sigmund Freud and the unconventional educational reformer Homer Lane. In his writings and in the co-educational boarding school he founded, Summerhioll, he emphasised pupils' freedom and self-government.

Thursday 14 November. ... A glorious moonlight night, nearly a full moon. It's 9.30 and Jerry has just gone over. Heard a bomb drop a few minutes ago (some were dropped last night during the raid warning). ... The *Jervis Bay,* an armed liner protecting a convoy of 38 ships was sunk yesterday by a German battleship in the Atlantic.[19] Shows how hard up for ships we are when a ship of this type acts as protector to so large a convoy. Got about 180 destroyers now to 450 when we started the last war; and no French, Italians and Japs to help us; they're on the other side. The U-boat campaign will tell its tale soon. Afraid we'll be starved. ...

Friday 15 November. A glorious day, sunny and bright. The river temperature was 39 after a sharp night's frost. The Granta is nearly in flood: very thick and muddy after the recent rains, but it's water so in I went at midday on the way home from work.

Last night there was a lot doing. It was a beautiful moonlight night and Jerry was over all the evening and all the night. The siren didn't sound, but I don't know why, as there were bombs dropped in the distance after we got to bed and enemy planes were oomping about just as they liked all the while. I wasn't surprised to hear in Fred's shop that the Midlands had had it bad and today dinnertime when I called at Langford's the leather and grindery shop for some rubbers, to hear that Coventry had had a very bad raid, suffering 1,000 casualties. Langford said he heard the news on the 1 o'clock broadcast, adding that the cathedral was down and that when he heard it he felt bad. He's an ARP warden and said the planes that kept going over last night were no doubt on the way there. There was a short warning here this morning from 11 to 11.15. I also heard several explosions, probably time bombs dropped last night. If I keep on listening as intently as I'm doing nowadays for oomping engines, whistles and hisses as a sign of enemy planes and bombs dropping, I'll soon have ears as big as an elephant. At night I'm often deceived by the sound of the cis-

---

[19] The *Jervis Bay* was attacked in the Atlantic by the pocket battleship *Admiral Scheer* on 5 November. The resistance of the outgunned *Jervis Bay* quickly ended with her being sunk, but it did enable most ships in the convoy she was escorting to escape.

tern flushing in the pub lavatory in the archway opposite [the Spread Eagle]. Its hiss and rush reminds me of a bomb on the way like the one that fell in Pemberton Terrace. ...

Saturday 16 November. ... In three hours this morning I soled and quarter-rubbered a pair of men's, soled and heeled a pair of women's, a pair of children's, stitched up the back of an odd shoe on the machine (quite a long job) and knocked out some studs in a pair of women's. Not bad going by hand for me.

It is now about 9 o'clock [p.m.]. There is a warning on, the siren going at 7.15. Frank Edwards and his wife were here and he and I took a walk round the town. It is moonlight, but rather cloudy. Things were pretty well the same in the town, buses running, plenty of traffic and people about. We talked about the war, wondered how long it could last at its present pace. A gloomy picture: the money question, the bombing, the U-boat menace, Transport Union demanding that the government provide better shelter than unheated halls and uncooked food for the homeless, Engineers demanding and being refused advance in wages, probable restlessness of many army men who are married with their families in danger areas, reputed poor food the soldiers are getting --- and much more.

... The dogs are snoozing in front of the fire, Jess is knitting, Young Jess reading the report of the County Boys' School Speech Day. Jack has gone to the shelter with some of his cronies, with orders from his mother and me not to lark about too much. All one can hear on every side is that this war must stop. And when people start talking like that it will not be long before it does stop. ...

Sunday 17 November. The 'All Clear' sounded last night at 12.20, but neither Jess nor I heard it. A record for us ... . We went to bed about 10.30 and tired soon dropped off to sleep. It rained hard during the night and several times I awoke and wondered that the siren hadn't gone ... .

Last night there was a faint trickle of light through the blind. A senior warden came and told us that the blackout was not effective. We put it right—there was nothing else we could do—but it was just silly. An insect on the ground might have detected a light, but German aeroplanes don't come so low (though I thought I saw exhaust fumes from one that passed over parallel with Saxon Street last Thursday night). Most of them [air-raid wardens] are just interfering busybodies making an exhibition of the human weakness for giving orders. ...

Monday 18 November. The siren sounded just after midnight last night. We kept abed. Waves of German aeroplanes passed over within a few minutes interval of each other until I went to sleep again at about 3 o'clock. ... I was awakened several times by exploding bombs. The 'All Clear' went at 6.15. ... Some evenings we get 'the listens'. Somebody keeps saying 'Listen, is that a German plane?' ... The *Sunday Dispatch* yesterday gave the death roll at Coventry as 200 and injured as 800.[20] Then they'd got in large letters, a front-page caption '223 killed in Hamburg raid last night'. ... How despicable it all is.

Wednesday 20 November. There was a warning last night just before 8.00. It lasted until nearly 5.00 this morning; the longest we have yet had. I got tired at about 10.30 and had a nap on the floor between Jess and Jack. ... Big Jess was reading and she said bombs dropped in the distance while I was asleep. I went to bed at 11.30 ... . It was a rather harassing night as planes were going over all the while. ... different enemy planes following one another on the way to the Midlands, ... Summer time was allowed to continue during the winter and now we get up in the dark and have to keep blacked out during the breakfast. ...

Soldiers drill in the streets round the shop; there's a big convoy of buses (RAF) round the Backs with sentries on guard. On the way home tonight [from the shop] it seemed all very 'war-y'. Soldiers are in billets again along Brookside as they were when I was a boy during the last war. And there's a convoy on Short Common with a mounted anti-aircraft in the

---

[20] Coventry air raid: in the night of 14–15 November the Midlands industrial city was attacked by 500 German bombers; owing to British errors they were not intercepted. Twelve armament factories and much of the city centre were destroyed; 380 people were killed and 865 injured.

centre. Twenty-five years ago there were soldiers' wagons and horses and guns on the same spot. ...

I am very hard up. Hardly know how to scrounge along. ... Still pegging away at the novel. Have now done nearly 100,000 words.

Thursday 21 November. The siren went last night at 20 to 12.00 when we were abed. The 'All Clear' sounded at 6.30 this morning. Planes were over all night and there was gunfire and the noise of exploding bombs. One stick of three or four got louder as they dropped—an indication the raider was coming this way—and soon after he was cruising overhead. ... As I write now of an evening all I can hear is the oomp, oomp, oomp of approaching raiders and then the wow, wow, wow, as they pass overhead and again the oomp, oomp, oomp as they recede in the distance. I've provisionally called the book I'm writing 'Tormented flesh'. Seemingly, it might be myself I'm writing about. ...

Friday 22 November. There were three warnings last night: just before 9.00 until just before 10.00: ... . During this warning there was a loud explosion, so loud we at first thought the bomb had fallen the other side of the town, but it hadn't. After we got to bed the siren went again; this was somewhere about 10.45: ... the 'All Clear' had sounded I learned today at about 12.20. While I was lying awake German planes came over and dropped bombs in the distance. At about 2.45 the siren sounded the third warning and shortly afterwards there were ten bombs dropped; ... . The 'All Clear' didn't go until 7.40. ... We heard today that bombs were dropped at Duxford and Linton. Both are about ten miles away. Surprising how close the explosions sound at night. ...

Monday 25 November. It's been a quiet time the last few days. The Germans have been busy bashing Birmingham, Liverpool, Southampton and probably Bristol. The Coventry casualties are now stated to be over 500 dead: ... . Frank Edwards had a sort of questionnaire on Saturday as a preliminary to his appeal as a CO. I have promised to go to London with him as a witness to testify to the sincerity of his pacifist beliefs. At the rate the affair is moving it will be some time yet. ...

The two Jesses are talking about Father Christmas to Jack. Jess had made her cake and pickled some onions and cabbages as a beginning, although there's talk of no Xmas holiday being observed.

Wednesday 27 November. ... It's 6.30 and I've just come in from taking the dogs for their evening walk. The searchlights are up (as we say now); they use the light we formerly used to light up the streets. ... Our gold holding[s] and securities will last out till the spring. We have other foreign holdings which can be sold, although with difficulty, but they are not limitless and would not last long. As we cannot pay for imports by exports, there being nothing to export now production is all war material, presumably America is being asked to finance our war. If they can all well and good for us, if they can't or won't ---.

Friday 29 November. The actual time of the warning last evening was 10 minutes to 7.00. It lasted till 5.15 this morning; the longest in Cambridge as yet. Bombers were passing over all night a little to the south of the town; evidently on the way to Liverpool, as they were heavily raided there according to the papers today. ... The shops are as bare as Mother Hubbard's cupboard. No wonder. We've lost 2,500,000 tons of shipping since the war; over 3,000,000 tons including allied losses. No imports of apples, bananas, peaches, grapes and apricots now; and further rationing on the board.

... Beverley Baxter MP, newspaper-article writer thinks history will prove that 3,000,000 men were necessary to beat the Nazis.[21] I wouldn't be surprised as the Nazis have about 12,000,000, especially as he thinks we're going to do the attacking ... And then after crossing France we've still got to take the Siegfried Line. Alas, I'm afraid it cannot be done; ...

Saturday 30 November. ... Had a walk round the town with Frank Edwards this afternoon. He's propping up his living room with stout timber in case of air-raids ...

---

[21] Arthur Beverley Baxter (1891–1964): born in Canada; a journalist in the UK from 1920; writer of fiction, plays and criticism; Conservative MP for several constituencies from 1935 until his death.

Jess [his wife] had the cheek to go and apply to a place for delivering papers the day before yesterday. The shop was shut. Damned good job, too. She wouldn't have gone anyway; I'd have seen to that. Didn't know she was so hard up. I seem a flop as far as making money is concerned. Not a great success in any direction if it comes to that. But I'll strike oil yet; then I'll pour the dibs into her lap. Think I'd even agree to her buying a fur coat, although I don't agree with them; she's waited long enough!

December 1940

Sunday 1 December. A frosty morning and after getting stupidly cross with Jess about a pair of undarned socks I took a walk around Long Common with the dogs. On the way back I took a look at the place in Barrow Road where the bombs fell a few weeks ago. Two barren plots of ground with a few bits of wood and bricks and iron were all that was left of two fine houses; a little miserable scene of desolation. There was a fair number of soldiers about; and, as usual, members of the Home Guard were playing at boy scouts, messing about in the fields and ditches and generally giving rein to their feelings, bottled up since they were boys and now allowed free play owing to the so-called military necessity of the occasion. ...

Friday 6 December. ... We listen to Lord Haw-Haw sometimes on the radio. ... Jess went to the Market Place the other morning and after a scramble in a big queue managed to buy a dozen eggs, half of which she sold to Mrs Cash. They were 4*d* each. I helped the war effort a week or two back: opened the gate leading into a field round the Backs for an RAF despatch rider. See a lot of them chasing about nowadays ...

Members of the ILP [Independent Labour Party] in Parliament — there's three of them — brought in an amendment to stop the war, which was defeated by, I think, 341 votes to 3. Two of the ILP members were tellers and their votes did not count, but a couple of Labour Party members voted for them: [David] Kirkwood, [John] McGovern and [James] Maxton were some that opposed the war. One of them said it was no good carrying on blindly, the Blitz would intensify probably in February and there wasn't much hope of big military victories; there might even be a Dunkirk 1,000 times over. Straight speaking. Attlee and others strongly opposed them, but time will show who was right. …

Monday 9 December. … Jess went for a walk with Mrs Edwards in the afternoon and came home with the cheerful news that the local authorities were building a communal grave because of the likelihood of aerial bombing. … There were two warnings last night: roughly 12.00 till 4.00 and 6.00 till just after 7.00. I missed the siren sounding the first warning, but was dreaming about bombing and woke up. … Soon after bombers came roaring over. I went to sleep … But I heard the next warning and the 'All Clear' … . The raid was on London; …

Wednesday 11 December. Last night for a change I walked to the Greyhound where Fred sat in the bar as usual swilling pints, just as Tom and many other Overhills have done before him. I had a couple of lemons, … . Just before 10.00 a young woman looked over the bar counter, smiled and said 'The siren is going ladies and gentlemen'. I left then to come home in order to be with the family, saying I was coming home. … The warning lasted about ten minutes, barely that. One often meets RAF lorries on the road carrying loads of twisted metal that were once English or German aeroplanes. … Jess is cooking sausages for supper. They smell appetising. They're beef sausages and cost 1*s* 1*d* a pound; the general price is 10*d* a pound; … . Jack has just told her to cook them in Persil, then they won't shrink. …

Thursday 12 December. … Now that summer time is kept on it is dark until about 8.30 in the morning … . The weather has changed and it is now very cold and frosty. There is almost a full moon. … The papers still say the morale of the people is high. Is it? All those I speak to are depressed and cheerless: absolutely fed up with the war and the misery it entails. … I've been busier at the shop this week. Progress on the novel is slow.

Friday 13 December. There was a warning last night at 8.30 lasting until 4.30 this morning. Waves of enemy planes went over for hours, but according to the newspaper this morning there was no blitz. … In the night we heard what we thought was gunfire, ... [but I] think the explosions were fog signals. ...

Saturday 14 December. A raw, cold day. Sleet fell on the way home at midday, but I managed to get in a dip without the dogs getting very wet. Went money-hunting this afternoon. A long journey, but I never got any dough; the chap was out. ... Did no writing today; felt stale.

Sunday 15 December. Had the busiest week at the shop since I've been there. After paying expenses ... it left me with between 45*s* and 50*s*. ... Took the dogs round the Fen and Green this afternoon. What a mess it is round the drift at the back of the Leys School where the army lorries have churned up the mud. The Backs don't look so beautiful now either since it's been made into a lorry (and tank) park.

Monday 16 December. ... [In the evening, on the way home from the Greyhound] Jerry was going over—another raid on Sheffield. There was a fair number of lights showing at the station as we passed, although I'm told they are hooded and cannot be seen from above. The 'All Clear' sounded as we were going to bed at 10.30. ... Am trying to write the book by the end of the year.

Tuesday 17 December. ... The blackout now lasts from 5.30 p.m. until 8.34—that is 15 hours 14 minutes; and the shortest day isn't here yet. ... The *Daily Herald* doesn't want Lloyd George to be the new ambassador to America. Too old and believes in a round-table conference with Hitler to promote peace. They [the *Daily Herald*] want to fight on to victory.[22]

Wednesday 18 December. ... Today I never went in the river. I hurried home, changed and went with Jess to hear part of a carol concert at the County Girls' School. Young Jess played three accompaniments on the piano as well as taking part in the singing. It was nice to hear the girls sing, ... Was great guns on the book today; wrote nearly a chapter. It was easy

---

[22] Despite the surprising offer of the ambassadorship to Washington in November 1940 (which he declined) David Lloyd George, 1863–1945, was in his twilight years widely suspected of defeatism, although timidity in the face of Nazi power was a likelier cause than sympathy with Nazi aims. In May 1941 Churchill brutally compared him to Marshal Pétain, the collaborationist leader of the Vichy government.

stuff—about racing. We've had two meatless days. Couldn't get any meat. The best apples like Cox's are 1s 2d a lb; ... cookers and so-so's 6d a lb ... .

Saturday 21 December. ... Last night the siren sounded just before 9.00. Jack [and others] were at the pictures ... . I was glad when they returned home (after seeing the picture through) shortly afterwards. I've never been at the pictures during a warning, but hardly anybody leaves although a notice that the siren has sounded is switched on the screen. We heard planes going over when in bed and were awakened by the 'All Clear', which sounded at midnight, for when the siren finished the Roman Catholic church clock was striking. ...

Read in the paper last night that Baird has invented television in colour. What things really could be like without war. Provided we get away with it, television will be the craze when peace comes, as wireless was soon after the end of the last war ... I bought Jack and Jess a fountain pen each for a Christmas present; also gave them 7s 6d each (as I type the siren is sounding a warning; it is just after 8 o'clock); I gave Jess one week's rent from Shelford Road—35s. ...

Monday 23 December. ... [There are frequent raids but] we always go to bed and carry on as usual. There is nothing else we can do—except watch out for incendiaries, as these are dropped first and followed by the high explosives; if this happens we shall have to make a run for it ... . There was a warning today between 12.30 and 12.45; the first we've had in the daytime for a long while. ...

Since typing the above I have walked along to the Craskes to take a pair of shoes home. While there the siren sounded: time 7.30 p.m.. As I came home it was still wailing, the night pitch black, snow slightly falling (a sudden change in the weather); before I got home, less than 100 yards, German bombers were passing over ...

Tuesday 24 December. The 'All Clear' sounded last night just as we were going to bed: 10.20 p.m. There have been no further warnings since and as it's Christmas Eve and about 9 o'clock we're wondering if Jerry is going to let us alone for a little while.

... [In the afternoon] we walked down the town, [and] went in Marks and Spencers where people were buying mixed nuts at 2s a *lb* and oranges at 5½d a *lb*. There was a queue waiting to be served with the oranges and people were almost fighting, being kept back by a man. Going from there to Woolworth's I bought Neil Bell's *The Truth about my Father*, one of Collins' sixpenny White Circle books (just what I wanted) and then walked through Boot's, Jack keeping me on the move and forbidding me to look at the books as we were meeting the Cash's [thus] in Petty Cury and we were already a few minutes late. We met them with Mrs Moore, when Bert stood treat of tea in Lyons … . I've registered a promise to take the Cash's for a fortnight's holiday to the seaside—Devon or Cornwall— if I pull it off with the novel writing, to level the score. ...

Wednesday 25 December. ... We got up fairly late. Jess gave me a cup and saucer and a shirt; Young Jess a pair of hand-knitted socks; Jack a tin of sweets. ... We had a good wartime breakfast: corned beef and egg. The corned beef Jess bought just before the war; a 4*lb* tin; there's none about now and it was therefore very tasty. ... I've stuck the year's photos in the photo album, wrote [to] London University transferring my Final B.Sc. Econ. examination to June 1942 (it was 1941) and sent a letter to Wolsey Hall about the self-tuition course I want to take up for it. ... Spent the rest of the day reading Neil Bell's *True Story of my Father*. A rather grotesque story. He dealt with the subject like the craftsman he is.

Friday 27 December. Yesterday, Boxing Day, I read Neil Bell's *The Seventh Bowl*. There was racing and I won about 30s. In the evening we went to a friend of Frank Edwards who has a talkie-cinema apparatus and he showed us the Pathé film of Jack and also the one made by the Tivoli. It was a treat to see them again. ...

Saturday 28 December. ... I heard from Neil Bell this morning. Said he'd made me a character in a new book of his: just a small part: did I mind? I've written back. Do I mind! ... Perhaps it's the only fame I'll ever get. I'd better snatch it. ...

Sunday 29 December. … Bombers were passing over when we came home [from the Greyhound] between 11.00 and 12.00, but there was no warning. … Expect we shall hear the bells ringing one of these nights before long as a sign of invasion.

Monday 30 December. The siren sounded last night at 6.25 p.m. the warning lasting about 25 minutes. I read *Traitor Class* [1940] today and finished *Merchants of Death* by [Helmut Carol] Engelbrecht and [Frank Cleary] Hanighan [1934]. The former, by Ivor Montagu, shows up the ruling class of this country pretty thoroughly; the latter is a record of the arms and munitions industry from the beginnings. Dreadful.

Today there was a warning just after 2 o'clock lasting for about a quarter of an hour, but before this there was some excitement in the town as a lone German raider machine-gunned Marshall's aerodrome. A man who works there told me he came Ditton way at about 1.30 and after his first attack circled four times, machine-gunning each time. The clouds were very low (it's been a mucky, rainy-on-and-off day), but he was well below them, so very low. Marshall's fired back with Bren guns and at the man who told me's suggestion [that is, at the suggestion of the man who told me] to some officers who seemed in a dilemma they telephoned to Duxford and a Hurricane was sent over. By the time it arrived he had gone. Tonight's paper says the raider machine-gunned houses and there was one slight casualty. My brother Fred told me bullets fell on Barton Road and Parker's Piece, but I don't know if he were repeating a rumour. …

… Roosevelt's made a big 'fireside' speech, backing up England. I'm not impressed and still think this country will conk out. Its ruling class will sell out when it suits them as the French ruling class did. They're championing their own interests, whatever they are; … . What hope is there for the future with so many evil forces at work?

In the summer of 1940 there was an appeal for aluminium for aircraft construction. In these pictures children at Milton Road Junior School are seen with the pots and pans they have collected, and the material is being delivered to the WVS headquarters at the Old Post Office.

Railings at Emmanuel College being removed for scrap metal to make munitions, July 1940. Many other railings were cut down for the same purposes.

1941

January 1941

Wednesday 1 January. ... It's 8.30; a plane is roaring over and we're speculating whose it is. Bought an Italian reading book today; one of the bilingual series. Neil Bell told me he'd mentioned my name—just a short part—in his new Puritan book. Do I mind? Do I!

Started checking over the novel preparatory to getting out a fresh manuscript. Is novel writing a hobby? Hardly. A hobby is a relaxation. Novel writing is intensive concentration. There's a difference.

Thursday 2 January. Last night there was an Alert from 11.00 p.m. until 3.10 a.m. then another from 4.10 a.m. until 5.50 a.m. ... also ... from 10.40 a.m. until 10.55 a.m. ... The meat ration is officially 1*s* 10*d* worth per person. The local butchers have put a notice in the newspaper that all they can allow customers is 1*s* 1*d* worth per head. In some places people are only getting 7*d* worth each. ...

Friday 3 January. The siren sounded last night at 8.50, the warning lasting until 11.40 a.m. Lots of stuff passed over and according to the papers it was Cardiff that got it. Have started retyping the novel. Trying to think of a new title as Bell told me to change 'Tormented flesh'. ...

Saturday 4 January. A warning from 11.40 p.m. last night till 3.50 a.m. this morning. No meat from the butcher's today. All we've had all week, the whole family is 8*d* worth between us. This with two ounces of butter a week and four ounces of sugar is getting down to the borderline. A lot worse to come yet, though, I think.

The call is for firewatchers now. A warden called tonight to ask if I would attend one lecture to learn how to put out incendiary bombs. I said yes. ... The Germans are using explosive incendiary bombs to make the fires spread quickly ...

Foundations for air-raid shelters being dug on
Parker's Piece, November 1939

Foundations for air-raid shelters to hold 1000 children being
dug at Brunswick School, 2 November 1939

Sunday 5 January. A warning last night from 11.30 p.m. till 4.50 a.m. The wail of the siren is a strange sound with which to be awakened in the middle of the night. Eerie to listen to. It must be terrifying to children. There will be a lot of neurosis in the coming generation. ... Jack and Jess have been skating this morning on the sewage farm. Jack said he got on well (he used my skates) but Jess not so well.

Big Jess told me of a conversation she heard between two women outside the window, who live in Gothic Street. One said the other should have heard what HE (a soldier) said. Apparently, the soldier had called on her at a quarter to one at night. 'Anybody would think we were bloody prostitutes', she said, 'the way he was speaking. Keep coming round talking like that he'll turn others away. He wants me to have my photo taken so that he can wear it next to his heart when he goes away. He didn't half know a lot about Hilda (her sister who lives with her) and I said "Well, you ain't married to her" and he said "No, I wouldn't like".' There was more which Jess forgets. They are married women. ...

Later: 9.30 p.m. ... [A] warning this afternoon lasted almost an hour. Hore Belisha, writing about the firing of the City of London in the *News of the World,* said our leaders should have been prepared for it and as the Germans will stop at nothing they should prepare against gas.[1] I've heard lately more rumours that our gasmasks are no good, so I wonder how he expects they'll set about it.

Day and night bombing, threats of invasion, gas attacks, indifferent rationing, poor food, and so on and on. What a world it is. ...

Monday 6 January. ... H. G. Wells is home from America. Says it's time for the RAF to join up with the air force of the USSR. That would stop Germany's *blitzkriegs*. I wonder what some of our leaders think. ... Am busy retyping the novel.

Tuesday 7 January. There were warnings today ... from 1.00 p.m. to 2.30 p.m., from 4.30 to 4.55 p.m., from 5.45 to 6.00 p.m.

---

[1] Leslie Hore-Belisha (1893–1957): Secretary of State for War 1937–40. His ruthless modernisation of the army and his sharp tongue set the generals against him. His resignation followed.

...

Wednesday 8 January. ... Jack spent the day with me at the shop, being still on holiday. Coming home tonight we went in the local library and borrowed Doyle's *The Hound of the Baskervilles* which I've never read. Late tonight we went up East Road to get fish and chips. Parker's Piece was a white expanse of snow. It's a wintry winter.

Thursday 9 January. Jack again came to the shop with me. He makes hot drinks, tea and Oxos [a meat-extract drink], and we have sweets and a wrestle or two. It's good living like that. He came round the Green with me at midday and watched me go in the river. Temperatures: water 33 degrees, air 29 degrees. ...

The siren is sounding: ... My word, Jerry is roaring over. Young Jess is reading *Paul et Virginie* [1788, by Bernardin de St Pierre] in French: part of her school work. ...

Friday 10 January. The 'All Clear' went at 2.15 this morning. It woke me up. The raid was general, the enemy planes splitting up. ... The paper is full of Italy's coming downfall. I think it's a side-issue of the war. Germany is the real enemy. ...

Monday 13 January. The 'All Clear' sounded last night between 11.00 and 11.30. ... A bit of racing today. Got a few shillings out of it. Jack minded the shop. A lot of twisting and turning and going to and fro doing a bit of this, that and the other nowadays to make ends meet. Want a lot of books for the degree work, but haven't the money to buy them. Been borrowing off Frank Edwards again for the rent [for the shop]. Owe him £15 now.

Wednesday 15 January. ... Can't get any pieces for Jim and Jock now from the butcher's. Can hardly get any meat ourselves; and it's scrap meat what we do get. One butcher complaining in the paper said the stuff sent him to make sausages broke the coarsest blades of his machine. He declared it was from a twenty-year-old boar. Rode to Pinks' the knackersmen this afternoon and bought seven lbs of horseflesh for the dogs for 18*d*. ... Jam's gone up another tuppence a *lb*, strawberry 1*s* 2*d*. ...

Thursday 16 January. ... Because of summer time it is still dark at 8 o'clock in the morning, but the nights are drawing out a little, although the blackout still lasts about 15 hours.[2]

There were two Alerts last night: 11.30 p.m. to 1.30 a.m. and 2.30 a.m. to 5.30 a.m. … We were warm in bed. Didn't want to get up either! During the night we were awakened by a loud explosion. It sounded like a gun going off, but might have been a bomb. (An Air Force man round the Backs told me today he heard five bombs dropped during the night.) Then Jess woke me up just in time to hear a burst of machine-gun fire. There was an enemy plane circling the town and she said she had heard quite a lot of machine-gun firing before waking me. I'd been dreaming that I was throwing myself down on my face in Trumpington Street because high explosives were being dropped. Had the curious feeling of being a bit numbed and looking at myself to see I was only scratched, when I said I was all right, anyway. This must have been round about 4.00 am when [the raid was] unbeknown to us until we heard people talking excitedly in the street at about 6.30 or 7.00. Scores of incendiary bombs were dropped on the town: Cam-Tax garage, the Perse School and a wireless shop suffered damage, and incendiaries were also dropped on a hospital (probably Addenbrooke's), a church (the Roman Catholic) and houses, but were quickly put out. About 50 fell on Parker's Piece. Jess and I went out and had a look at the firemen at work on the Perse which was still blazing at 9 o'clock. Traffic was very disorganised and gave a good idea of the chaos a big fire 'Blitz' must cause.

Our descendants will bless this generation for the wanton destruction of the heritage of our forebears. Actually, it's not ours to place in jeopardy and cause to be destroyed. …

Friday 17 January. I was up at 5.30 this morning to go to London with Frank Edwards as a witness before the London Appellate Tribunal for conscientious objectors. A bitterly cold day, the weather frosty, frozen snow crunching underfoot, moon shining in a clear sky was how the world struck me as

---

[2] During the First World War it became the practice to advance clocks by one hour on Greenwich Mean Time to extend the evening light. From February 1940 until October 1945 this practice was imposed all year round, and was supplemented from 1941 onwards by moving the clocks forward two hours rather than one during the summer months.

I walked to the station ... The journey was cold, the carriages unheated, and our feet were like ice. Outside the white waste of the fields looked as if we were travelling to Siberia.

We got to London at 9.45. Eric met us at Liverpool Street. ... [We met him by chance] as we came out of the refreshment room, where we'd had a cup of Bovril and a cheese sandwich.

We walked to Aldgate, through the Minories to the Tower on to Billingsgate fish market. ... One of the Tower bastions was down. ... [In the Tower] the rooms revealed were small and dingy in appearance. Going on to the Bank we saw men of the Pioneer Corps working with huge excavators on a big [bomb] crater in the middle of the road where a subway had been blown up a few days ago, causing a lot of deaths. Across the Royal Exchange nearby was a large, green banner with big white letters 'Dig for Victory' on it. Cheapside was almost in ruins; St Paul's Church [cathedral] was scarred by high explosives. Ludgate Circus and Fleet Street also had their scars; so did the Strand. [John] Lewis's [store] was down in Oxford Street, and everywhere back of the main streets were gutted buildings, heaps of rubble, craters and ruins that made me think I was living in a world run by lunatics. A strong smell of disinfectant came up from the Tubes: purification after the shelterers for the night had left.[3]

Before [the appeal] coming down Charing Cross Road to look at the bookshops, I bought an Italian dictionary in Foyle's for 1*s* 3*d* and managed to get a *lb* box of chocolates for Big Jess, a fancy cake for Young Jess and a jam roll for Jack at an A.B.C. [Aerated Bread Company] shop. The few sweets and chocolates on sale were too dear to buy.

[The appeal] took place at Ebury House, near Victoria Station: [it] lasted about ten minutes; ... [and the panel had three members]. I think I did well with my testimony. ... The chairman looked impressed after I finished speaking. But Frank didn't do so well. He hummed and hawed over some silly questions about ARP work and was, I thought, insolent in his

---

[3] From the start of the London blitz thousands of people slept on Underground platforms deep beneath the street; there were for example 177,000 such sleepers in September 1940. Bunks were provided from December 1940. Conditions were often primitive.

bearing, sitting with his hands in his pockets, feet sprawled out in front of him, rarely saying 'sir' as a sign of respect when answering the chairman.

The proceedings abruptly ended. The chairman said he saw no reason for altering the decision of the Cambridge tribunal; the appeal was dismissed. ... Frank didn't seem to mind. Said now they can get on with it. ...

Saturday 18 January. ... There's been two warnings: the first starting at 12.40 at dinnertime lasted about half an hour: the second during the afternoon was from 2.20 p.m. to 4.05 p.m. We marvel at Jerry coming over in this weather and tell one another he must want a job. ...

Down a lavatory in London when in London I read some writings on the walls. Thinking about them and those I've read in similar places, I thought a book could be written about them. Be very enlightening. Be interesting to laymen as well as psychologists.

Tuesday 21 January. ... Four warnings: 10.10 a.m. to 10.50 a.m., 11.40 a.m. to 12.30 p.m., 2.40 p.m. to 3.10 p.m., 3.40 p.m. to 4.15 p.m. Looks a bit like a railway timetable. ...

Jack and I walked to the fish shop for chips. The fishman said he would soon have to shut up; he couldn't get enough fat. I said I thought the government were subsidising fried-fish sellers. He laughed and said 'They'd do something, they would'. ...

Wednesday 22 January. Frank Edwards rang up this morning to say the *Daily Worker* and *Week* had been suppressed.[4] Democracy is gasping for breath. ...

Friday 24 January. Bags of sand are being left at all houses and shops to put out incendiary bombs. They are also being tied on to lamp-posts: two on each.

---

[4] Between the Nazi–Soviet pact and the German invasion of Russia in June 1941 the *Daily Worker* (and usually Claude Cockburn's maverick journal *The Week*) argued that Britain was fighting an imperialist war; they were studiedly vague about whether the war should be fought more intensively or not at all. The two journals were suppressed under Defence Regulation 2D; the ban lasted for eighteen months.

Saturday 25 January. ... The sandbags are already dropping off lamp-posts; or, perhaps, they are being knocked off by children. ... They'll not stand up to the weather, a heavy bag tied to a post with string. No. I'm wrong, it's thin rope. Must state facts as they are. ... Bought seven books at Bowes and Bowes today for examination work — second hand — for two guineas. ...

Monday 27 January. ... Students are about the town with posters protesting against the banning of the *Daily Worker*. There was a 'severe' letter about them and their action in tonight's local paper.

> *The letter, from 'Disgusted' of Cambridge, reads*:
> *I have today witnessed a disgraceful exhibition by students (male and female) carrying sandwich boards with signs protesting against the Government's suspension of the* Daily Worker. *When will these misguided people understand that their fellow men and women are fighting and dying for freedom? The abuse of freedom is quite another matter, and should not be tolerated. The sooner these people are placed under military discipline with a double dose of intensive training the better.*

Tuesday 28 January. There was a warning this morning at 11.50 for 12 minutes and another this afternoon at 2.50 lasting 25 minutes. ...

Thursday 30 January. There was an Alert this afternoon at 3.45 pm. Immediately, there were explosions. ... the bombs were on Mill Road, near the railway bridge. One man, a crane driver, was killed and several people injured. ...

Friday 31 January. Three warnings today: 11.58 a.m. to 12.18 p.m., 12.22 p.m. to 2.58 p.m.; 8.40 p.m. to 9.30 p.m. ...

February 1941

Saturday 1 February. A warning from 11.50 a.m. to 12.45 ... p.m.

Sunday 2 February. ... I went for a walk. It was cloudy, but fairly bright. Overhead — bombers, fighter planes and Marshall's trainer planes. Along the road — barbed wire, signposts down, holes and trenches beside the road. On the Fen — tanks. On Short Common — motor transports and stuffed sacks for bayonet practice.[5] Soldiers and RAF men about. ... Looks as if the crisis will be here soon. Then we shall hear the church bells ringing and will know the second battle of Britain is on. But whose Britain is it, that's what I want to know. ... I don't think Great Britain will win the war, never have, but if it did I'd be surprised if the ruling class that lords it here changed things in a way that would materially affect the workers for their good. ... So I'll go back to my novel writing and examination studies feeling smaller in a fast-moving world than Tom Thumb.

Monday 3 February. ... There was a warning this morning from 11.00 until just after 12.00. Heavy explosions sounded. Heard later the bombs fell at Waterbeach. There's a 'drome there. ...

Sunday 9 February. Afternoon. Jack and I have been as far as Newmarket Road trying all the shops to buy a few sweets. Got a quarter of pre-war twopenny quarter-pound sweets for 9*d* at last in Fitzroy Street. All the other shops, about a dozen, were sold out; some shut up. ...

Monday 10 February. ... Just heard Haw-Haw on the wireless. He called Churchill 'the old man of the sea' — a take-off for Winston's peaked cap and general liking for the Navy, I suppose; ... There was a warning last evening from 7.10 p.m. to 8.35 p.m. Another ... from 11.55 p.m. to 12.55 a.m. There was also a warning this evening from 7.30 p.m. to 9.30 p.m. Heard lots of enemy planes go over. Jerry's usual answer to a broadcast of Churchill's, saying what we're going to do. ...

Wednesday 12 February. A bomber roared over the house last night when we were abed and coming out of a sleep I said to Jess 'Is that one of ours?' She said the usual 'I hope so', and I wondered that some of the low-flying planes never hit tall buildings ... . We heard today this was one of ours, a bomber. It crashed after the crew had baled out, into some houses on Histon Road, killing three old ladies and injuring some others ... Jess and I went to have a look at the damage done. A sorry sight ...

Thursday 13 February. ... The siren sounded tonight at about

---

[5] Short Common has not been securely identified. It was perhaps the piece of land west of Trumpington Street opposite the Botanic Garden. I am grateful to Mr Chris Jakes of the Cambridgeshire Collection for this suggestion.

7.50. The warning is still on. A flare was dropped in the west just after the Alert sounded. We all went to the door and saw the sky lit up over Scroope Terrace. ...

Friday 14 February. ... Jess and I went to see Charlie Chaplin in his picture *The Great Dictator* ... [As Hitler orated in the film] the siren sounded. We could plainly hear its wail and a notice came on the screen saying a warning was sounding and patrons could leave if they wished. ... A fair number left. The exit doors were all opened. ... [It's] the first time I've been in a cinema when an Alert was sounding. ...

Sunday 16 February. I went over to the Greyhound to see Fred last night. ... I called in Fred's on the way home. Didn't stay long though. Jerry was over all the way coming home, searchlights up. Then in Cavendish Road there came a crack in the heavens and a whine and I knew a bomb was falling. I went flat on my face. There was an explosion and a chap half-drunk—it was about 10.30—said 'Was that a Jerry, mate?' ... ARP wardens were blowing their whistles and the sky was lit up Hills Road way. I was glad to get over Hills Road bridge—a danger spot—and away from the hiss of train engines, which the mind associates with falling bombs. Near the line it is noisy too, with engines shunting. One's ears are keyed up for sounds which cannot be heard in the neighbourhood of a railway station. There were more than a dozen explosions soon after the bombs fell, but whether they were bombs or gunfire I don't know. The rest of the journey home was just darkness, searchlights, bombers droning overhead, people listening at doors (plenty strolling about the streets unconcernedly, especially couples) and ears straining for any sound that indicated bombs dropping. ...Heard today, h.e. [high explosive] and incendiary bombs were dropped on Hills Road ...

Monday 17 February. The bomb on Saturday night fell ... somewhere near Perne Road, ... Nobody was injured ... . The people in the neighbourhood are getting together to protect themselves against incendiary bombs. I have been approached and agreed to patrol the immediate neighbourhood on Sunday nights during blackout hours if the siren sounds with three others as fire-watchers. If incendiaries are dropped

On 30 January 1941 a bomb fell on a terrace of cottages at the side of Mill Road bridge.
See the entry for 30 January 1941.

Bomb damage in Huntingdon Road.
Houses were damaged in a raid on 29 September 1941; repairs were soon undertaken.

we get to work with stirrup pumps and/or sand. ... There was an Alert this evening from 8.10 p.m. to 10.05 p.m.

Tuesday 18 February. ... The siren sounded last night at 2.10 a.m. The warning lasted till 6.0 a.m. We had a very disturbed night. Heard a plane or two buzzing about, ... and had to put up with a couple of owls hooting, answering each other, for hours. ... There was another Alert at 7.45 a.m. for a quarter of an hour. And then another this afternoon from 3.0 p.m. till 4.55 p.m. ....

Tuesday 25 February. My eyes and throat feeling rough last night we went to bed at about 10 o'clock. Soon after we got there 'planes roared low over the house. We thought they sounded like Jerries. Just dozing off there was the sound of an exploding bomb. It startled both of us and made Jess feel bad. No sooner had this bomb gone off than the plane roared over us and we knew it had fallen pretty close. Talking about the incident as we lay there, there was the whistle of another bomb falling, then the crash. This sounded close and Jess lost herself for a short while. I patted her and gave her a drink and as soon as she was herself I said we'd better get up, there looked as if there was going to be plenty doing. We got out of bed and started putting on our clothes, planes roaring overhead all the while and then came the familiar whistle and we both crouched low beside the bed.

  Then the bombs started to fall, nearly a score of them. I had one arm round Jess; she whimpered a bit and I said they were some way off; but we thought they were all in the town and that Cambridge was being blitzed. The lull came and we hurried downstairs. Young Jess was under the table, Jack still abed. I told them to dress. Planes came low over the house, flares were lighting up the sky and there was the repeated plopping of incendiary bombs. I went to the door once or twice and looked into the street. Planes diving low made me hurry in and the family got under the table. Big Jess said 'Hark at the incendiary bombs falling' and I went to the door again. Roaring planes and plop, plop, plop was all I could hear with a bit of shouting from Gothic Street. Then a plane dived and I rushed in. The family got under the table again and I crouched beside it, waiting for the bombs and probably the end. I think we all thought it was up with us, but the plane roared upwards again after almost skimming the roofs.

We ran for it then to the shelter in Trumpington Street, expecting bombs to come down every moment from the planes buzzing over. The telephone rang four times some time after we were there and a warden told me it was from the Observer Command [Royal Observer Corps][6] or something like that and meant that the raiders were within 15 miles again. Then it rang once to say they were outside that radius. The 'All Clear' went at 12.30 or thereabouts. The two Jesses went to bed, but hearing Hills Road had got a pasting Jack and I went to have a look. A row of about 26 shops had been badly damaged. The scene was people, cars, wardens, police, wreckage, glass smashed all over the place and little craters in the road. We couldn't find out about casualties. A boy of about 14 picked up something outside a newsagents — a souvenir probably — and the newsagent caught him and made a fuss. Another man supported him; shouted a lot of ballyhoo about getting six months for looting (this man owes me nearly £2 for betting …) and a policeman came up and started to follow the boy, gone down a side street. I soon ended the chase; said loudly it was only a bloody kid looking for souvenirs, he wasn't old enough to pinch, which made the policeman grunt and turn about. …

These are some of the facts gathered since from various people and the newspaper. Twelve dead in Hills Road. … No record of the injured. Two women killed when a bomb demolished a house at Newnham near Grantchester Meadows. Hundreds of incendiaries dropped. H.e.s [high explosive bombs] dropped on the cattle market, at the back of the Eastern Omnibus Company, Newnham, a lot down and round about Cherryhinton Road way, falling mostly in gardens. … According to the newspaper a bomb fell on the Roman Catholic church. Windows suffered badly everywhere the bombs fell. Hills Road now roped off. Suggests they are digging for dead people.

The reason for this attack: probably due to a convoy of tanks

---

[6] The Observer Corps (later the Royal Observer Corps) was formed in the 1930s by civilian volunteers. During the war it supplemented the radar network by reporting the number and nature of hostile aircraft.

that came into the town last night and wound its way along Hills Road, over the bridge with lights on and looking like a bloody great snake according to a chap who told me about it. The tanks are still parked round Cavendish Avenue and a convoy of lorries is along Brookside, so we're wondering if we'll get it again tonight. ...

Wednesday 26 February. There was an Alert last night at 8.25 p.m. and as enemy planes were continually going over after we were a bit jumpy. Firewatchers outside patrolling the streets were laughing and talking as they passed. One of them said he didn't think HE meant business tonight. We heard two or three bombs explode in the distance and the ring of the firebell as the fire-engine went rushing by. ...

The wireless has just faded out; it's nearly 8 o'clock. Means a raid is on in London, I suppose. ... Terribly hard up scrounging odd bobs [shillings] off the children to pay for the next meal. If I don't earn we're sunk.

The siren is sounding. It is nearly 8.00. We can hear people outside shouting 'Come on' and feet hurrying by the window. They're off to the shelter. Children's voices chattering. Poor little tots. ...

Thursday 27 February. ... Forgot to mention that as we neared the shelter on Monday night I told Jack to hurry on and get down it. He purposely dawdled as though indifferent; haste was not the right thing. Boylike, of course, ...

The 'All Clear' sounded last night at 10.10 p.m. There were warnings today as follows: 8.20 a.m. to 8.55 a.m., 9.35 a.m. to 9.50 a.m., 10.35 a.m. to 11.35 a.m., 12.50 p.m. to 2.30 p.m. ...

A new bill is going through Parliament permitting a member to retain his seat even though he goes abroad as a paid official—like [Stafford] Cripps now in Russia and [Malcolm] MacDonald (whom it is all about) either going [to] or in Canada so that they can be both administrators and officials.[7] The

---

[7] Malcolm John MacDonald (1901–81): politician and diplomatist, son of the Labour Prime Minister James Ramsay MacDonald, was educated at Bedales School and the Queen's College, Oxford. MP from 1929 to 1945, latterly for Ross and Cromarty. After the political crisis of 1931 he was one of the few MPs who followed Ramsay MacDonald (to whom he was very loyal) into the National Labour rump which supported the Conservative

bill was opposed by all classes in Parliament, but Churchill wanted it and had his way by saying that if it was passed he would regard it as a vote of confidence in the Government. This country decries dictatorship (What about Cabinet dictatorship?) and will still do so, no doubt. …

March 1941

Saturday 1 March. … Had a walk down the town this afternoon with Young Jess. Bought her Shakespeare's *King Lear* (6d Penguin) for school work. … Then I went up Fred's with the dogs and talked over last Monday's raid. He said 13 bombs were dropped on Hills Road. … A warning this evening from 9.05 till 9.30. …

Monday 3 March. … There was a warning last night at 9.15, my firewatching duty night. I went out and patrolled the street with three others, until 10.00 when the 'All Clear' went, much to my delight. … As I looked up at the stars, thinking how quickly everything could be ended … everything seemed silly, futile. …

Had talk with Mr Humphries on the telephone tonight. He made me feel gloomy. Thought the war would perhaps last ten years, being carried on from Canada. …

Wednesday 5 March. … Couldn't get any segs from the leather shop today.[8] They told me they can't get anything from Sheffield now. The firms have ceased production owing to bombings by the Germans. … The production of ordinary goods is to be heavily curtailed. Factory workers are to be shifted over to war work according to the newspaper today. …

Thursday 6 March. There was a warning today at 12.45 p.m. lasting till 2.15 p.m. Soon after the Alert I hear a bomber go over and went to the door of the shop to have a look at it, as a bomber passing over during a warning seemed strange. …

---

governments. In the 1930s he held various positions in the Dominions and Colonial offices; in 1940 he became Minister of Health, and in 1941 High Commissioner in Canada, unusually combining it with his membership of the House of Commons.

[8] Segs are small pieces of steel driven into the heels of shoes to prevent them wearing down.

because of its queer shape I thought it was a German Dornier. Shortly afterwards two fighters whizzed past in the same direction and they strengthened my conviction that it was an enemy bomber and they were after it. So it proved. ... in the paper tonight the report said it machine-gunned the Market Square and a woman was injured. ...

Saturday 8 March. ... After tea Jess and I went and changed the wireless battery. ... It seemed a queer Saturday evening. Nearly all the shops shut and those that [were] open with very little to sell. A find at Hyde Park Corner — chocolate for sale. ... An Alert at 8.20 p.m. A moonlight night: planes keep coming over. Feel a bit jumpy and been to the door several times to listen to them passing over. ...

Sunday 9 March. The 'All Clear' went at 11.05 p.m. last night. ... A misty morning and two early Alerts: 8.15 a.m. to 8.30 a.m. and 9.15 a.m. to 9.45 a.m. Went for a walk round Brooklands Avenue after breakfast. ... How the old men cling to their gasmasks. They carry them much more than young people. ... [and] old women. ...

The tempo of the war is increasing again. ... Sooner or later, I feel Russia will have a hand in the game. Just a matter of time before she becomes involved.

Monday 10 March. There was a warning last night from 9.45 p.m. to 10.45 p.m. It was my night for fire-spotting so I had to turn out for a couple of hours. It snowed for the first hour. Jerry planes went over several times, Huntingdon and Waterbeach way ...

Tuesday 11 March. Bombs went off last night soon after we got to bed. ... Heard today bombs were dropped on the railway line at Fulbourn. Children buy carrots nowadays instead of sweets: 2*d* a *lb* ... .

Wednesday 12 March. The 'All Clear' went last night at 12.30. Bombers were going over all the while. Raids were on the Midlands; ... . The siren sounded this evening at 7.55 p.m. — that's almost as soon as it's dark — and the Alert is still on. ... Done a lot of shoe-repairing today and spent all the evening on the novel as usual. I'm tired, too tired to write about things I want to write about.

Thursday 13 March. ... The siren has just sounded again—at 8.30 p.m. ... . Jess tells me that people now queue up for fish paste and tinned stuff (no tinned salmon now). Stocks are gradually being exhausted and people go for what they can get. ...

Friday 14 March. The 'All Clear' went last night at 3.40 a.m. Bombers were going over all the while. ... The siren has just sounded again: 8.35 p.m.

Saturday 15 March. ... Jam is to be rationed from Monday next—eight ounces each a month! Lately, we've been eating as much as four *lbs* a week as we've been unable to get more than very little cheese and the butter ration is only two ounces a week, so I don't know how we'll get our bread down now.

We're bashing Germany with our bombers and they're bashing us. A fine game ... .

Sunday 16 March. ... More invasion talk with newspaper instructions [on] what to do. We have the right, for example, to defend ourselves in our own homes! A lot of talk too in the papers (and Bevin on the wireless) about the registration of men and women up to 60 for war work. ...

We're always hearing bombs exploding in the distance. Enemy planes trying to find the 'dromes around here. ...

Wednesday 19 March. ... Last night at about 9 o'clock one of my sisters-in-law came round with her sister and said the old man was very ill. I rang up the doctor and found out about him and then went to Wellington Street where he lives. It wasn't a bad little room. He was abed and they never let on who I was, but he peered at the foot of the bed where I was standing and asked if that was a policeman. 'I see', he said, then 'a bloody listener', adding something about getting the key of his door and he'd keep them out. Another look towards me and he said 'Is that Jack?', and my sister-in-law said no, it was her son Albert. ... I slipped out of the room and after a few words with Jess went to mother's at Chesterton and told them he was bad. My sister Mabel decided not to go near him. Back to Wellington Street. Jess and Glad (sister-in-law) said they would sit up with him as he was evidently worried about my presence. Heard a lot about him while there from a woman.

He'd refused to go into the infirmary, accused people of stealing his money and his medical papers and of cutting the buttons off his coat and sewing them on again (same old accusations) .... Impossible to do anything for such an awkward old man. We were both glad to be coming home and said so. Felt our place was with the children during an Alert. ... Jerry was going over as we walked home. ... I would like to help him, have always tried to do so. He just won't let me. ...

Thursday 20 March. The 'All Clear' went soon after Jess got home: 11.00 p.m. I woke up in the night, heard bombers flying low and thought they were Jerries. Then the siren went again. Immediately the Catholic [church] clock struck 1.00. The warning lasted till 2.15 a.m. There was a very bad raid on London. Five hospitals struck. The worst raid since the fire blitz. ...

Saturday 22 March. ... Finished the book this afternoon. Just checking over now. I dropped Neil Bell a postcard with the words 'done it' on it as the message.

Sunday 23 March. ... Heard a funny noise. Like a newspaper man having a fit, as I was coming home in Panton Street. I looked round and a couple of hundred yards away a squad of soldiers were being put through their paces by a man with a voice. Talk about fighting for freedom. Looked—and sounded—as if they'd lost their freedom in the doing of it. ...

[At his mother's house] there was a Jewish woman there and her daughter. The mother had lost her husband in an air-raid and both had been bombed out. After a talk they both declared strongly in favour of the war. The people of this country would never yield to Hitler. Understandable as they were Jews, as they obviously feared persecution in the event of Germany winning the war. I could have said a lot, but didn't, but when the daughter said I belonged to the British Empire I answered that I owned none of it; not a bit. ... none of the British Empire belongs to me. Wells says the Jews have asked for much of their persecution. They think they're God's elect, the chosen race. If they didn't they would have become absorbed in the nationalities of the countries in which they sought refuge long ago. A very sensible argument to me. ...

Monday 24 March. The siren sounded last night just before 2.00, so I had to get up as it was my night for firewatching. It was very cold (a sharp frost this morning) and we heard a Jerry or two oomp over in the distance. Had a chat with a soldier on guard in the 'Plant'un' [the trees by Hobson's Brook, Brookside] and a senior ARP warden, … The 'All Clear' went at 3.00 o'clock — and was I glad. Went back to bed like a slab of ice. …

Tuesday 25 March. … Saw in the newspaper this morning that Lord Woolton, the Minister of Food, says there's too many dogs in the country (three million); they're eating too much food. … This made me concerned. I and the family don't want to part with Jim and Jock. No fear. This urged me to ring up the Guildhall and fix up to take an allotment. Get plenty of spuds; it might help. …

My age-group registers on the 12th April. This dinner-time I rang up the local Labour Exchange and found out that shoe-repairing is at present a reserved occupation at the age of 30. Tonight I've just sent the following letter to the Central Board of COs, 6 Endsleigh Street, London WC1. 'Dear Sir, I am a 38 year-old shoe-repairer and shall be registering as a conscientious objector on the 12th April. As shoe-repairing is a reserved occupation at the age of 30 and I do not wish to go before the CO tribunal until it is necessary, will you tell me just how I stand and the procedure I must follow to put this into effect?' …

Saturday 29 March. … Didn't get an allotment. All they could offer was a piece of ground sown five years ago with sans foin. Roots as long as the arm and as thick so the secretary of the allotment committee told me. I gave it a miss. …

Sunday 30 March. … I spent the morning clearing up papers and books and notes ready for a beginning on exam work and another book. I want to finish the 'Big Bastard' novel this year if I can and next year write an autobiographical novel. Have found a title: 'No bed of roses'. …

I've heard from the CBCO. They say that COs in reserved occupations are normally notified that unless their occupation ceases to be reserved or the age limit is raised they will not be called on to state their case before a tribunal. …

Monday 31 March. The siren sounded last night at 2.35 a.m. and as it was my night for firewatching I turned out with the others. ... Jerry went over several times. There were flashes from the west once and a sentry on guard over the convoy to whom we were talking at the time said it was ack-ack (anti-aircraft fire). About 5.00 there was a terrific explosion. ... It was miles off, sounded Fulbourn way, and made the windows of the houses rattle near us. ... This morning, Bob the milkman, firewatching in the next street said his pal found it so cold he put his gasmask on to keep his face warm! ...

April 1941

Tuesday 1 April. Heard from Neil Bell. He thinks 'Tale of a Taylor' a remarkable book. Said send it to Michael Sadleir; I ought to pull it off.

Bevin says he cannot accept the principle of conscientious objection to civilian work. Every citizen must be on equal terms as far as work is concerned (Cheers in the Commons). Why all this concern about people working while the war is on and not when there was peace? ...

Wednesday 2 April. ... I wrote to Neil Bell today. Said his letter didn't inflate me (he said don't let it) but it made me very happy. All those grim sittings, night after night after the day's work, with enemy bombers roaring over, seemed worthwhile.

Thursday 3 April. ... A chap has just come in to ask me to sign a paper for compensation in the event of injury during firewatching. I refused. The signing would have made me a Civil Defence Volunteer, liable to 48 hours duty a month for firewatching, including 'pool' [away] service. Told him I was only doing it in my own neighbourhood. ...

Friday 4 April. German and Italian forces have taken Benghazi, the Libyan port.[9] This is a shock to people, who are wondering how the German forces arrived without any comments being made about it. One man I spoke to this morning who

---

[9] In December 1940 to February 1941 British troops pushed the Italians back 400 miles in North Africa. The removal of many British troops to defend Greece, and the arrival of the Afrika Korps under Rommel, led to the German advance in which Benghazi was recaptured.

has had a lot to say about the brilliance of the imperial forces, seemed to be in despair. He said it was funny how soon our troops crumpled when they came up against Jerry. ...

Saturday 5 April. I walked over to the Greyhound tonight. Saw Fred. He was half-sozzled. Had been scrounging round the shops and had managed to get half a pound of chocolate, some cheese and some bacon. He was well pleased with himself. He registered today under the new act for workers (he's 43) and kept emphasising that he registered, but he wasn't doing anything; and he wouldn't have registered at all if it had been for military service. ...

Tried for fish and chips on the way home, but though the shop was cooking when I went and had fish and fish cakes, just over an hour later when I returned it was sold out and shut. Got some chips at another shop and we had an egg with them when I got home (no buttered bread though these days). Bought Jack Hugo's Latin today to pull him up a bit. ...

Monday 7 April. ... Heard a lot of bombers going over in the night about 1 o'clock. Thought I would have to get up and go firewatching, for when our planes are buzzing around the siren generally sounds. It didn't, however, and I was able to keep snug in bed.... .

My comments the other day about the situation in Serbia still stand, ... There has been a coup d'état there of a sort, but it's merely one ruling class for another.[10] We've opened up another front to gain time. Germany has taken Benghazi to split our forces. That, I feel sure, is the position. ... Germany hopes by delaying reinforcements to push into the Mediterranean Sea. I think they'll do it, too. ...

Tuesday 8 April. The siren sounded last night just after we got to bed: 9.0 p.m. The 'All Clear' went at 4.45 a.m. Bombers kept going over for hours. I think Merseyside got it; and some

---

[10] Prince Paul, ruling Yugoslavia as regent for King Peter II (b. 1925), concluded a pact with the Axis powers in March 1941. Anti-Axis conspirators seized power on 27 March, abolishing the regency and declaring Peter to be king. Conquest by Germany followed.

places in East Anglia. ... The firewatchers in the street packed up at 2 o'clock. Didn't blame them. ...

Wednesday 9 April. There was an Alert last night at 8.55 pm. It lasted till 4.30 am. We heard bombs going off round about 10.30 before we went to bed and after we got there. ... Squadrons of bombers passed over both ways and we heard today that Coventry had been blitzed again. Portsmouth, also, according to the German radio.

I heard today that some of the Cambridge AFS [Auxiliary Fire Service] men were sent to Yarmouth yesterday, where fires from a raid were still burning. Cambridge was covered in smuts today. Long, thin wood ashes something like blackened curl-papers they seemed to me, came down and blew about the streets. A big fire somewhere, or fires. I wondered if it were Coventry as a strong north wind is blowing. ...

Jess paid 1*s* 9*d* for a tin kettle yesterday: pre-war price 9*d*. I read in the papers that production is restricted to 25 per cent since the war for these articles and that it will be increased to 50 per cent in July. How do these facts square with the price she paid?

I feel very tired these days. Don't know if it's lack of sugar. Could sleep on the proverbial clothes line. I went to see the relieving officer last night about E.T.O. Said I would pay 5*s* a week towards his upkeep in the infirmary ... . Fred has offered to pay 2*s* 6*d*. I wrote a letter for him to that effect and took it over to the Greyhound tonight. ...

Thursday 10 April. There was an Alert last night at 9.45 p.m. lasting until about 5.10 a.m. again. Bombers passing over all the while; Birmingham and Newcastle were their objectives we learned today. An East Anglian town also had its worst raid of the war. I heard this was Ipswich. ... Last night the *CDN* [*Cambridge Daily News*] was talking about the 'lovely bombs' we had been dropping somewhere. ...

Fred told me this morning that his daughter saw a bomber in the searchlights brought down Newmarket way last night. Said there was the sound of a rocket exploding when it happened, which made the people run out of their houses. ...

Every night when I'm abed and I hear the oomp oomp of the German bombers I say to Jess 'Hear that?' She says 'Yes' and we lie and listen. I think of the children downstairs and hope if Jerry intentionally or accidentally slip[s] a bomb they make a clean job of a messy one. And then I turn over and go to sleep, which is all I can do. But nowadays the feeling that one has seen another night through grows with successive days.

For some days men have been working on painting and erecting a flagpole round the Backs in the field at the back of King's College. ... they are men of the RAF. A flag fluttered there for a few hours: Union Jack in the corner and the red, white and blue rings of the Royal Air Force below. All in honour of the convoy of lorries parked there, I suppose. ... Jess tells me that the food queues in the town are getting longer. Women nearly get afighting.

Friday 11 April. Good Friday: a day of rest. There was an Alert last night just before 10.30 p.m. lasting until about 4.30 this morning. ... roughly the warnings are from just before before dawn, as the nights are shortening and the mornings lengthening, summer time just making itself felt to our benefit. Soon another hour is to be added to summer time. We heard bombs go off last night while in bed. ...

I spent the morning writing to Neil Bell. Then Frank Edwards and his wife and daughter came round in his car and he took Jess and me for a drive to Shelford round Hills Road home. ...

A short while ago the Londoners round here were rowing. Calling one another bloody cows, and stinking bloody bitches. Even the siren going off didn't stop their shouting and swearing and fist-shaking under one another's noses. I believe they did a bit of scrapping, too, but I didn't see that. The next morning some waylaid others and then they started all over again.

There's been a great to-do lately according to 'Cameronian' in Reynolds [*Reynolds' News*]. Officials of the Ministry of Health sat down in solemn conclave to decide whether the words 'Always wash your hands after using the W.C.' should be included in some of the Health Ministry's advertisements on hygiene ... They've at last included it in the national press advertisements. What courage!

Saturday 12 April. I went to the local labour exchange today at 3 o'clock and registered with the Os — as a CO. I was astonished at the appearance of most of those with whom I was registering; they were fat, bald, grey, veritable old men in many cases, and I thought 'Do I belong to this lot, this category? My word, I must be getting old! ... while I was reading a large, blue-coloured envelope before signing it a clerk asked me what I thought was the matter with it and I answered pretty tersely that I never signed anything without reading it. ...

Sunday 13 April. ... I've told a lot of people lately that if I didn't believe in Germany marching into Poland and making Europe an economic unit, I should believe in fighting still taking place on the Scotch and Welsh border; or nearer, between Cambridgeshire and Essex. Somebody asked me why should Germany be the controlling force; I said why not? I said it was central and nobody could deny the Germans had marked abilities and the aptitude for organisation likely to make the attempt a success. And, I added, it was about time our intriguing to maintain the balance of power, came to an end. ...

Tuesday 15 April. ... Heard today and saw it confirmed in tonight's *CDN* that a stick of seven bombs were dropped on Chivers jam factory yesterday. A little boy slightly injured. ... Started going in the water again today. ... [after] several weeks.

Thursday 17 April. The siren went last night at about 9.30 pm; the 'All Clear' at 5.15 a.m. A plane roundabout 4.00 a.m .sounded ominous, roaring over low. ... I bought *Morals, Manners and Men* [1939] by Havelock Ellis in the Thinkers' Library today. ... I wrote Dr Alex Wood asking if he would write me a letter that I could hand to the CO tribunal; I received a very good one from him today. ...

Sunday 20 April. Morning. Got up fairly early and worked a long time on the bets for yesterday. A lot of doubles and trebles at complicated odds. Wrote H. L[ionel] Elvin, a member of the Cambridge Anti-War Council years ago, asking him if he'd write a letter to give the CO tribunal.[11] …

There was a lot of stuff fell around outside the town after we got to bed last night. Awful crunches shook the house. But people don't take so much notice nowadays and we could hear them walking about and talking and the strains of a piano-accordion in the streets after turning-out time. The 'All Clear' went between 11.30 and 11.45…

The Jesses have gone to the pictures; Jack's out; and I feel a bit depressed. Got no appetite for writing or reading. And there's nobody to turn to for a chat. When I count up my friends I have very few. Not because I don't think friends an asset; I've always been too bookish to go about and make them. A mistake, I'm afraid. …

Monday 21 April. … I saw a small collie dog on Coe Fen today wearing a gas-mask … Have just got a pamphlet telling how to make a gas-proof box for the dogs. I shall have to find out more about dog gas-masks. …

It is easy to conclude by the papers that we are slowly being pushed out of Greece. Empire troops' heroism and so on are the headlines, but they are continually taking up new positions, which tells its own tale.[12] …

Tuesday 22 April. Everybody I spoke to today about the war seemed depressed and thought we were rapidly losing it if we hadn't already done so. … it is significant how the attitude of the public is changing. Now, the people are more than war-weary; they're war-sick.

Apparently, Australian forces were sent to Greece without the Australian cabinet being consulted. People and Parliament in Australia are demanding news of what's happening

---

[11] The Cambridge Anti-War Council was a pacifist group of the 1930s. H. Lionel Elvin, a Fellow of Trinity Hall and an English Faculty don, was a pacifist and socialist prominent in the CAWC, as was Alex Wood, a Scot, a devout Christian, Fellow of Emmanuel College and a University Lecturer in Physics, and a Cambridge city councillor for many years. Elvin came to accept that it was necessary to fight against Hitler, but Wood remained a pacifist.

[12] Following the German invasion of Greece on 6 April Britain sent some of its North African forces to defend it. They were unsuccessful in resisting the Germans.

in the Balkans. All being kept very quiet. Churchill was very evasive about it in the Commons today ... And there were lots of questions; more doubts than I've seen expressed about him and his ways for a long time. Soon, his popularity will wane. No leader could keep popular long in this country [in] the state it's in; Churchill least of all.

Jess got three little packed cheeses from our grocer yesterday: the sort that used to be sold in boxes before the war for about 6*d* a box, each box containing about eight of them. She also queued up in Sainsbury's for two sausages! Some people only got one. Sainsbury have brought out their own system of checking customers over supplies of unrationed foods.[13] It's on a points system and depends on how much there isof the rationed foodstuffs for which consumers are registered with them.

Wednesday 23 April. There was an Alert last night from 10.20 p.m. till about 11.45 p.m. We were abed when the siren sounded and I was so tired I never heard the 'All Clear'. Today I was told a German plane kept hovering over the town and a new searchlight that lit up the place like day was put up to find him with other searchlights and then he cleared off. The King's Royal Rifles have been in billets along Brookside; they are now gone; and with them the convoy parked on the 'Plant'un'.

Since writing the above I've had a walk with Frank Edwards who dropped in to see me. As we parted on Hills Road at 8.30 pm the siren sounded the Alert. A few seconds later the 'All Clear' went; a few seconds later a siren sounded, but whether a warning or the 'All Clear' I didn't know; a few seconds later another siren went for a little while and faded again. People were asking what was what; maybe some of the wardens were drunk. Jack has just come in to say it's a warning, a warden having told him to take cover as enemy planes are right overhead. ... As I type the 'All Clear' is sounding — 8.50 p.m.

---

[13] The official scheme for 'points' rationing, which followed Sainsbury's, was introduced in October 1941 for canned goods, cereals, dried fruit etc. Consumers were given coupons, or points, which might be surrendered for such goods at any retailer. The points required for any specified item might be varied by Whitehall in accordance with national supply. For these matters and rationing in general see Ina Zweiniger-Bargielowska, *Austerity in Britain* (Oxford, 2000).

Thursday 24 April. … A lot of planes about last night. Woke up and saw a light on in the house opposite. They've got a poor blackout in the shop windows and the other night during an Alert a light went off and on quite a score of times and Jess and I have started looking on the house with suspicion and thinking spies are there!

I sent in my form to the CO tribunal today. The following is my statement: My objections are based on moral grounds. My pacifist beliefs date from the last war, when as a youth of 14 and 15 I read and was greatly impressed by Ramsay MacDonald's pacifist articles in the *Labour Leader.* Subsequent reading showed the futility of fighting to solve the world's problems. In 1934, to further the cause of peace, I became a member and eventually secretary of the Individual Members' Section of the Cambridge Anti-War Council. More recently, to shape my ideas, I have worked for a degree and I am now reading as an external student for the final B.Sc. Economics examination (June 1942) of London University. None of my studies have weakened my pacifist convictions, but much that I have learned has strengthened them.

Jack Overhill also enclosed letters from Dr Alex Wood and a Mr Humphries, which he cited in the diary, testifying to the sincerity of his beliefs. He had also asked for a letter of support from Lionel Elvin of Trinity Hall. Elvin's cautious reply affirmed that he had known Jack for a short time only and that he would be bound to admit it to the tribunal if Jack continued his request for support; in addition, Elvin believed it was necessary to defeat Hitler by military means. Jack's reply to him stated that he had wanted no more than a brief letter of support, and continued:

The weakness of your argument that now we are in the war we must fight our way out of it, lies in the fact that the other side can so easily engineer a war and see you're in it, that if you're going to fight every time they land you in trouble, you'll certainly never stop fighting. …

Friday 25 April. Newspapers have recently been reduced to four pages; Sunday newspapers to eight pages. There is now a milkless day: everybody to go without one day's supply a week. An unfair rule, as there is no equitable rationing about that; for example, a household of four that has had five pints a day now has thirty pints a week instead of thirty-five. ... Basing present supply on past supply is absurd. Why not half a pint a day each person, or something like that? ...

Two Alerts last night: 11.40 p.m. till 12.40 a.m., 2.30 a.m. till 4.30 a.m. ... very tired these days. ...

Saturday 26 April. There was a warning last night from 3.40 a.m. till 4.20 a.m. I was awake and listening to the wail of the sirens spoke to Jess about the terror it must generate in little children. There will be some neurotics in the coming generation ... Britain has come undone again in the Balkans. Failure in everything we touch.

In the hunt for scrap metal railings are being taken down. In every case I've seen of them removed I think appearances have been bettered by it. Railings in the Victorian era must have been a mania. ...

Young Jess came over the shop this morning and told me E.T.O. died early this morning. I thought about him and me living together a lot after she'd gone. Wished things had been different. ... I can only say I always did my best. ...

Sunday 27 April. ... There was an Alert last night, the siren sounding just before 10 p.m. The 'All Clear' went at 2.0 a.m. the Roman Catholic church clock striking just after the 'Raiders Passed' signal. ... Another lot of King's Royal Rifles in billets along Brookside and so the lorries are again on the 'Plant'un'. ... When I see the barbed wire about the Fen in readiness for invasion and think of the German troops forcing their way through the mountainous country of the Balkans I have to smile. ...

Tuesday 29 April. I heard from the Ministry of Labour today. I am not to go before the CO tribunal provided I keep at my trade as a shoe-repairer, shoe-repairing being a reserved occupation at my age. If I change my occupation I must notify the authorities; if shoe-repairing is removed from the reserved occupations list, I can state my case before the tribunal. ...

Wednesday 30 April. There was a warning last night from 12.05 a.m. till 12.35 a.m. A man told me he saw a couple of flares in the sky towards Chesterton way; ...

May 1941

Thursday 1 May. … Fred and I went to Haverhill today, where E.T.O. was buried; so I fulfilled his wish, made to him as a boy. Fred was well oiled when we went to the cemetery as he had drunk seven pints … . First, he had to be told by an attendant to put out a cigarette; … [in the church] he cursed loudly and luridly all the while. Useless to repeat it. … We had a walk round the town, met a man named Basham who was in India with my uncle Charlie, one of the old man's brothers (bought him a drink or two) and then Fred had another two pints in the Woolpack and we came home. We did both journeys by rail. I drank many lemonades, but never equalled the number of Fred's pints. Possibly his behaviour will be noised around Haverhill. If so, I have no doubt, it will be looked upon by those who remember the old man's family, as traditionally Overhill.

Friday 2 May. People to whom I have talked today have generally showed apprehension about the Heidelberg bombing; fearing reprisals on Cambridge. … The siren has just sounded: 9.50 p.m. …

Saturday 3 May. There were two warnings last night for after the 'All Clear' was sounded of the Alert mentioned above [on 2 May] at 1.45 a.m., the siren went again at 3.30 a.m. the warning lasting till 4.15 a.m. I thought when I heard the 'Raiders Passed' signal (a warden told me this is the correct name, as the 'All Clear' is signalled by the ringing of handbells, which I thought was the 'All Clear' only for gas. As I've never heard handbells yet there has never been an 'All Clear'! …) that there would be another warning before long as no sooner had it sounded than a German bomber came oomping along over the town, followed by a flash. He soon went off, but it made the 'Raiders Passed' signal sound a bit weak. …

Sunday 4 May. A warning last night: 10.55 p.m. till 4.40 a.m. The time was put forward another hour last night, making two hours summer time. … A big advert in today's paper showing how to wear gas-masks and use them effectively; … .

I saw sheep and baby lambs on the playing field of the Leys School, now an annexe of Addenbrooke's Hospital, this morning ….

Monday 5 May. As soon as my head touched the pillow last night at 10.50 the siren sounded, so as it was my firewatching night, up I got again. … The warning lasted until 4.50 a.m. and there were plenty of bombers about in the early hours of the morning. Merseyside and Belfast had heavy raids. …

Tuesday 6 May. Two warnings last night: 10.50 p.m. to 11.55 p.m., 4.15 a.m. to 5.00 a.m. … People are queuing up outside the fish and chip shops now. … The queue for eggs was so long on the market this morning that Jess gave it a miss. …

Wednesday 7 May. A warning last night: 11.45 p.m. to 3.00 a.m. We heard a stick of five bombs go off and a firewatcher outside say 'I wonder where they fell'. Rumour today said Oakington. … Heard nothing from Sadleir, feel a bit frettish about it at times, but on the whole don't hope for good news. The general outlook is too gloomy to aspire in that direction.

Thursday 8 May. A warning last night: 11.25 p.m. till 4.45 a.m. … Jack has just shown me an advertisement in an old *Gem*. It is a reproduction of the front cover of the first issue of the *Magnet* (the *Gem* is offering congratulations to the *Magnet* on its thousandth publication in 1927) on Tuesday February 11th 1908. It is of particular significance to me as it gives me the day of my fifth birthday—a Monday. I started school that day: and I didn't like it; I still remember repeatedly throwing my cap on the ground as I was being taken to school as a sign of rebellion that I didn't want to go. I think mother and the old man separated the day after I was five. …

Friday 9 May. A warning last night from 12.10 a.m. till about 5 o'clock. A lot going over the town; scores of planes, incendiaries dropped on Hills Road setting fire to Homerton College and doing considerable damage to it. Many houses in that direction also set alight. High explosives were dropped round Coldham's Lane; and an RAF private told me that some heavies fell Waterbeach way, badly shaking the guardroom round the Backs. … Slack at the shop this morning and [I] wrote up the beginning of the 'Big bastard'.

Saturday 10 May. Two warnings last night: 12.10 a.m. till 1.40 a.m., 2.30 a.m. till 5.00 a.m. ... Had a mooch round the town late tonight. A lot of soldiers standing about at street corners. ...

Sunday 11 May. A warning last night: 11.15 p.m. till 5.05 a.m. There was another big blitz on London. ... If Hitler makes a going concern of his new order in Europe, what then? Maybe, the countries will rally to the Reich and will actively and effectively co-operate in making the task a success. And if we are strong enough to bomb Europe, what will Europe do to Britain? Blast it off the face of the earth? The cause of this country is a hopeless one, has been from the beginning. The capitulation of France put finishing touch to our intrigues and balance of power politics in Europe. The old order has gone; great events are taking place; I hope for the better; but, doubtless, there's a lot to go through yet as the controlling class will not yield without struggle. But finally it will be eclipsed. The sense of right in the people will triumph over that of wrong immediately they are aware of what is right and what is wrong; that is becoming increasingly evident every day; I mean this new sense of awareness that everything is not what it should be—even apart from the war; that those who work should also play, not pay, pay, pay—in blood and sweat and tears as Mr Churchill oratorically puts it.

Wednesday 14 May. ... [On Sunday night, 11 May] there were two warnings: 11.45 p.m. to 3.50 a.m. and 5.10 a.m. to 5.30 a.m., my firewatching night. Out till 2.00. Plenty doing. Flares, heard two burst of machine-gun fire in the sky, lots of heavy crumps round about, and saw a German bomber pass overhead parallel with Saxon Street. One chap walking about, the bloke with the stirrup pump who would love a fire, with a white enamel bowl on his head for a steel helmet. Enemy bombers buzzed about all over the place. ...

A sensation Monday night which I first heard on Tuesday morning: Hess, a prominent German leader flew by plane from Germany to Scotland.[14] I think this might mean Germany going in with Russia. ...

Friday 16 May. I woke up last night and heard the chimes sound 2.00. Lay and wondered if the Hess affair [were] a pointer to peace as no raids for four nights. I was too optimistic for at 3.0 am the siren went, the warning lasting till about 5.00 a.m. Heard a few planes, probably ours. ...

Hess is receiving the treatment of a prisoner of war: as an officer and gentleman. As he is in hospital and faddy about food he is having chicken and rice. The people I've spoken to don't think much of it. ...

Saturday 17 May. A warning: 12.10 a.m. till about 4.30 a.m. I don't think I heard the warning, only the 'All Clear'; ... .

An undergraduate came in and had a bet this afternoon and he told me that racing created a utility of satisfaction.[15] ... I slated him a bit; stopped his talking down to me. He was 19; loftily conscious of his knowledge. Most of us are at that age. Of course, he believed in racing for the reason stated. I was going to tell him that sellers of opium and keepers of red lamps also created utilities of satisfaction — what about them? Should they be allowed? But I didn't get the chance between telephone calls before he went.

Sunday 18 May. A warning last night from about 1.25 a.m. till 3.55 a.m. Never heard anything doing though. Had a walk up Long Common with the Jesses and the dogs this morning.[16] Soldiers had camped in one of the plantations there (mentioned in 'Adolescence')[17] overnight and we were diverted from the path coming back by a sentry because we should

---

[14] Rudolf Hess, nominally Hitler's deputy but losing influence with him, flew to Scotland on 10 May, most probably in a madcap scheme to unite Britain and Germany in an attack on the USSR. Britain declined to take the idea seriously. Hess was incarcerated, and at the Nuremberg trial sentenced to life imprisonment. He died in Spandau prison in 1987, aged 93.

[15] An unusual way to describe the pleasure which racing gives to its spectators.

[16] Long Common, officially 'Empty Common', lay to the East of Trumpington Road, south of Brooklands Avenue, between Vicar's Brook and Hobson's Brook. I am again grateful to Chris Jakes for this identification.

[17] 'Adolescence' was one of Jack Overhill's unpublished novels.

have passed a temporary latrine! We came home Coe Fen way and the daisies were glorious. ... Went and had a chat with Bert Cash repairing his punt in the evening. ...

Monday 19 May. Heavy clouds and raining this morning and as I crossed Sheep's Green coming home to dinner the siren sounded. The warning was from 1.05 till 1.25 p.m. ... the siren went off once more. The warning lasted from 1.45 till about 2.20 p.m.

I am getting ready some of my schoolbooks and old manuscripts for binding in order to preserve them better, if it is possible to preserve anything these days. ...

Thursday 22 May. ... Bert Cash gave me an address in Wales to which Young Jess can go in August for a leaders' course in gym training. I'm not keen on it; not just now. There might be an invasion of this country in August; and what if she was there when that happened? I like us to be together, just in case. ...

Did a pair of hand-sewn at the shop today. I'm much quicker doing them than I was, but sewn work is still slow work with me; and consequently bad[ly]-paid work as it takes so long. ...

Friday 23 May. ... Horse meat is 1*s* 1*d* a pound at the animal shop in the town. I'm still getting it at Pink's. He charges me 8*d* a pound and told me it's fetching 1*s* 4*d* a pound in London for human consumption.

Sunday 25 May. Frank Edwards rang up this morning to tell me HMS *Hood,* the largest battle-cruiser in the world, was sunk in an engagement off Greenland with the German battleship *Bismarck*. ...

Monday 26 May. ... 80,000 German troops are in Norway, apparently ready to invade Great Britain. ... 14,000,000 leaflets are being distributed telling people what to do in the event of invasion. ...

Tuesday 27 May. A woman told me in the street rather excitedly today dinner-time that she had just heard on the wireless that the *Bismarck*, Germany's big battleship, was sunk. ... Revenge for HMS. *Hood*.[18] ... Got the notice by post this morning telling us what to do in the event of an invasion.

Friday 30 May. The book came back from Constable today ... . Michael Sadleir suggested cutting out some of the dialogue of Dennis Porter, one of the main characters, and redesigning the end of the book, as the light ending was out of keeping with the first half. I wrote back and said I couldn't do it: that when I rewrote stuff I made bad worse. ... I'd sooner write another book. ... Now I'll forget 'Tale of a Taylor' and get on with something else.

Saturday 31 May. ... This afternoon I saw a telegram boy pull up outside the house and knew it was a reply from Bell to my telegram. It was. The message said 'Merely a setback to your success is certain writing Neil Bell'. He's a great chap. I felt very heartened and always do after hearing from him.

I went to the fair on Midsummer Common with the two Jesses tonight. We had a go on the darts without any success. I listened to the band on the 'Prom' as we were going and coming back. Finished off the day with a sausage supper. ...

June 1941

Sunday 1 June. Sensational headlines in this morning's newspaper: 'Clothing is Rationed'. ... the rationing — by coupons — looks adequate enough to cover my requirements, although at present I have only the clothes I stand up in.[19] ... I saw a queue outside a cigarette shop the other day. ... Everything is gradually being rationed. What about beer?

Tuesday 3 June. ... Our troops have evacuated Crete. The fighting lasted twelve days. The *Daily Herald* is asking the usual lot of 'Whys?' ... I borrowed a couple of pounds off Jess today

---

[18] Germany's 42,000 ton battleship escaped into the Atlantic to attack Allied convoys. She was engaged by the *Hood*, which unluckily was hit by a shell that caused it to blow up. There were only three survivors. The *Bismarck* was sunk on 27 May; of her crew of 2222 there were only 115 survivors.

[19] Clothes were rationed on the same principle as the points system for foodstuffs. An annual allocation of coupons had to be exchanged for individual garments.

and £3 10s off Albert Digby, which, with some other money I raked up, I managed to pay the bill for E.T.O.'s funeral. The undertaker gave me 10s for a drink! Discount, I suppose. ...

Wednesday 4 June. A local rumour: Hess is in Cambridge. More likely Berlin! ...

Thursday 5 June. A warning last night from 12.35 to 3.30 a.m. Haven't heard the siren lately and it gave me [a] nightmare. ...

Saturday 7 June. ... The lilac, laburnum, may and chestnut blossom is now glorious; but the appreciation of its full beauty is marred by the weather—still dull and gloomy. The highest temperature registered at Sheep's Green of the river this year is 53 degrees.

Monday 9 June. Jess came round to the shop with calamitous news this morning: Joe Bennett, the bookmaker, had packed up! ... He's given me a bit of commission on my covering bets for years and it came in very handy. Now we could do with it and shall miss it. ...

Wednesday 11 June. Eggs are to be rationed on the 14th of this month. We have 200 or 300 in waterglass for the winter. I wish we had had some jam by us when the rationing of it started. I miss it. We manage on the meat ration and that's about all. Butter is scraped on the bread; a mouthful of cheese a week, a teaspoonful of jam a day; half-sweetened tea because of little sugar; that's how it is nowadays. And there's no cooking fat to make anything with. ... Coal, gas and electricity are to be rationed. I expect the Italians are burning the coal we should have had. We sent them enough in the hope of keeping them out of the war! ... There's talk now of a run on soap. It'll be rationed. ...

Parliament held the inquest on Crete yesterday.[20] Little came out that we didn't already know. Churchill's dictatorial powers were more in evidence. The man's a positive menace to the common weal. A god with clay feet. He'll come tumbling

---

[20] 35,000 Allied troops retreated to Crete after being defeated in Greece. They lacked co-ordinated command, artillery and transport. The island was conquered in May by 17,500 German troops. More than 3700 Allied servicemen were killed and 11,000 taken prisoner. Three British cruisers and six destroyers were lost during the evacuation.

down; nothing so sure. ... It's striking 10.00 as I type and it's broad daylight. It's daylight now until nearly midnight because of the two hours summer time, ...

Thursday 12 June. There was an Alert last night: 1.30 a.m. till 4.15 a.m. ... Russia is in the news: Germany is massing troops on her frontiers. ... I think if Germany tackles Russia she'll get the worst of it; and communism in Germany and Great Britain would be the result of it; but I doubt if Germany will try. ...

Friday 13 June. ... There was a warning last night from round about midnight until a few minutes before 4.00 a.m. ...

Saturday 14 June. A warning last night from about 2.00 a.m. till about 4.00 a.m. ... I am rearranging ready for re-writing 'The big bastard'. Have changed the title to 'The chancer'.

Monday 16 June. A day of glorious sunshine. What a welcome change. In view of the weather people were surprised when the siren sounded today at 11.55 a.m. The warning lasted till 12.35 p.m. ...

Tuesday 17 June. We heard eight or nine terrific explosions in the night and heard today that a German bomber followed a Stirling bomber home and unloaded when Oakington aerodrome lit up to receive it in. ...

Friday 20 June. ... I went and bought a pair of flannel trousers today; the price was 36s. I nearly fell through the floor; but I had them; had to, as I've hardly any clothes at all. But I gained a bit in buying a sports coat, as I allowed about 55s for this and got a good one for 46s. The purchase tax of $33^{1}/_{3}$ per cent does the damage; and, of course, prices have risen since the war started. ...

Saturday 21 June. ... Bought a shirt today, for which I gave up five coupons. Thirteen coupons yesterday for my coat and eight for my trousers, uses up my twenty-six coupons, the number allowed till August. Then we get forty more to make a total of sixty-five per person per year. The shirts were 8s 6d each, a fair price for these days, as the shopkeeper let me buy two; which shows how easy it is to get round rationing. ...

Sunday 22 June. It's about 9 o'clock; a glorious morning. I got up and made the family a cup of tea this morning for a change (Jack often does it). Since then I've had my breakfast and I am now in bed again, sitting up typing, as I've been doing a bit on the novel.

While I was having breakfast, Frank Edwards rang up with sensational news: Hitler is attacking Russia. Hitler says ... he is going to rid Europe of the communist menace. ... So at last we have the solution of the riddle that's been troubling people like me. German national socialism and communism were not merging together.

One can feel more certain that Hess came here on a peace mission. That the lull in the air war was because Germany didn't want to bring about our defeat; that would mean a victory for communism. ... the leaders of this country have a tidy problem to solve. Do we fight for Russia and communism (not likely!) or do we forgive Germany the merciless bashings she has given us? ...

[In the afternoon] I went for a swim. On the way I thought about the WAR. It seemed remote, as in those sunny days of early September 1939 when war was declared, the day being bright and sunny with a soft breeze blowing and the air heavy with the scents of summer.

Monday 23 June. ... While at the Red Lion at Grantchester, we joined the crowd listening to Churchill's broadcast on the war situation; he surprised me in a way by saying that we were going all out to help Russia. He seemed sincere, but whether or not the future will tell. ... I think Russia will put up a show that will make numerous people ready to decry them sing another tune. The Germans included.

Tuesday 24 June. The evacuated Londoners round here are a motley crowd, filthy in their habits and disgusting in their ways. The children are uncared for, given a piece of bread and marg[arine] to eat in the street for dinner; the younger ones foul the streets like dogs and the whole neighbourhood is like a refuse tip. Breaking bottles, milk or beer, is a pastime with the children, all seemingly as cunning as the proverbial waggonload of monkeys. ...

Saturday 28 June. There was a warning last night, starting about 1.15 a.m. and lasting for nearly an hour. ...

Eggs are being rationed: one each a week! With regard to the rations we make shift with the meat, get along all right on the milk allowance and find the tea ample; the butter, cheese, jam, sugar and fats are quite inadequate. Often the cupboard is bare and it's a job to find something to eat. ... I managed to get a pound of extra jam out of the grocer today. We're going without sugar in our tea in order to keep it for making jam.

Monday 30 June. ... The other night between 11.00 and 12.00 there was a knock at the front door. I called out 'Who's there?' and got out of bed and looked out of the window. It was a half-drunken soldier, he's got an address! After fumbling for it to see where it was he said 'Gothic Street'. I told him further along, first turning on the left; and off he clumped. Soon there was laughing and shouting in Gothic Street and we heard him clump off again. Perhaps the lady of the address was already engaged ... We had a good laugh over it. They're a tribe round here nowadays and no mistake. ...

July 1941

Thursday 3 July. There was a warning last night at 2.00 a.m. I was uneasy as the children were sleeping upstairs, but urged by Jess to let them lie and to wait and see if there was anything doing, I didn't disturb them. There was a flash between 2.30 and 2.45 and I hopped out of bed and waited until a German bomber approaching in the distance had come up and passed over. Jess said 'Now don't get windy' as I jumped out of bed. I said I wasn't; but I was anxious about the children. ... Soon afterwards we heard the clock strike 2.45 a.m. and almost immediately the 'All Clear' went.

It's another perfect morning; a glorious blue sky. ... I'm working steadily at examination work, including Italian, and the book. I bought a secondhand copy of Hawtrey's *Currency and Credit* [1919; also later editions] yesterday for 12s. Couldn't afford it, but must have it. ...

I'm beginning to think the Russians will come out on top. So I might have to change my opinion about the war ending this year. ... if they hold the Germans it might drag on, with us still involved either belligerently or passively.

Evening. Went to Grantchester, the old spot, with Big Jess and Jack for a swim this afternoon. Water 64, the weather hot. It seemed strange to be down there again; and coming home through Trumpington seemed stranger still. It seemed years ago since we were there and brought back memories of many happy times. ...

Friday 4 July. A banner floats across St Andrew's Street telling people their railings will build a destroyer. ... Much of the bread we eat nowadays is dry, such as dry bread and chips, dry bread and egg ... and so on. A man asked Jess yesterday had I decided what day I intended to eat my egg. He intended to save his until he had two and so have a good blowout every fortnight!...

I went to the County Boys' swimming sports this afternoon. Helped to judge the diving. Jack won the 30 yards race he was in pretty easily; ... .

Saturday 5 July. I heard what I thought was an enemy bomber go over in the night and soon after there were a couple of crumps in the distance, which rattled the window frames. Then the Roman Catholic [church] clock struck the quarter past something and I grumbled to Jess about the siren not sounding. A few minutes later it went off and later I heard the clock strike 3.00. The warning would be at about 2.20 a.m. and it lasted until about 3.50 a.m. I could hear Jerry several times in the distance and there was another explosion while the warning was on and a night fighter or two went over. I was relieved when the Jerry bomber finally oomped off as the children were sleeping upstairs. I've told them (at breakfast) they're sleeping downstairs again in future; had enough of being on edge as I was last night for an hour and a half ...

Sunday 6 July. ... Big Jess and I went to the old spot at Grantchester yesterday afternoon from 4.00 till 8.00. I had a couple of dips. Tea was good and varied for wartime: bread and cheese and spring onions, bread and jam, choc roll and biscuits; Jess had tomato sandwiches (I don't like tomatoes). And we had a drop of sugar in the tea, although now we're saving the sugar for jam. (This month everybody gets half [a] pound of sugar each week above the normal ration of half [a] pound for jam-making.) ...

A communist woman came into the shop yesterday and asked me to join the People's Convention.[21] I said I didn't belong to any party and wouldn't join; I preferred to be independent. This, in order not to be compelled to adhere to policies of which I don't approve. And all parties have their programmes. I don't think she liked it. I approve of the P.C. though. ...

Tuesday 8 July. Last night after Jess went to bed I biked down to the river and had another dip [after six in the day]. It was very refreshing. I was soon back and getting into bed as the clock struck 11.00. ... Jess queued up for everything this morning: strawberries, gooseberries, potatoes, peas ---

Wednesday 9 July. ... Now, I spend my day as follows. Clear up all the repairs in the morning, work on two subjects and Italian down the cellar at the shop (it's cool down there) for the exam in the afternoon; more Italian in the afternoon, usually beside the river when I go out for a dip and a walk with the dogs in the evening. When I come home, just before 9.00 as a rule, I settle down to the novel. All I'd written seems to be dud, so I'm doing it again. ...

Friday 11 July. Jam is to be half the present fruit standard. Heaven help us! ... Still very hot, but there was a shower this evening. ...

Sunday 13 July. ... On the way home [from the doctor's] I saw a man I know named Jack Lavender, the first man I saw doing the crawlstroke. He's become a father at last; he's fifty-two; was pushing a daughter, aged three, in a pushcart. ...

---

[21] The People's Convention, promoted by the Communist Party, first met in January 1941. It called for the defence of living standards and democratic rights, friendship with the USSR, and a People's Government, claiming that Britain had 'the same kind of leaders who brought France to defeat'. It was hoped that popular agitation would bring a new government, and stimulate the German workers to overthrow the Nazis. Peace would follow.

Tuesday 15 July. ... Jess went to Histon yesterday and heard that a young man there in the RAF had been in the habit of driving from his home to Cottenham by car and going on bombing raids to Germany. The other day his parents took him the usual cup of tea upstairs in the morning and he wasn't there. The father then went to Cottenham and learned that the bomber in which his son served had not returned. That happened about a week ago and they've heard nothing since. He'd been on 29 bombing raids. And RAF men are often buried from their own homes; Young Gigney, who used to be a member of the Granta Swimming Club, was the other day, after crashing upon landing in a night-fighter. ...

Wednesday 16 July. The willow wort [probably great willowherb, *epilobium hirsutum*] is coming out. What a beautiful flower it is. My earliest recollections of Coe Fen and Sheep's Green are associated with it: hot, summer days, on the way to and from the river, just a pair of bathing slips in my pocket, looking at the willow wort growing across the ditch near the bathing place, sensing rather than appreciating the beauty of small pink flowers ---

Thursday 17 July. ... Today, I said to Jess that my trying, hurrying, scurrying and sticking at it, year in and year out, hadn't got me very far. One never knows though; perhaps it's got me further than I think.

Friday 18 July. There was a warning last night from 2.20 a.m. to 3.00 a.m. ... A billetting officer came here the other day; Jess saw him. It doesn't matter now about the stairs of the shant we live in being dark and winding and there not being enough air space; the authorities would foist lodgers on us. I'll see they don't; will go to prison first; there's plenty of big houses in Cambridge that can shelter evacuees and war workers; let them take them.

Wednesday 23 July. ... About Perce [his brother]. He died with diphtheria in 1912; I was always worried for years afterwards as the anniversary of his death approached, watching for signs of a sore throat and very scared if I happened to have one. I forgot if he died at a quarter to three or a quarter past, but to make sure never felt quite easy until the quarter past had passed on the day. I remember lying on Parker's Piece one Saturday afternoon welcoming the time when the ordeal was over and looking at the Catholic clock with satisfaction because it registered a time later than that on the way home. ...

I heard a stick of bombs fall in the night not long after the Catholic clock struck 3.00. Heard today the bombs were dropped at Oakington. No siren.

Friday 25 July. ... Jess had a fairish report with praise for steady work, which is worth a lot. There was a suggestion on the report that she takes more subsidiary subjects next year. I asked what that meant and she told me that's to satisfy the examiner in case the pupil wishes to enter a training college, in case he (or she) doesn't get the Higher School Certificate. I said I wasn't agreeing to that; she's staying on for the Higher School Certificate and she can keep trying if she doesn't pass first time. ...

Wednesday 30 July. ... [In addition to extolling the quantity of Britain's war production] Churchill also said that if we (Great Britain) falls, they all fall. 'They' presumably is inclusive of any other countries opposing Germany. What he should have said is if Russia falls the rest falls; that would have made sense. ...

August 1941

Friday 1 August. ... Jess is tired of hearing me say I'm hungry; but she said it herself yesterday. Sometimes, we get an egg with dry bread. Butter, cheese, fats, fruits — but what's the use of naming them — we can't get them; can't get nuffink nowadays. ...

Wednesday 6 August. Jess said soon after we got to bed last night that it must be a fortnight since we heard the siren; I said it must be; then we went to sleep — to be awakened by a stick of bombs falling outside the town. Shortly afterwards, at 2.50 a.m. the siren sounded and another couple of sticks of bombs fell. It was pouring with rain and I wondered aloud how the bombers would find their marks on such a sticky night, ... I heard the bombs — about 20 h.e.s [high explosives] and 20 incendiaries—were dropped at Rampton, near Cottenham. They fell in a cornfield, and did no damage.

Thursday 7 August. I saw dessert gooseberries marked up today at 3s a *lb* … . It gave me a shock. Unripe apples are 8d a *lb* and unripe small pears 9d a half-pound. Babies are to have blackcurrant juice: as a substitute for orange juice, I suppose. …

Friday 8 August. I woke up last night just in time to hear a stick of bombs fall. (I heard today at Oakington.) Then the siren sounded; 2.30 till 3.00 a.m. the warning lasted. I was told, also, today, that the bombs on Tuesday night did not fall at Rampton, but at Smithy Fen, where I worked on the farm at the beginning of the war. Jess's sister told Jess they were aimed at a dud aerodrome there and were bombs of a new sort, jumping about on the ground exploding like a jumping cracker, setting fire to things as they did so. Well, you've got it as I got it. Rumours are legion nowadays. …

Saturday 9 August. Two warnings last night: 11.50 p.m. till 1.05 a.m., 4.0 a.m. till 5.0 a.m. …

I've decided to change the title of the book I'm on to 'The Cordwainer'. Third time lucky! Had a walk round the town with the two Jesses late this afternoon: queues outside the tobacco shops; Lyons full up; queues in Marks and Spencer for cakes and fish; Sainsbury's nearly sold out of everything. Jess bought [a] half-pound of German sausage—not bearing that name now—and I think from the taste of it the Germans would have been indignant about our calling it such. It was 10d a *lb* and would have been dear at half the price. We came home nearly empty-handed, … .

The time is put back an hour tonight to normal summer time, so now it will be an hour in advance of Greenwich time. I haven't cared much for the two-hour summer time system: too tiring.

Monday 10 August. … I'm reading and enjoying one of the Penguin *New Writing* books.[22] … I wouldn't know what to do with myself if I wasn't a bookworm.

---

[22] Forty volumes of these very popular collections of short stories and essays were published by Penguin Books 1941–50: John Lehmann and Roy Fuller, editors, *Penguin New Writing 1940–1950* (1985).

Tuesday 12 August. ... We get a double ration of jam this month, four ounces each a week instead of two; the fruit standard is now very, very low. There is to be an increase shortly in the cheese ration, three ounces a week instead of one. The meat ration is 1*s* 2*d* worth each person a week now. ...

Wednesday 13 August. ... There was a warning last night from about 11.30 p.m. till a little after 2.00 a.m. and I think I must have had a nightmare, for although a large number of bombs fell outside the town, making the windows rattle loudly, all I heard, or a lot of it, must have been fancy. Anyway, I heard the siren go off and the Catholic church clock strike midnight and bombs exploding in the distance and the windows rattle. Then I heard a w-h-e-e-e-e-e and a bomb just missed the house. I waited for the explosion, but it didn't come. Then I heard running footsteps and looking out of the window saw a prostrate figure on the path at the top of the archway and somebody carrying an object that looked like a hurdle to put round it. A crowd was forming and I knew the person was either seriously injured or dead. It was snowing furiously as I watched and then I started to dress. As I put my clothes on I said to Jess 'I think you should know there's a bad raid on' and she set up sharply in bed wearing a black nightdress with white spots, looking as though she hardly knew where she was. I said 'take it easy, there's no need to get flurried' and — woke up! But so convinced was I about the bomb whistling by the window that hearing voices in the street I got out of bed and questioned the firewatchers, asking them if 'that bomb' fell in the town, the one that had just whistled by the house! They said none had fallen in the town and I asked them if they'd seen the light switched on in the pub bedroom window as an enemy bomber was going over. They had, as that was a fact, the incident happening as I got out of bed. ...

Thursday 14 August. ... Attlee, Deputy Prime Minister, was speaking [on the wireless at 3.00 p.m.]: a declaration of war aims; Churchill and Roosevelt ... had met at sea on the quiet.[23] I didn't hear all he said ... as the battery petered out and

---

[23] They met off the coast of Newfoundland and proclaimed the 'Atlantic Charter'.

the wireless faded, but it was no disappointment. It's taken Churchill and company a couple of years to make up their minds what our war aims are; and now they're rather tenuous. The warlike nations are to be unarmed, and this time, the peaceful nations (that's us!) are to remain armed! And Nazism is to be destroyed! Well, well, well. What hopes of a settlement and peace. ...

Sunday 17 August. ... Roosevelt says that the Lease and Lend Bill does not apply to Russia; she has the money to pay ... . Looks as if America is on the make; just out to profit from the war. ... Evidently she [Russia] can have the help if she pays for it.[24]

A warning last night: roundabout 10.30 p.m. to 12.10 a.m.

Tuesday 19 August. ... Three Cambridge COs sent to prison today by E. O. Brown the mayor for failing to take their medicals, so I suppose Frank [Edwards] will be for it soon; maybe myself as well later; can never tell.[25] I didn't envisage Germany attacking Russia when I made the bet with Frank that the authorities wouldn't touch him before the war ended. I thought the war would end in our defeat this autumn—it might yet!—but there's a big chance of it dragging on now, with Britain more or less looking on, and in that case it looks, at least, a show must be made with COs who refuse their medical examination. ...

Wednesday 20 August. A warning last night from 1.00 a.m. till 3.00 a.m. Soon after the siren sounded, enemy bombers passed over; then the sky was lit up in the north. We heard today that incendiaries were dropped at Chesterton. ...

The milk ration is to be a gill [¼ pint] a day for adults, [a] half-pint for those under 17, a pint for babies and nursing mothers. ...

---

[24] The USSR paid for goods supplied until October 1941. The USSR became eligible for Lend-Lease aid from then onwards.

[25] During the 1930s pacifism grew in the University and to some extent in the city, partly in consequence of the growth of Communism, with which it was linked: T. E. B. Howarth, *Cambridge Between the Wars* (1978), pp. 218–20. Jack's friend Frank Edwards was a hairdresser in Mill Road. His pacifism eventually took him into Bedford prison. See the entry for 8 September 1941.

Thursday 21 August. ... [After a cycle ride to Newmarket and back with Jack, and a swim] as a relaxation I read five tales of W. W. Jacobs in the bilingual series of Italian and English. ...

Sunday 24 August. ... The nights are not very good. As soon as we get abed there's calls of 'R-o-s-i-e' from the evacuees next door (Rosie is with the soldiers up Brookside), then there's calls for 'E-i-l-e-e-n' (probably in the same place) and various calls for other girls round here whose ages range from 13 to 20 and who, very likely, are playing peep-bo in the dark with the soldiers in billets along Brookside. Then there's the pubs turning out, the Spread Eagle and the Cross Keys. The 'Spread' is the worst; youths and girls, singing, whistling, shouting, giggling. --- How they dramatise themselves; their actions and talk based on that of the most popular film stars, is nauseating. Frequently, they sing snatches of sentimental songs; but I believe croon is the right word. They all fade away, there's a brief spell of peace; and then the cats start. ... In between times, there's rows and the wail of the siren. ...

Tuesday 26 August. Last night I went to post a letter between 9.00 and 10.00. Pitch darkness everywhere except for the twinkling lights of cars and lorries. The searchlights started to stab the sky in every direction; one, Duxford way, was particularly powerful, seeming to have a double beam. Planes were droning over, some low; and one suddenly appeared like a big, black bird against a smudgy white outline of sky just above the housetops over Scroope Terrace. ... A nightmare sort of world; unreal. ... By the bye, I'm paying 3*s* 7*d* a pound now for leather, but I think it was dearer than that during the last war.

Wednesday 27 August. [After a warning at about 12.30 a.m.] I went to sleep and was awakened by an awful crump in the distance; it sounded like one big bomb, but was no doubt a stick going off almost together (I heard today the bombs fell between Oakington and Longstanton). [After the 'All Clear' there was a second warning.]

Friday 29 August. There was a warning last night at 12.45 a.m. lasting for about half an hour. In the night, Jess said she had heard some bombs fall; ... . There were many planes about.

Today we heard that the bombs fell in the Great Eastern Street area, killing an old lady and a child. ...

Saturday 30 August. ... A newspaper item: melons £2 each, peaches 5s each, grapes 17s 6d a *lb.* ...

Sunday 31 August. A heavy explosion startled us last night round about 9 o'clock. We heard this morning that it was one of our bombers that crashed at Oakington. There was a warning last night: 10.50 to 11.50 p.m. ...

September 1941

Wednesday 3 September. ... I spend a restless night, not going to sleep till past 2.00. Thought a lot about Jack. Wished he would work harder and try to make a success of his studies. There were a lot of planes about and one roared over and circled round very low. They give me an unpleasant feeling night and day; ... .

It was a very hot, still night, and sound was intensified, especially the sound of footsteps. Three times I got out of bed just before midnight to watch an officer patrolling up and down the archway opposite, obviously looking for 'stray' [presumably 'other ranks']. I got fed up at last and when he walked called out 'left, right, left right'. He looked up at the window, turned and started to walk off and I called after him 'left, left, left', timing his footsteps. Then he went on tiptoes and sheered off. ...

Thursday 4 September. Eric, Jack and I went to see Shaw's *Major Barbara* at the Victoria cinema last night. It was good, but too long. And there were too many set speeches. At the end Barbara's conception of right and wrong seemed a bit mixed up, her acceptance of a husband who was inheriting a huge armaments industry conflicting with her character and outlook.

The walk home in the moonlight was grand. Jack came into bed; Eric and I talked for a while on Trumpington Road seat about the religious feelings of people who suddenly find God. He thought there was something in their claim about being happy because something had entered into them. Maybe there is. I had a queer feeling like that myself once, several years ago. But I didn't feel happy about it. It was one night when alone late in front of the fire in Shelford Road. I was reading about religion in a *Daily Herald* encyclopedia and for the first time seemed to be in touch with God coming on earth in the form of Jesus Christ. I say 'in touch', but that's rather vague, as an intense feeling of association with God took possession of me. It was strange and thinking that forces beyond me were at work, I was rather apprehensive for a minute or two and went up to bed.

Saturday 6 September. A hard week's work at the shop. Earned, after expenses, nearly a fiver. ... The title of the book I have in mind to write next, 'No Bed of Roses', has already been used I find when looking it up in the English catalogue of books. This made me swear. I was very keen on it.[26]

Sunday 7 September. ... Whether we are bombed or not this winter will be a pointer of our intentions to open a Second Front and wage seriously the war with Germany. Did I mention that bread is to be rationed? So Eric tells me. Eric [also] tells me the German sailors on the *Bismarck* mutinied and flung their officers overboard. This was the first I'd heard of it. ...

I don't know what to make of the war in Russia. ... but the Russians are still vigorously fighting; and Leningrad and Odessa haven't fallen, while Moscow is a long way off.

Monday 8 September. ... I went to hear his case [Frank Edwards's, for refusing to take a medical examination for military service] at the court of summary jurisdiction this morning at the local Guildhall. Bert Cash and a man named Harry Paul, a friend of Frank's, also turned up. Frank's case was taken first. He pleaded guilty and asked if he had anything to say said 'My views are well known. I don't think there is anything I can usefully say at this stage.' The verdict for his offences was a nominal fine of 10s; then he was detained for medical examination. He refused it and got three months. ...

The magistrates treated him in a very human way; there was no bullying, no ranting, no homily from the bench: just the remark that he'd had his chance; so that was entirely a factual

---

[26] The title had already been used three times.

statement. I gathered the impression they were carrying out an unpleasant task; I wouldn't be surprised if he had their sympathy. Anyway, the sentence was light, as the court could have imposed a fine of £50 and given him twelve months. I inquired of a policeman what would follow. The prisoner would be taken to Bedford prison that afternoon. If his wife wanted to see him she could be at the police station up to 2.30 p.m. Harry Paul said the policeman said 'Come on, Frank', when he took him into custody. Frank obviously knew him; probably as a customer. ...

I rang up Mrs Edwards and she seemed fairly perky; said her birthday was November the 12th and hoped he would be home by then; she would have her hair permed, face lifted and everything else lifted as a welcome. ...

There were two others charged with the same offence. One didn't turn up; a warrant was issued for his arrest. The other, a man from Ely, was an irresponsible sort, seemingly a bit religious. He said he was a hard-working chap (kept on saying it) didn't see why he wanted [needed?] to take a medical examination, he was well enough; and his firm dealt with 60 tons of coal a week, worth £180, and a lot of flour and stuff, and all that created beauty and loveliness ... and so on. He was cut short. Would he take his medical? He didn't mind, couldn't see the reason for it though. Obviously, he didn't know the medical made him a soldier; ... .

Tuesday 9 September. Planes were flying low over the town very low last night. At 3.00 in the morning, a bomber seemed to scrape the housetops and I wondered to Jess if it was one of ours returning from a bombing raid and in difficulties ... Then there were explosions. We wondered if it had crashed, or if it was a German bomber [that] dropped a stick of bombs. We heard today it was a Jerry; the bombs were dropped Ditton way. ...

Wednesday 10 September. ... [Jack] reminded me of the cricket we had chirping outside the house a short time back. But, thank goodness, that's gone. It was in a crevice of the house wall one night and I tried to frighten it off by swooshing water up the wall, it was so irritating, but the trick didn't work.

Thursday 11 September. Altogether, there were about 60 replies to my advertisement about 99, Shelford Road being to let furnished. Jess let it yesterday to a young married woman after showing her round; the best thing she COULD do. The rent of two guineas is a fair charge. We could get a lot more, but I don't believe in extortionate rents. Why should I? a man with socialist views. Jack and I went over to do a bit of clearing up in the garden. Managed to get a few bars of chocolate on the way. …

Friday 12 September. There was a warning last night: 10.15 p.m. to 12.30 a.m. Humphries called in the shop today. We talked about firewatching. I thought the CO had a hard case to make against it, or when his house caught fire why not stop in bed and burn. But I didn't like the idea of its becoming compulsory. …

Wednesday 17 September. The manager of the Cambridge branch of the Midland Bank and I exchanged a few words in Fred's shop yesterday. I said there would be a patched-up peace at the end of the war. He said never, the Democracies were out to smash Germany. I reminded him that in 1939 he said to me that there would not be a war. He was wrong then, he admitted, but he was certain he was right now; … . I wondered if he were including Russia in the Democracies! But I let that go and asked how they would do it in view of Germany's self-sufficiency plan. …

  It's nearly 9.00 in the evening. I'm upstairs, pegging away at exam work and the novel. … How the nights draw in.

Saturday 20 September. I registered for firewatching today. Am now thinking a way out. It doesn't look possible. Don't want to do it outside my own neighbourhood if I can help it.

Sunday 21 September. Spent a restless night thinking about firewatching. Said I should register as I was already doing firewatching, but I would refuse to enrol, objecting to conscription. Will I? Are second thoughts best? Don't like the idea of going back on myself, but going to prison for such a miserable affair hardly seems worth it. It's not like refusing to kill, … . Today, sidestepping, I wrote to the local authorities, requesting to be posted to this district on the grounds of hardship.

[That is] my studies for the B.Sc. Econ. final examination! Don't think it will wash, but I tried.

… Jess, I know, would be prostrate if I went to clink. And there'd be money worries while I was there. Then there's my old bugbear, claustrophobia, to think about. Prison, I think, would make a wreck of me, and though I'll take that chance when it comes to refusing to go into the army, I'm wondering if a showdown about compulsory firewatching is worth it. …

Monday 22 September. A policeman told me today that the normal population of Cambridge is 74,000 and that its present population is 230,000. …

Tuesday 23 September. … Allen [an acquaintance] told me there's big notices up in Pye's [factory, Chesterton] to the effect that every tank turned out this week is for Russia.[27] …

Thursday 25 September. The weather was fine this afternoon and Jess and I walked to Grantchester with the dogs. I bathed them and had a 'soap' there myself as well as a dip. …

Saturday 27 September. When I arrived at Lensfield Road corner last night on the way home there was a big crowd opposite Downing Archway (facing our house in Saxon Street) and I thought there had been an accident. I hurried home to see if the family was all right and as nobody was in hurried up the archway—to meet Jess coming down with Jim (Jock was in the house). A Hurricane had crashed in an alley between two houses in Lensfield Road, knocking part of a wall down as it fell in a garden. I heard all about it from Jack, first on the scene with Webb, a window-cleaner round here (he of stirrup pump fame!) and an airman, who telephoned for the ambulance. The Hurricane got in a spin, partly straightened out over Sheep's Green (so Ted Clee the custodian at the Sheds told me), and crashed.[28] Jack said they couldn't get anywhere near to assist the pilot and they could not see him because of the flames from the wreckage. The ammunition exploded and I told Jack that it was dangerous to go near; … . As I type I can see part of the wrecked plane on a lorry at the top of

---

[27] In peacetime Pye and Co., based in Chesterton, manufactured wirelesses.
[28] Changing sheds: men and women swam at different places from the bank of the Cam.

the archway. A soldier guarding it keeps shooing children, souvenir-hunting, away ... the distance it crashed is barely 50 yards away from the house. I was told the incident happened at 10 minutes to 5.00. ...

Sunday 28 September. ... I read in the evening paper the other evening that Maurice Cornforth, a prominent local communist who belonged to the Cambridge Anti-War Council when I did, was talking on Parker's Piece about the creation of a Second Front *now* to help Russia. Humphries told me that Cornforth is working on a farm roundabout here somewhere. I wonder why such an enthusiast wasn't already fighting Germany; the armed forces are open to him;[29] ...

Monday 29 September. At 11.05 last night we were awakened by several loud explosions to hear a plane approaching over Scroope Terrace. There were continual flashes of light and much running about and excitement in the street. It was pouring with rain and as black as pitch. There were more explosions, farther away and the sky lit by flares and flashes.

We wondered if it was gunfire, feeling no vibration and I thought it was Chesterton way. A Londoner in the street said 'There's no bloody siren in this town'. At 11.20 p.m. the siren sounded, and as it was my firewatching night I got up, walked round to Bebee, a fellow firewatcher, talked to him and his wife in his house for a few minutes to let him know I was on tap (though I didn't think anything else would happen and believed it was all over whatever it was) and strolled up the street. I was hoping the warning would be a short one, as it was still raining fast when the 'All Clear' sounded; it was then about 11.40 p.m. I returned to bed, ... The explosions turned out to be bombs, dropped on Huntingdon Road, near the corner of Histon Road: high explosives and incendiaries. There were no casualties. ... Some damage was done to property and one or two fairly big craters made in gardens and the

---

[29] Maurice Cornforth (1909–80): a British Marxist philosopher; educated at University College London and from 1929 to 1932 at Trinity College Cambridge, graduating in Moral Sciences. In the early 1903s he was a follower of Wittgenstein; later he became in effect the official ideologist of the Communist Party of Great Britain. He worked as a farm labourer in East Anglia during the war.

road. I went to have a look this morning, it not being far from the shop, but didn't get very near, the way being barred and a policeman on duty. ...

Tuesday 30 September. ... There is newspaper talk of an increase in the cheese ration to four ounces a week. English and German wounded prisoners are to be exchanged. This made me think a lot. ...

October 1941

Wednesday 1 October. As I walked across Coe Fen with the dogs this morning on the way to work I suddenly remembered the date. It was ten years since I put the old Morris car on the road; ten years to the day. What memories! In the September of that year I had mumps and Jess carried on the bookmaking. She had a pretty good time and as a result we bought the car, secondhand, for £12. It was a roomy, two-seater tourer, 13.9 h.p. And did I get about in it; did we all get about in it. It was probably one of the best times in my life. Then I was 28; now I'm 38. Memories, memories ---

They are holding gas tests in the town (tear gas): last Sunday, and again on Monday; probably more to follow. ...

Thursday 2 October. There was a warning last night: 12.20 a.m. till 2.10 a.m. According to the *Cambridge Daily News* there was a burst of machine-gun fire over the town in the night, which they attributed to one of our night fighters chasing an enemy bomber over the town.

Jess and I went to London today and had a look round at some of the ruins Hitler's knocked abaht a bit. I saw plenty of tobacco in the shops. It's very scarce in Cambridge — but we had to queue up for a quarter pound of mint sweets in Selfridge's. There were also plenty of tarts and cakes in the shops; also scarce about here. The restaurants hadn't much to offer, however. ...

Friday 3 October. I'm busy on the novel and tucking in at the exam work, which gives me little time for anything else on top of shoe-repairing; ... .

The army is manoeuvring around here. Jack tells me they've retreated 50 miles, the 'Germans' are advancing. Anyway, the town is full of soldiers, lorries and tanks. This morning it was very foggy, but there were army vehicles drawn up even on Parker's Piece. I could just distinguish the outline of them in the fog, although they were only a few yards from the road. ...

Saturday 4 October. Two warnings last night: 9.18 to 10.30 p.m., 10.50 to 11.30 p.m. I heard bombs drop during the first warning and was told today they fell at Waterbeach. ...

Sunday 5 October. I'm on the last chapter of the novel; although I have two of the earlier chapters to revise before getting out a fresh manuscript. ... I've just heard a question answered by the *Brains Trust*, a Sunday afternoon feature, on the wireless. How I would like to kick Professor Joad up the backside for his pedantry.[30] His voice and manner always give me this feeling.

Monday 6 October. I finished the last chapter of 'The Cordwainer' today. I can't tell what sort of book it is yet, but I don't think it's a mucher. ...

Tuesday 7 October. The swopping of wounded prisoners has fallen through. It was on and off for a day or two, with much newspaper talk about 'mercy' ships, and after the German and British governments had broadcast to one another, it's finally off; at least, for the time being.[31] ...

---

[30] The *Brains Trust*, named after Roosevelt's panel of advisers in the early years of the New Deal, was broadcast on the Home Service and attracted many listeners in wartime Britain. Usually three regulars drawn from a panel of about nine discussed abstruse and philosophical questions. Dr C. E. M. Joad was a 'regular': head of the Department of Philosophy at Birkbeck College, University of London (though he was never a professor) he became famous for his sharp and precise utterance.

[31] There had been protracted negotiations through the embassies of the USA and Switzerland for the exchange of sick and wounded prisoners of war. The British assumed that the exchange would affect all such prisoners, as the International Convention on Prisoners of War laid down; this provision would have meant the exchange of 1200 Britons and 150 Germans. On 7 October, as hospital ships were about to sail from Britain, the German government announced it would countenance only a numerically equal exchange. Britain then withdrew from the plan, accusing Germany of 'bad faith'.

A row in the house tonight. Jess [his wife] called me a liar and lazy and smacked my face over some tinpot business to do with blacking-out. Of course, I clouted her; couldn't stand that; and then Jess fainted. I'm all regrets now; anything rather than that. …

Wednesday 8 October. I keep having irritating spells of toothache; some teeth I had cleaned out years ago (they are dead) seemingly having arrived at the stage when they are best out. But I've got to rake up the money to pay a bill for [his wife] Jess's teeth (nearly £6) first, before going to the dentist. … It's a job to make ends meet, though one way or the other I rake up pretty good earnings. But there's four of us to keep, all adults in size and appetite, and things are dear. …

Thursday 9 October. I went to the Regal with Jack and Tom tonight … to see Nelson Eddy and Jeanette Macdonald in *Bitter Sweet*. The singing was nice, but what a poor, uppish sort of story; the usual sort of Noel Coward stuff. He can't get away from himself and his class; well, I can't either, if it comes to that; but his crowd seem a vapid lot to me.

Monday 13 October. … The Germans are heading for Moscow. A terrific thrust … everybody is asking—will they take Moscow? I think very likely. But Russia will fight on a long while yet. The Germans will never succeed in occupying her. The country is too vast. And she has plenty of men and munitions with which to fight on yet, which makes occupation a remote thing. I think so anyway.

Tuesday 14 October. It is 8 o'clock in the evening. Jess and I have just returned from taking the dogs for a walk round Brooklands Avenue. The searchlights are up and planes are continuously passing over. … The 'All Clear' went last night when we were in bed: at 11.20 p.m. …

Wednesday 15 October. I heard the 'ghost' voice on the 9 o'clock news of the BBC last night.[32] An undertone; somebody interjecting remarks like 'It's a lie' and 'Sez you'. All very childish, I thought. …

---

[32] The 'ghost voice' was William Joyce, 'Lord Haw Haw'. See the entry and note for 20 October 1940.

[I] caught the bus to Bedford with Mrs Edwards and Harry Paul to visit Frank in prison. We saw a crashed bomber on the main Huntingdon–Royston road; … A man on the bus told me the pilot mistook the landing field there for the new one at Hardwick, nearby, this one being for small planes like Moths, … .

We arrived at the main entrance of the prison at 2.10, showed the permit and were told to wait in a room, evidently one used by warders, by a warder. … after a wait of 20 minutes (during which time all we heard was the rattle and jingle of keys during the locking of doors and the gate inside the prison) we were taken to another room where Frank was waiting. With the warder in the room (a pleasant fellow) we sat and talked across a table. Frank had grown a moustache to save the use of the safety-razor blade allowed him each week out of the lot his wife had sent him, and looked pretty fit. He told us the routine; Joan smuggled across to him a bar of chocolate; and after talking for half an hour we left. … He expects to be out on November 8th. …

Friday 17 October. Tommy Handley on the wireless is raising a lot of laughs and I'm joining in.[33]

I wish all I had to do was write novels for a living. What a dream!

Saturday 18 October. A letter from Neil Bell: a homily. Whatever I do, I must guard against going to prison for my convictions. Swallow them first, as it was my job to hang on to life and to my sane, normal self with hands and feet, teeth and toenails. This was in reply to a letter of mine telling him that I thought that even a month in jail would finish me as I suffer from claustrophobia. …

Monday 20 October. I had a nightmare last night. Woke up sobbing and kicking and shouting. Terrible things dreams, sometimes. … Just been for a walk with Jess and the dogs. Saw the bombers going off on their deadly work, moving slowly as if very heavily loaded, towards the east on the way home.

---

[33] Tommy Handley was the star of the radio comedy show *It's That Man Again* (or *ITMA*). It was almost a national institution during the war years.

Thursday 23 October. … Jess and I had a walk up Long Common with the dogs this afternoon. Army huts of some sort — they are cylindrical in shape — are being rapidly shoved up by soldiers (not at tradesmen's rates) on Short Common. Goodbye to another bit of 'common' rights (no pun intended) as I don't suppose Short Common will be returned to the people again after the war; unless there's changeovers and the people inherit the land! …

Saturday 25 October. A lot of running about today, much of it for nothing. Lately, I've made five journeys to get some glass for the kitchen window. I managed to get it today and this afternoon I put in two large panes of glass in the rotten frame of the back window. One of the windows I repaired had to be done in two pieces; owing to the glass shortage that was all I could buy — odd pieces.

I then tried to have a squint of the old inn sign of the 'Man Loaded With Mischief', now preserved in the Cambridge Museum of Archaeology and Ethnology (wanted for 'The Cordwainer'), but it was shut. An uncivil porter didn't know whether for [the] duration or not.

Then a journey to the reference room of the local library to find if the name of the murderesss that was Silas Lucas's accomplice in 1850 (also wanted for the book) was Reeder or Reader.[34] I couldn't find Cooper's *Annals*, however, so I rang up the library when I got home and asked them if they could tell me. They said they would ring me, but didn't do so, thinking, I suppose, that any old time would do for a nobody. They'll probably let me know during the week.

I think the system of reference at the local library an insult to a man's intelligence. Whenever I go there and look up the index numbers I can never find anything. The books are higgledy-piggledy, all over the place; or so it seems to me. There's groups of this, that and the other and it's a case of find the author and the book if you can. True, the grouping of arts and sciences has its advantages, but it would be a treat to

[34] Mary Reeder (or Reader) was with Elias Lucas hanged in April 1850, in the last public execution in Cambridge, for the poisoning of her sister Sarah Lucas in Castle Camps. The book Jack was seeking was C. H. Cooper, *Annals of Cambridge*.

go and look under an author's name for his works as is done with the fiction department.

I then went and looked up Lambeth, the curator of the local folk museum for something also connected with the book. He was out, so damn and blasting it I came home to tea.

Wednesday 29 October. ... Tonight I called to see one of my old headmasters, Mr Chandler. He's 80 and failing rapidly, being a little, wizened old man, crouched up in an armchair. We had a long, pleasant talk, his two daughters — friendly sorts — joining in. I told him about my efforts to get published and take a degree and he was greatly pleased by it, liking to see his old boys do well; or try! ...

Thursday 30 October. This afternoon I biked to the Cambridge and County High School for Girls to see the headmistress about [his daughter] Jess's future.[35] I asked was it possible for me to apply for a State loan in order that she might go to a training college [for teachers] for two years and learned that loans were granted at interest by the County Council, not the State. The school would also advance £50 free of interest redeemable at any time (some of the girls she said took seven or eight years to pay back a loan).

Big Jess doesn't like the idea. We can't afford it; where do WE come in and so on? But I'm seeing it through if possible. Jess [daughter] has nearly £100 in the Cambridge Permanent Benefit Building Society and as a last resort that will see her through; though I would like to do it myself without touching that; anyhow, it's a sound speculation. Money can't be better spent than on education, especially when it means a good job at a decent rate of pay. Jess is keen to go on to a training college.

Friday 31 October. I've written to the County Council about the proposed loan. Strike while the iron is hot. ...

November 1941

Sunday 2 November. I've just written off to four training colleges for prospectuses and entry forms for Jess. Now off for a dip.

[35] In Collier Road; it later moved to Long Road.

Evening: Went to the pictures with Jess: saw the *Ghost Train* again, this time featuring Arthur Askey. He was funny, but the theme of the film was so ridiculous it hardly bears writing about. This time to bring it up to date, 'Fifth Columnists' were introduced, which made it sillier than ever, for they were making rifles to send to the Nazis!

Monday 3 November. ... Slack at the shop, so I've pushed in six typescript pages of the novel today. My average is three.

Tuesday 4 November. We've heard from two of the training colleges to which I wrote. The fees are £100 for a two years' course. A clergyman's reference is needed for both places, which sets a poser, as I'll not humble myself to their sort. Maybe I'll manage without them. ...

Wednesday 5 November. Russia and all about her is all to the fore nowadays; of course, because she is fighting our war. Even my wife has a hat to match her overcoat a la mode Russia! A great, noble, inspiring people, the Russians; look at the newspapers (and forget what they said about her and Finland nearly two years ago) and see if she isn't. ...

Thursday 6 November. We were up till nearly midnight last night, filling in the entry forms for Jess .... I'm ever so slack at the shop, which makes me uneasy, as I must earn my living, quite apart from upsetting my routine for snobbing, writing and exam work, as I have to do the repairing in patches instead of straight off.

Friday 7 November. ... The searchlights are up; a starry night; the moon rises late; bombers keep roaring over; I don't know whose. ...

We get less milk now, Jess and I a half-pint a day between us, the children a half-pint each ... I've bought three quarts of cod-liver oil lately. Jack, Jess [daughter] and myself take it; Jess can't; or won't.

The evacuee children love smashing bottles, beer and milk; even chuck them out of the windows to the peril of passers-by.

Saturday 8 November. ... Newspaper news: conscription from 15 to 65 for Home Guard duties. (Without comment—from me! I'm speechless!)

A dip in the river. An argument there with a fellow about the war. I said I thought we would be in a bad way very likely if, should we lose the war, we were left to stew in our own juice; it would be better if we were incorporated in the Third Reich! Impossible to relate arguments about the war; they're too long-winded. ...

Monday 10 November. A man from the Electric Light Co. came in the shop today and handed me two forms: one requesting me to economise with lighting and the other to fill in and return to the company to say I would. All this and the shortage of paper is getting so serious that there's newspaper talk of compulsion to make people save waste paper. ... there's a new system of points rationing for tinned foods coming into effect about the middle of this month.

Tuesday 11 November. Armistice Day. They sold flags, although there seemed few sellers about, and as usual I didn't buy one. Wasn't asked this year. ... We made one of our biggest raids on Germany the other day. I'll expect we'll be paid back in our own coin ... although some people think we're paying the Germans back in their own coin.

Wednesday 12 November. ... I'm hard at the novel. No time for anything else after the day's work, except a walk with the dogs....

Saturday 15 November. ... [Daughter] Jess hopes to become a physical education teacher. ... As a gym mistress ... she would start at a rate of pay at which most young women aspire to but never reach. I hope she makes a good marriage; that's the best job for a woman; but the job of schoolteacher is a good alternative.

Sunday 16 November. ... War news: the *Ark Royal* is sunk at last.[36] ... America and Japan are at daggers drawn. Might get at it any time. ... And, of course, there's still a war between Germany and Russia. That's not for me to relate: too big; will leave it to the history books.

Wednesday 19 November. I went with Frank Edwards to a talk on Justice given by Chas Raven, Regius Professor of Divinity

---

[36] *Ark Royal,* an aircraft carrier completed in 1938, was torpedoed 150 miles east of Gibraltar.

at Cambridge University this evening at the Friends' Meeting House, Jesus Lane.[37] (A black night; I fell over a bike resting against a kerb on the way.)

I didn't get much change out of it. The talk resolved itself into a long abstract dissertation upon the Apostle St Paul. Cobblers are not the only ones that stick to their lasts! I have all the 'little' man's shyness at meetings, but at question time I had a thing or two to say. I said that if all the facts were known about every case (**all** included the biological and economic facts) few would ever be punished.

In answer to this the chairman (Dr Alex Wood) said that people were not punished because they had done wrong, but because they had broken certain rules. I couldn't see the connection between my question and the answer, but in reply said that was hair-splitting, and merely shifting the argument a stage further back as presumably the rules were based upon right and wrong in the beginning. …

I'm afraid I haven't an audience manner. I'm gruff; almost growl.

Thinking it over: it was all moonshine — I mean what they were talking about. Elastic principles of justice could very well be applied to guilty people living under the present social system that largely makes them guilty; but they never will be. And under a better system they wouldn't be needed. There'd be nothing to go to prison or be punished for.

Tuesday 25 November. Done nearly £3 worth of work in a couple of days and got out an eight-page chapter of the book. I shall be glad to get the latter off my hands (it's going well) and get down to the exam work. It will be a chance to sit over the fire and read instead of always banging away at the typewriter. …

Electric light is being put in the house under the two-way tariff scheme.[38] And it's being done for nothing, in wartime, and a condemned house! …

---

[37] Charles Raven: Regius Professor of Divinity 1932–50, and Master of Christ's College 1939–50.

[38] Presumably this cryptic remark refers to the practice of charging more for an initial number of units (e.g. 100) and less for succeeding ones.

Wednesday 26 November. ... We're overrun with mice. It's a wonder they don't eat off our plates. Anyway, they trip about the rooms while we're in them. Tonight, I kicked one with my foot, as three scuttled out of a sack of dog biscuits I moved, and killed it. Didn't care to do it, but it is impossible to make pets of them, bonny little things though they are and with no awareness of private property.

Friday 28 November. Newspaper news: conscription up to 50. ... men up to 50, women for the forces up to 25 and for other work up to 30 and so on.[39] ... I'm beginning to think this is all bunk; [it's a] shout to make out what we're doing [is] to frighten Jerry. ...

Much of this ballyhoo about call-ups is no doubt to keep the people in subjection. Men and women are naturally inclined to worry about things personally affecting them—and they do; consequently, the real evils of this war are apt to be overlooked. But once the war ends, this regimentation stops; which with the fear of Hitler, invasion, bombing and other unpleasant facts removed, will bring the people's minds to bear on things likely to be unpleasant for our present leaders and the system they are trying so futilely to uphold.

Saturday 29 November. ... A walk round the town with Jack. Couldn't buy any sweets; only apples at 9*d* a pound. ... And—record it!—[I had] a bath.

December 1941

Monday 1 December. The Russians have recaptured Rostov so the newspaper said yesterday. ... They're doing great things: putting up a fine show. The Germans underestimated their morale. Communism was more stable in Russia than the German leaders thought and this might be a costly mistake to make; [it might] mean all the difference between winning and losing their war with them. ...

---

[39] By the National Service (No. 2) Act women aged 20 to 30 were to be liable for service in either the three women's military forces or a wide range of jobs, from the munitions industry to forestry. Women married to servicemen or with young children could not be asked to work away from home. Britain was the first country to conscript women.

Thursday 4 December. Went to the Regal with Jack; saw *Ziegfeld Girl*. A local councillor came on during an interval and appealed for 'Warship Week' (being held this week in Cambridge: [he] wanted £700,000 for a destroyer).[40] ...

Saturday 6 December. ... A Home Guard test is on. I was asked for my identity card on Hills Road bridge this afternoon, the first time I've been asked for it since I've had it.

Sunday 7 December. There was no end of banging and buggering about last night: the Home Guard up and at it. They had a nice night for the job, as it rained cats and dogs. ...

Monday 8 December. I heard a plane go over last night and shortly afterwards some crumps followed and the room was lit up as if flares were being dropped somewhere; more explosions in the distance and the room was lit up again; and then there followed another explosion and another terrific one that always [almost?] rattled the window out. Soon afterwards it struck 3.00 a.m. There was no warning. We thought it was a raid, but all we can learn today is that one of our bombers crashed at Waterbeach. Maybe they jettisoned their bombs first. I heard there were six killed.

Newspaper headlines this morning told that Japan had declared war on America and Britain, and that the Japs had attacked Hawaii. Today America and Britain reciprocated. ...

Today at the river a young fellow there said it would be a good thing if there were no national boundaries after this war. I agreed, but didn't welcome his idea of the Church taking control with bishops over districts. I said the Church actively encouraged war, egged on both and all sides in the name of God and the right. There was a doctor there, and he broke in; said war was a disease and had to be treated as such (I ought to have said prevention was better than cure, but you never think of these things till afterwards). There was some further talk and he asked me rather aggressively what I was anyway. I said a pacifist. He said that if I was in Germany I would be exterminated like a worm ... . I said that to defeat Hitler we

---

[40] A week in which citizens were exhorted to save, often through the government National Savings scheme, to meet the costs of war. There were several other such periods.

had to adopt his methods and so defeat ourselves in doing it. He was fed up with us bloody pacifists; we were either cowards or Hitler's agents, trying to rot the guts out of the country. ... Other people were fighting for me, he said. I answered that I didn't want anybody to fight for me. ... He said I should not receive any rations, he'd seen hundreds of men drowning trying to bring me food. ... Would I succour wounded? he asked. I said I would help anybody that was hurt. Then why didn't I join the R.A.M.C? Because it was an organised unit. ...

He said look what Hitler was doing. I said I had no room for the German system and repeated my statement about beating ourselves to beat it, adding that our propaganda department was at work, don't forget. He said it was true what they were doing; I could make inquiries of many hounded out of the country now living in Cambridge. I repeated I wasn't bolstering up the German system. How could we have stopped all this? he asked. I said it was the result of bad leadership. What would I have done[?] I answered that I was no politician and I couldn't give him a review of English politics in a few minutes in a public bathing place. (I should have told him to read Palme Dutt's *World Politics 1918-1938*,[41] but forgot, of course; I could also have mentioned we needn't have kept the blockade on Germany long after the last war and caused so much suffering; nor need we have sent them scrap iron right up to the year the war started. Forgot, of course; everything was so scrappily and hurriedly said as we were dressing.)

He said D.O.R.A. [Defence of the Realm Act][42] and conscription and all the other restrictions we suffered during the last war were removed. I said not permanently, they were all back again and worse; ... . There was no proof all this regimen-

---

[41] Rajani Palme Dutt (1896–1974): the son of a Bengali doctor practising in Cambridge and a Swiss mother, was educated at the Perse School and Balliol College. A founder member of the Communist Party of Great Britain in 1920, he was an inflexible Stalinist till his death, convinced that capitalism meant servitude and authoritarianism. Until June 1941 he regarded the war as an 'imperialist' conflict. His views and Jack's were similar, despite Jack's refusal to join the CPGB.

[42] The Defence of the Realm Act of August 1914 had granted the government sweeping powers to govern by regulation during the First World War.

tation would cease after this war. Depended how it ended. Suddenly, I thought he would strike me. He said he didn't want to talk to me. I said I reciprocated. But then we started off again until abruptly he said once more that he didn't want to talk to me. I replied that I wouldn't and as I was dressed came away.

What a man to win freedom for you. There wouldn't be much difference between his victory and Hitler's! He had no room for minority opinion, the root of democratic government. ... I heard the other day he's night surgeon at Addenbrooke's [Hospital]. (Hope I don't come under him!) and that he'd been (I think) to New Zealand as a ship's doctor during the war and torpedoed twice, seeing lots drown. Probably, the reason for his bitterness and intolerance.

If he had set about me I shouldn't have stood much chance. Apart from his size, he's been a county and hospital rugby player and runs five miles stripped down the river these days before going in! A lot fitter than I!

Tuesday 9 December. ... About the incident at the river yesterday. Castle, the other chap there, said the doctor thought I was going to hit him, not him hit me! Didn't know I looked so bellicose in argument. ...

Castle—he's about 18—is going to be a parson. Thinks I'm a heretic ... I told him I didn't think much of Bible-punchers who crammed their creeds down people's throats. They were the worst of the lot.

Wednesday 10 December. Two battleships, the *Prince of Wales* and the *Repulse* sunk by the Japs is today's news.[43] ... Hard at the book. Want to finish it this week.

Thursday 11 December. Went to the Central to see Gordon Harker and Sidney Howard in *Once a Crook* ... . The News was all encouragement to boys to join the RAF; some form of training scheme; all set out as something glorious and wonderful ... Reminded me of the schoolmaster in the film ver-

---

[43] The battleship *Prince of Wales* and the battle-cruiser *Repulse* had been sent to Singapore to act as a deterrent force against Japan. Lacking air cover they were sunk on 10 December to the east of Malaya by bombs and torpedoes from Japanese aircraft.

sion of Remarque's *All Quiet on the Western Front*. He told his pupils how noble war was; they didn't think so when they got at it; nor much of him either, if I remember rightly. …

Saturday 13 December. … Went down the town with Jack this afternoon. He weighed in Boots: 10 stone 6½ pounds. He's about 5′ 10″. What a giant for 14. We couldn't buy anything to eat in the town at all. What a sell! Take your son out and you can't treat him to anything when you've got two or three bob [shillings] in your pocket. Managed to buy a quarter-pound of jelly cuttings for 5*d* in Marks and Spencers at last!

Monday 15 December. I was up to midnight on the book ['The Cordwainer']. Took it to the bookbinder's this morning. As a favour because I worked there they said they would get it bound for me by Thursday so that I could send it off so that it arrived before Christmas. I wrote Neil Bell about it and said I believed I was sending him a book with a kick in it, but I was prepared for anything (except publication!) …

Tuesday 16 December. … They're still sending local COs to prison for refusing to take their medicals. Makes me wonder about my own turn, whether I'll land in jail or not.

Wednesday 17 December. … I disturbed a soldier and a girl inside a [telephone] kiosk, evidently the modern stand-stills for couples.

Thursday 18 December. Finished reading *Guilty Men* by 'Cato'.[44] The guilty men that led this country into war are well known, but unfortunately most of them are still at the helm.

Wednesday 24 December. … down the town with the family for a look round the shops: … . We had a cup of tea in Lyons and some unappetising fancies: hardly 'tackable' even in wartime. There were few people about for Christmas Eve … [at home] fish and chips; had a regular blow-out. …

Thursday 25 December. It's 10 o'clock in the evening and the pickles have just been put on the table for supper by Jess: Jack is gloating over them and hopping about now with the cups

---

[44] 'Cato' was in fact three Beaverbrook journalists, including Michael Foot. *Guilty Men*, an indictment of the policy of 'appeasement' 1936–9, was published in July 1940.

and saucers, which Jess is bringing in from the kitchen. The time-pips have sounded on the wireless as I type and now the programme is *The Old Town Hall*[45] —

How have we spent the day? This morning I took the dogs for a walk round the 'Green'; up Long Common this afternoon; tonight, a little while ago, we all had a walk in the moonlight round the 'Avenue' [Brooklands Avenue]; a lovely night, dry underfoot, cool, but not cold; there's been plenty of 'eats' for all [despite] the war: poached eggs for breakfast, chicken and plum pudding for dinner with roast potatoes and sprouts and for tea, salmon, Christmas cake, mince pies and biscuits; as titbits during the day — cream soda for drinks, sweets, chocolate; and I've had a big apple and juicy orange. I've read Dickens's *Christmas Carol* and found it excellent entertainment. ... As presents, in addition to the [HMV 12"] record Jess bought me ['The Holy City' and 'The Star of Bethlehem'], she also gave me an enlargement of a photo of [daughter] Jess and some chocolates (a rare present these, nowadays). Jack gave me one volume and Jess the other of *Roget's Thesaurus* in the Everyman's Library. I gave Jess a quid [£1] and the children 10s each ... A very quietly enjoyable day.

Saturday 27 December. ... Had a lemonade in Marks and Spencers, a cup of tea in Woolworth's and bought some peanuts. Nothing else going in the eat and drink line. (Jack had Bovril though, not tea; must be exact these days to picture war conditions properly.)

Sunday 28 December. ... The Japs have Hong Kong.[46] Singapore is threatened. ... Lots of heavy explosions in the town today. Heard it was the Home Guard practising with a new kind of trench mortar. Strange how Sunday loses so much of its significance during wartime.

Monday 29 December. My holiday is over and I'm back in harness. Up this morning at 7.00 and on with examination work:

[45] *Christmas at the Old Town Hall*, on the Forces Programme (which later became the Light Programme) was broadcast from 9.30 to 10.15 on 25 December. It was a variety entertainment, with Clay Keyes as Master of Ceremonies and Richard Goolden as Old Ebenezer.

[46] Invaded by a superior Japanese force, the British possession of Hong Kong was forced to surrender on Christmas Day 1941.

On 27 September 1941 a Hurricane crashed in the garden of 5 Bene't Place, at the bottom of Lensfield Road. The pilot was killed.

currency, principles of economics, Italian reading, Italian grammar work, Italian verbs, French reading, French verbs — now there's the other subjects, industrial history and so on —
   I'm trying to get Jack to do a bit more work on his music, French, Latin and English.

Tuesday 30 December. Churchill spoke to the Canadian Parliament at Ottawa tonight and we heard part of the broadcast.[47] — Beer is to be weaker, margarine is to have its vitamin D content doubled, milk is to be distributed more evenly. …

Wednesday 31 December. I must guard against getting examination fever; the work gets on one's brain; for that reason Jack and I are going over to the Greyhound. …

---

[47] In his speech to the Canadian Parliament Churchill spoke of the French in the spring of 1940: 'When I warned them that Britain would fight on alone whatever they did, their generals told their Prime Minister and his divided Cabinet, "In three weeks England will have her neck wrung like a chicken". Some chicken, some neck.'

1942

January 1942

Thursday 1 January. ... [In 1940 he had dreamed about his son Jack.] I dreamt he was killed in an air raid ... and awoke to hear somebody saying 'next year' ... Superstition. Maybe. But parents worry about their children over anything. I'll say no more about it except that I'm glad 1941 is over for that reason alone, which is the best way of measuring how much I've been worried about it. Now for some examination work. ... A walk with the Jesses and the dogs round the 'Avenue' [Brooklands Avenue] this afternoon after a cup of tea round the fire with the wireless playing (have I mentioned we've got the radiogram on the go now with the electric light in the house? — which, of course, is much better than the Pye battery set). ...

Saturday 3 January. ... We queued up for biscuits in the town. And saw one of Fred's children refused biscuits after standing in the queue. This, I suppose, is done so that mothers of large families shouldn't have an advantage by sending out children to line up in queues to save them doing the job themselves. ... presumably the large families will get no 'extras' at all, for how can women with large families hang about in queues? ...

Sunday 4 January. This morning I've been turning over old notes and papers with a view to getting out another novel, not immediately, but in order to make a start as soon as the examination is over ... .

Monday 5 January. Studying hard: six to eight hours a day. ...

Wednesday 7 January. I'm learning about 'pure' economics. What rot. All moonshine. I've learned nothing about economics since I matriculated. It's put differently: intentionally made abstract, that's all.

Thursday 8 January. Been working at the foreign exchanges until I'm nearly potty.

Is Germany in a hole? I'm beginning to think so although her essential war productions are three times that of Russia's.

Sunday 11 January. I went into the river again this morning, the first time for about three weeks owing to a cold. The morning was very frosty, the grass white and the river covered with a thin sheet of slow-moving ice. I daren't risk a dive and went down the ladder. I felt the ice tickling my ribs a bit sharply as I went through it.

Rations are to be cut again. A short time back, about two months ago, they were increased, but now we are returning to half a pound of sugar each a week, six ounces of fat, not more than two ounces of butter to be included in it; and in February cheese rations are to revert to two ounces per person per week instead of three, which we are getting now.

I had a couple of hours this morning framing a new book; a weekly Sunday morning two hours I've planned in order not to waste time. I forgot to mention that Jim [one of the dogs] caught fire at the shop on Friday morning through rolling close to the gas stove while warming himself. He flared and I worked quickly to put him out, you bet! ...

Monday 12 January. I've been wondering. How does Russia regard the USA war programme? Surely, it's not very appetising to know that she'll be at her weakest and exhausted say in another two or three years just when the capitalist powers are at their strongest. I can see further complications arising out of this war; lots.

The river is frozen over. Air temperature today at the 'sheds' was 23 degrees, water 33 degrees. I had to make a hole, go down the ladder and duck. ...

Tuesday 13 January. A wintry day; a little snow on the ground this morning, then intermittent downfalls of sleet and snow. How I long for the summer — and more leisure, as it's been another tearing sort of day — 26*s* worth of shoe repairs together with a good six hours exam work. ...

Saturday 17 January. Don Varley gives Jess [his daughter] an egg sometimes: sign of the times; if the war lasts long enough young men might very well offer their girls a bit of bread instead of box of chocolates. ...

Sunday 18 January. … I had a walk round the Fen this morning with the dogs. The Home Guard were about: in ditches and any old place that would do, apparently; and I felt a bit uneasy when I saw so many guns poking at me from every direction. One of the guns might easily go off! …

Monday 19 January. Young Jess caught me up on her bike this morning in Fen Causeway as I was going to work to bring me two letters one to say I was now registered for firewatching and must take orders from wardens of various sorts; and the other from Neil Bell. I felt a bit excited as I opened Bell's letter; wondered what he would have to say about 'The Cordwainer'. A hay lorry was passing and turning to see where Jim and Jack were I saw the back of it and superstitious-like remembered a saying something like you mustn't see the back of a hay cart and thought the report couldn't be very good. But it was: very good, indeed. He said I can now write a novel, that the book was a workmanlike and competent novel --- that no-one can teach me anything --- and that I must now go my road and make my way --- That's something, even though he thought chances of publication were almost too remote to think about. I've sent the book off to Michael Sadleir as he suggested. …

Monday 19 January. A warning—the first for months: 10.37 p.m. to 11.00 p.m …

Tuesday 20 January. … The weather is bitterly cold; a little snow on the ground frozen solid with frost makes the world look wintry. The river was frozen over today and I could only have a duck down the ladder.

   Managed to buy a film for the camera today. Got it as a favour.

Thursday 22 January. … Skaters were on the ponds in the Botanical Gardens.

Friday 23 January. A wintry day: frost and snow; the river is frozen and the snow pretty deep on the ground.

Monday 26 January. Churchill's stock seems to be falling.[1] There's a lot of criticism over this country's policy, especially with regard to Australia. He is attempting to tone down public opinion by asking for a vote of confidence. I suppose it will come off and he will linger in power for a time; then, like the rest of the public idols, he will be set aside in favour of somebody else, who, in turn, will have his day and be set aside for somebody else; ...

Thursday 29 January. ... Benghazi is in the news again.[2] Rommel — already defeated — is attacking again in Libya. ...

Jess and I had a walk up Trumpington Road late this afternoon with the dogs. The weather was raw. Hedges, houses --- everything seemed derelict and neglected; ... I was reminded of the war atmosphere during 1917; ... .

Friday 30 January. The Germans have taken Benghazi again. This is so sudden. And the people I've spoken to are marvelling what we're up to. It's changed hands four times.

Saturday 31 January. Dried fruit and cereals have come under the points rationing scheme lately; which means that if a person has these he must go without other tinned stuff like salmon and meat.

February 1942

Sunday 1 February. This morning as I lay in bed I took notice of the noises outside: cawing rooks, motor engines, the voice of the milk girl and children, a dog barking, the bawling commands of an NCO or officer to soldiers on the 'Plant'un'. --- There were others, but I forget them; inside the house, downstairs Jess [daughter] was talking to Jim, and there was the sound of the wireless playing in the front room. It was strange how these all suddenly broke into my consciousness;

---

[1] Churchill was given much of the blame for the Japanese successes in the south-west Pacific from December 1941 onwards. In Britain and Australia it was said that the British Government regarded that war as a sideshow. A vote of confidence in the House of Commons on 29 January 1942 was, however, won by the Government by 414 votes to one.

[2] Rommel recaptured Benghazi during his advance in 1942 which took the Afrika Korps into Egypt.

… it was snowing fast at the time and watching the flakes coming down and hearing that bawling voice of the soldier I think I became aware of external things by reason of my own snugness as I lay in bed listening to his orders. How silly they seemed; I could picture it all: a line of khaki-clad men standing stiffly in the falling snow, getting ready to march to church. ---

We've retreated in the East and now making a final stand at Singapore. …

Monday 2 February. … Tonight I read in the *Cambridge Daily News* of a young man of 19 getting two months' hard labour for absenteeism. Two months for not working; not so long ago they didn't want people to work --- a lot of them at least.

Thursday 5 February. A surprise: receipt of Neil Bell's new book *Tower of Darkness* this afternoon. He said he thinks it will be 'my cup of tea'. …

Saturday 7 February. Round the town with Jess [wife] and Jack this afternoon …; it was bitterly cold. Jess bought me a secondhand copy of [G. D. H.] Cole's *Intelligent Man's Guide Through World Chaos* [1932 and later editions] as an advance birthday present; got it for 3s 6d. I've read it twice, but intend going through it again for examination purposes; it's so readable and so complete.

Sunday 8 February. … A lot of talk in the papers about victory over the Germans this year; this because of the Russian successes; certainly not ours. A bit optimistic, I think; … Cripps has just given the *Postscript* on the wireless; all about Russia and the war effort.[3]

I've spent an enjoyable day. After trying to get at Bell's book and reading it in snatches I took Jess's tip this morning to settle down and enjoy it. It's a grand book and I wrote and told him so tonight. … Ronnie Spink one of the main characters

---

[3] *Postscript* was fifteen minutes of commentary, often given by well-known public figures, broadcast after the 9 p.m. news on the Home Service on Sunday evenings. Sir Stafford Cripps MP, prominent on the left wing of the Labour party, had just returned from Moscow where he had been British Ambassador to the Soviet Union. In this *Postscript* he called for sacrifice and total commitment in the cause of victory: Clarke, *The Cripps Version*, pp. 263–4. On 9 February he joined the War Cabinet as Lord Privy Seal and Leader of the House of Commons.

will live in my mind as one of the most outstanding characters in fiction. I was pleased to notice how much liberty Bell has been allowed in 'these Gestapo days' as he called them in the letter he sent with the book. There's still a lot of freedom left when a writer is permitted to say so much; it's a happy augury for the future. ...

Monday 9 February. I met an antique furniture dealer, aged between 50 and 60, I know in the town today. He looked ill and stopping for a short chat I learned that he is suffering from neurasthenia. At once, he had my sympathy. ... I walked back with him to his shop, had a talk with him there and he revealed the trouble was largely domestic following an attack of nerves over the bombings. I called on him again coming home and he walked as far as the house with me. I told him to give me a ring any time he felt really in need of company and I would go to him straight away. I think he's now well-to-do, but he said he would give all his money for a return of his former happiness, which would mean the return of his wife. ...

Tuesday 10 February. My birthday! Thirty-nine years old! I received three birthday cards, one from each member of the family, and nailed these up in the shop after taking last year's down to keep amongst my hoard of treasures. Jess's card was strikingly attractive: an open book with a picture on its pages of flowers, an arched bridge, rustic houses and village church all in colour. The wording was good, too.

And I had a surprise. ... home first at dinner-time I found a greetings telegram from Neil Bell on the mat. ...

Looks as if we're losing Singapore.[4] ...

---

[4] Singapore had been regarded in Britain as impregnable, and its loss was described by Churchill as 'the worst disaster and largest capitulation in British history'. 35,000 invading Japanese troops faced 70,000 British, who were badly equipped and led, lacked air cover, and were increasingly demoralised. After the surrender on 15 February, 62,000 British and Commonwealth troops were taken into captivity. They included men of the Cambridgeshires and other East Anglian regiments only recently arrived in Singapore: Colin Smith, *Singapore Burning: Heroism and Sacrifice in World War II* (2005).

Soap is rationed as from yesterday. There's an excuse for not washing at last. A woman who came in the shop said we'll have to shake our shirts now.

Wednesday 11 February. On and off for months and all out since Christmas I've been typing out examination work and finished it today. ...

Thursday 12 February. Spent the afternoon arranging the typed papers I mentioned yesterday and then took them round to the bookbinders to be bound up. An enormous wad; nearly 400 pages all told. I've got to memorise it now as part of the examination work; ...

Friday 13 February. A big scrap in the straits of Dover yesterday, hundreds of planes engaged in trying to sink three big German warships being shifted from Brest to Heligoland. The Jerries got through and we lost a lot of bombers and planes; 42 was the report I saw.[5]

I heard bombers going over in the night, the first for a long time; probably ours setting out on a bombing raid.

Saturday 14 February. There looks like being a stink over the German ships escaping. ---

... When I came home in the blackout I saw flashes in the north-west. Must have been a bit doing that way. Hadn't seen anything like that for some time; ... Passing traffic lights I saw a little army convoy passing at 'red' without any hold-up of the traffic by scouts; nearly a mix-up and a woman got away with her skin in the nick of time.

Sunday 15 February. Teatime: just heard on the radio that the Japs have given it out that we have surrendered unconditionally in Singapore. ...

Tuesday 17 February. ... The newspapers are gloomy about Singapore (the Cambridgeshires were there with other East Anglian regiments), the escape of the German warships from Brest and other wartime setbacks. ...

---

[5] The battleships *Scharnhorst* and *Gneisenau* and the heavy cruiser *Prinz Eugen* succeeded in sailing, with some damage, from Brest to Germany through the English Channel. The British lost 42 planes sent to intercept them.

Thursday 19 February. ... This examination work is a lot of nonsense. The memorising—and who can sit an exam without it?—is exhausting too.

Jess tells me the audience sang the 'Internationale' in the pictures the other night when she was there. ...

Friday 20 February. The book came back from Constables today. There was a long letter from Michael Sadleir apologising for sending it back for no other reason than its lack of contemporary appeal; he would be unwise to publish it at this critical juncture of a great war; a war-racked and escapist public wouldn't want it. He said its technique was better than many novels that are published, and given normal conditions he would have published it if for no other reason than the vitality of the animal passages (whatever they are!) but in texture it resembled my other books; he would like a change in KIND as well as handling. ...

I wrote [to] Neil Bell right away. Told him I couldn't write drawing-room stories and wouldn't want to if I could: that I had very abruptly changed my opinion about waiting till Constables gave me a chance; they had had five of my books and as I hoped to continue writing the same sort of stuff there was little likelihood of them giving me a start if it was the KIND of books I write that's balking them. ...

[Talking to Humphries] I told him it was a rum bloody world (he knows it) and that I didn't seem to be making a job of things when my wife wanted to go out to work. --- He sympathised; thought I worked too hard. ...

Saturday 21 February. ... Last night in bed the theme of my next book came to me. A skit on the present system: two brothers, one tries and gets nowhere by traditional straightforward methods; the other, less clever, does a lot better by the traditional not-so-straightforward methods. A lot of the book will be autobiographical. I think I can make a job of it.

I went to the Borough Library to read *The Economist* for exam purposes this afternoon. Didn't get a lot of change out of it. ...

Sunday 22 February. ... Spent a large part of the morning seeing about my entry for the examination and taking that survey of the work necessary to get the whole into perspective with the requirements of the examiners.

I wonder for what purpose: this year, anyway, as my failure with 'The Cordwainer' hasn't cheered me up for making a success of it by any means. I keep plodding along, but I still don't get very far: hence the novel I intend to write. You see, I am always urging Jack to 'get on'. If I am an example of effort I don't wonder he doesn't try! And, alas, I'm afraid he does not try. At times I fear for his future, he makes so little attempt to help himself. And in this devil-take-the-hindmost system one has to fight to remain at subsistence level, let alone rise above it. After the war it will be no different for a long time, not even though radical changes take place, as periods of transition are always bad. ...

Neil Bell is 55 today and I sent him a greetings telegram yesterday afternoon with instructions for it to be delivered today ... 'Greetings Neil Bell --- Many happy returns --- light reading for today *The Flying Fifty-five* by Edgar Wallace --- Jack Overhill.' I've just mentioned this to Jess; ... I told her to think of a better one applicable to my birthday; she couldn't; so I suggested *The Thirty-nine Steps* by John Buchan.

Monday 23 February. Everybody I meet seems depressed: the war and the weather. There's been some government changes (Cripps—the next Prime Minister, I suppose; if there is another—is in the [War] Cabinet, now numbering only seven); as if mucking about and ringing the changes with a few so-called leaders can make more effective the country's half-hearted efforts to win the war. To beat the enemy Britain must adapt itself to total war, and torn between Capital and Labour it can't; if it did it would by becoming a totalitarian state beat itself, for that's what she's fighting against; and why fight to prevent it in order to become one?

Tuesday 24 February. I'm finding the going with Economics pretty hard: Keynes's 'Pure Theory of Money' and what not --- A lot of ballyhoo of course. Being clever about money is like being clever about religion. It could easily be simplified under another system.

Wednesday 25 February. ... I heard from Neil Bell this morning and wrote to him tonight. He said among other things 'You have the satisfaction (and that is a hell of a lot when you come to consider things calmly) of knowing that you can do the stuff; that circumstances beyond your influence prevent your work being published now; and that as soon as those circumstances vanish you will without doubt achieve your aim — probably all you hope for in your wildest moments of optimism'. --- He bucks me up no end.

Friday 27 February. The newspapers state that Germany is building submarines on an unprecedented scale. We shall starve yet. Speaking to Frank Edwards about it I said if we lived on rats they wouldn't last long in this thickly populated island; and he replied that I mustn't forget the members of the Conservative Party.

March 1942

Monday 2 March. ... I forgot to mention that the siren went off yesterday dinnertime. It startled us at first; and then we remembered it was the first of the month tryout.

Wednesday 4 March. ... Queues are forming outside the fish and chip shops again. ... Only one baker allowed now, delivery every other day. Butchers are not to be allowed to deliver at all. But the rich still have servants.

  Railings are disappearing. Most places look better without them. The Victorians had a craze for railing, walling and hedging themselves in. ...

Thursday 5 March. ... I sent 'The Cordwainer' to Joseph's [Michael Joseph, the publisher] the other day at Bell's suggestion; ...

Friday 6 March. Everybody is to be conscripted for non-combatant work in the event of invasion. This is a new Defence Regulation. What powers ministries have that questions like this, or rather orders like this, don't need to go before Parliament because of widely framed acts.

  It's bitterly cold again: frost and snow. It's the worst winter I've experienced as the cold spell has been intense and lasted since the beginning of the new year. ...

New orders about waste paper: people can be fined and locked up for throwing an empty cigarette box down in the street; and dustmen can give householders away (I loathe this informing business) for putting waste paper in the dustbin. It's a queer sort of freedom we're striving for and no mistake.

Sunday 8 March. ... Less on a lot of the points scheme for meat and fish, and a few extras for currants and beans to balance. ...

Sunday 15 March. When I started to keep a diary I wrote when I felt like it, which was when I had something to say. Because of the bombings and in order to make a record of air-raid warnings I developed the habit of writing down something every day. Now, finding that's an ordeal, I'm dropping it and instead of putting down a few lines, largely about nothing, every day, I'm going back to my old habit and making notes now and again; but I'll try to do it at least once a week. ...

Black market racketeers are to get 14 years and a fine three times the value of the goods. (Then why don't they start by pinching some of the big hotel proprietors? I heard last week of a chap who went into a hotel and saw oranges being scoffed in a luxury mixture by the diners. Reserved for the children! Anyway, poor people can't buy in the black market; they can't afford to. Obviously the culprits are the rich.) ...

There's to be an all-round reduction in the number of coupons for clothes and boots. ... white bread gives place to brown next month.[6] ---

I've just written [to] Neil Bell; and now as it's fine and sunny—the weather has changed—I'm off for a walk, letting all those things I could write about slide. What do they matter anyway, when the sun is shining?

Sunday 22 March. Mr A. B. Chandler, one of my old headmasters (St. Paul's) died on Friday 13 March, aged 81. His death brought up a lot of memories of St Paul's Evening Classes, which I attended for three years without missing a lesson, beginning in October 1917. ...

---

[6] To conserve food, the wartime National Wheatmeal Loaf was made with a higher extraction rate of flour from wheat than before the war: Zweiniger-Bargielowska, *Austerity in Britain*, places this expedient within a discussion of rationing as a whole.

The book ('The Cordwainer') came back from Michael Joseph's this week. I'm sure it hadn't been read; I had it rebound before sending it off and it was as spick and span as when I sent it: condition impossible had it been handled for five minutes. Perhaps, things are so bad in the publishing world nowadays they don't trouble to read manuscripts sent in by new authors;...I went to the Guildhall to hear J. B. Haldane speak on Friday night; Jess came with me;[7] ... The meeting was for the purpose of getting the ban removed from the *Daily Worker*. Haldane's appearance belied his photos; or those I've seen of him; he looked an old man, although I should think he's only in his early 50s. There was a full house: sympathetic. And there was good response at the call for funds (£40,000 is the crusade figure) nearly £25 being subscribed in £1 and 10s notes from Girton girls, college men, young free Austrians and free Germans (self-styled: I wonder what their freedom really is!) soldiers (several just in front of me had a whip round and raised 30s among themselves) and such a miscellany of persons that there was clear evidence which way the wind is blowing politically nowadays: Leftwards. Bert Cash sent up half-a-crown with a note, which the collector on the platform read out with the rest: it said 'two-and-six from a teacher who nearly got the sack for telling his pupils that Hitler's secret weapon was Chamberlain'. There was a loud laugh from the audience and the collector, a communist named Bill Rowe, said it was worth inclusion in Cummings's notes in *World News and Views*. So Bert had his half-crown's worth.[8]

Haldane made reference to the *Daily Mirror*, threatened with suppression over a cartoon this week by the Home Secretary. If things are allowed to go on this way, only the *Telegraph*

---

[7] J. B. S. Haldane (1892–1964): geneticist, was educated at Eton and New College, Oxford; he was a university teacher at successively Oxford, Cambridge and University College, London. A liberal socialist in the 1920s, he became sympathetic to Marxism in the 1930s, largely because of the Soviet Union's opposition to Nazi Germany; he joined the Communist Party in 1942 but resigned from it c.1950 because of Stalin's repression of scientific freedom.

[8] Arthur John Cummings (1889–1957): a journalist of pronounced radical and anti-Nazi views who wrote for the *Daily News*, later renamed the *News Chronicle*, 1920–1955. His political commentaries were very widely read.

would be left, he said. There was the usual demand for the opening of a Second Front, but I thought his answer to his own question 'Who are they to ask that young men should sacrifice their lives for this cause?' (asked by pacifists) rather specious. It was to the effect that five workers on the *Daily Mirror* had given their lives and he himself had been to Spain and been unconscious half-a-dozen times fighting Fascism. That was no answer to the pacifist. Those men have every right to sacrifice their lives; it's no reason for others doing so who don't believe in that method — a very silly method — of righting wrong. 'I go you follow'! Nonsense. …

Sunday 29 March. There was a raid last Monday night on a SE coast town on a bigger scale than any since last May. And as we have been making another raid on the French coast this week I would link the two events as follows: possible preparations for a large-scale attack on France. …

The British Empire (upon which the sun never sets) is collapsing after a short-lived spell (there's men alive who fought in the grab for Africa) without people realising it. …

I mentioned, I believe, the other day that an old lady in the shop said what we want is some good organisers. As if their blatherings made any difference. Might as well try to stop the tides. … Talk about missing buses. There's some of our leaders couldn't catch a tortoise. …

Last night the comics in *Saturday Social* were faded out just before 9.00 in order that the BBC could put on a record of majestic tone and martial taste to herald the king speaking. He couldn't follow straight on from the comedians. As if he isn't one!

I sent for some past exam papers for a lookover for the examination in June. I stand a fairish chance of getting through, I think.

Jess went to the Labour Exchange yesterday and got an afternoon job. I had a row with her about it. … The title I was going to use for the fresh book, 'Devil take the hindmost', has been used — worse luck! …

April 1942

Monday 6 April. My nerves were a bit rough last week so packed up work at the shop on Thursday evening determined to have a rest over Easter. I have; although I've done a little Italian and read a very useful book, a Penguin Special by J. Keith Horsefield called *The Real Cost of the War* [1940]. On Good Friday Jack and I tried but failed to get in the Central [cinema] and so went into Lyons, where the cakes for wartime were of good quality. On Saturday morning I had a walk round the Green with the dogs and then down the town with [daughter] Jess. We bought three pounds of good hardboiled sweets on the market: cheap: 5s. ...The weather has been so so: Aprilfied: rain, sleet, sunshine, cool winds; but on the whole fairish and bearable after a rough winter. ...

Monday 13 April. Sunday wireless programmes are a hotchpot these days: highbrow and lowbrow music, religious services, jazz bands, music hall broadcasts, brains trust talks and exciting descriptions with incidental noises of wartime activities like the commando raid on St Nazaire.[9] The noises include shells bursting, machine-gun fire and the sounds of personal combat (one man hitting another on the head with a club?) and a relay of a 'Sunday broadcast 100 years ago' in 2042 will I am sure bewilder listeners. They'll think us less civilised than the Ancient Britons, I'm sure.

Jack started work last week: newspaper round in the mornings at 7s a week. And Jess [wife] is an insurance agent starting this morning at 45s a week. Did I mention that Jess [daughter] had a very good school report last term? Jack's was only so-so; 20th in exams. ...

---

[9] The dry dock in St Nazaire was the only one on the Atlantic coast big enough to hold the battleship *Tirpitz*, which it was feared might be used to attack Allied convoys. On the night of 27/28 March 1942 a destroyer packed with explosive rammed the dock, putting it out of action. At the same time 268 commandos landed to destroy essential machinery. Casualties were heavy.

War news: no agreement on India; Cripps coming home.[10] Three big ships of ours sunk by the Japs last week.[11] A bit of an inquest in the Commons, but not much. ...

All work and no play makes me a dull boy. I've done 22*s* of work today (15*s* net) and six hours studying. It's 2 o'clock and I've still another six hours' work to do: banking. Every day is much the same.

Sunday 19 April. ... Last Thursday afternoon Young Jess and I went for a walk to Byron's Pool (Jess being at work and so unable to come).[12] We called on her old headmaster [P. R.] Robinson at Trumpington School on the way and he told us how he's ousted the ARP workers from his school, being fed up with them about the premises. At the 'Pool' I read Italian while Jess picked violets and celandines. ...

Fred told me yesterday that a local signalman on the railway told him that he had had removed by making complaints 36 trucks full of debris from bombed sites in London that stood near his signal-box. They stank so much containing bits of human bodies. The debris was finally tipped into a refuse pit at Chesterton.

We seem to be bombing Germany on a fairly heavy scale, so I suppose our turn will come again. France will soon be presenting us with further problems by the look of things. Laval has taken over and he's no friend of this country. The question is whether the French fleet will be used against us. Our fleet is stretched out enough now and that would be awkward if French sailors will do it; and they might; after all, we clouted them some time back.

The flowers are out round the Backs, especially in St John's Wilderness. How they remind me of the days when Jess and I were courting in 1923. It was this time of year. ...

---

[10] In India Britain faced acute danger from Japan, and also growing Indian demands for independence and American criticism of British imperialism. Stafford Cripps was sent to India in March to negotiate with the Congress Party. Britain was prepared to concede a promise of postwar independence, but the negotiations failed in bitterness: Clarke, *The Cripps Version*, pp. 257–370.

[11] The cruisers *Dorsetshire* and *Cornwall* had been sunk by Japanese aircraft in the Indian Ocean, and the aircraft-carrier *Hermes* similarly off Ceylon.

[12] The poet is thought to have bathed in the pool, in the Cam near Grantchester, while he was an undergraduate at Trinity College.

May 1942

Sunday 3 May. During the past fortnight the RAF has bombed the German towns of Augsburg (a suicide flight), Kiel, Lubeck and Rostock, making such a mess of the last two that the pretence of 'military objectives' bombing has now finally gone by the board. The Germans, as reprisals, have badly bombed the English towns of Bath, Norwich and York, and these hitting-back tactics are called by our newspapers 'spite' raids.

Apparently, many old-fashioned buildings were knocked down in Lubeck (a sort of return for those knocked down here eighteen months ago) and rumours have been going round, having as their basis our newspapers and the German wireless, that English Baedeker towns, i.e. towns which have buildings of ancient and historic types, were going to be systematically bombed by the Germans. Apparently, [since] Cambridge is one of them, and [has] the initial letter of the town following that of (B)ath , local people have been on their toes during the past two nights, expecting something to happen. There might be something in all this as Bofor[s] … guns have been placed in the town (one or two on Parker's Piece). …

I've looked all round, wondering what we can do in the event of a heavy raid. There's no public underground shelters near here (we don't fancy the shelter we used to go to in Trumpington Street in the event of a blitz as it's only cellars under a big house: the last thing to take refuge in, burying alive being too unpleasant); surface shelters are being built on the 'Plant'un' round the corner (after nearly three years of war!) but they're not very inviting things either (granted they're finished in time) blast settling them very easily. Finally, there's the question of the dogs; we don't like leaving them to it. So it looks as it we shall have to run for it: Coe Fen, or somewhere like that, to be in the open, away from flying debris. The ground will be softer for the bombs to go in (all concrete in this neighbourhood), and a hollow or dry ditch (find one) MIGHT protect us (of course I mean the family) from blast; but there's getting there and shrapnel falling from the guns. ---

… What will happen in the spring offensive in Russia? For here lies the deciding issue of the war: unlikely of being settled by political upset (rife in Germany — the newspapers think!) and aerial bombing.

I'm bankrupt of ideas. Head filled with too much nonsense about economics, banking and credit and what not. ---

Sunday 17 May. Churchill spoke on the wireless last week; talked about gas. I suppose that's what it will come to, next. Neil Bell thinks so in a letter a few days ago. And he added that he put the autumn of 1944 as the extreme limit of the war owing to a general petrol shortage on both sides. That's a year less than he thought some months ago. I still think the war will end next year, probably the latter end. …

Thursday 21 May. I had the afternoon off today and Jess having other irons in the fire I decided to walk to Grantchester for a swim. I took some grub and a flask of tea; also managed to get a few hard-boiled sweets and a half-pound of prunes to chew on the way. The day was mild and warm and setting out with the dogs I had a pleasant time. On the way — wallflowers and tulips in the gardens, cow parsley under the hedges; lilac, laburnum, may blossom, chestnuts in full bloom; lush grass, buttercups golden in the sunlight, daisies. ---

I gave the dogs a wash, dropping the soap in the water before I began. Then a dip in the river, a cup of splash [tea], something to eat, a read (an old *Gem*!) and then another swim. On the way home I stopped at the Green Man in Grantchester and had a couple of grapefruits. I met [daughter] Jess beside the river along the Meadows on the way back. Altogether a pleasant afternoon; one the dogs enjoyed as well as myself.

Sunday 24 May. The 19th anniversary of my wedding day, Empire Day and Whit Sunday, all rolled into one, and by way of celebration I've spent a fair part of the day over the fire; eating chocolate (Frank Edwards brought a box of ration chocolate round; very acceptable at four bob) [4s] and studying the usual bunk for the examination. Note I say fire, as the weather, although sunny, turned chilly today, after a rainy night, and Jess lit one to make it look cheerful. What can I say about it being my wedding day except that it's amazing how the time has passed so quickly. ...

The Russians have abandoned Kerch. Fighting is now round Kharkov and the Central front. This summer will tell the tale on the Russian front. Soon we shall know whether it is to be Nazism or Communism as the dominant world force.

Lord Nathan said in Parliament last week that we shall keep an army of occupation in Germany after the war (apparently, to re-educate the Germans — how much we hear of this; anybody would think Englishmen don't want anything of the sort). Talk about counting your chickens before they're hatched. But the BBC and the Press have so painted the picture lately that the Germans are already on their last legs, if not completely beaten. I don't share this view by any means. ...

Sunday 31 May. ... Leather seems to be getting short; no more long-soling to be done and boots and shoes to be pieced if possible. Milk rations: these are finished for the time being; though I don't believe the number of cows in this country can give very good milk to 48 million people! Cheese rationing is increasing to four ounces per head from tomorrow — for a time. ...

I went to see the headmistress of Jess's school last Thursday afternoon about borrowing £40, part of this year's fees for Jess at Avery Hill. Just paid two quid [£2] for 99 Shelford Road and just over £1 on 7 Saxon Street for last year's compulsory war insurance. ... I'm all the while heading off bills of this sort. ...

Last week Frank Edwards had a bit of argument with a Leeds graduate about examinations. Apparently, some men can pass with honours at Cambridge and Oxford (and no doubt other places) by doing half-an-hour's work a day while I slog my guts out with six hours a day and sweat on getting a pass. Of course, it all boiled down to ABILITY. Oh yeah! I took up the cudgels on Frank's — and my own — behalf, since when the opposition has wilted.

My own examination is approaching. What are my feelings? A wish to finish with the job. I have up-and-down moods: I'll pass; I shall not pass and so on. And there's time when I wonder. Suppose I suddenly forgot all I've learned; suppose I miss the train or get held up any day—easily done in these rather risky times; suppose there's a blitz when I'm up in London to put us all out. So much can happen about seeing it through this year, apart from temporary sickness putting an end to one's chances and ability to pass the examination.

Jess is nearly full out as a full-time agent for the Prudential. She's been appointed to an agency Harston way … .

I forgot to mention that there were no end of our bombers passing over last night. I met a London policeman I know down here for the weekend this morning and he said he counted 70 going over as it was getting dusk round about 11.00 p.m. in less than half-an-hour. They were mostly passing over in threes. …

June 1942

Monday 1 June. According to the news we raided Cologne on Saturday night. The biggest raid ever; sent over more than 1,000 planes. I suppose there will be reprisals.

Wednesday 3 June. On Monday night the Germans raided Canterbury. And we made another mass raid of more than 1,000 aeroplanes, this time on the Essen district. American papers say that 20,000 were killed and 54,000 injured in the Cologne raid. It's too ghastly for words. …

I forgot to mention Jess [wife] bought herself a new bike last Monday: nine guineas [£9 9s]! Talk about profiteering. And she paid for it. What a husband!

Sunday 7 June. Jess and I went to London on Friday: a tryout to see if there was a good service to South Kensington for the examination. We missed [one] by a few minutes just before 7.00, but caught the next at 7.30 and then got to the examination rooms at 10.00: the hour the examinations start each day. It was a sweltering day. We had a look round. The cakeshops had plenty to sell; some difference from here; and tobacco and cigarettes seemed plentiful. I bought a bathing costume, or rather, Jess bought it for me, in Selfridge's for 5s 6d; cheap; they're ten bob [10s] in Cambridge, the cheapest. And combs that are sold in the town at 2s 3d were on sale for 7½d. I came home well stocked with grub. ...

Wednesday 24 June. Well, the examination is over and I am at the shop snobbing again. ... I scribbled down in a notebook all that happened during a rather hurried ten days and I will set it down in order ... .

> *Saturday 13 June.* ... I cleared up all the work at the shop on Friday night, put a notice on the door window saying I was closed till June the 13th and packed up. ... I went down the town with Jess in the afternoon and bought her a birthday present (umbrella) and had a squint at *The Economist* in the public library.
>
> *Sunday 14 June.* I studied all day, but managed to mend a puncture in Jack's bike and take the dogs for a couple of walks. ... Fearing I would oversleep, I slept downstairs on a camp bed, fixing it up with the telephone company and Frank Edwards to ring me at a quarter to 6.00 in the morning.
>
> *Monday 15 June.* I had a bad night; slept rotten; I found out that camp beds are cold things to sleep in. The draught gets underneath and the bedclothes easily roll on to the floor. In the morning I noticed that I had slept with the window shut; and there's gas in the room. Showed my state of mind. I took the family a cup of tea up, just to start off well; then off to the station to come face to face with my old bogey: a non-corridor train; but corridor or no corridor I meant to go through with it and in I got and off to London I went; which was much more heroic than it sounds, as people who suffer from claustrophobia will very well know. At the Examination Halls in Imperial Institute Road the lights had fused and as the place was blacked out students were blundering round downstairs in the dark. An attendant told me half the building had been taken over by the Office of Works, whatever that is.[13] Anyway, the place was a shant. No drinking water handy (I went into a workman's mess room for a drink as I was very thirsty after the journey) and only a couple of the lavatories with toilet paper in them (this gave out before the end of the week; and students sitting for their final! Talk about hygiene; and I expect some of the chaps were doing papers on hygiene, too!)
>
> The exam was held in the Great Hall. An attendant told me it held about 1500. But there were many desks empty. I did pretty well with the paper on Economics in the morning. During the

---

[13] It was the department responsible for buildings in government ownership.

midday break of one and a half hours I sat on the grass outside, eating sandwiches and revising, watching a lot of airmen cadets parading in gasmasks in between times. I wasn't at home with the Banking and Currency paper in the afternoon; had to draw on all my knowledge for it. … but reviewing the paper as a whole afterwards, I felt I had done a satisfactory one. Jess was still out on her insurance round when I got home … . This was about 9 o'clock. … the children going to bed I got on with revising for the next day (I always did this backwards and forwards in the train). It started to rain and I was beginning to get anxious just after 10.00, when Jess came in. She brought some eggs with her and I had a couple, which were welcomed. We swopped news. A hard day for both of us.

Tuesday 16 June. Another uncomfortable night. Found my glasses had slipped out of my pocket on the way to the station and not looking forward to the day's work without them I borrowed a porter's bicycle when I got there and returned home for them, just beating the train. While revising in the cloakroom at the Examination Halls a raised nail in the chair I was sitting in tore the hole in the backside of my trousers (I'm the ragged-arsed philanthropist these days) a little farther. I did very well with the morning paper: Economic History of the Great Powers; but noticed afterwards that I had misread one of the questions. … I don't think, however, that the slip would make any difference to my paper as a whole; it was, I think, a good paper. …

In the afternoon I wrote a rather provocative essay on 'A New Policy for Education'. I did this in about an hour and a half and then, keeping an eye open for the [in]vigilator, took a shorthand copy of it. I suppose I should have been better set to work to have re-written my essay for the examiner; I had plenty of time; instead I preferred to leave it as it was with the adjustments and alterations and have the copy of it; after all, it was about the only bit of creative work during the whole examination. It contained a spelling mistake. I couldn't think if the word 'diffusion' had one or two fs in it, and although I wrote out the word and pondered over it, couldn't decide and put one 'f' in, which, of course, was wrong. And I tagged an 'of' at the end of a sentence unnecessarily. Beyond that and a phrase I could have left out, the essay was pretty well as I wanted it. I don't know if it was long enough; not much more than 1,000 words; still, I'd said all I had to say, and as it was very much to the point, I'm satisfied about it, chance whether the examiner is. (I've decided to type it out and include it in these notes for reference.)   Felt tired and dazed on the way home, but kept at it. …

Wednesday 17 June. I made a good job of the French translation, but there was a lot of it and it took me an hour and five minutes. But this gave me nearly two hours for the Italian translatio-n instead of an hour and half as I had planned (the two were to be done in three hours) and I started, only to come to a full stop before doing the first paragraph; I couldn't find out a word. Foolishly, then, I tried the other piece to see if it was easier (there was a choice of two pieces) and finding it wasn't I switched back to the first, wasting over half an hour. Then, with only an hour and 20 minutes to get the translation done I was in a sweat, a regular panic. I have never felt like it before in an exam and in despair I almost got to my feet and shouted: 'You bastards, what have you made it so bloody hard for?' But I pegged away, desperately, leaving out what I didn't know and going back to fill in afterwards. The result was I finished on time, but the writing was ragged and I wouldn't call it a good translation. There were four pages of it and during the dinner interval I went carefully over the paper again. I spent half an hour on it, but couldn't better what I had put, so at least I have the consolation of knowing that I couldn't have bettered what I sent in. I did pretty good with the Modern Economic History Part 1 paper in the afternoon (this was my special subject: three papers). I was up till midnight, helping Jess with her books [as an insurance agent]. She didn't balance to the amount of 30*s*. The camp bed collapsed. What a day!

Thursday 18 June. Jess made up the camp bed and I had a better night. The day's revision work was enormous; I had to slog all day. It was continuation of Modern Economic History: Part 2 in the morning and Part 3 in the afternoon. I did pretty good with both papers; and excelled myself over one question in the morning paper asking if the period 1700–1750 could be called decadent. (Of course, it wasn't: it was a necessary prelude to the Industrial Revolution.) …

Friday 19 June. Another cold night on the camp bed. A RAF chap was cleaning out the lavatories at the Examination Halls just about the time students were using them. He was busy with a hose and the lavatories were ankle-deep in water; no toilet paper in any of them. I did pretty good with the paper: Constitutional History since 1660, excelling myself over one question by showing what happens inside and outside Parliament have relation to each other; i.e. Parliament can have no separate existence (as the question seemed to indicate), that it is called into being through external factors and that these factors and the functions and organisation of Parliament are simply reflections of one another. I bought cakes and a porkpie in London to bring home, there being plenty of that sort of stuff up there and none in Cambridge. Had two more punctures to mend. ...

I gave 1s to the porter I borrowed the bike from. Over the weekend I studied up for the final paper: Political History of the Great Powers since 1815. I went with the Jesses and the Cashes as far as Paradise up the river on Sunday afternoon ... It was sunny and pleasant. On Monday I went to London again and sat for this paper and did pretty good. I had a sweltering ride home in the train as the weather had changed to heat, and arriving in Cambridge with a few eatables, went straight to the river for a swim. ...Summing up I think I did well on nine of the eleven papers, my Italian was only fairish, and I could have done better with the Banking and Currency paper. ...This does not mean that I think I shall pass; far from it; I haven't thought at any time since my many failures that I'd get through this year and per-haps not next; maybe the year after. I look upon it as a contribution to the time when I do.

Anyway, it's over until another year. And soon I shall be thinking about another book. I don't want to waste the year. ...

As an experience? Well, I know to the full the deadening effect of examination work. It's annihilating; and no good to anyone. After all, nine-tenths of it is memory work. ...

The war: this is going disastrously for us. Rommel's forces have taken Tobruk and Bardia; an assault on Egypt is imminent.[14] This together with shipping losses and the German offensive at Sebastopol have made people gloomy again; and Parliament is rising on its hind legs again; though to what effect remains to be seen. But I do think we are entering on the last stages of the war. Another 18 months will see it over: and perhaps before.

The normal sequence of the diary is resumed:

Thursday 25 June. There was a warning last night from just before 2.00 a.m. until about 3.00 a.m.; the first for a long while. ... [The family rose] ... before we had finished dressing German bombers were going over and the searchlights were up. It was a fairly light night, though cloudy. We came downstairs and I went out and put up the blackout and blacked out a light

---

[14] Tobruk, having resisted Rommel's advance in 1941, fell to his renewed assault on 20 June, with the capture of the garrison of 35,000 men. These events caused especial.dismay in Britain.

that was showing through the door giving on to the passage. Then, we waited. Planes still passed over, going, I thought north-west (this was right, as we learned today that Birmingham was attacked). I walked as far as the end of the street, came back and after a short wait decided to go back to bed. We did so and the 'All Clear' went soon afterwards. Our attitude was, of course, all based on our wondering about Cambridge getting its promised bombing: we didn't know what to do. ...

Friday 26 June. ... Bought Pepys' *Diary* secondhand for 18*d*; cheap; I've never yet read it. ...

Saturday 27 June. There was a warning last night at 2.10 a.m. lasting until about 3.00 a.m. We got up for a little while and then went back to bed. While down I walked on to Lensfield Road to see what the clattering of hoofs was and found a lot of horses making up the road. Evidently, they had got off Coe Fen or some neighbouring common. They were soon driven back. ...

[On the river punting with Bert Cash] Bert had a few rows going and coming: with fishermen about the joys of fishing ('Your idea is: it's a nice day; let's go and kill something' was one of his exchanges with a group of youths on the bank); and continuing his vendetta against another Grantchester youth for chucking clods the day before at some ATS girls he deliberately punted over his fishing line!

[On the punt] I made use of the time: preparation for the new book. I've found a new pastime—sleeping my blooming head off.

Sunday 28 June. ... [Eric visited.] When I went to see him off I saw the Home Guard Parade on Parker's Piece: several thousand Home Guards and crowds of onlookers ...

Tuesday 30 June. There was a warning last night: just before 3.00 a.m. until just before 4.00 a.m. A lot of planes passed over and we could recognise the oomp-oomp of the German bombers. I believe a number of our night-fighters were up as well; I thought I heard one of Marshall's trainer planes droning round. ... It's a tiring business getting up, but we're a bit scared of lying abed now since the threat to Cambridge as a Baedeker town. Often as I sit and listen I wonder if I'll see the dawn of a new day: ...

It seems I've roused a nest of hornets. Frank Edwards: noising my opinion of exams to the COs of his gang, has upset the apple-cart of several who regard it as a slight upon their intellectual achievements. Me, disparaging their ability, talking about university degrees like that! The outcome is that I've been challenged to debate it — it being all about education and what not — with THREE of them at Frank's house on Thursday 16 July. These three are graduates from Oxford, Cambridge and Birmingham; or is it Leeds? I've accepted. What ho! So hurrah for the snob! (that's me!) I'll let 'em have it. All their ballyhoo about culture, scholars before socialists and the like — in the words of the song 'Who do they think they are?' Anyway, we shall see, arrogating to themselves silly airs because they've memorised and written a lot of tosh in an examination room. I've done it, so I know all about it. ...

July 1942

Wednesday 1 July. After the lapse of a week I started Italian again this morning. And I am now kicking off with the new novel, 'Whims of the Father'. It's about half-past 9.00 [p.m.]. Just an hour at it to make a start and then kip. ---

Saturday 4 July. A political upset in the Commons over Libya. Churchill, back from America — where he was apparently running the war when it went so badly! — talked over the Opposition and there were only 25 votes against him. But for all that he's tottering. Another bust-up or two and he'll fall....

The Russians have evacuated Sebastopol after an eight months' siege and the Germans have now begun their delayed summer offensive. The next few months will tell the tale. Jess and I had a cycle ride round the houses tonight. Too blustery for the river.

Thursday 9 July. ... Turning in to Sheep's Green round Newnham Mill from the Backs in my dinner hour a few days ago on the way to river (dogs plodding behind) I saw the rosy-pink flowers of the willowherb showing for the first time this year among the rushes of Snob's Stream.[15] How they stirred me (they

---

[15] 'Snob's Stream': snob was Cambridge slang for anybody not a gownsman; a townsman.

always do) and back went my mind to 1911, the year I learned to swim [he was then eight]. Again I was walking beside the ditch on Coe Fen on the way to the river looking at the pretty flowering willowherb amongst the green of the opposite bank: little girls, such dainty little things, in summer dresses, wearing large coloured hats (then fashionable), passed me, some on bikes, some walking, as they went to the ferry (now done away with) to be taken over the river to the ladies' bathing-place for a swim. It seems a long cry from those days, as wearing thick, heavy, hobnailed boots and a corduroy suit, I looked rather wistfully after those little girls; they seemed very remote from me, a shabby little fellow with nothing in his pockets except a pair of home-made bathing drawers (I always wiped [my body] on my shirt), but once at the men's bathing-place and stripped off my boots and suit, I felt their equal; anybody's equal. ---

I always think of it as I pass along that way: often it seems but yesterday; and then I remember it is now 31 years. --- Which reminds me that the other night I had my old dream feeling, when bordering between sleeping and waking, that I was 39 and there were only 30 years more before I had lived the allotted span—if I got so far; then, no more wife and kids and mates; just black-out—and I was in a panic (as usual) about it and became fully awake, when (as usual) all the horror I experience over this feeling during sleeping and waking, vanished. Queer, isn't it, that when I'm wide awake and in full possession of my senses I regard the matter dispassionately and with none of that terror-stricken total eclipse feeling that I have when only partly conscious? …

Sunday 12 July. … 'The enemy has long ears' (large letters) 'guard your conversation' (small letters); and 'Don't take chances in the blackout' (large letters) 'always cross the road with care' (small letters) was the notice on the back of a couple of bus tickets I found hanging on a nettle on Sheep's Green the other night. …

Paying back £14 to Frank Edwards reduces my debt [to him] to £12; but now I owe some money to Jess, as I've done a bit of borrowing off her; however, I'll pay back in time. …

I'm finding it difficult to shape the novel; I mean the first chapter or two; soon though I'll have it going. Big battles are raging in Russia. Still, for all a bit of scrapping, a lull in Egypt. Shipping is very serious: a debate is coming off in secret in Parliament about it.

I'm beginning to loathe conscientious objectors! Heard so much about them lately from Frank Edwards. The religious sort are the worst. I expect what it amounts to is that the best sort of COs are sent to prison; the worst — and this is the religious, bible-punching kind — are let off. Frank tells me they are as self-centred as hell; will almost fight for the best seat in the lorry. And as for kindness — they've never heard of the word. One of them, speaking of examinations and degrees said that when ONE had forgotten most of the subjects studied at a university there is always something left: CULTURE.

Friday 17 July. The other day a CO who had served three months in prison was given another six months and Dr Alex Wood wrote a letter to the local paper about these cat and mouse tactics, saying he felt sure this was not the intention of the legislators when framing the act to protect conscientious objectors. His letter had two replies and according to the one last night COs stink. This person would put all conscientious objectors in a box and drop them to the bottom of the ocean to remove the stench of them. I wonder why a chap like this wants to wage a war with Hitler. Obviously, he doesn't believe in minority rights and as Hitler is reputed to believe the same thing they're blood brothers, not sworn enemies, as the mutt, by the rest of his letter, would have us believe. Anyway, he'd missed the point. Wood was aiming at the misuse of the judicial power delegated by the Government to the ministry concerned. Lord Hewart in his book *The New Despotism* [1929] and Ramsay Muir in *How Britain is Governed* [1930 and later editions] had a lot to say about this.[16] Not only the rights of

---

[16] Gordon Hewart (1870–1943): first Viscount Hewart, was educated at Manchester Grammar School and University College, Oxford. After some years as a journalist he was called to the bar. As an 'advanced' Liberal he was MP for a Leicester seat 1918–22, serving as Attorney-General. In 1922 he became Lord Chief Justice, serving until 1940; frequently rude to colleagues he lacked political judgement. *The New Despotism* attacked

COs but the rights of every individual are involved. ... The savage in me made me feel like going round and beating him up ...; the pacifist in me urged me to write a flaming letter to the paper; Jess told me not to do anything of the sort and so I decided to let sleeping dogs lie; mustn't forget there's a war on. ...

Sunday 19 July. ... Fuel is to be rationed; and the police are to have power to enter houses and see how much is being burned. ...

Today I heard the Sleeping Beauty waltz twice on the radio ... . This song always reminds me of a swimming club concert in which Dunlop Kidman took part ... . Now Dunlop's gone, killed at Dunkirk. He was boy diving champion of Cambridgeshire, the Midlands and England in 1929 and gave Jack a lot of coaching with his diving. I remember swimming in a race against him round the backs about 1930 time; it was 50 yards and he won on a wrong decision, as I finished first but the judge standing on a punt—the finishing post—never noticed me coming up on the outside. The people shouted at the decision from the bank, but it was made and had to stand. Dunlop knew my views about war. When he joined the Air Reserve force [Royal Air Force Volunteer Reserve] just before the war and we talked about it, he said he hadn't joined to fight, just for fun; but he was wrong; they got him; they had him. I still remember his delight when I met him just outside the railway station when he told me he'd just conquered air

---

the growth of delegated legislation and the assumption by civil servants of decision-making powers rightfully belonging to the judiciary. Its arguments had much merit, but they were undermined in the 1930s by the book's cantankerous tone. Ramsay Muir (1872–1941): was educated at the universities of Liverpool and Oxford; he taught at Liverpool and Manchester, resigning his professorship there in 1921; he then dedicated himself to work for the revival of the Liberal Party as an instrument of change. Suspicious of State intervention and socialism, he put his faith in rational progress and enlightened capitalism. His book *How Britain is Governed* criticised a parliamentary system that did not reflect the wishes of the electorate or give the House of Commons control of the Executive; a powerful Cabinet in effect controlled the majority party, while party funds were too dependent on Big Business and Trades Unions. Muir also, like Hewart, attacked 'delegated legislation'.

sickness during acrobatics with glucose. Poor Dunlop: a good fellow if ever there was one. ...

According to the papers yesterday, Paddy Finucane, England's ace airman was killed a few days ago:[17] ... He was only a youth; about 21; everybody's upset about it; but could they expect anything else; he's brought down 32 enemy planes and it was only a matter of time before his turn came; ...

Tuesday 21 July. Another recollection: running along Panton Street, late for school in the drowsy heat of a summer afternoon, I entered the shadow of a big tree; time stood still; it must have done, as I have since crossed that patch of shade a thousand times, seeing the blue of the sky between the green of the leaves, feeling the guilt of my solitary, hurrying self and HEARING the stillness of the sun-drenched street, so full of charm that for all my fears I was filled with a hallowed sweetness, rarely equalled, never excelled. --- (I was about seven.) ...

Wednesday 22 July. My brother Perce died 30 years ago today at quarter past 3.00 [p.m.] with diphtheria and I remembered it this afternoon in the shop. And my fears for years afterwards on the anniversaries that I would die on that day, too. I can remember my relief at hearing the Roman Catholic church clock strike the quarter past as I lay on Parker's Piece one afternoon; and in other places. ...

Thursday 23 July. There was a warning this morning: 9.05 a.m. till 9.25 a.m. It was very cloudy and there was the roar of a lot of planes: nothing else. ... Just been to the Vic [Victoria Cinema] with Jess to see Arthur Askey; quite good. ...

Friday 24 July. ... There was a warning last night from about 12.15 a.m. to 1.15 a.m. A lot of planes over. A stick of bombs went off in the distance and then Jack came into our bedroom; [daughter] Jess remained upstairs in her bedroom. I thought after a while it was all right and Jack going back to his room I turned over and was about to go to sleep when there was the sound of another exploding bomb, this time much nearer. I got up and had a walk into the back room in my shirt, feeling

---

[17] Wing Commander Brendan 'Paddy' Finucane DSO, DFC, aged 21, was shot down over the French coast: D. Stokes, *Paddy Finucane* (1983).

very uneasy, but went back to bed and lay there till the 'All Clear' sounded. ...

Tonight Jess and I rode over to Chalmers Road; I wanted to see a chap that lived there about some money he owed me; ... didn't get the money. A not very nice ride for all the pleasant evening as I had a slow puncture and had to keep pumping up the tyre and we ran into an ARP gas test. Men standing about, dodging about, biking about, car-ing about, all in uniforms; enjoying themselves it looked to me. ... Luckily we missed the gas they were letting off, as we hadn't our masks. ...

Sweet rationing starts shortly: two ounces each a week. Jess left school today ... She received her reference from her headmistress, a very good one; and her gym stripe from the gym teacher, Miss Rodwell. She was going to work at a place in the holidays — clerical work — for £1 a week (for a month), but I stopped that. People are not exploiting my children. £1 a week! She can do with a rest; she's worked very hard and it's been a strain. I know. She's talking about doing a half-day's work a day at Chivers' [jam-makers at Histon], sorting fruit. I don't mind if they pay her a fair wage, but want her to enjoy herself after her labours more than anything. ...

Saturday 25 July. ... A short talk with Charlie and Ken Craske to wind-up the evening. War talk. When is the war going to end? Will there soon be a compromise peace? Both reckon that morale is lower than at any time since Dunkirk. Very likely.

Sunday 26 July. ... A very restless night last night: bombers roaring over all night — and occasional night-fighters passing over — so I should think we made a big raid on Germany.

Monday 27 July. It was pouring o' rain this morning when we woke up; a fine start for the day; for Jess's big round [as an insurance agent] is on Mondays, [daughter] Jess was starting at Chivers, three miles away, and Jack had his paper round to do (he's still sticking it: because he spends the money, I'm sure). Jess [daughter] started out on her bike and almost immediately the siren sounded: it was then 7.15 a.m. I was glad to see her return. The 'All Clear' went at 7.45 a.m. She then made another start. ...Jess tackled her round, but when I came just after 1 o'clock I met her; she'd got as far as Lordsbridge the first time and drenched to the skin had come home. She managed to do her round for the day however, as the weather cleared up. ...

It isn't often I crave to be a despot, but when I read in the paper a couple of days ago that 400 munition workers had made a deputation (to Downing Street, I believe) urging that a Second Front (all the craze nowadays) be formed, I wished I was. Then they'd have got their Second Front; I'd have seen to it; and they'd have been there, whether halt, maimed or blind, as they might even then stop somebody else getting killed. They actually promised to work harder so that the soldiers could fight harder. Fancy that! I haven't seen any deputations from soldiers who will have to do the stuff. Some are ready, I know; and I can appreciate their principles though they don't agree with mine; but these people who keep talking about a Second Front annoy me. Everybody who wants one should fight in it. I doubt if they'll ever come back. ...

Tuesday 28 July. Jess and I went to bed last night just before midnight. The siren sounded at 1.45 a.m. A glorious moonlight night. We lay abed for a while, hearing planes go over, not knowing which was which. Then there were three explosions, not so very loud, and we hopped out of bed. I thought they were bombs in the distance, but agreed that perhaps it was gunfire from Grantchester. Immediately the bombs went off a plane seemed to scrape over the house and outside a warden told me it was Jerry scampering over the top of us. At 4 o'clock I went back to bed, so did the children, but Jess stayed up and talked at the door to one or two people. The 'All Clear' went at 4.15 a.m. and we heard by then that bombs had fallen in the neighbourhood of the Round Church and Thompson's Lane. Details today: the raider was a Junkers 88; he was so low the number could be seen and people thought he would crash; at one time he put his lights on; Spitfires chased him; three people were killed and some injured, six seriously, is the present statement of the casualties, and a lot of damage was done, including some to the Union Society: a cobble weighing about two pounds was flung as far as the house in which Charles Lamb lived on King's Parade (said to be half a mile by the local paper, which I doubt) falling through the roof and rooms to the scullery sink. ...

Wednesday 29 July. Last night as we were going to bed after 11 o'clock the sky northwards was suddenly lit up with a bright crimson glow that repeatedly blazed and faded. We wondered what it was. Had the siren gone and we hadn't heard it because of the radio playing and were flares burning a little way off? The light disappeared and we went to bed hoping for a quiet night; we had one; and felt better for it. Heard today this light was caused by a Stirling bomber crashing at Oakington. Don't know whether it's true or not; can't believe all you hear nowadays; far from it. ...

Thursday 30 July. 1.45 a.m. Here we are, all up, downstairs in the front room, for the siren sounded at 1.20 a.m. and after lying abed for a few minutes we were almost shaken out of it by gunfire. Thought at first it was bombs (at least, I did), but then realised it was the guns going off, probably on Parker's Piece. Just had a walk on the 'Plant'un' where several stand talking and listening. ---

Friday 31 July. Tired out we went to bed early last night: 10 o'clock. The siren woke us at 1.15 a.m. I and the children got up, Jess, worn out, stayed abed. Planes passed over but the expected gunfire never happened. Eventually, we went back to bed again. Soon afterwards an enemy plane went over and the guns opened up. First, the Bofors on Parker's Piece: a series of pop, pop, pops; then heavier guns, which sounded like bombs (probably those at Grantchester). A second or two after these have gone there is the distant explosion of the shells. Now we know the difference between bombs exploding and gunfire. With bombs there is the whine and then the explosion; with the guns there is a flash and then the explosion, light travelling faster than sound.

Some people like the guns; think they're a protection; I'm one who doesn't think anything of the sort. Arguments are easy to counter. It drives enemy planes higher; I say they can still drop their bombs however high they are. It turns the enemy planes; other places, say I, can turn them on to you. Further, it's dangerous then to make a run for shelter owing to falling shrapnel; the bomber has to fall somewhere if brought down, there's no sleeping through a warning if the guns open up, and, lastly, the enemy is less likely to treat a defended town lightly. …

A warning not to carry gasmasks owing to shortage of rubber was issued today; might wear them out quickly and it be impossible to replace them. Sign of the times. We're running down. And if it was unsafe to go out without a gasmask last week it is now. What'll we do … if our rubber peters out …?

August 1942

Saturday 1 August. Eric unexpectedly came down for the weekend … . Eric and I talked about the war. Would the Russians hold? Lady Astor's outburst against the Russians (silly woman); how long would the war last?[18] ---

Monday 3 August. The siren sounded at 3.00 a.m. this morning. We didn't get up; heard a couple of queer-sounding planes go over, which Eric said he thought were ours, as they had single engines. I heard the 'Raiders Passed' signal; think it was round about 4 o'clock, but don't quite know and didn't bother to find out today. … There was another warning this evening at 6.00 p.m. or just after, lasting half an hour. …

Tuesday 4 August. Today is—unnoticeably—the 28th anniversary of the Great War. Not a word about it in the newspaper today; …

Loss of sleep through air-raids and lowered vitality through lack of sugar and fats, imperfect substitutes and shortages of all sorts must mean bad temper and bickering among people. I'll bet there's lots of disharmony in most homes nowadays. I'm going by my own—measuring other people with my rods? You bet! There's plenty, heap big plenty, disharmony at 7, Saxon Street these days; none of us seem to agree five minutes.

---

[18] Nancy, wife of Viscount Astor, was Conservative MP for the Sutton Division of Plymouth, an ardent Protestant, Christian Scientist, and advocate of Temperance.

I'm de-reserved as from the 1st of this month and have been notified to that effect. I got a form from the Labour Exchange, filled it in and sent it off a couple of days ago requesting exemption in the usual manner. Dunno if I'll be lucky.[19] ...

Sent the first year's fees, £42 10s, for Jess to Avery Hill. And sent Jack a card and ten bob for a birthday present. ...

Wednesday 5 August. There was a warning during the early hours of this morning—about 2.45 a.m.—lasting for half an hour or so. ... Fred called to see me this morning. He's in a tangle over the Home Guard; wants to kick but can't because of his big family. I framed a claim for exemption for him, basing it on his varicose veins, long hours, large family and dysentery contracted during the last war. ...

Thursday 6 August. Heard this afternoon as I was grooming Jock that I had failed in the B.Sc. (Econ.) final examination in Economic, History and Constitutional History. Very well failed by the look of it. ... I passed in Italian and the Essay I was windy about and failed in those subjects in which I thought I'd excelled. ... Well, better luck next time! ... I wondered this year should I have any luck with 'The Cordwainer' or my final B.Sc. Econ. examination. Should I get away with both, or one, or neither? Now I know.

Friday 7 August. This very long entry (it contains about 3700 words) begins with a copy of a letter he had just written to Neil Bell. The letter starts with an account of his daughter's being upset by his examination failure. He also describes the debate forecast in the entry for Sunday 28 June.

> ... But I told her it wasn't the first time, and very likely wouldn't be the last; it was OK. I would pass; that was something only delayed; there was a lot of punch in me yet. I wondered if it worried her because of her own examination. Once or twice before she'd passed when I've passed and failed when I've failed. I hope the sequence is now broken. Examination failures are more shattering to youngsters than to an old man like me. ...
>
> Later I went along to meet the graduates and other fellows who came along to listen. This didn't pan out quite as Edwards hoped. The Cambridge graduate dropped out and I

---

[19] If Jack was de-reserved he would become liable for national service like other men in his age-group.

think there must have been some hesitation on the part of those that turned up: a London graduate (Internal) with honours and a Leeds graduate, also an honours man. Apparently, the Leeds fellow was at a meeting at which I asked some questions (I wrote to you some time back; it was to do with Justice) and he must have thought I was a bear because he frankly confessed to Edwards that he was nervous of me; he knew just the sort of fellow I was and wouldn't know how to handle me at all.

Well, I wasn't so very bearish; and frankly I misjudged them, for they were both nice fellows and I liked them very much indeed. I spoke for nearly two hours (what a gasbag; …) and they made notes, occasionally questioned me, while the others (non-university men, but all COs) listened. From the beginning I knew their type; they just knew nothing of life as it's presented itself to me; their path has been made easy by money and indulgent parents; but they had a sense of humour and took my knocks (the heaviest raised roars of laughter) in good part. … the biggest laugh was when I jeered (lightly, I hope) at their culture. I'd seen it, I said — on the walls of the lavatories at the Examination Halls, at South Kensington: …

As I talked so long they had no time to make an answer before closing the meeting at 10 o'clock (necessary because they have to get up at 5.30 a.m.) so I suggested they thought over what I had said (they had their notes) and they could then say it at any time to suit themselves, as I would come along whenever they wanted … All I had to say and show (and I took plenty of my work along) rather disorientated them. And they agreed with a lot, most of it, once it was said, and thought education and examinations wanted a good overhauling. What surprised them was not so much that I had failed, but what I had attempted and so far done. It was too much, far too much, they said. The London man said he knew my remarks about the Ph.D. examiner I met in the train saying seven minutes was as much as an examiner could give any paper was true … . And both agreed that I had slipped through; they were certain of it. To which I replied that it was a bit regular then (twice entrance exam, three times Part 1 Inter, twice Part 2 Inter, and the Final still in the air) and it must be a bloody big mesh. … I didn't let on that I had failed in the Final till right at the end. It was a thunderbolt. But what struck them most was that a chap could turn up and talk like I had a couple of hours after hearing he'd failed in the final examination for a degree. They marked that up very highly to my credit. …

I went home, went to bed about half-past 11.00. The siren had us out at 12.55 a.m. and it was warm until 2.30. We ran to the surface shelters, some protection being better than none, and stood huddled there in the dark (no lights, no benches) while the flames and the flares lit the skies all round us and the guns roared at Jerry enjoying himself overhead. ...

After the conclusion of the transcribed letter to Neil Bell the entry continues; Jack reverts to his address to the graduates.

Back to the graduates. I remembered their shaft that it was 'all a question of ability' and said that although I wanted to write a novel and sit for the B.Sc. Econ. Final again next year, I was prepared to postpone both of these for the purpose of finding out. I would take up the study of Chinese, or any other subject, with any of them (particularly the one who said it) for a year and at the end of that time would have a try-out with them without any examiners; we could find out ourselves easily enough who was the best. I was in earnest but they didn't take me on. What else can I remember that I said to the chaps at Edwards's last night? ...

I began by saying that there was a reason for us being there: I'd said things with which they disagreed; and they'd said things with which I disagreed. I was there to justify my attitude; and I should expect them to do the same. I said I thought it would be best to state the cause ... for my attitude; that would best be done by describing the ways in which I had tried to educate myself. I thought my education began when I was seven as it was then I first started reading the newspaper to my father, who could not read. I mentioned my scholarship, its unfortunate ending, my going to night school for three years without missing an evening of any session; named the subjects I studied; mentioned that I went to Emmanuel College under the WEA when I was 19 for a course of economics (not very advanced: matric standard) my teachers' diplomas for shorthand and typewriting, my application to London University in 1929 to sit for their entrance examination (refused because I was a bookmaker), then later, after London University, as a democratic institution, had thrown open their exams to anyone, encouraged by the advertisements of Wolsey Hall in *John O' London's Week-*

ly, I made a start.[20] I gave them my experiences of the exams I've sat for (mentioned in this diary); mentioned Bert's photos of me at Grantchester as evidence of the way I worked; that 'Queen Street' took me 500 or 600 hours to write, while, all told, I gave 3,000 or 4,000 hours to the Inter B.Sc. Econ.

Continuing to revisit his words to the graduates Jack Overhill described the ease with which university degrees might be acquired by some: internal students, but not external, were permitted to graduate after two years' study during the war; at Cambridge 'boatrace men, footballers, cricketers and the rest of the sporting fraternity' all seemed to graduate, while it seemed possible to gain an honours degree on one hour's work a day 'roundabout midnight'.

Passing the exam was all that mattered to most of them, which defeated the real object, that of acquiring knowledge. The universities were bound up with the public schools; parents wanted something for their money and wouldn't support either by sending their children to them if they were not granted (given) degrees. ... There was no room for genius; a moderate man could reach a dead level in all subjects and pass, a brilliant could fail in one subject after doing fine in all the others. ... Being a parrot — and who could study for a degree without? — wasn't the way to acquire knowledge ... I could have asked what had London University done for me except take my money and make a profit out of it; and reckoning the part services of a[n] [in]vigilator (or [in]vigilatress), some writing paper, and the services of a seven-minute examiner, and probably those of a seven-second questioner, a good profit. ...

Now for a bit about the raid on Cambridge last night. (The German radio claims to have bombed Cambridge and Edinburgh in tonight's paper). We lay abed after the siren went, but the sky was so lit up with fires that we got up and went outside into the street. ... Lots of German planes were over so we went into the surface shelters; but the guns were firing be-

---

[20] Wolsey Hall was a correspondence college aimed at those wishing to improve their qualifications. *John O' London's Weekly* was a literary journal, 'middlebrow' in its aesthetic character, and circulating widely among self-educated readers and writers like Jack Overhill.

fore we did so. Heard today h.e.s [high explosive bombs] fell on Stourbridge Common and incendiaries on the town were as common (almost) as blackberries. The paper said only four people [were] slightly hurt and a cow … was killed; that it was our worst bombing; and that a new fire bomb — phosphorous — was used by the Germans. As there were no benches to sit on in the shelter I fetched two chairs and a warden came after me thinking I was a parachutist. …

Saturday 8 August. Another letter to Neil Bell:

… The Leeds graduate I wrote to you about is, or rather was, a public school teacher, and it suddenly occurred to me today that he was defending himself against a shoe-repairer. Just think of it. Nothing can more strikingly illustrate the changes that have taken place during the past 30 years. Impossible to convey to you the local awe of the undergraduate before 1914. In those days they all wore cap and gowns and the apocryphal air of learning they diffused humbugged the townspeople to such an extent that what with the 'cleverness' and the 'class' of the young men they almost went in fear and trembling.

I shared that feeling to some extent, but there was no respect in my awe or in any of the gang of which I was a member. The 'toffs' (our term for them) were never particularly generous to us. Once, my brother and I earned sixpence fielding tennis balls for them on Downing grounds; and I remember my ninth birthday [1912] as a beano because with others I scrambled for cake thrown to us by them out of a window and got a piece; significant as an indication of their lavishness. Our usual greeting was the long-drawn chant 'Hello, Sproggins (it was always Sproggins), when are you going d-o-o-w-w-w-n?' to which they sometimes responded with 'Catch the little devils' … but they never did … . And we hurt their dignity. Now, I realise just how much. 'Carry your bag, sir' sidling up to one. 'N-o-o-o', in a high-falutin' voice. 'Toss you off for tuppence, sir?' with a lewd grin; and the bubble was burst. Even then I could sense their discomfiture. …

Now, to come to the point. Any of those students might have been the father of this public-school teacher and it is inconceivable that he could have envisaged his offspring arguing with one of that gang of microbes. But it has happened and it is a sign of change of such magnitude that it's worth thinking — and writing — about. …

Monday 10 August. There was an Alert last night at 12.15 a.m. lasting about an hour. Uneasy about the planes passing over, I got up; so did the children, but Jess stayed abed ... After a walk outside and finding it quiet, I decided to go back to bed; so we chanced it and did so. ...

Double summer time ended yesterday. It's blackout again now round about 9 o'clock. Makes one think of the winter.

What about the war? Well, there's trouble in India. Gandhi has been arrested with some other leaders, which I think is an unwise move .... Rebellion and revolts are breaking out. We'll certainly not be able to hold India down with one hand and fight the Japs there with the other. And effective co-operation doesn't seem possible. ... German troops are advancing in South Russia, which means Russian troops are retreating. ...

Tuesday 11 August. A warning last night: 1.10 a.m. till 1.50. We didn't get up; and I didn't hear the 'Raiders Passed' signal. ... I went after some horse flesh at 7.00 this morning and met nine buses on each other's tails on Mill Road taking workers to work; war workers, I suppose. Men gossiping in shop doorways looked Victorianish and the scene, so much life at such an early hour, women in overalls as well as men, and smoking too, as they walked along, seemed in keeping with wartime. ...

The Americans have taken the offensive in the Pacific: Solomon Islands. ... All I hear is grumbles about the war. And everybody seems to be a communist, unbelievable though it might seem. Certainly people are sick of our setbacks. ...

Wednesday 12 August. A warning last night: 2.00 a.m. till 2.45 a.m. We didn't get up. There was nothing doing locally. Round the Backs today: soldiers (airforce men) doing the dead march; and some of them doing physical training. ...

Thursday 13 August. A warning last night: 2.30 a.m. till 3.30 a.m. We didn't get up; but I feel uneasy about it. According to reports the explosive fire bombs that are being used call for one being on the alert. ...

Sunday 16 August. ... [In a letter to Neil Bell Jack wrote:]

> I've always been a teetotaller and non-smoker. In the beginning my father urged me to be; and as a small boy I always did as he said. (I was very loyal; too loyal I believe now.) Then my beery

family sickened me of booze; so did a beery neighbourhood. Another thing, and enough to help me along as a youth: everybody seemed to smoke and drink; well, let 'em; I'd be different. So I grew up with it thoroughly out of my system. ... But I'm no crank about it. I buy chaps drinks and give cigarettes as presents. Every man to his liking. Sometimes, feel glad about it e.g. when I read what Wells had to say about the harmful effects of drinking and smoking in *The Science of Life*; when I hear smokers coughing their guts up; and when I look in to the bleary, dazed eyes of a sozzled man or woman. They're not living then; not really; and I'm sorry for them. Perhaps you've guessed it: I've an acute sense of awareness of myself and my surroundings; and I wouldn't be robbed of this for anything. And I've got my appetite in the mornings, getting some of those pleasures of taste drinkers tell me I lose the night before ... Don't forget too, that first and last in my life — and it takes precedence over everything — writing, reading, sex and the rest of it — I'm a swimmer, right to the marrow of my bones; and smoking is definitely bad for the wind; ... I can think of no greater pleasure than swimming along in a green-banked stream with the sun shining down ... then soaking the sun into my body on the bank. ---

Why am I so keen on a degree? It's probably my plebeian nature at work: apeing my betters. But I don't want to keep [remain] a snob and a degree is still a qualification for a job in this rum world of ours; and likely to be in my time. Those two things apart, I've only been at it six years and think I'm on the last lap; while I've been writing for 26 years; and I never go back; I always plough forward. Once I start retreating I'm finished; I know that; so I don't mean to give an inch while I can gasp. ...

Sunday 16 August. I went with Jess [daughter] to Haslingfield to buy her a secondhand travelling trunk for when she goes away. Got it for half a crown [2s 6d]: and from such a queer couple living in a caravan in the corner of a field. They had numerous cats and dogs and a horse and an old fellow showed me inside his home: an untidy bedroom littered with bedclothes and a hot, stuffy little kitchenette. He also showed us the old-fashioned carriage he got in when there was an Alert; why he gets in it I don't know as it's obviously no safer than the caravan; not so safe. He called this carriage a hearse and it very well might be. It was a primitive way of living and something like the old-fashioned squatters lived at the time of the enclosure acts, I should say. ...

Monday 17 August. An Alert last night; 11.45 p.m. till 12.15 a.m. We didn't get up, waiting to see if the guns went off. It was very quiet, but immediately the 'All Clear' sounded bombers roared over for an hour. We thought these must be Germans, the time being too late for ours to start out and too early to return home. We heard today that the RAF and the Americans were manoeuvring; don't know how true it is. ...

Tuesday 18 August. ... The graduates still can't get over some of the things I said ... And a most heinous offence on my part was to call Rupert Brooke's poem 'Grantchester' a lot of doggerel. So it is. There's bits in it a kid could write better. Frank told them today he dare say I knew and liked Grantchester as much as Brooke. I dare say, as I lived near it for 13 years and I don't suppose he lived there any longer than 13 months; ... I still think Brooke died himself into fame; and that Winston Churchill helped him on by his dramatic 'Rupert Brooke is dead' remark at the time. To jar them a bit more I told Frank to tell them that once I get on the go I'll write Brooke right off the map as far as Grantchester is concerned. I'll write half-a-dozen books about the place that'll so eclipse his poem that it's my name and not his that will be identified with the place in the future! ...

Wednesday 19 August. ... We've made a super-commando raid on occupied France, landing at Dieppe. Fighting still continues, with the Canadians doing most of it according to all accounts.[21] I suppose there will be several hundred casualties and then in less than a week a withdrawal: result nil.

Another note in about firewatching. I've got to fix up two others to do a four-hour spell on Thursday nights. I bought my monthly ration of a half-pound of chocolates last Saturday and gave them to Jess [his wife]. Next month we're to get three ounces a week. But fats and sugar and meat rations are

---

[21] The raid on Dieppe, launched on 19 August, was designed primarily to test the German coastal defences. It was ill conceived and had little chance of success.

to be cut down. We're being recommended to eat more potatoes: good for the figure --- so they say.

Friday 21 August. The Dieppe raid is over. We achieved a lot according to the press, but blessed if I can see it. Don't want to see it, perhaps!

Young Jess had fixed up to do a night's firewatching at the County Girls' School last night, and not wanting her to tramp lonely roads these days at night time I went with her to the school. She had her mother's trousers on and we walked, I pushing her bike so that she could ride home in the morning, Jock following. It was moonlight, bombers continually passing over, but we couldn't pick them out; they were ours; or, we thought so. When we got to the school we couldn't make anybody hear and after ringing the bell and trying the door, came away again. I was very pleased to do so, not wanting her to stop there all night. Where the caretakers, regular firewatcher (male) and the other girl that had promised to turn up had got to I didn't know and didn't care; she'd done her bit by going. We got home just before 11.00, tired after the day's work and the long walk. ...

Sunday 23 August. There was a warning last night just after we got to bed: 10.45 p.m. till 11.35 p.m. ...

At home, while having supper, we heard a bit on the wireless that was laughable. It followed a musical programme and had something to do with the British army; normally, that would have been turned off, but too lazy to get up over it while in the kitchen it was allowed to drag on: drum music, talking and shouting the odds generally. Now and again we caught snatches and just before the end we heard something to the effect that Great Britain was not military-minded. I said of course; that's why we'd held India in subjection for so long; ... [Then we heard] 'Salute to the British army (or was it soldiers?) for their victories over the Germans in the Great War, Salute to the' and so on and so on 'for their victories over Napoleon, Salute for ... Marlborough, Salute to the Bowmen of

England'. --- We laughed then and spoiled the rest, but heard the finale --- 'Salute to the British Army'.[22] ...

The 'Rule Britannia' stuff dies slowly; but nevertheless, it is dying; slowly, but surely. ...

Monday 24 August. There was a warning last night: 10.15 p.m. till 11.55 p.m. The pubs had just turned out when the siren went and people stood about gossiping and laughing without taking notice of the Alert. Planes went over and they sounded like enemy ones. Then there was a row at the top of Gothic Street. Not a scorcher like some of them, but a tidy one with a good bit of bad language. It closed with somebody turning the conversation, saying that he (Jerry) was over here a fortnight ago, nearly landing on Parker's Piece: he must have been after his (the speaker's) cheese ration. It's queer how people adjust themselves to war. There was always the chance of a bomb coming down, but they carried on with their petty little quarrels as though there wasn't a war on.

A punt round the secondhand shops this afternoon to buy Jack a jacket. Got a pretty decent one for 10*s*; lucky; and he paid for it out of his earnings at Chivers'. ... Coupons don't have to be given for secondhand clothes up to 51*s*. ...

Tuesday 25 August. ... Mrs Sale thinks Alan Sale, her son, might shortly have to go abroad. I read the letter he sent her: a manly letter, saying he would always think of her lovingly and she was to look on the bright side: it made me feel sad: how glad we shall all be when this wretched war is over. ...

Wednesday 26 August. There was an Alert last night as I sat at work on the novel; about 10.15 p.m. It lasted under half an hour. The Duke of Kent was killed yesterday.[23] The *Herald* gave it front-page prominence, but I noticed they were very reserved about it in the leading article; ...

---

[22] *Salute to the British Army* was a morale-boosting programme broadcast from 8.45 to 9.00 p.m. on the Forces Programme. There were other programmes of the same type throughout the year.

[23] The King's youngest brother, the Duke of Kent, held the rank of Air Commodore in the RAF and was killed in a plane crash in Scotland while flying to Iceland.

Thursday 27 August. ... Also a long letter from Neil Bell about my review of his book. [Jack had written about 2,500 words on Bell's *Peek's Progress* in the middle of August.] He said this was first-rate and paid me some flattering compliments. Finished up by saying: 'There remains a mystery: why you're still unpublished. It's the war: there's no other sane answer. But you will be: no doubt at all there.' ... He also said 'Quite obviously you could this very minute step in to a job as a professional reviewer in any paper and hold it'. I wondered if he were kidding me (suspicious devil!) but Frank Edwards thinks not. Said he wouldn't waste time writing me letters in the way he does unless he had faith in me. Well, there's something in that. And sometimes I feel I deserve a bit of praise. I don't get much for all my failures! The world has no room for anybody except those at the top. And there's quite a lot of people who could win swimming championships — if they tried; I've just tried and shown that I couldn't. And there's quite a lot of people who could pass examinations for a degree first time — if they tried: and I've just tried and shown that I couldn't. And there's quite a lot of people that could write novels and get them published; I've just tried and shown that I couldn't. And look at the trashy novels that are published; if mine aren't published they must be duds --- and so on *ad infinitum.* Poor old me!

I went to work early and did 26*s* worth by 11.30, when I left off, hurried home, had dinner and a wash and with Jack caught the 12.15 p.m. bus to St Neots. A lovely, hot, summer's day; and we had a fine time. ... Had minerals in a pub on the way to the river (the Ouse): four dips in the river, eating our tea in between times: ...

We talked to a fellow named Smith lying on the bank, and he told us that the electric company buildings where he worked (we could see the chimney stacks) were bombed, cannon-shelled and machine-gunned about 18 months ago by a lone raider in broad daylight; no-one was hurt, although 300 worked at the place, and little damage was done; ... The chap said he was a communist; was from Glasgow; and growled at the upper classes wanting men to risk their lives at 2*s* a day; said he would be in the front of a revolution; and prophesied that it would come. We left the river just after 5.00 and going into the town had a walk round Woolworth's, bought some apples and a big jam tart each and ate them in a churchyard; then went into a pub for a grapefruit (lot of grapefruit in it!) and a fish and chip shop for a bait of fish and chips (6*d* piece of fish each, 4*d* chips for Jack, 2*d* chips for me). Got home again just before 8.00, when we went to the Sheds and had another dip. ...

This is my firewatching night. Now for a bit of work on the novel. ...

Saturday 29 August. ... There was an Alert this afternoon from 1.56 to 2.31. I was surprised to hear the siren go off ... [a warden] said a bomb had been dropped in a field at Histon; no damage done, no casualties. He thought they were trying for Chivers' factory. The newspaper told the same story tonight, without naming places. ...

Sunday 30 August. ... Read a bit of Pepys' *Diary* and am beginning to like him. War news is all about the defence of Stalingrad and the Caucasus. Will they hold? seems to be the question. ...

Monday 31 August. ... When I came home tonight I picked up the *Cambridge Daily News*. It contained the result of the Higher School Certificate and eagerly I looked at the results, my heart thumping. Alas, Jess's name wasn't there. It thoroughly upset me. --- ...

Jess was on the river with the Cashes. She cried when she heard the news. I told her to pluck up, she's got nothing to cry for. And she hadn't. She worked like a Trojan, tried hard, and if she failed well, dammit, she did her best, and nobody could do more. I hope she can weather it, take the clout and punch back. After all, character can be moulded on failure as well as success. To help her I recited some of my own failures and setbacks. ...

September 1942

Thursday 3 September. We were awakened last night round about 1 o'clock by gunfire: a Bofor[s] (probably Parker's Piece) and heavies (probably Grantchester). The siren didn't sound. I thought I heard a bomber going over. Jack and Jess came down and lay on our bed for a little while and then as it was quiet after a burst or two they went back to bed and I again went to sleep; ...

So we enter today the fourth year of the war. It's been a day of national prayer. Saw and heard Dr Temple, the Archbishop of Canterbury, on the pictures tonight: it was all the Empire, the Allies, the King and the Lord's Prayer. Of course, it would be. ... The film we saw (I went with the Jesses) was called *One of our Aircraft is Missing* [1942].[24] Propaganda. Some of it silly. Germans portrayed as windy cowards as our bombers bombed them in Holland; the Dutch delighted in being bombed by the RAF. ---

Saturday 5 September. ... [Jess's] boy-friend Don Varley got a County Major scholarship to Trinity College on the result of the Higher School Certificate examination. ...

Tuesday 8 September. ... I thought the siren would go off. So it did. The noise after the pubs turned out had hardly died down when it started: the warning lasted from 10.40 p.m. till 11.55 p.m. Raiders passed over; bombed Bedford according to a German claim; and the guns went off. Jess [his wife] thought she heard shrapnel falling and hitting the window like fine rain; ... I got up after Jack and [daughter] Jess came into our room; and as Jess's [wife's] head was so bad I bathed it in hot water. ...

[Evening] Feel very tired after finishing my day's writing; hope to get a good night's rest. The hope of everybody these days.

Wednesday 9 September. There was a warning last night round about 11.00 p.m. lasting until just before 12.00 p.m. We got up after hearing enemy planes going over followed by a couple of heavy crumps. Going outside to the surface shelter we saw the sky lit by flares Madingley way. ... They went out, planes

---

[24] *One of our Aircraft is Missing* was made by Michael Powell and Emeric Pressburger; it recounts the fortunes of the crew of a bomber returning from a raid on Stuttgart, and forced to bale out over Holland. Befriended by Dutch people, they make a dangerous return to Britain. The last scene is of their taking off for a new raid on Germany.

kept droning over, but the guns, firing earlier, had stopped. Suddenly, the sky Barton way flamed a dull red, flickered and returned to normal: starlight. Soon afterwards the 'Raiders Passed' signal sounded and we went back to bed. We heard today that the bombs were dropped on an experimental farm: Madingley; and a bomber was brought down at Orwell (that was the red light in the sky), all the crew of five being killed. ... It's 10 o'clock [p.m.] and I can hear our bombers on the way to Germany. ...

Thursday 10 September. We all went to London today for an outing; 8s 9d railway fare for each of us; next month excursions end. We had a look round; went and had a swim at Marshall Street baths; then had a look round Selfridge's bargain basement; not many bargains there now though. The shops were full of eatables and we had a blow-out. Coming home I rowed with a smoker in the train; his wife wanted the window shut; I wanted him to put his pipe out: he wouldn't, so the window kept open. All rather childish, but I'm bludgeoned into doing too many things I don't want to do by the State these days, without putting up with any Tom, Dick and Harry riding roughshod over me.

Friday 11 September. ... I had a letter from the Ministry of Labour today giving me six months' exemption from call-up. The ban is now removed from the *Daily Worker*.[25] I've just read a copy of the new issue. Not like the old. It seemed strange that it should be all for the government instead of against it. Frank Edwards said they've got to do it to be published. I said better remain unpublished and retain their laurels. I shall soon cancel my order for it. ...

Sunday 13 September. ... Ten of us walked to the Red Lion at Grantchester and we had tea. We shied for walnuts coming home at the trees near Charterhouse Terrace; plenty fell, but not quite ripe.

---

[25] The *Daily Worker*, a communist newspaper, was suppressed under wartime regulations by the Home Secretary Herbert Morrison from January 1941 to September 1942, for allegedly undermining the war effort. Jack's mention of 'the first few copies' on 24 September refers to its renewed publication.

Monday 14 September. ... [Jess, Jack's wife] passed the place where the bomber was brought down the other night on her round today. She heard comments about it; only two bodies found, chaps of 18 and 20; bits of others were spread over a wide area and one woman related how a friend of hers while crossing a field found a finger with a LOVELY ring on it!

Tuesday 15 September. ... I've completed my quota for the day of the book I'm writing ... . The day's date reminds me of Sunday, 15 September 1940, the day when 187 German bombers were brought down at the end of the Battle of Britain.[26] I didn't record this day in the diary but remember it well: Eric came down and we (the family) spent a quiet day beside the river at Paradise. Peter Brading, Jack, Tom Cash, Gerald Best and Jess [daughter] sat and sang, accompanied by a ukelele, round a camp fire there that evening. Later that evening Eric, Frank Edwards and I went into the Northern Hotel for a drink and while there the radio gave out that 180-odd bombers had been brought down that day; the people, men and women, in the lounge clapped. ...

Wednesday 16 September. As I type the 'All Clear' is sounding. The siren sounded the warning at 9.30 p.m. and it is now just after 10.00. The last notes die away in a mournful wail. ---
...I can hear our fighters going over. ---

Thursday 17 September. I saw a drunken American sergeant, pistol in holster round his backside like any swaggering Jesse James, making overtures to different women — any one would do — today. ... Went to see *How Green was my Valley* with Jess. Fine. One of the best pictures I've ever seen.[27]

I am reading a couple of chapters of a sociological book a journalist that comes into the shop has written and can't get published. I don't wonder. Strikes me as pompous, pretentious rubbish. When three words will do instead of one, he uses them. ... I hardly know what it's about; and what I do

---

[26] On 15 September 1940, afterwards celebrated as 'Battle of Britain Day', it was claimed that the Luftwaffe lost 185 aircraft. The claim was due to mistaken counting, not mendacity. German losses were in fact 62 aircraft.

[27] The film, based on Richard Llewellyn's novel of the same title, concerned coalmining in South Wales and gave a sympathetic view of the miners themselves.

know I disagree with. Don't know what to say when I hand it back.

I've written 50,000 words of the book: still unnamed. Jess bought a couple of towels for [her daughter] Jess to take away with her [to Avery Hill Training College]: 9s 11d each. Spoke to Frank Edwards about it: six towels represent his week's wages.

Friday 18 September. Stalingrad fills the news. And there is now some speculation of what will happen if it falls.[28] ...

Monday 21 September. We saw Jess off at the station this morning for Avery Hill. ... This afternoon I walked to the shop ... and did a pretty good day's work. But I was heavy-hearted, being chockful of memories: Jess as a little girl, growing up, a thousand scenes; finally, I went down to the cellar and wept. ... With Jess going away a phase of my family life seemed to have ended. ---

... Jack got a distinction in French today. Hip, pip, etc!

Thursday 24 September. ... Just had a walk round the houses with the dogs. There's a glorious harvest moon. I could hear bombers passing over, probably ours, although there were repeated flashes.

Stalingrad still holds.

Lady Astor's on the go again about [how] Russia is fighting for herself and the British communists are Russia's worst enemies. The *Daily Worker,* which is improving since the first few copies, says 'Lock her up' in the leader, a sign of progress, anyway.

Friday 25 September. Went to Lyons for tea with Jess and Jack; but the cupboard was bare; so we just had a cup of tea and a look round the town and had tea at home.

Tuesday 29 September. ... I went to Mrs Wonfer's in Gothic Street today to take a pair of shoes home. She's one of the two

---

[28] The battle of Stalingrad, the turning-point of the war, began in the summer of 1942 as German troops advanced towards the city on the Volga. In September both Hitler and Stalin forbade their armies to retreat. In the next three months occurred the fiercest fighting of the war, in the streets of the city. After the encirclement of the German armies in November, the struggle ended with their surrender in January 1943.

remaining in the street since I lived there and I had a look at the illuminated address presented to her through the death of her son Cecil, killed at Devils Wood in the last war. ... She showed me a large commemorative medal, also; and there was his 1914–15 Star and two war medals framed, ... She then told me of her husband's desertion of her during the last war and wept a little. It was sad and I apologised for evoking such unhappy memories; but she smiled through her tears and said it was all right; and I think she meant it, knowing I was sympathetic. And I was; only too true I was, poor woman. ...

A letter in tonight's paper from a CO turned down by the tribunal. He said he was still free and would be if the Appellate Tribunal decided against him—free to go to prison! Somebody else wrote a letter about the surface shelters; said they were as free from ventilation as a frog is from feathers; he was told there will be no door so fresh air can get in; very likely, but where foul air will get out is what puzzles him. ...

Wednesday 30 September. ... A lot of talk again about the Second Front. The *Daily Worker* and the communists are whipping up people's enthusiasm for it. Churchill said in Parliament today that nearly half the force at Dieppe was lost. I took that as a warning to the public to leave well alone; and maybe it will act as a saver for Churchill when things go wrong. He can then say 'I told you so'. Frank Edwards thinks it will come off or why continue the war; that's why it's being continued for the American and British armies to have a go. He also thinks it will be mass slaughter. Well, if the Second Front takes place the war will soon end .The casualty list will be so high that what with the people's moral[e] being so low, it can't be off it [it can't be ignored?]. ...

October 1942

Thursday 1 October. On the novel again; and made a fresh start on examination work. ...

Friday 2 October. ... Stalingrad still fighting back.

Saturday 3 October. ... Went to a Boy Scouts fete at the County School; really at Don Varley's invitation; ... I guessed the weight of the cake, the name of the doll, the age and weight of the rabbit—all wrong. Took part in the treasure hunt—and didn't find the treasure (half a crown). Knocked the top hat off Ken Snelson, Don's friend, as he walked behind a screen, but it cost me a bob at a penny a time to do it because of a lot of narrow misses. I flung darts at potatoes suspended on string—and missed (Bert speared them twice). I tossed tennis balls in a pail and saw them bounce out. I went in the wrong end of the ghost hole and howled to frighten the ghosts—and was turned out; tried the other end and it was shut down. Paid a penny to see where the pretty young lady (as depicted in the painting on a card hung outside the tent) had her operation and after peering into a little cigar box lit up by electric light for the purpose and read[ing] the words 'Addenbrooke's Hospital' printed inside it, realised I'd been sold a pup—for one penny. Still, I enjoyed the outing and it provided me with good story material, as I'm always finding it difficult to name the games played at fêtes.

Sunday 4 October. Jess registered for firewatching this morning at the Newnham School; she went off cursing; and at midday a lady called and asked her if she would join the WVS (Women's Voluntary Service) and undertake to give tea in this street to air-raid victims …, and she would, I believe, have committed herself had not the lady said that perhaps she was disturbing our dinner and she would call later. I've talked it over with Jess; she has a home and family to see after, works for the Prudential, has now to do firewatching, all on poor food and under the stress and anxiety of wartime condition—raids and the rest of it: no, she's not undertaking to do work of that sort; she has enough, and more than enough, to do already. Lately she's lost a lot of weight and will need looking after herself unless I keep a watchful eye on her, let alone looking after other people. …

Tuesday 6 October. … I told Jack tonight he must be in by blackout. Don't like to lay down the law, but though he's big in size he's young in years and I fear for his moral as well as his physical well-being. Suppose the siren sounds and the guns start blazing and he has to come home through shell-fire. And suppose he starts straying a bit under wartime conditions. I don't want him to burn his fingers before he knows where he is. …

Saturday 10 October. ... India is in the news.[29] Imperialist Britain hanging on like grim death. Our newspapers shout about the number of Norwegians and others the Germans are executing; I wonder how many are being executed in India. ... And Stalingrad is still resisting.

There was a warning this morning: 8.20 till 8.35 a.m. There was nothing doing here, but Jess heard an enemy plane was brought down at --- now she doesn't know if it was Ramsey (Hunts) or Ramsgate!...

Sunday 11 October. ... I don't think I mentioned that Neil Bell was kind enough to send Frank Edwards a copy of *Peek's Progress* in return for a tin of Four Square tobacco Frank sent him as an appreciation of the pleasure he got in reading Bell's *Tower of Darkness*. ...

Have I recorded that when there's a raid it's my diary I always collar. We leave money in the house, but take the diary! But it's part of us. I can earn some more money, but that's not replaceable ... .

Tuesday 13 October. ... German prisoners taken by us at Dieppe were tied; Germany as reprisals has tied up some of the British troops they have as prisoners; now Britain has tied up German prisoners as a reprisal for that reprisal. So it goes on.[30] ...

Wednesday 14 October. ... A man speaking to me about the Russians holding Stalingrad said 'that's the way to fight for your country'. I had a good mind to say 'fight for yourself', but let it go. The twist would have been lost on him as he believes he's part of this country, whereas I don't, of course. ...

Thursday 15 October. I heard the reveille sounded for the soldiers this morning. The town's full of them again. It reminded me of the last war.

---

[29] In 1942, as the Japanese threatened India from the east, the Congress Party increased its demands for independence in the 'Quit India' movement. But insurgency was suppressed by the British, sometimes brutally.

[30] German allegations that their soldiers captured in raids on Dieppe and Sark were bound, contrary to the Geneva Convention, led to the manacling of Canadian and British captives, and further reprisals by both sides. The matter was eventually resolved through the good offices of the Swiss government.

There is Civil Defence practice going on outside tonight. This is my firewatching night, so I was luffed [cajoled] in for it a bit between 8.30 and 9.00 p.m. Three of us put out smoke bombs at the sound of a whistle with a stirrup pump and water. The first time (in Doric Street) the bomb wasn't out properly as the chap handling the pump gave it another dose. Suddenly, Jack watching, said 'What's he doing?' I said 'Putting the bomb out'. He grinned and said 'Puzzle him; here it is' and showed it to me. I nearly collapsed with laughter, took it from him and when the cry went up 'Lost bomb' dropped it near enough to the spot where it was supposed to be to avoid suspicion. Twice more the whistle went and we hurried off (I lugging two pails of water each time) and put out a bomb in Panton Street and another at the corner of Pemberton Terrace. They were off our beat, but we were the smarties and outshined the others. …

Friday 16 October. … To save coal I put a new firebrick in the fireplace yesterday and cemented it round. Made a workman-like job of it. The typewriter fell out of my bike basket a couple of days ago. And it still works! A big day's snobbing today; but I've done my quota of the novel.

Sunday 18 October. I went out with Frank Edwards on his tandem this morning: to Hardwick, where we called on my nephew Henry and his wife Olive. He played a guitar and mouth organ, both at the same time, to us, and ranted against authority, particularly over his objections to vaccination, in real Overhill fashion. When I heard him I thought there must be something in the breed: all the Overhills object to authority: I mentioned it to Jess and she said yes, they were just ag'in everything … .

Monday 19 October. … Tonight I have had a quiet hour or more reading through many of his [Don Varley's] examination notes and essays. … As far as I can judge his education has given him a big start over myself. He is better informed than I was at 18. Perhaps, I knew more about life and less about literature, art and economics. …

Tuesday 20 October. All on my own. Jess at the pictures, Jack at the Band of Hope. Just been listening to some musical comedy memories on the wireless. The pieces were fine, especially one about the 'aggravating moon' which came out in 1909. I think the old ones the best. I would like a good gramophone selection of them; and of the many ballads I like.

Wednesday 21 October. Don Varley brought a book to the shop for me today on the English Constitution by Maurice Amos.[31] ... Carrying on our Sunday evening talk where we left off, I said ... that it was believed that he [Edward VII] made a lot of money through dealing in armament shares. As an interesting book on these things I recommended *The Merchants of Death.*[32]...

Thursday 22 October. Jess sent us a photo of herself today, which helped to break the monotony of the day's doings. ...

Saturday 24 October. Jess and I chased all over the town this afternoon to buy a doormat. Jess got one at last up Mill Road on her own as I came another way to get the Sunday joint (shops close early these days having nothing to sell). The cost of the mat was a few coppers short of 10s, but cost isn't taken into account now, the buyer is always glad to get it—whatever it is he (or she) wants.

Tuesday 27 October. As I sat working in the shop this afternoon I had one of my occasional fits of gloom; I was suddenly aware of the rich gift of Nature: LIFE; and how it is squandered; not, however, through any fault of our own, but through the faulty workings of an obsolete social system. ---

Thursday 29 October. ... Stalingrad holds; the Eighth Army is attacking in Egypt ...; the Americans and the Japs are still at it in the Solomons; it's difficult to assess what's going on in the Pacific. ...

Friday 30 October. ... Among other things he [Don Varley] suggested to her [Jess, Jack's wife] that she bought me a suit. She had a good laugh; so did I; he's a lad. ...

Saturday 31 October. ... There's a lot of American soldiers in the town. A rum-looking lot.

[31] *The English Constitution* [1930].
[32] H. C. Engelbrecht and F. C. Hanighen, *Merchants of Death: A Study of the International Armament Industry* (1942).

November 1942

Sunday 1 November. Funny I should mention the American soldiers in these notes yesterday, for last night while I was having a bath in the kitchen, a couple of them, three parts drunk, hearing a piano playing in the house (Jack was playing) opened the front door and walking along the dark passage tried to get into the kitchen. At the sound of their voices Jess pressed the door back and kept it shut. They were swearing and inquiring about somebody called Gilmor, and she told them to scare them off that she'd got a dog in the kitchen and they replied that they had one out there. Wet, I hopped out of the bath and pulled on my overcoat; then I opened the door and told them they were in a private house and mumbling the pair withdrew. To cap the affair, Jess fainted! But she soon pulled round. …

Wednesday 4 November. … I received a notice from the Board of Trade today to say I have been registered as a shoe-repairer. … [Frank Edwards] said he's driving Italian prisoners backwards and forwards in a lorry to their work on farms. …

Thursday 5 November. … our troops have won a big victory in Egypt. … This time instead of shouting the odds and not doing the stuff we've done the stuff and haven't shouted --- till now! And now the enemy is beaten according to the old women shouting to one another over their backyard walls. …

Friday 6 November. Jess, Jack and I went to see the much advertised picture *Gone with the Wind* last night. It was a trite story; too much of the same thing; … It lasted about four hours; and we sat in the picture house three quarters of an hour before it started and paid 2*s* 6*d* for the cheapest seats. I certainly grudged the money and the time.[33]

Saturday 7 November. … Last week I thought of the title of my next book: 'Prisoner in the Pie'. It will be the story of a provincial bookmaker. I've had it in mind a long while.

---

[33] The colour film from the novel of the same title by Margaret Mitchell combined romance and the American Civil War. Though very successful at the box-office its sympathetic view of 'American values' was certain to be unappealing to Jack.

Frank Edwards thinks it's possible that the Germans are letting us advance in Egypt so that we can get into a stronger military position to talk peace terms with them. I've seen this suggested — I believe in *Peace News*. There might be something in it.

Monday 9 November. Fred came round to the shop this morning about young Fred's exemption form for his call-up, which I wrote and told him to get yesterday. … [Tonight] young Fred, who is 18¼ and registered for military service on Saturday, came round to fill in the form. He handled a pen like a truncheon, jabbed out the letters, chucked blots, spelled words wrong and didn't trouble much. I told him not to treat the authorities with too much indifference, they might resent it --- with consequences disastrous to him. I added that it was all a very serious thing, perhaps a matter of life and death, but I don't think he was very impressed. Boys are like that. I wished him luck.

Tuesday 10 November. Churchill says he isn't the king's first minister to see the liquidation of the British Empire. What we own we hold. ---

[In the morning] a chap named Mark Horner gave me a look in. He's nearly blind and after much effort and the enlistment of the aid and signatures of six doctors is to be aided in becoming a masseur. He has to pass an education test and wanted to know if I would give him a hand with some practice essays. Of course, I said yes.

Wednesday 11 November. Poppy Day. No, I didn't buy one. Have never done so and don't intend. Such spurious patriotism helps to perpetuate wars.

Today I saw where I was heading with the novel I'm writing: Nowhere. So I changed the theme. Very few alterations were needed and now it's a book about myself and E.T.O. [Jack's father]. One I'd always wanted to write. In writing the background of a book about twins, one being honest and hardworking and getting nowhere and the other being dishonest and getting somewhere by the time they were 40, I wrote so much about their father (my father) that he dominated the book. Here was my chance and I switched over. Now I can see where I'm going, which I couldn't before, and think I'll make a good book of it. The book about the twins I'll do later, probably in association with the examination swindle.

Thursday 12 November. ... Heard from the income-tax authorities. No allowance is made in respect of a mortgage; mortgage interest charge; or war damage insurance; so really a person pays income tax on money they never receive; e.g. a man paying £20 war insurance on property is liable for income tax at 10s in the £ on it, so the insurance really costs £30 and not £20. Obviously, this is taxation gone mad; no system that promotes it can possibly last.

Today, Jess heard an old man question a girl of about 12 in the street: had she got over her fright? Then, what did the soldier say to her? The soldier wanted to take her on the Fen. What for? For dick. For what? For dick. And she made an old-fashioned gesture. The bad, wicked man, he said. ...

Sunday 15 November. The church bells were rung today to honour our victory in Egypt.[34] A bit of Churchillian melodrama; he loves it. I believe Britain's success in North Africa of more strategic importance than the destruction of a few Axis divisions indicates and that if we can manage to clear the enemy out of North Africa it will have far-reaching effects on the war, but to celebrate victory with 240 Axis divisions still fighting in Russia is rather premature. I liked to hear the bells, however. They rang as we lay abed (we were up late) and sounded very Sundayfied and old-timish. Bow bells also rang on the wireless between programmes this morning. May the bells soon ring in peace, but before that happens there's to be much fighting done yet. The newspapers today talk of conscription of married women with no children for the forces and an extended age-limit for them; and further comb-outs of men in unessential industries. ...

---

[34] The church bells were rung to mark the victory at El Alamein of the Eighth Army under Montgomery over Rommel's Afrika Korps. Forces in Egypt at this time were British and Commonwealth 195,000 and German and Italian 154,000. On the Eastern Front Germany and the USSR both had more than 6,000,000 troops. Jack's contention about the importance of the desert victory is questionable.

Tuesday 17 November. ... [In the evening] after a walk round the houses in the moonlight with the dogs I settled down to the book and did the usual 1500 words.

Friday 20 November. ... I've just been round Brooklands Avenue with the dogs. Moonlight glowing golden on the edge of the clouds, the evening mild; and still, except for our bombers roaring off on a raid, following one another at about a minute intervals.

Monday 23 November. The war is going better for Britain and today a man asked me if it would be over by Christmas. I said there was a leading article in the *Daily Herald* which said that many people were in prison for spreading despondency, but many should also be there for spreading complacency.

Tuesday 24 November. Cabinet reshuffled: Morrison in, Cripps out. A bit of Churchill wangling. Cripps' stock was high after he came back from Russia: it fell owing to his mission to India being a failure; and since then he has failed in the House of Commons because of his policy to bring the Tories and Labourites in step by his suggestion that the former should speed up and the latter slow down in their policies. Thus the moment was ripe for machiavellian moves on the part of the Prime Minister to remove a formidable rival. I always thought Cripps was specially selected to go to India to bring about his downfall. Churchill knew no Englishman could solve the Indian problem satisfactorily to himself or the Indian and English people; it would want a magician to do that at present; and so Cripps has gradually fallen in favour and he is turned out of the Cabinet without a word from anyone. What changes are wrought by time.

Wednesday 25 November. Now the Russians are attacking and according to the papers have the Germans on the run round Stalingrad! ...

Thursday 26 November. There's another lot of evacuees next door ... .

Friday 27 November. ... I think there will be an armistice with Germany and Italy by Christmas next year whatever happens about the fighting. The people will be ready for it by then and that's what ends wars.

Saturday 28 November. I had a walk round the town with Jess this afternoon; almost a strange place nowadays, as there's nothing to buy without coupons; and everything is marked up at excessive prices; much more than I can afford. The Government wants to stop people spending to stop inflation; it's effective where I'm concerned; but, there, my earnings go in other ways. …

Yesterday the French sank their own fleet at Toulon, as it is reported that Jerry was after it.[35] We hail it as a victory. Maybe, but I still remember the French as our ally, and in that sense it's a loss.

December 1942

Wednesday 2 December. The Beveridge Report is out.[36] There is much comment in the papers about it. It will be contested by the insurance companies; and vested interests of all sorts. I've ordered a copy: 2s: 150,000 words. The Russians are advancing on three fronts. …

Thursday 3 December. Jess was further notified this morning that she'd been enrolled for firewatching duties. …

Friday 4 December. Don Varley looked in at the shop. His first term at Trinity is over. He didn't think anything of Wells's *Love and Mr Lewisham*, which I think is grand and one of the best love stories I've ever read. I lent him my 6*d* copy thinking he'd like it.[37] …

Saturday 5 December. … The Beveridge Report is being much discussed in the papers. My prediction: It will be adopted

---

[35] In November Unoccupied France, nominally under the control of the collaborationist French government at Vichy, was occupied by German troops. On 27 November, as German troops were approaching Toulon, the large French fleet in the naval base was scuttled to deny its use by the Axis.

[36] The *Report on Social Insurance and Allied Services* by a committee under Sir William Beveridge, Warden of University College, Oxford, laid the foundations of the modern Welfare State.

[37] Probably the London Book Company's 'Novel Library' edition (1929).

by the Tories; for if they don't the socialists will do; this will carry the Tories back into power, and discredit the Labour Party; and keep out the Labour Party. The Report will be used as pretext: it is the New Order: and people will believe it is: when really it's only an old order been patched (as the Labour Prime Minister of Australia has already said, adding that the workers are easily satisfied if they accept that in return for the sufferings inflicted on them by this war). And so the old gang will keep in the saddle ... and fascism described as Progress and called State Planning will bolster up Capitalism, when there will be another and greater world war, which will extinguish it, in another quarter of a century: for then it will be ready to be extinguished.

What a gloomy outlook. What a pessimist. ...

Wednesday 9 December. ... Hannen Swaffer said in today's *Daily Herald* that Neil Bell's latest book was one of several lately banned in Ireland. It was too frank. ...

Thursday 10 December. To the pictures with Jess and Jack. Was struck by the remark of Claudette Colbert's. She said men don't get cleverer (for moneymaking) as they get older, they only lose their hair. It made me feel I've paid too little attention to making money to apply myself to other matters, putting up with much shabbiness and shoddiness in consequence. Have I done right? I wonder.

Friday 11 December. ... I saw in tonight's paper a report of Mr Murfitt's attendance before the Eastern Area CO tribunal. He's a farmer I know, about 50, living Royston way, and objects to service in the Home Guard. He was a CO in the last war and [then] sentenced to two years' imprisonment. He was registered CONDITIONAL UPON HIS REMAINING AT WORK ON THE LAND. A face-saver upon the part of the authorities; I mean a condition of that sort. Nevertheless, I was glad they decided to let him alone and wrote him a letter to that effect. Fancy, a CO twice in one lifetime. A sign of progress!

Saturday 12 December. Jess has bought me Fowler's *Modern English Usage* [1926 and many later editions] as a Christmas present. I called in Fred's shop. Young Fred has received his call-up papers for the army for next Tuesday. Fred was very gloomy; said 26 years ago he received his own call-up papers for the army at the same time of year; …

Jack went to Letchworth to play Rugby. His team was defeated after being unbeaten this term. The master had already written up the match as a victory to go in the school magazine!

Sunday 13 December. Last night I finished writing the first volume of the book; about 160,000 words. I shall start on the second volume tomorrow and hope to have written it by the middle of April. I shall not get out a fresh manuscript till I've done this in case I make adjustments. Jack hit on a title after hunting in *Roget's Thesaurus* for a phrase that would adequately cover the theme: 'The Kiss of Judas'. I wrote and told Neil Bell this morning, adding that I didn't yet know if it was any good or not as I HADN'T YET READ IT; I had simply turned on the tap for so long each day. …

The papers are full of reports about the demands for manpower that are likely to be made in the New Year. It sounds ominous in both its particular and general aspects. Sometimes, peace seems as far off as ever. The real struggle at present is taking place in Russia. …

Tuesday 15 December. … Today, I started volume two of 'The Kiss of Judas'. Pipes are being run into the streets of the town from the river in case of a fire blitz. They are a fair size; about a foot in diameter; and they run along the gutter, being sunk under the surface at street openings. …

Wednesday 16 December. There was an Alert last night just after 2.00 a.m. lasting about a quarter of an hour. We heard nothing except some planes go over after the 'All Clear'.

I've just been for a walk with the dogs and hearing a man threatening to fetch a policeman to some little boys carol singing round his door ('Carol singing isn't allowed now,' he said) I called out 'Shame on you, turning the kids away'. He laughed and went in. …

Don Varley came in the shop as I was finishing in semi-darkness this afternoon. … He delayed me till almost dark (I had no bike lamps) with an argument about the British Constitution. … briefly, he defended and I attacked. He taxed me with being biased (as usual) and the talk ended by my saying that many things had not been done in this country preceding the war as our social system was economically at an advantage over the Germans', which had disrupted and produced Hitler and all he stood for, but that didn't mean to say Britain wouldn't be in the same boat before long and that events would not shape themselves in the same way in this country.

Friday 18 December. Jess came home: end of term. ... I called in to see Fred this morning. Young Fred went yesterday [called up into the army] and he was very cut up about it: broke down whilst talking to me. He's a man very fond of his children, concealed by an assumption of roughness that often ill fits him.

Sunday 20 December. Jack has bought me Henry Williamson's *The Beautiful Years* [1921] as a Christmas present. ...

Monday 21 December. It may be wartime, but the Christmas fever is in the house: presents, Christmas cards, planning how to make a cake and pudding on rations and the rest of it. ... I sent Neil Bell a copy of a composition I wrote at evening classes in January, 1918, entitled 'My Opinion of the War'. It's a gem. ... Now for the book.

Wednesday 23 December. Jess [his daughter] has bought me [C. E. M.] Joad's *Guide to Modern Thought* as a Christmas present.[38]

Thursday 24 December. We were awakened last night by a motor starting up in Gothic Street, Mrs C. ... shouting out insults and (presumably) a soldier shouting back. Evidently a lady in Gothic Street had had a late caller and he was rousing the neighbourhood on his departure. ...

Had an argument just before leaving off this afternoon at the shop with a theological student, aged 30, of Westminster College. Too long to repeat; it lasted well over an hour; but I told him the Church in this country and Germany both egged on men to fight in the name of God and the Right; that I didn't think much of the Church's attitude to VD (opposing enlightenment of the public); and that his (and others' like him) interpretation of what God did and didn't want was blasphemy, as he (and they) were subordinating God to themselves; for all any-

---

[38] See note 30, p. 122.

body knew God might want evil and not good in the world. ---

I read in the *Cambridge Daily News* tonight that we're dropping clothing cards on Germany to upset [the] German economy. I sent the cutting to Neil Bell with the words 'You were right. Monty Norman and Dr Schacht have evidently decided against treasury notes'.[39] This, of course, all has to do with the currency theme for a novel and his short story 'The Root of all Evil'.

Friday 25 December. I got up at 7.00; and while making a cup of tea for each of the family to take upstairs to them in bed, serenaded them with carols ... . (I got a shock when I heard as I switched on the wireless that Darlan had been assassinated.)[40] I then lit the fire and went in the water [the river, to swim]; it was moonlight; a full moon shining through mist and making the Causeway road look silverish; there had been a frost; I could just discern the whiteness on the grass (it wasn't quite light) and the cement was frozen and slippery. I gave the custodian [of the swimming pool at Sheep's Green] half a crown for a drink; he gave me a couple of yule logs. Then home again. The family were still in bed. Jess [his daughter] got in my place with Jess. She gave her mother a handbag and necklace she'd made her as Christmas presents; ... Jack said I might become famous in the following manner: 'Jack Overhill, the father of Jack Overhill, the jazz pianist'.

---

[39] Montagu Collet Norman (1871–1950): banker, governor of the Bank of England 1920–1944, advocate of the gold standard and balanced budgets, and therefore widely blamed for recession and unemployment between the two wars. Hjalmar Schacht (1877–1970): financier, 1923 President of the Reichsbank, and founder of a new currency which ended the hyperinflation of the mark—hence Jack's remarks about his opposition to paper currency. In 1939 he was dismissed by Hitler over his disagreement with rearmament expenditure. At the time of Jack's remark Schacht was interned by the Nazis. He was acquitted at the Nuremberg trials.

[40] Admiral François Darlan: a leading member of the Vichy government, he negotiated a ceasefire with the Americans on 10 November after their invasion of French North Africa. Shortly afterwards he defected to the Allied side, a *volte face* which astonished many people. He was assassinated on Christmas Eve by a young French royalist who was trained by the British Special Operations Executive but not acting on its orders: H. Coutau-Bégarie and C. Huan, *Darlan* (Paris, 1989).

Sunday 27 December. … Listened to the *Brains Trust*.[41] Joad was good. And Gould. It's been a quiet Christmas; a nice time; good fare for the fourth Christmas of the war (Jess made a fine cake and mince pies; and we had pork and a rabbit). …

Monday 28 December. The Americans about here talk the English language in a foreign voice. They're a flatfooted, round-shouldered, slouching lot of blokes.

Tuesday 29 December. My fingers are cracking again; so are Jess's. Lack of fats? I've tried cod-liver oil, but it doesn't suit me. Makes me liverish and anything that upsets my liver and digestion upsets my nerves: that's how I've worked it out, anyway.

Thursday 31 December. More snow. Only 34 degrees in the water. … I also met my nephew John. He told me a tale of his effort to get 14 sheets of asbestos for his firm from a local aerodrome. The job took two hours on the spot. He was directed from one to another, all the men (he said) seeming to be in the canteen, or behind tins and doors to be out of the way; all were drinking tea and smoking. …

Just been to see the film *Mrs Miniver* with Jess.[42] Very proper-gandish is all that can be said about it. …

[41] For Cyril Joad and the *Brains Trust* see footnote 30 on p. 122 above. Lieutenant-Commander R.T. Gould RN (retired) was a prolific author, an expert on the marine chronometer, and a frequent broadcaster on astronomy on the *Children's Hour*.

[42] *Mrs Miniver,* a popular morale-boosting wartime film with Greer Garson and Walter Pidgeon, imagined the involvement of a British housewife in the Dunkirk evacuation.

1943

January 1943

Friday 1 January. I had my dream feeling between waking and sleeping last night about life being over in another 30 or 40 years at most and appalled at the thought I abruptly came to as usual; but the feeling lingered long after I was awake (I lay awake a long while) and I cuddled to Jess for comfort. It's queer how this thought affects me at night times. In daylight it dwindles to insignificance — though its significance still remains. …

I don't intend to write regularly in this journal this year. By regularly I mean every day in the way I have during the past year or two. I fell into the habit in recording the times of air raids, but I like my old habit of writing when I have something to say; not forcing myself to say something.

Sunday 3 January. Frank Edwards and I rode to Harston on his tandem this afternoon.

Talking about prison life he said that all judges should serve six months hard labour to fit them as judges; they'd then know what a sentence meant to a prisoner.

Wednesday 6 January. … The blackout is still 15 hours a day: and rations are to be cut down, a belt-tightening process according to the papers. …

Friday 15 January. Tonight soon after the ITMA programme ended on the wireless we heard the siren sounding. It was a surprise, as there's been nothing doing lately, and we were more surprised than ever when Jess said 'It's the "All Clear"'. It was. We hadn't heard the Alert go. Making inquiries we learned that the warning was a short'un, lasting only a quarter of an hour: 8.50 p.m. till 9.05 p.m. There was a glow in the sky Huntingdon way.

Saturday 16 January. I heard today that the above-mentioned glow was a bomber that crashed. Don't know whose, whether ours or a German. … I believe there's a fair amount of bombing going on, especially on our coast towns, but we don't hear a lot about it.

Jack Ryder called in this afternoon; he's called up; has to go next Thursday. He thinks now there's only one thing for the world: Communism. He doesn't mind going in the army; he's hard-up financially and his family life has broken up (his wife's in Reading and he's been sleeping at the office, often several days without taking his clothes off, at which he works in London) and feels he might meet people in the army from whom he can obtain introductions to get a better job after the war. He's had a lot of ear trouble and intends to use it as an excuse to get out of any fighting that might come his way. He said he's long since given up believing in anything we're supposed to be fighting for, and I concluded from his manner that he thought there was truth in some of the things I said to him ten years ago.

Sunday 17 January. ... The Russians are advancing, which is like saying the Germans are retreating, but it's too soon to say what it all means. We still get three ounces of sweets a week, [a] half-pound of sugar a week, and a pound of jam a month, per person. ...

Jess's [his daughter's] holiday ends today and she goes back to Huddersfield tomorrow.[1] ... from what I can see of their love affair [Jess's and Don Varley's] I am reminded of Dickens's remark in the *Pickwick Papers* that 'the course of true love is not like a railway'. ... I bought a packet of razor blades [from Frank Edwards], and it reminded us that I bought a lot from him when the war started and we wondered if it would be over by the time I used them all. I've got to hurry up as there's only three left.

Monday 18 January. We went to the Red Lion [Grantchester] for tea yesterday afternoon. ... There was an Alert soon after we got home: from 8.55 p.m. till 9.25 p.m. ... Last Saturday night British bombers raided Berlin; they returned the compliment by bombing London on Sunday night; when our bombers were again over Berlin. We lost 22 bombers on this

---

[1] Jess's teachers' training college was evacuated to Yorkshire during the war.

trip. So it looks as if the bombing is starting all over again.

According to the wireless the siege of Leningrad has been raised.[2]

Tuesday 19 January. Applicants for the house on Shelford Road [which was vacant again] are numerous. I spent the evening answering telephone calls about it. ... Jess still gets hurt about the condition of the house and furniture. I tell her it doesn't matter, we can start again.

Wednesday 20 January. Twenty-four German bombers escorted by sixty fighters attacked London this afternoon. It is reported that only six got through and that fourteen were brought down. A school was hit and there were many casualties. There was a warning tonight from about 10.30 p.m. till 11.15 p.m. ...

Thursday 21 January. I heard the raid was on East Ham. Nearly 50 children killed, 6 teachers killed, and 50 children injured at the school that was hit. ...

Friday 22 January. I haven't mentioned that last week I concluded reading Henry Williamson's *The Beautiful Years* [1921]. A beautiful book. It made me eager to read the other three that form the novel *The Flax of Dream* [1936], and I have got from the library and am reading *Dandelion Days* [1922] which although not as good as the first, is an enjoyable book and one I'm always keen to pick up. These books are lightening a dreary hard-going time in my life.

Saturday 23 January. ... Don [Varley] came into the shop yesterday to lend me a history book by Lipson.[3] He also left me one of his essays to read and today dinner coming home from work I leaned against the railings of the old iron bridge on Coe Fen in the sunshine and read it; it was well put; and I agreed

---

[2] The siege, better described as a blockade intended to prevent supplies from reaching the city so as to permit its obliteration by German forces, lasted for 900 days from autumn 1941. Some supplies reached the city across the ice of Lake Ladoga, but 900,000 inhabitants died from starvation and disease during the siege; according to some sources it did not end until 27 January.

[3] Ephraim Lipson, *Economic History of England* was published in three volumes between 1921 and 1934.

with the content of it. He should do well, if he pulls through the war all right. ...

We've let the house at 45s a week—a 3s increase—on a fortnightly tenancy, rent payable in advance. ... A deputy fire warden called on me this evening from the senior fire guard, who had, in turn, been instructed by the local authorities to ask me to take over the leadership of this street for firewatching. I declined; said I couldn't make a case against firewatching and so had done it before compulsory registration; in fact, since its inception; but becoming an organiser was a different thing: I would then as an organiser be actively co-operating in the war effort, which as a CO I could not do, as it would conflict with my pacifist opinions.

Monday 25 January. I tried to re-arrange my hours today, doing shoe-repairing in the morning, exam work in the afternoon, and writing in the evening: it didn't come off, as I lost Jim on the way to work this afternoon and it put me all out. ... I looked for him on and off for the rest of the afternoon, so did Jack after school, in the raid, and I found him just before blackout turning into Silver Street, apparently on his way to the shop. ...

Tuesday 26 January. I worked till 2.30 today to clear up 46s worth of repairs: then had a dip on the way home; Jess wondered where I'd got to. But it put me out for the day and I'll give that up; must do if I'm to follow my programme.

The bombing has dropped off again. I think the reaction to the bombing of the school in London, in which so many children lost their lives, has something to do with it. People begin to think that sort of thing wouldn't happen if a game of tit for tat wasn't being carried on. It seems that the Alert was sounded after the bombs fell on the school, and many people have been killed in London by AA fire owing to the shelters being locked.

It's very difficult to get leather and I am turning away some of the roughest repairs as it is essential to conserve what stuff I can get. Today, I couldn't get any rubber: the shop had sold out: a run on it owing to the leather shortage.

Wednesday 27 January. I tried to get down to Lipson's *Economic History of England* (volume 2) in the shop this afternoon, but Mark Horner came in and spoiled it. I got two bends of leather today; S. African stuff, yak, or some such name, they told me in the shop.

The Russians are mopping up the last of the Germans at Stalingrad; we seem about to push them out of Tunisia. Churchill has met Roosevelt at Casablanca.[4] They're going to pulverise Hitler and Mussolini: unconditional surrender. Stalin refused to join in the talk: too busy, I suppose, doing the job for them!...

Sunday 31 January. Last Thursday Jess and I went to see a navy film in which Noel Coward figured [*In which we Serve*]. I didn't like it. Too much public school spirit about it --- bits of boys dying as heroes with the captain (Noel Coward) telling them how proud of them their people would be.

As I refused the street leadership for firewatching I received a letter from the authorities to say I had been detailed to the Devonshire Motor Works [in Barnabas Road] for one night's firewatching every week: Saturday nights. I don't particularly mind this; the alternative to refusing to do firewatching seems to be to lie abed and burn; and as somebody else keeps an eye on my shop there seems to be no logical reason to refuse to do the same for somebody else; so, apparently, I have no case to make against it; and if I said I had a shop of my own to look after, I'd be given the chance to do so, but it would be every night instead of once a week, or pay a man for watching when I wasn't there; what I object to is forming part of an organised body to help the war effort; but I thought they'd done the dirty on me by sending me to a munition factory, as so many small motor firms are these days. I went to find out when I came out of the pictures ... and upon meeting the fire guard there told him I was a CO and refused the job if it was a munition works; but it wasn't; just some lock-ups. I went

---

[4] At this conference in French Morocco the Combined Chiefs of Staff were also present. The Allied policy of insisting on the unconditional surrender of the Axis powers was agreed, as was the launch of the combined bomber offensive; Germany was to be bombed by the RAF by night and the American Eighth Air Force by day.

last night at 9.00; the conditions were good: electric light and gas and three decent beds; but I had a ragged night; slept an hour; I studied the rest; all because one of my fellow watchers snored his head off and talked aloud in his sleep. I left at half-past five, wanting a breath of fresh air. This chap told me it was his last night there as he's going in the Home Guard, and I now feel relieved about it.

A woman (who has done nothing to help the war effort except talk patriotically) told me one day that I have no respect for my wife and children or I wouldn't be a CO! So now we know. I reminded her that her husband was skulking out of the army; she said he was doing his best; I think she meant to keep out of it! …

Don Varley called in the shop and told me that because of service in the navy he will be excused Part 1 of his exams. I told him his degree will signify nothing. He agreed. I added they didn't excuse me, a snob, but put me to the trouble of repeatedly taking my exams.

My hands are full of cuts and cracks and in a rough state for shoe-repairing and typewriting; they often keep me awake at nights. … My finger nails are like celluloid and bend at a touch. What deficiency in the wartime food is causing this, I wonder? …

As 'The Kiss of Judas' had been used I've been trying to find a title for the book I've written. I hit on the 'Sins of the Fathers' as being more applicable to it, as the book shows how Tom Cash's family is affected by his actions: but the title has been used: so now I've got another, the 'Whims of the father'; this is even more apt; and original (I hope), as it was the old man's whims rather than his sins that caused all the trouble.

I've done 50,000 words (about a half) of the second volume and as its theme seems to be John Cash running counter to his father's warnings against women (he marries at 20) I've used one of the old man's catch phrases as the title: 'Children can't be told'. I'll probably call the third volume the 'Stain of Judas'.

February 1943

Monday 1 February. Don Varley came over last night through a heavy downpour of rain. He stayed till nearly 12.00. I wrote while he was here, but after Jess and Jack went to bed we had a short talk about the Beveridge Report and he read out some notes he had made of a lecture given by Mrs [Joan] Robinson, an economist, on it. Then I looked up my notes and was able to give him some facts for an essay on the rise of prices in the 16th century.

I worked till 3.00 today, doing 51s worth of work, and then left off, going in the water on the way home. ...

Tuesday 2 February. I did £2 worth of work in four hours this morning: enough for the day — at snobbing. Since then it's been exam work and writing.

It's still hard to get leather; and rubber soles have run out; but the leather shop has 100 hides in, and now they mustn't release them till they have permission owing to some mix-up about the price. The couple of bends I got from them last week were out of this quota and they let me have them before receiving the letter. Many snobs are idle according to the man in the shop.

Evening: Beaverbrook calls for the Second Front. He ought to be in the first wave; anybody does who advocates it, as it's tantamount to swearing other men's lives away. ...

Sunday 7 February. ... I've chucked taking the *Daily Worker* in case it makes me a Tory. I like *The Economist* and *Peace News* the best of the weeklies. The public library don't reserve books and send out cards to the effect that they have them waiting for borrowers so they told me yesterday, so there's no hope of getting examination books, as they're never in the racks. Don Varley has recently got me a couple of volumes of Lipson's *Economic History of England* from the University Library. I can't afford to buy textbooks; wouldn't buy them if I could as it's the same stuff rehashed as those in the books I have.

I went firewatching last night, but although pretty comfortable I didn't sleep, just lying down from 12.00 till 4.00; I left at 6.00. ...

Wednesday 10 February. ... I woke up this morning and knew the great day had arrived. Forty! Incredible! Unbelievable! But true nevertheless. I resent it. ... the swift passage of time and the realisation that I am forty is a shock. Thirty years ago I was in the Fourth Standard at St Paul's under Jerry Watson: it seems like yesterday; ... Alas, life is short. --- ...

I did a bit of stitching and reading at the shop; and made myself a couple of cups of cocoa as birthday treat. ... Home again: ... Jack brought out a parcel from Don Varley; I opened it and inside was an egg [a birthday present] ... . Tonight: I've done my quota of story and eaten Don's egg — and some chips — for my supper. ...

Sunday 14 February. Last Thursday: to the pictures with Jess; one of the films was called *Those Kids from Town* [1942]; about evacuees; laughable; but the socialist in it didn't know what he'd put in the place of the aristocracy when they were swept away (as he put it);[5] film producers don't credit the lower order[s] with much sense. Jack asked me what would be put in their place; or rather what could be; I said the answer was Russia; nothing else need be said. ...

I went firewatching again last night; two fresh fellows there: an ex-miner and a chap who had been badly wounded at Dunkirk. They didn't leave off swearing about conditions today and neither believed in the brave new world after the war. ... The Russians are still going great guns: but they're trusting in themselves and not us and the Americans.

I forgot to mention that I received last Thursday the *Autobiography of Mark Rutherford* [a pseudonym of William Hale White] from Neil Bell as a birthday present. ... He said perhaps he should have sent me a barrel of Guinness or a bottle of halibut oil instead of Mark Rutherford! ...

Monday 22 February. In a letter to Neil Bell copied in the diary Jack Overhill writes that for some days he had suffered from a badly poisoned finger and swollen glands, and that though he wrote 500 words on his novel on Saturday 19 February, 'indolently putting it

---

[5] Leslie Halliwell, *Halliwell's Film Guide*, 7th edition (1989), comments on the film: 'An earl takes in a group of nosey Cockney kids evacuated from the city. Sentimental wartime crowd-pleaser.'

off *he wrote nothing the following day, the first he had missed since Christmas. The letter continues:*

> I've written 75,000 words of the book and hope to have it done first time round in three weeks. I've got a title for it (if it hasn't been used): 'He Couldn't Leave the Pretty Girls Alone'. ... Today, I sent off the six guineas [£6 6s] entrance fee for another cut at the B.Sc. Econ. Final. I am still very slowly reading Mark Rutherford. It gives me the queer feeling that I wrote it (as far as I've gone; nearly 100 pages). ..

The transcription of the letter having been concluded, the diary continues:

... Yesterday Sir John Anderson took the salute outside the Fitzwilliam Museum to celebrate the 25th anniversary of the Red Army. There was a procession of all sorts of units, men and women. I told Jack as we walked round the Fen with the dogs it was the 'Uniform Age'; they should have brought the convicts in to make it complete; ... The people round here got a ladder and climbed on to the top of the [air] raid shelters [the] better to see the procession. ...

Saturday 27 February. ... Don Varley looked in twice, but didn't stop long. He borrowed my examination notes for an essay he's doing on chartered companies a few centuries back. ...

Sunday 28 February. [There follows an] Extract from a letter I wrote to Neil Bell last night before setting out firewatching: ...

> My grounds for conscientiously objecting to play a part in the war? Don't you think I am playing a part? Think of it: keeping nearly a hundred people dry-footed every week. The other day a woman told me I had no respect for my wife and family or I wouldn't be a CO. Her husband (my age) has spent all his days since the war playing cards in an RAF depot.
>
> Yes, the basic reason is that I believe all modern war is double cross on the common man. I say modern as the old-fashioned mercenary had pillage and rape as his reward. Your questions (a) do I advocate submission to Germany? (b) would I submit as a nation in all circumstances in preference to resisting? are thus answered. How? Well, is a person who believes he is being double-crossed likely to identify himself with the nation? and if he doesn't, is the phrase 'submission to Germany' likely to mean anything to him?
>
> I am, as I have said before to you, often at cross-purposes with myself. Often the Jack Overhill that scares me would love to do a

bit of killing and I have to say 'Hook it, you murderous bastard' and reason. There are fundamentals I cling to. One of them is that large-scale finance (big business), the root of all evils (war is one of them) knows no frontiers. Another is that democracy is dying; to wage a war to revive it will only result in the totalitarianism it is fighting against.

Submission to Germany implies rule by foreigners. But Churchill and Co are as foreign to me as Hitler and company. I have nothing in common with them; they have nothing in common with me. The real political leaders of this country don't care two straws about me or my kind. They want England to go on (as it was) for ever and ever Amen. Their England mind you. And that's not my England. What I think doesn't matter in the least. My job [their view of my job] is the out-of-date one of to do and die, not to reason why. But I want to know what I'm fighting for; and wanting to know now means all the political, economic and moral aspects of the question. I haven't worked them out yet; nothing near; and I don't suppose I ever shall. ...

If I believed in war I'd fight. I'd want to do the rough stuff; not make munitions or repair shoes; there's enough about who don't believe in it, or don't want to do it without having any beliefs at all, to do that sort of work. ...

These are some of my thoughts, chucked down helter-skelter as they have popped into my mind. Do they clear the air at all? I will answer any questions in like vein; which is not rule of thumb, but according to my mood. The next batch of answers will probably be altogether different; but that's because I try to answer every question straight and fair according to the facts in mind at the moment and not to any fixed rule (e.g. like the 'What would you do if your mother was attacked by a German soldier?' question of the last, and this, war CO tribunals').

[*So ends the extract from the letter to Neil Bell.*]

Firewatching again last night. The three of us there had fish and chips for supper; and we made tea last night; no bolster; tried my boots under my pillow; still too low; then my overcoat; not altogether a success; and the room was stuffy; yes, an uneasy night; home just after 6.00 and then to bed till 9.30 when I took Jess and Jack tea up. I wrote [daughter] Jess this morning; sent her rail fare to come home next Friday for half-term; ... I'm just back from a mooch up the Common with the dogs: ... I'm now going to have a bath on me owny-o; and then tea; then I hope to do a bit of writing (neglected a couple of days because I've been so busy) before Don Varley comes round.

[*Extract from a further letter to Neil Bell:*]

I've just been having a bath and while rubbing down I suddenly remembered that I said in my letter that the common man is double-crossed in all modern wars. This is rather sweeping. Russia is at war; and it's a fact I forgot she was! and a Russian might well and truly say not in his case; and I'd agree with him. ...

March 1943

Wednesday 3 March. ... I'm still slogging away at the book. Done about 84,000 words now; but I think it will work out to a bit more than 100,000. ...

After writing the above I set out to Frank Edwards' for a haircut. The siren went when I was in Russell Street and ... I returned. The time was 8.40 p.m. and the warning lasted an hour. ...

Thursday 4 March. Another warning during the early hours of this morning, 4.45 a.m. till 5.30 a.m. I heard a stick of bombs in the distance. ...

Friday 5 March. [*Extract from a further letter to Neil Bell:*]

Britain was forced into alliance with Russia by Germany's action in attacking her; and they're uneasy bedfellows.

I believe peace by negotiation will be the outcome of this war; I believe there will be epidemic wars for at least another hundred years; and that capitalism in this country will see me out though I live to a ripe old age.

I prefer democracy to fascism (with the reservation that I would like to know more than I do about the latter), but not at the price; which is the lives of probably millions of innocent men and women. ...

[It's quite possible that the political situation will develop in this fashion]—a conscientious objector that had changed his mind because of Russia's entrance into the war would soon learn that he was (and had been) fighting for Britain, not Russia and what she stands for. The army would be sheer martyrdom for a man of my temperament; I'd be in the glasshouse [military prison] in five minutes. Can a forty-year-old leopard change its spots? I doubt it.

Tuesday 9 March. ... I seem to have a lot on hand one way and another; hardly a minute to breathe as the saying goes. But I must do a lot of shoe repairing to level off my many bills; and then there's the novel, exam studies, the reading and reviewing of Neil Bell's *Cover his Face.* ...

Wednesday 10 March. ... I walked back to work this afternoon Midsummer Common way with the dogs; a glorious afternoon; sunshine; light clouds; a little East Anglian breeze that made me sniff at it as I walked beside the river Cam and which took my mind back to Coldham's Common (not far from where I was) which I used to roam around with the big boys when I lived near there; I was then under five. I read *Cover his Face* at the shop, having done a good morning's work. Don Varley came in; said term ended next Saturday, but he'd gone down today as it saved five bob [5s] a day for the cost of his meals in hall at college, he could feed cheaper at home; he has a last lecture for the term tomorrow and a naval exam next Monday. He brought a *Daily Telegraph* round here last week; he mentioned it; his father reads it; thought I might like it as it has good reports of parliamentary debates; I said I didn't like newspaper reports of these debates; too one-sided; I'd read *Hansard* if I had time; and anyway, I read newspapers for news only and not knowledge. ...

Thursday 11 March. To the pictures with [wife] Jess. There was a collection for British prisoners of war and she was shamed into giving a few coppers. I rebelled; said it was cadging and prisoners of war shouldn't depend on charity. The programme was nauseating: soldiers, sailors, flagwaving, military bands, arm-swinging, quick marching and the rest of the usual wartime provender. And when we came out into the moonlight bombers were roaring away on their bashing expeditions to Germany. How they roared; there must have been scores. There's no escape from it except death; at every turn war stared one in the face. ...

There's some sort of manoeuvres going on round about here. Is it a try-out before an attempted Second Front?

Sunday 14 March. ... I've got a new sports coat and flannel trousers; 30*s*; cheap. Jack had his eye on them, but I managed to get them on before he did, so they're mine!

Started exam revision work today. Been at it on and off all day, so done no writing except about Neil Bell's *Cover his Face*.

At this point there follow c. 4000 words about Cover his Face, *cast in diary form and intended to be sent to Neil Bell; they are described by Jack in a covering letter as 'less a review than a ramble'. Some of that writing is included below, within square brackets.*

[27.2.43. *Jack explains that he has had no time to read* Cover his Face *today, but continues*: I went to Bowes and Bowes to buy my daughter Jess Shelley's poems for a birthday present. ...

13.3.43. Today I went to Bowes and Bowes, where I bought Sayers' *Modern Banking* [1938 and later editions], the Macmillan *Report on Finance and Industry*[6] and Thorold Rogers' *Six Centuries of Work and Wages* [1884]. ...

14.3.43. I went firewatching last night (Saturday). My two companions, a little ex-miner, wounded ten times in the last war, and a labourer, badly wounded at Dunkirk in this war, were talkative as we sat and ate chips and fish cakes round the gas fire. The ex-miner said that Germany had had four cuts at world dominance and had once fought Britain under Bismarck with 70,000,000 men! ...]

Wednesday 24 March. ... We heard bits of Churchill's talk on the wireless: he said we might beat Hitler next year or the year after (two more years and a 'might' beat him; that's a bit thick, but apparently the best he can do) and talked of a Four Year Plan after the war. ...There's oats and barley in the bread now; but it's eatable; rye has still to come!

A man, an author called in the shop on Monday to have his shoes repaired. His name is Martin Boyd and a Miss Sindall, the woman who delivers *Peace News*, had mentioned him to me; he said he heard I wrote books and so made himself known to me; he told me he's written eight novels; Consta-

---

[6] The Committee on Finance and Industry, chaired by Lord Macmillan, was set up by the Labour Government in 1929, at the start of the world economic crisis. Its *Report*, published in 1931, recommended that Britain should join in concerted international attempts to expand credit to boost trade. It was 'nothing less than a grand design for world reflation' to cure the depression; it therefore paralleled Keynes's reflationary proposals: Robert Skidelsky, *Politicians and the Slump* (1967), esp. Chapter 11:2.

ble's published the first three under another name; Dent's publishes him now. He lives at Great Eversden and is having trouble with the Ministry of Labour; they want to make him an agricultural labourer; he's refusing; he's about 50; and he keeps appealing.[7] He said there's fascism in this country now; there's the proof, his own case, he's just [a] chattel ordered about by the State. ...

Tuesday 30 March. I heard the announcer say on the wireless yesterday morning that our planes had been dropping food cards over Germany to disorganise their system of rationing, which the German authorities say will be met by the death penalty on people guilty of using them. Some time back we did this on them with clothing cards, but apparently treasury notes [German money] are taboo. Why?

There was a warning last evening at about 9.15 p.m. lasting for about a quarter of an hour. ... Things have slowed down in Russia. They [the Russians] seem to be holding the Donetz and slowly advancing in the direction of Smolensk. The spring thaw no doubt has something to do with it; and exhaustion; and a re-grouping of forces. Yesterday it was announced that we'd captured the Mareth Line in Tunisia.[8] ...

Jack's just in from the Band of Hope; it's about half-past nine; and am I tired; but I've still to do my quota on the novel to keep pace with my work; examination studies gulp all my spare time nowadays.

Wednesday 31 March. A representative from the District Manpower Board called on me today regarding my application for deferment from call-up. He came in just after 12.00; looked a proper old-school-tie waller [wallah]; ex-army major with a

---

[7] Martin Boyd (1893–1972): an Anglo-Australian novelist who lived at Plumstead, Little Eversden from 1939 to 1948. His dislike of Churchill, his pacifism, and his especial hatred of the RAF's bombing of German cities, is described in his 'Anglo-Australian Memoir', *Day of my Delight* (1965). Boyd's best-known work of fiction is *Lucinda Brayford* (1946).

[8] After their victory at Stalingrad the Russian forces steadily advanced westwards (with occasional setbacks). The Mareth Line in southern Tunisia was a prewar defensive system, built by the French to prevent Italian incursions from Libya. In March 1943 it was defended by the German and Italian forces against Montgomery's Eighth Army, which outflanked the line at the end of March.

severe countenance and a stiff moustache; aged about 55. He asked if he could come round the counter (he called at the shop) to do some writing; I said yes and asked if he minded my keeping at work; he didn't mind, so long as I answered his questions; they were a rigmarole wanting to know what I'd been since I left school; at the end I said it was a bit of an inquisition; and it's a wonder I didn't add it was a bit of fascism, too; he also filled in details about name, address, age, was I union or non-union (non-union) [and] hours put in a week (I said 44)[;] after he'd written it all down he asked my output; I told him, but he didn't enter that item. Then he gossiped a bit about the heels of his shoes seeming to be high after recently being heeled, offered me a cigarette, and commented about the money a boy paid me for soling and heeling his shoes, thinking it was too much; it wasn't and he blamed his glasses for mistaking two 2*s* pieces for half-crowns [2*s* 6*d*]. (During the inquisition he also asked if I did any government work and the answer was no, all civilian.)

He spoke about my provisional registration as a conscientious objector and although I had intended to put a leash on my tongue, it wagged when he asked what were my objections to war; if they were religious the Bible didn't say we mustn't kill. (Mentioned this to Jess and she asked what about the commandment 'Thou shalt not kill'); … I said I objected on moral grounds and sitting on the counter talked at him rapidly for a few minutes; but I've forgotten something else before this happened; I asked when would I hear the result of this; he didn't know; might be days, or weeks; I said I hoped to sit for my degree and interested he took out his notebook from his case and wrote in it that I was sitting for the B.Sc. Economics final examination for London University in June; he said as he put away the book that shoe-repairing and sitting for a university degree was a contrast; but to go back to what I was saying above: I said I dare say I believed in God, but it was an impersonal God, not a personal one; Christ may or may not have lived; I didn't know and wasn't very interested; that the Bible could be interpreted to suit whoever read it.

He looked a bit surprised; and then he said this wasn't a war for territory, but my rejoinder was that it might be one to hold what we have (Churchill said so the other day) and what was the difference? He then spoke of what the Germans had done to the Czechs, Austrians, Poles and so on; didn't I think they would do it to us? I said I was 40; I remembered the atrocity stories of the last war; they weren't gospel; Lord Ponsonby had written a book proving them largely lies;[9] I believed there had been persecution in this war on the part of the Germans, but it was exaggerated; and we were not stainless in this respect ourselves; what about India? and the upset at Nassau in the Bahamas last summer.[10] He said you wouldn't do anything if we were invaded? and I said no; I preferred democracy to fascism, but not at the price of millions of innocent people. I added that as a CO I was often at cross-purposes with myself, but the war was a big thing.

He went looking rather serious. I suppose this all means that soon I'll be going before the tribunal. ...

I've done no writing on the novel today because of this rather detailed record of the affair, but I've managed to get my examination work done. ...

April 1943

Sunday 11 April. ... Jack has bought me Henry Williamson's *The Dream of Fair Women* [1924] as a birthday present; a bit

[9] Arthur Ponsonby, 1st Baron Ponsonby of Shulbrede (1871–1946): the son of Queen Victoria's private secretary, was educated at Eton and Balliol College Oxford. He served in the diplomatic service and resigned in 1902 to enter politics as a Liberal. An MP from 1908 to 1918, he opposed war in 1914. As a pacifist he was a member of the Union of Democratic Control and emphasised the place of moral force in international relations. After the war he joined the Labour Party and was elected MP in 1922; between the wars he voted for disarmament and supported Chamberlain's policy of appeasement in 1938. He resigned from the Labour Party in May 1940 because it joined Churchill's coalition government to prosecute the war vigorously. His book *Falsehood in War-time* (1928) states that lies are told by every side in war; but the 'myths' denounced in his book were all allegations uttered against Germany, for instance that English POWs had been tattooed with the German eagle.

[10] In the Bahamas a rich white élite ruled over a native poor and local labour in the building trade was paid much less than American. Over 2,000 locals marched on Nassau on 1 June 1942. The riot was settled, largely by the efforts of the governor, the Duke of Windsor: Ashley Jackson, *The British Empire and the Second World War* (2006), pp. 87–92.

late in the day, but I say what I want to him and [daughter] Jess when I feel like it. I've read a couple of chapters and like it very much. ...

Horse-racing started yesterday; I took a few bets, stood them all, chancing my luck, and won 10*d*. ...

The war: I made a wrong forecast (one of many!) a time back in these notes, about our forces being kicked out of Africa as it looks as if the Axis troops will soon be staging a Dunkirk there. But Russia wasn't in the war then, and that's made all the difference, to forecasts as well as our chances of pulling off some sort of victory in the Second World War; or, at least, emerging as a power to be reckoned with, if not a first-class one. This remark can be challenged, I know, but I don't think Britain will ever be able to rank on a par with Russia and America; or, later, China ... and Germany. ...

When I came home from firewatching this morning just before dawn our bombers were returning from their now daily and nightly bombing raids on the Continent. Some had lights on (I marvelled at this; a short while ago they daren't have exhibited lights in case German fighters were on their tails), some hadn't; and I heard the engines of one coughing as though missing and wondered if it had run (literally) into flak and was staggering home with difficulty. One I could just distinguish as a faint outline against the greying sky looked like a huge bird of prey; and it suddenly struck me as one of this age; a particularly dreadful type of one, too. A few searchlights were up and as I turned into Hills Road and looked towards the Roman Catholic church two searchlights straddled the road far in the distance in the shape of an inverted V (the victory sign upside down!). I went to bed for a couple of hours when I got home and they were still roaring homewards. Our bashing of German towns now must be terrible and I hope they'll never be able to pay us back in coin. ...

Thursday 15 April. There was a warning last night: 12.40 a.m. till 1.25 a.m. It was moonlight. I asked Jess if she was getting up and she said no so I stayed in bed. I heard a few planes in the distance, that's all. ... We heard last night that Dunlop Kidman, missing in a Spitfire over Dunkirk nearly three years ago, is buried near Dunkirk, his body having lately been washed up on the beach. ...

Friday 16 April. A glorious day; I had half an hour's sunbathing at the sheds [at the swimming pool] this afternoon and a dip; then back to the shop to study history and banking. Mark Horner came in; he's reading 'Tale of a Taylor' and likes it. While we were talking the siren sounded; it was then 4.50 p.m. and the warning lasted ten minutes. ... it's about 10 o'clock and our bombers are roaring outside as they set off from the 'dromes around on their raiding expeditions to Germany. The din from them is terrific.

Saturday 17 April. A warning last night: 12.35 a.m. till 1.23 a.m. Six hundred of our bombers raided Germany last night and we lost 55 of them. Another warning this afternoon: 3.10 p.m. till 3.25 p.m. ...

Sunday 18 April. Palm Sunday and [daughter] Jess and I went for a ride into the Fens on Frank Edwards' tandem. We went through Histon and Cottenham on to Wilburton and Haddenham, where I called on Norman, the farmer, who was going to employ me when the war started but the distance was too far. We had a talk over a glass of milk; he's a friendly sort; and then returned via Milton. The day was glorious, but there was a strong wind on the way home and the journey of about 15 miles took us an hour and a half. We're both stiff and sore now. The siren sounded on Milton Road on the return journey: the warning was from 1.50 p.m. till 2.00 p.m. There were a lot of our bombers up, but we saw and heard nothing; probably a stray raider in from the coast. ...

Tuesday 20 April. I went to a firewatching practice at the back of the Broadway, Mill Road, last night. One of the NFS [National Fire Service] men said in a short open-air lecture that firewatchers are not supposed to wait seven minutes to see if fire-bombs contain explosives, they are supposed to tackle them at once! One man there snarled about looking after other people's property instead of his own; I agreed with most of what he said, but it was his argument and not mine and I just listened. The siren sounded today: 11.50 a.m. till 2.00 a.m. [rightly p.m.]. ...

Saturday 24 April. A warning last night: 11.05 p.m. till 11.45 p.m. We were abed and heard people in the street saying they could see shell fire in the distance. Maybe they were seeing things, however, as they hadn't long turned out the pubs. …

Sunday 25 April. … Home from firewatching this morning at 6.00 I went to bed till 9.00; it's now 9.00 at night and I've studied for the exam all day. The Jesses (home now) went to the Red Lion [Grantchester] for tea; Jack went to the pictures; and so my companions have (as usual) been the dogs; dear old fellows, both of them; how fond I am of them, and they of me. …

Today, I saw a young man and his wife carrying their baby on an improvised chair; this is because prams are scarce; he was a fat fellow, but wearing narrow Utility trousers without turnups his legs looked like pipestems.[11] …

May 1943

Sunday 2 May. … I forgot to mention last week that permission was given to ring the church bells again (in time for Easter) it being judged no longer necessary that they should be reserved as an invasion warning.

A few days ago it was reported in the paper that the king was in Newmarket, watching horses in training. Was his journey really necessary! Perhaps, I should add, so that the joke doesn't fall flat, that the question 'Is your journey really necessary?' is one of the many wartime slogans; and that there's a real hullabaloo about people using petrol for journeys not directly connected with the war effort or essential work; drivers are summoned nowadays for going a few hundred yards out of their course.

Wednesday 5 May. I had a letter from the District Manpower Board at Luton on Monday morning granting me the maximum period of deferment from call-up (or, as far as I am concerned the start of the ball rolling for a lot of trouble for them and for me) which is three months … .

---

[11] The Utility scheme was devised by the Board of Trade to concentrate the production of a wide range of items, from furniture and clothing to pencils, on simple and economical designs which would make optimum use of material and labour.

Last night there was a warning. Soon after it went I heard the Roman Catholic [church] clock strike 3.00 a.m. and a few minutes after the 'Raiders Passed' signal I heard the chimes sound the half-past 3.00, so it must have lasted about half an hour. It was a still night, the siren sounded loud both times. We heard a fighter dashing over once or twice and a heavier plane, perhaps a bomber, but whether *ours* or *theirs* I can't say.

Saturday 8 May. There was a warning this morning: 7.35 a.m. till 7.50 a.m. The weather was cold and dull.

I had a soldier call on me tonight to say he could let me have, or rather a shoe-repairer he knew in Kettering [could let me have], as much leather as I wanted; he'd heard I was short and could only get rubber. I looked at his samples of men's soles marked 1*s* 6*d* a pair and women's soles at a 1*s* a pair and women's top-pieces 2½*d* and knowing it was stolen Services stuff declined the offer with thanks. I said my conscience wouldn't permit it; and it wouldn't; I'm not made to withstand the worry transactions of that sort involve.

Sunday 9 May. ... Our troops have captured Tunis and Bizerta.[12] The news yesterday morning was a surprise. It looks as though the Axis forces will soon be cleared out of North Africa. What then? Of course, our next enemy will be America. There must be a showdown with them within a few years; perhaps over the gold standard; or colonies. We're in pawn to them and it's bound to happen.

Tuesday 11 May. Jack had a cheque for a guinea [£1 1*s*] from Neil Bell this morning as 25 percent commission on his idea for the short story 'Root of all Evil', which has been accepted for publication for four guineas [£4 4*s*]. Neil said it's obviously a highbrow periodical that's taken it, for had it been a lowbrow the payment for it would have been four times as much. ...

Friday 14 May. The weather suddenly changed yesterday and in the afternoon I walked to Grantchester (to the old spot) with the dogs. The buttercups, the hawthorn blossom and the fresh green of the grass and trees and hedges were a picture; and the laburnum, drooping golden in people's gardens with the

---

[12] The capture of the two cities was followed by the surrender of the last Axis forces in North Africa on 13 May.

lilac, red and white may, and spring flowers, made the walk a pleasant one. I spent a few grand hours in the Meadows. For a while I read and talked to an ex-public school undergraduate, who hadn't much time for the common man which made me strongly champion his cause even more than usual, and then I had a swim and tea, Jim and Jock helping me eat it. ...

There were a couple of warnings in the early hours of this morning: 2.00 a.m. till 3.00 a.m., and 3.20 a.m. till 3.40 a.m. People told us they heard bombs in the distance and it's reported that Chelmsford was bombed.

Tonight an old lady fell down outside in the street. I went outside to assist her. She smelled of drink. I was going to help her home; she wanted to give me money in order that I drank her health; I said I was a teetotaller; she said 'Non-smoker as well?' I said yes; when she said she didn't like men who didn't smoke and drink and she certainly didn't want me to take her home, I didn't. ...

Saturday 15 May. ... I am systematically revising all my work for the examination next month. I have written for bed and breakfast to an address in London for the period as I am a bit concerned about the trains during Bank Holiday, the first day of the exam falling on Whit Monday. ...

Monday 17 May. There was a warning last night from 12.45 a.m. till 2.05 a.m. It's moonlight these nights and we're heavily bombing the Continent so reprisals are taking place. ...

Tuesday 18 May. Three warnings last night: 11.25 p.m. till 11.40 p.m.; 1.45 a.m. till 2.10 a.m; 2.50 a.m. till 3.05 a.m. A lot of planes were roaring over; some of them sounded as though they might have been German bombers; but it's hard to say. All I went on was that our bombers at night time seem to go over one at a time when going to and from a raid from the aerodromes around here; and last night a crowd of bombers went over together, something like they used to when we were being heavily raided a couple of years or so ago. Fighter planes don't make the noise of bombers and pass over more speedily. The Germans say Cardiff was bombed by them.

It's ghastly to read the newspapers nowadays: 26 ATS girls killed when a bomb fell on a hostel; 9 children killed when a plane of ours crashed on a cricket pitch.[13] --- It makes heartrending reading and though there's so much of it, I don't get hardened to it. With our heavy raids on the Continent it must be a hundred times worse there. Our bombers let loose thousands of tons of bombs in a single raid, and nowadays they're raiding day and night, France, Germany, Italy. ...

Thursday 20 May. There was an Alert last night: 2.30 a.m. [to] 2.45 a.m. I only heard the 'All Clear'. I went to work this morning without troubling about breakfast; there wasn't a sight [of anything] in the cupboard, rations having given out, though Jess would have made me some scrambled egg out of dry tinned eggs (on the points); but I didn't feel particularly hungry and wanted to clear off a lot of repairs at the shop and have an afternoon in Grantchester Meadows. I started work at 7.45 and finished just before 2 o'clock and I did £2 16s 6d worth of repairs in that time. ... [Later, in the meadows] The weather was grand and I enjoyed a couple of dips in the river; in between I studied and gossiped to a fellow I met there.

Saturday 22 May. Churchill made another broadcast from America the other night and among other things said that Germany was hard to get at; and so Britain will concentrate on bombing to see if that will bring victory.[14] Looks as though the Second Front might not come off after all. As for the threat of bombing Germany into submission, Germany has still a lot of cards in hand and the boot may conceivably be on the other foot. ...

Monday 24 May. ... *The Overhills' wedding anniversary, a day's outing in London*: What did we do? In and out of shops and restaurants. Food is more plentiful in London; much. I bought Jess a dress ring. And she bought herself a dress, a pair of shoes, a handbag (24s) and nearly 15s worth of face powder and cream; this latter she thought cost five bob [5s], taking no notice of the change, and was flabbergasted when she got

---

[13] The death of the members of the ATS occurred when a 'hit and run' raider bombed a hostel in an unnamed East Anglian town during the evening of 11 May. Search has failed to reveal details of the UK plane crash.

[14] During Churchill's visit to North America the decision was taken, as he urged, to follow victory in North Africa with the invasion of Italy. The American preference had been to invade France in 1943.

home to discover how much it really was. We went into an exhibition, thinking it was the real thing, only to discover it wasn't, the skeleton man, fat boy, ugly woman and the rest being only pictures; but the fault was ours; we misread the notice outside, as it plainly said what it was. ... It was our intention to have a dip in the Marshall Street baths, but as the day was coolish didn't feel like it and gave it a miss. I wish we had gone to a show, but found out too late in the train on the way home by reading the *Star* that some of the theatres (e.g. the Windmill) open in the afternoons. Anyway, we had a busy day and couldn't do everything. It was just a little celebration.

As an afterthought: I bought Michael Sadleir's *Privilege* [1921]: a shilling copy.

Sunday 30 May. ... I've been firewatching at the Devonshire Motor Works [in Barnabas Road] 18 weeks and last night for the first time there was a warning: 1.0 a.m. till 1.20 a.m. We went downstairs and heard a plane go over that we thought was a German. I then returned to our room and read banking till the 'All Clear' sounded. ...

Don [Varley] called for a last revision from my notes yesterday afternoon. He takes his university exams the next two days. He told me he was sixth out of 120 in his naval exam [for entry to the navy] last week. I explained a bit of banking to him, but told him to keep to banking history (history is his subject) and not delve in to banking and economic theory, of which he knows very little, or he'll get tied up.

June 1943

Sunday 6 June. ... Don's been in the shop once or twice and he spent Thursday evening with us. I gave him a busman's holiday by talking constitutional history most of the time, for last Monday and Tuesday he sat for his Preliminary examination. He brought me the test papers to see and didn't seem satisfied with his answers to the constitutional history paper, but I think he did pretty well. He's expecting to go away into the navy in about another ten days. I hope he keeps well.

We're still heavily bombing the Continent; and there's a lot of short sharp raids on this country, mostly by small forces of enemy fighter-bombers on coastal towns, whom the newspapers call 'sneak raiders'. ...

Saturday 12 June. The day has turned out gloriously fine and on the eve of a second cut at the B.Sc. (Econ.) final I might as well record my feelings. Well, what do I feel like? Not very hopeful! But I've been working consistently and I shall do my best. It will be a relief to have it all behind me again; lately, I've worked at it all hours without stopping, at times lying on the bed awhile to rest; and (I must admit it) sometimes falling asleep through sheer boredom of revising stuff that's as dead as ashes to me; perhaps, my snoozing has also been the result of overtiredness. ...

Sunday 13 June. Eric met Jack and me at Liverpool Street. We went to the YMCA central hostel and fixed up lodgings for a couple of nights. The clerk told us the place was bombed a couple of years ago, 100 of the public being killed and 40 injured; he said it was kept quiet. We then went to the Serpentine where Eric and Jack had a swim while I revised. In Hyde Park I saw a touching little scene: an old man kissed his sailor son goodbye. A couple of sheep dogs minding sheep showed themselves to advantage. Talk about knowing their job. Back to the YM for dinner: 1s 9d; cheap. Eric and I talked in the lounge while Jack mooned about the streets. ... In the evening Jack and Eric went to the pictures; they saw one about Stalingrad. I tried to study in my bedroom at the top of the building; but I'd overdone it but couldn't absorb a word; my mind was just a blank; I tried to sleep and couldn't, so wrote to Neil Bell while downstairs a gramophone played: Gigli singing the serenade from Drigo's *Les Millions d'Arlequin*;[15] which soon changed to hymns: 'O, hear us when we cry to thee': ... There followed 'Now the day is over', which reminded me of how I stole a leaf out of a hymnbook, when I was at St Paul's School

---

[15] Riccardo Drigo (1846–1930): Italian composer. His ballet *Les Millions d'Arlequin*, also known as *Arlekinada*, was first performed in 1900; the 'Serenade' from it was very popular.

at great risk of the cosh because I liked it so much; but it fell flat then.

I then lay on the bed and dozed off till 9.00, when J[ack] and E[ric] returned. Eric went home and Jack and I went and had a short stroll round while I went back to the YM. There I bought a couple of jam tarts and two mince pies in the canteen before going upstairs. ... I lay awake till about midnight. The bed and room were fine, but the noise of people bathing, going to the lavatory and trooping up and down the stone-flagged corridor in heavy boots (soldiers) and gossiping in loud voices in adjoining rooms kept me awake. Two gossiped so loudly I got out of bed and opened my door and shouted 'goodnight', which shut them up. Then at 1 o'clock the siren went (and an alarm bell in the YMCA); a notice in the bedroom said we were to go down to the gym; I'd arranged for Jack to see me and together we went downstairs, first by the wrong staircase, in pitch darkness following the handrail; we had to give it up and return and descend by another staircase. There was only one other fellow in the gym and we learned that boarders need not go down unless the alarm bell sounded twice; we lay on beds till the 'All Clear' went a quarter of an hour later. Back to bed; I awoke at 5.00 with the stomach ache and had to make two trips to the lavatory (the jam tarts and mince pies?) I revised then till 8.00; met Jack; a wash and brush up; breakfasted after a fashion in a café; ... I set out for South Kensington.

I'd better break off here to mention that there was also an Alert in Cambridge on Sunday night: 2.10 a.m. till 2.35 a.m. ...

Monday 14 June. I had a headache most of the day, but I soon settled down to the examination. I came away feeling I'd done pretty well at the day's subjects: Economics and Banking and Currency. Back at the YM I revised in the lounge, and although I had sent Jess a couple of letters, noticing a telephone box in the building I telephoned her; I got straight through and she told me she had managed to pull through with the day's racing. After Jack and Eric came in and Eric had gone home, I revised till about midnight. Then, in bed holding a post mortem on the day's work, it suddenly dawned on me that the first question of the day on the Economics paper about interest had caught me napping; I had approached it from the point of view of a model answer on a Wolsey Hall paper, which, I felt sure, was the wrong angle. What was wanted was an exposition of Keynes['s] and Hayek's theories on interest (with which I am acquainted). Especially Hayek's, for he's a London University lecturer and he probably set the question, as his name was down on the paper as an examiner. I regarded this as serious; enough to plough me; and had half a mind to pack [it] in for the year and try again next; but I decided to see the examination through; I'd paid my fee!

Then, the siren sounded an Alert; I went to Jack's room and met him and before we were properly dressed the guns started and the second alarm sounded the order to go down to the gym. We went; and neither Jack and I felt comfortable as we did so: the narrow corridors, the big building, the alarm bell ringing, the guns booming made me long for the wide open spaces — e.g. Coe Fen in Cambridge! The 'All Clear' went soon afterwards, but we hadn't been long abed before there was a second Alert and downstairs we had to go again. … Back to bed again I slept till 5.30 when I was awake and revising Economic History again for the day's paper on the subject.

Tuesday 15 June. (Again I had better interrupt my narrative to say that there was an Alert on Monday night in Cambridge: 3.20 a.m. till 3.45 a.m.). The morning was sunny and parting with Jack who was meeting one of his cronies at Liverpool Street so that they could have a day together in London I set out for South Ken., I thought I did pretty well with the Modern Economic History paper in the morning; but I found afterwards I'd missed an implication about Russia in one of the questions. (Funny this, for last year in the same subject I missed part of a question; but I passed in the subject.) In the afternoon I adopted different tactics with the essay from last year, when I wrote it and took a shorthand copy; instead I quickly wrote the essay, corrected it and then rewrote it, presenting it to the examiner without any alterations; I then kept the original and a copy of it is included in this diary. … Jess had set out to meet me with the dogs, but coming home we missed each other; a neighbour told me she'd gone up the station and I returned to meet her in Bateman Street; ... Don Varley biked up as we met. Later I read my essay to him; he was horrified; fancy presenting that to an examiner! What I ought to have done was an argument for and against religious teaching in schools (the subject) in true academic style. Oh, yeah! I'd sooner pay six guineas [£6 6s] and have another cut! Probably shall!!

Wednesday 16 June. I slept comfortably in my own bed, but was up fairly early to read through some of Don Varley's notes. ... This morning was languages, but as I'd passed these last year I didn't have to go in and so was able to catch an 11 o'clock train to London. ... I was too late for dinner at South Ken., so went without. I thought I did pretty well at History I. ...

Thursday 17 June. Awakened by a call on the telephone at 5.30 a.m. Off again: History II in the morning; History III in the afternoon. Seemed to do pretty well. Home again; up till 1 o'clock revising Constitutional History, keeping myself awake by strolling round the houses and having a cup of tea. (By the bye, the journey home was awful; people, myself among them, stood two deep in the train corridor.)

Friday 18 June. Again roused by the telephone at 5.30; had a look over some of Don Varley's notes; and then off. Finished dinnertime; thought I did well. ... It rained fast coming home — to kippers for tea.

Saturday 19 June. No exams today. I went to the Senate House to look for the result of Don's exam, but it wasn't out. A severe-looking old man saw me nosing round with the dogs and showed by his manner that he didn't like it. Wonder I didn't have words with him --- the cuss. Who the hell is he? says I to myself. Professor Oojah? Yah! Somebody just riding on the backs o' the likes o' me. Do him good to do a little hard work; and a lot more of the brainy'uns, too. ...

Sunday 20 June. Spent the day on Ketelbey's *History of Modern Times* [1929, and later editions] and my notes for the morrow's subject: Political History of the Great Powers since 1815. ... The rest of the week's doings ... . Nothing outstanding happened. I met one or two chaps who had sat two and three times for the Final, so it didn't make me feel very hopeful. One fellow named Roland Hughes, from Blackpool, a Wolsey Hall student (aged 38) had sat three times and was thinking about packing in. The lavatories were still ankle-deep in water (I mean those at the examination halls) and in most cases there was no toilet paper; when there was it had usually fallen into the water. One fellow told me he did the essay on religious teaching in schools and he said on his paper that there should be religious instruction in atheism and agnosticism to do the job properly. ... By the way, with regard to the interest question on the economics paper this shows exams are no true test of ability for according to my showing I know nothing of Hayek's theory of interest and most emphatically I do.[16] Is just failing to cotton on to a point at the right moment so important a test of ability? for that's what it amounts to.

Wednesday 23 June. There was an Alert last night; 3.25 a.m. till 4.05 a.m. I thought I heard enemy bombers passing over; people in the street thought so, too, by the sound of their voices.

Mrs C. ... was on the go again the other night at the top of her voice at an American soldier FLIRTING with a married woman in one of the houses down Gothic Street. Mrs C. ..., short, plump and very loud-voiced thinks the morals of her neighbours are her affair; yet on and off she lives with a man! The American answered quietly. Upon the whole they are very quiet, goodhumoured, tolerant and well-behaved.

Bombers are passing over (thousands of them!) night and day on their raiding expeditions to the Continent. ... Don Varley got a 'Second' for his exam. ...

Thursday 24 June. ... I had a 220 yard swim and a few good laughs over an *American Freeman* Neil Bell sent me some time back. This is an atheist newspaper and many of its stories are very funny. ...

---

[16] Friedrich August Hayek (1899–1992): Austrian economist and political philosopher; a lecturer at Vienna, and from 1932 to 1950 professor of economics at the London School of Economics. He became a British citizen in 1938. An iconoclastic thinker of prodigious output, he is best known for *The Road to Serfdom* (1944), an attack on the idea of a planned economy; he was therefore opposed to the collectivist current of British opinion during the war years.

Friday 25 June. ... Jess and I had a walk round Midsummer Fair; there were no stalls and only two side shows; the amusements were of the roundabout type for the young; there were no coconut shies; only bottles; and they had few prizes to offer for them and the darts; she didn't get a prize; little short of a miracle would have won one, the numbers to make up the requisite 25 with three darts being too low. We walked round the town afterwards longing for the time when we could buy what we liked again.

Saturday 26 June. Peter Quick came in the shop today (I think I've mentioned his name in these notes before) to borrow four of my manuscripts. He and his girl (who works for Chatto and Windus) are going to try to set up as publishers; I was dubious about them making a success of it; he said it was possible provided money was spent on the right sort of advertising and the critics like Desmond MacCarthy could be got to review the books, the first of which they hoped to get Joad to write for them. He thought they'd pull all that off (and get the paper); I don't; but good luck to them.

Sunday 27 June. ... I've started picking up the threads of 'He Couldn't Leave the Pretty Girls Alone' with a view to finishing it shortly and making a start on 'Judas Stain'. The siren sounded tonight at about 10.15 p.m. lasting about ten minutes.

Monday 28 June. Peter Quick came in today and I record details of our conversation as I hope to use some of it later in a novel I intend to write about a man becoming a famous author. I have often wondered how to give the character a start; now I know; by a pioneering venture in publishing of the sort which Quick has in mind, so that instead of the publisher establishing the author he establishes the publisher; and at the same time himself.

  Peter Quick is 22; he has fair hair and blue eyes; he appears to simper; offset by an engaging grin; and he lisps. After my talk with him yesterday I judged him one of the 'art for art's sake' sort (they're not much in my line!). He gave me his opinion of my writing; said 'The Cordwainer' was much better than 'Jim Baxter' (so did Michael Sadleir; and I'd shown Quick Sadleir's letter!). He suggested I rewrote parts of 'Jim Baxter'. I said not so likely; and then he started talking about the perfect novel; the usual trite stuff. I told him I didn't want to write a perfect novel; who did? He admitted that was an unfortunate remark of his; then he named James Joyce's *Ulysses* [1922] as the probable best novel of this century; had I read it? I said I had — after a fashion. What did I think of it? I said if everybody started writing like Joyce the whole world would soon be cuckoo. Reverting to 'Jim Baxter' — there were things I could have left out; many of the scenes wouldn't have been missed. I said all of them were reflections of Jim Baxter's character; did he mean some of them; did he mean some of them were trivial? He was wary. No, he realised trivial things were often important in developing character. Well, what was to be left out; and he mustn't forget an author has to write about something. (Come to that all of it might have been left out and the book need not have been written.) Again he talked vaguely of an 'integral something'. I knew what he was getting at: only that which is essential should go in a novel. What is essential? Who's to say what should be put in and what left out [?]

Of course, it was all a matter of selection (Neil Bell said that to me long ago in a letter), but I said different people would have different ideas of what should be left in and what should be taken out and I was certain that if I sent out a questionnaire to Peter Quick, Michael Sadleir, Neil Bell and half a dozen others who had read the book asking for replies on this point, they would all answer differently. He admitted it. Well, who is to decide? I asked; and he rather lamely answered 'You'. I told him I didn't want to be orthodox; I wanted to write readable books. He talked about the lasting value of books; I said it was best to let posterity look after itself; I could have added a lot; e.g. that Chaucer had lasted 500 years, Shakespeare 300; and what of it? How much will be left of what's written today in 10,000 years' time, a mere flash in time? But I didn't trouble; I didn't think the topic worth pursuing. I said I wrote about the things I knew; I still couldn't see what he was getting at. He tried to explain by saying that with a piece of sculpture, say of a kneeling figure, it had meaning --- but only meaning in that posture (or something like that); I picked him up. Meaning? What exactly did he mean by meaning? ... Take a dozen different people looking at a statue, all might read different meaning into it; that rather showed the meaning was imposed upon the statue instead of belonging to it. I wasn't being wilfully stupid. I just couldn't understand what he was driving at; and I don't think he was quite sure himself.

Then, he had to get on with his work for the War Agricultural Committee and I with my snobbing. Thinking things over I thought there's nothing like the cocksureness of young men. There he was 22 years old limited in experience (admitted by him) and with no knowledge of working-class life and so entirely ignorant of the subject matter of 'Jim Baxter'; and he's written nothing; and yet he criticised my writing with a sublime assurance of knowing all about it. Would he tell a bootmaker how to make a boot, a barber how to cut hair? I didn't think so. And yet with a difficult trade like novel-writing he knows all about it. Funny.

July 1943

Sunday 4 July. ... Last night firewatching: I was tired after a glorious afternoon on the river (I had two longish swims) and was dozing when Jim Long, the little ex-miner drifted in half-cut as usual, at about 11.30 and insisted on making me a cup of tea; I agreed to be matey and while he made it (bombers all the while roaring overhead --- there must have been a terrible raid on as they were passing over all night long) he chattered like a magpie ...; and then the tea drunk (not bad cup of char) we settled down for the night (I had a rough one). As he stretched out he said he always said his prayers before going to sleep and I heard him murmuring the Lord's Prayer. I was touched in his faith in God who has so obviously deserted him. Poor, credulous, abused little fellow. How cruelly society has wronged him (ten wounds in the last war, starvation, unemployment, the loss of his pension and goodness knows what) and yet he still pins his faith in God. ...

I'm on the novel again. Shall change its title to 'Square peg' (of round hole fame) if this hasn't been used as it's more suitable. Peter Quick came in the shop again on Friday. He'd read 'The cordwainer' and thought it fine. This was a surprise after our previous talk. He seemed quite wrapped up in the book.

I had a letter from Neil Bell, to whom I sent a copy of the essay I wrote for the examination, roundly abusing myself for queering my pitch again. I told him I couldn't help it. If I promised to be 'goody-goody' next year there'd be something I'd fall for; and I'd mentally shout 'Well, it's the bloody truth, anyhow', and down it would go, for nowadays I was so much out of harmony with the times, that every time I sat down to write I was unable to resist sticking my fingers to my nose and saying 'Yah'. ...

Sunday 11 July. I met my father in a room at the top of this house; spoke to him and came downstairs and he was in this room; I said he could deatomise and reatomise himself, be in two places at once; he looked at me old-fashioned, rubbed his chin and said he couldn't, but he would do a bit in that line; he would show me himself being hanged. He got up, pulled a face and pointed upwards --- and there he was suspended from the wall with a rope round his neck. I was horrified, but poked at the hanging figure with a stick --- and there was no figure, only a suit of clothes. I then woke up; it was 4.30 a.m; and came home from firewatching.

In bed and asleep again I dreamt I had a terrible skin disease; that when my body was touched the skin just peeled off raw; I bled; and I wept — because I wouldn't be able to work and pay my debts and keep Jess at college. Stumbling my way across Parker's Piece (why Parker's Piece?) I was refusing to be ill; and then I woke up. A few minutes later, Jess brought me up a cup of tea and I lorded it in bed. Grand! Three cheers for Sunday morning!

Jack won the school swimming championship. ... I gave him five bob [5s] for old times' sake. ...

We've invaded Sicily; the news came through on the wireless yesterday morning. The Germans are launching an attack in Russia and are gaining some ground.[17] ...

---

[17] The invasion of Sicily coincided with a crucial phase of the battle of Kursk, the largest tank conflict of the war, and a Russian victory.

Extracts from my letters to Don and Jess today: yesterday, a man told me that 'they're prepared to lose 2,000,000 men in opening a Second Front'. This angered me. ... Who are 'they'? Are they forming part of the 2,000,000? That some forked animals like ourselves should have the nerve to arrogate to themselves such rights and power --- an even greater puzzle is that the majority should so philosophically accept it. ...

Another busy week at the shop: £15 worth of repairs again. I keep steadily on with the novel. The weather is very poor: dull and showery.

Tuesday 13 July. There was an Alert last night: 1.27 a.m. till 1.55 a.m.

Wednesday 14 July. Another Alert last night: 12.18 till 12.48. The guns went off at a plane picked up in the searchlights. The plane dropped flares; it was one of ours. ...

Some Americans in the street talking to some women round here were asked what the medals were for that they were wearing. One said that one of them was for being a member of the American expeditionary force (thus confirming Jack's opinion that the Yanks were given a medal when they set out for war!), another for good conduct and the third for bad conduct.

Friday 16 July. Two Alerts last night: 12.33 till 12.58; and 2.45 till 3.00 a.m. There was nothing doing round here.

Saturday 17 July. Jess came home last night. I met her at the station at a quarter to 1.00, walking there with Jim and Jock in the moonlight. I carried a bag for her friends Jean Partridge and Joan Band (who arrived with her) to Newnham, after we got here, and on the way back a policeman asked for my identity card. I hadn't it with me: one of the few occasions I hadn't carried it since the war (due to the Utility sports coat I was wearing which doesn't have an inside pocket for a wallet) and (I think) the only time I've been asked for it. I explained things; and he was all right as he's seen me carrying the bag and asked if I had a fag; I said I hadn't as I didn't smoke. ...

Tuesday 27 July. There was a warning last night: 12.20 to 1.10 a.m. The guns went off. Jess [his wife] was brazen; wouldn't get up till the last minute; she must have felt like it; or tired. I heard one of the quick-firing guns called a rocket gun by people outside.

Today, Jess heard the Alert last night was a try-out associated with Home Guard practice. A policeman told her. Yet people say bombs were dropped. Talk about conflicting reports.

August 1943

Sunday 1 August. I've done little writing this week and the last chapter of the novel still isn't written. Reasons? The weather has been sweltering and I've tried to soak in a little sun for the winter, going on the river most days in the afternoon and evening; and in it several times every day. And I've been a bit broody about the swelling in my back [diagnosed as a benign fatty tumour]; …

My examination result comes through this week. Has the age of miracles passed or hasn't it; by which I mean have I by some stroke of luck passed and finished with the thing? Somehow, the result of the examination has seemed a little thing and of no consequence during the past few days.

Big happenings this week about the war. Mussolini has resigned; Italy will probably soon be out of the war.[18] In a letter Neil Bell said prophets like himself can now shuffle the cards for a fresh divination and that the most cautious might risk a pound or two on a general crack-up before the leaves fall. Let's hope so and get it over. …

Monday 2 August. Dull weather for Bank Holiday. I finished the novel by putting on a spurt all the morning and till 3.00 this afternoon. …

Thursday 5 August. … There was a big holiday-at-home swimming gala at Jesus Green this afternoon, followed by another below Victoria Bridge this evening. Jack won his two events: a 50 yards race, which he did in 29.6 seconds; and the men's

---

[18] Repeated Italian defeats and the Allied invasion of Sicily prompted King Victor Emmanuel III to dismiss Mussolini and have him arrested; he was rescued by German forces in September. He was shot in April 1945 by Italian partisans while attempting to flee to Switzerland.

open diving. ... There were enormous crowds during the afternoon and evening. A pity there was no band. ...

I thought I might hear about the exam today, as I did on this day last year, but it hasn't come through yet. I'm getting quite excited; I don't know why as I'm intent (more or less) on failure.

The Germans have evacuated Orel, which means another big Russian success; and we've taken Catania in Sicily and absolutely bombed Hamburg to the ground. But the Italians haven't packed in yet. There seems to be widespread resentment at the suggested registration of women between 45 and 50 and the compulsory direction of youths between 16 and 18 into the [coal]mines.[19]

Monday 9 August. I didn't feel very grand last Friday dinner-time with my back so I had a lie-down after dinner for an hour. There was a rush on the stairs and Jess, [daughter] Jess and Jack came tearing in the bedroom with the examination result ... I took the letter and as it was thin said I'd failed (the letter telling of a pass contains a pass list and that's fat); I was right and their faces fell. I failed in Economics and History, passing in Constitutional History, in which I failed, together with these other two subjects, last year. So all these stupendous efforts eliminated one more subject, and I've now narrowed down the examinations to two subjects.

What have I to say about it all? Next to nothing, except can so much labour result in so little return! I wrote and told Neil Bell, Don Varley and Wolsey Hall, the interested ones and then turned my mind to the novel ('Judas Stain') I am writing. Another change of title with the one I've just written: 'Only Begotten Son'; it hasn't been used and is better than 'Square Peg'.

---

[19] A decree of December 1942 made all women aged 16-45 liable for war service, and the liability was in due course extended to women aged 45-50. The partial immunity given previously to certain younger women was extended to similar groups over 30. Following the failure of the voluntary recruitment of young men to work in the coalmines a compulsory scheme was instituted for men younger than 25 who were not yet enlisted. Ten per cent of such men were selected by ballot to serve in the mines—the 'Bevin Boys'.

On Saturday I sent off three of my books to publishers; Peter Quick suggested that I did so when returning several manuscripts. I'm not very hopeful of publication, but I will put my name in front of them. …

Sunday 15 August. … I've spent rather a lazy week, doing only work at the shop and hardly any reading and writing. I've passed the time strolling around with Eric (who returned to London yesterday) gossiping about the many things there are to gossip about. …

I wrote to London University the other day asking if I might make application after two attempts at the B. Sc. Econ. Final to sit only for the two subjects in which I failed in order to relieve myself of the deadening effect of many years of constant repetition of subjects in which I've passed. I had a reply and a form showing that war concessions are only available to students doing approved national service, which cuts me (a CO!), out. I also asked them to name the most modern books on Economics and History; they referred me to my correspondence college (according to regulations — in order not to confuse students receiving instructions from two different sources).

Neil Bell's postscript about the exam in a letter last week: 'Good God, I nearly forgot it. … Shows the importance I attach to it in your career. I'll tell the examiner to kiss your arse only that would be honouring them too much.'

I wrote to Roland Hughes (who passed) and had a very friendly reply.

Wednesday 18 August. Last night there was an Alert: 11.55 p.m. till 1.00 a.m. I heard the 'All Clear' go and then we went to sleep; it was moonlight; then suddenly there was a terrific crash and I almost fell out of bed. Jess jumped and clutched me with an 'Oh, Jack', obviously thinking it was a bombing (as I did) and then became strangely quiet; I spoke to her; she did not answer and I felt her heart; then I hopped out of bed and ran round to her side of the bed speaking anxiously to her. She'd fainted. But only for a few moments, for when I put my arms round her to lift her up she spoke. There was a flash and another crash; voices sounded in the street; and unable to make head or tail of it I called Jack and [daughter]

Jess and came down and looked at the clock; I then went upstairs again (the time was 1.15) and Jack and I dressed and came down and had a look out the front door. Rain started to fall; there were more jagged flashes and thunderous crashes and at last we decided it wasn't a bombing, nor gunfire, but a thunderstorm! And so back to bed again. ...

Sunday 22 August. ... I'm working on 'Judas Stain' and have written 14,000 words, most of them last week. Whatever would I do if I didn't read and write and didn't have the dogs; for Jess never wants to go out with me these days? Without those interests my loneliness would be appalling.

Monday 23 August. There was a warning last night: 1.50 till 2.40 a.m.

Tuesday 24 August. A warning last night: 11.45 till 2.00 a.m.

Sunday 29 August. A rather quiet week: shoe repairing, reading and writing. ... This morning Jess and I biked to the Pike and Eel to look at a little houseboat named Tiny, owned by a fellow that comes in the shop. He's thinking about getting a bigger one. I don't know whether we'll buy it; it's certainly a nice little boat.[20] ... We are doing a lot of bombing, and constantly, day and night, there's the roar of bombers passing over. Berlin and Nuremberg have been bashed: and places in Italy, with whom the war drags on in half-hearted fashion. King Boris died yesterday, after being shot in the stomach; he was king of Bulgaria; one by one the big noises are passing from the scene; no-one can regret their going either.[21]

September 1943

Sunday 5 September. Last Friday, the fourth anniversary of the war, we invaded Italy. Yesterday, I had a form from the na-

---

[20] Jack did not buy the boat.
[21] King Boris tried to keep Bulgaria neutral in the war, despite strong German pressure and the pro-German sympathies of many army officers. Bulgaria succumbed, to the extent of helping the German conquest of Greece and Yugoslavia. The death of King Boris, aged 49 (almost certainly due to natural causes) and the loss of his negotiating skills, meant that Bulgaria was forced to join the Nazi attack on Russia. The country perforce fell into the Soviet camp after the Russian victory.

tional service office telling me it was being considered whether I [should] be directed into civil defence. I wrote back and said I was provisionally registered as a CO. Until I'm erased from the register of conscientious objectors they cannot do this, as I have all the privileges of a CO. I'm only liable for firewatching (nobody's exempt) and I'm doing it. ...

Tuesday 7 September. Two Alerts last night: 9.55 p.m. till 10.23 p.m., 3.27 a.m. till 3.45 a.m. I heard bombs were dropped round Haverhill.

Wednesday 8 September. All alone at tea today I picked up the evening paper (*Cambridge Daily News*). In the Stop Press column it was said that Italy had unconditionally surrendered.[22] ...

Thursday 9 September. An Alert last night: 10.20 till 10.55 p.m. ...

Friday 10 September. Don [Varley] arrived last night [on leave]. I went to the station with the Jesses in taxi to meet him at 10.30. He came in the shop today with Jess [daughter]. I thought he looked tired and ill. He doesn't like the navy. Said it's a very rough life. ...

 I dreamt the other night that my spate of words is the result of a spirit from **the other side** named Maijisa, an adult-minded female child wearing skirts about two feet six inches high! She demonstrated her control by levitating me through the air and sending my head through the ceiling without hurting me. I objected on the grounds that I didn't like heights! She assured me that our association was of the friendliest and only good would come of it. What we dream!

Saturday 11 September. The other day I had an interesting peep into the mind of a religious Victorian; a man, aged 76, an all-the-year-round bather, whom I met when going to work along the Backs. We talked and one thing leading to another, religion became the topic. He was surprised that a man of my sort (he knows I'm a teetotaller and non-smoker) didn't believe in

[22] Few Italians supported the war against the Allies. Mussolini's successor, Marshal Badoglio, negotiated with the Allies in the summer of 1943. The Italian surrender on 3 September was not announced until a few hours before the Allied invasion on the 9th.

God. But what a Christian he turned out to be. He was unable to define his terms (God, sin, etc.), knew nothing of the writings of Huxley and Darwin and Keith, disbelieved in Pavlov's and discredited Haldane's works, and showed an entire lack of faith in his own kind; so much so that by a devious path I got him to admit that he thought human nature was fundamentally rotten. Weak in economics and with no knowledge of biology and psychology he was all the while groping in the dark. I told him that those who perpetuated the present social system were more guilty than those who violated it: but it was obvious that brought up in capitalist traditions he believed in 'what I have, I hold' and thought the present social system a fine one. He thought it was a sin to steal a loaf of bread. I said character depended on heredity and environment; that a different type would evolve once the evils of these days are removed; and that the bulk of the men, women and children that fill our prisons and reformatories were there largely because of [a] faulty economic system, the rest being largely due to diseases of the human body and needing, not prison, but the attention of physicians, psychologists, geneticists, biologists and others like them—none of which he believed a little bit. No wonder there's been two world wars in my lifetime following a generation of that kind of men.

Monday 12 September. ... Jess and I had a walk round the town in the afternoon. We didn't manage to buy much: no sweets, even though I had some coupons; and little else. Most of the shops shut at 5.00; they've nothing to sell.

I went firewatching just after 9.00, talked to another fellow there till 1.30, left at 5.30, came home and went to bed at 6.00, dozed till 8.45 when Jess got up and brought me up a cup of tea. I came down full of a short story, gobbled my breakfast and then wrote for three hours the short story I had in mind. I called it 'An Accident for Design' and sent it to Neil Bell for his opinion. I feel full of short stories, but don't know whether I have the knack to twist them into shape. In any case, I haven't the time to write them, all of it going on novels. ...

The war has sent morals all to pieces. All the women round here carry on with the Yanks; except about two; married women included; many of them have illegitimate children and most of the husbands are in the Middle East. One girl married; her photo as a bride appeared in the local paper; a week later she was in the archway opposite kissing an American soldier.

Sunday 19 September. Jess went back to Huddersfield last Tuesday morning. Don saw her off. She looked a little tearful ... . She doesn't like the North of England, nor the people much. She thinks they're not quite as civilised as southerners.

Jack passed the School Certificate: seven subjects out of eight. He only got one credit and no distinctions, ... Well, now he's in 6B at school and I hope he starts to work in earnest. I've started saving to send him to Cambridge. He's taking English, French and History as principal subjects and Latin as a subsidiary subject for the Higher School Certificate. By the bye, it was Latin in which he failed and as this is compulsory for the entrance to Cambridge University I've arranged (by telephoning his headmaster) for him to have special coaching for it so that he can sit again in December. Don Varley tells me this costs about £12; but it's worth it, as he'll not do any good with Latin without a good grounding in the subject; and he hasn't got that now.

Neil Bell didn't think much of my short story. And offered to send four of his latest; an offer I accepted. I read them yesterday (three round about midnight while firewatching); three were fine; one only so-so. He said they were all tripe and he was money grubbing. I wrote to him about them today. ...

The war: Russia still making headway. Our troops and the Americans are now fighting the Germans round Salerno in Italy.[23] There's a lot of unrest in this country as the many strikes show. ...

Wednesday 22 September. There was an Alert last night as I was going to bed; 11.00 till 11.50 p.m. There were a number of planes about and I went and had a look outside. It was a starry night. They're ours, I thought; and went upstairs. ...

---

[23] Salerno, where the Allies invaded Italy on 9 September, is south of Naples. A fierce German counter-attack was beaten off by 16 September, and the advance north began.

Thursday 23 September. An Alert last night: 12.50 till 1.12 a.m. ...
Friday 24 September. An Alert last night: 12.13 till 12.40 a.m.

An English and History master named Hollingworth at Jack's school, who has had several thrillers published, has read my book 'The Cordwainer'.[24] He didn't seem to think a lot of it, judging from the long letter he wrote me. There wasn't enough detail. ... He overlooked the fact that I was writing a book of a length suitable to wartime publishing (though it didn't come off). Apparently, he wants everything described in a novel: the room, the dress, the furniture, the tone of voice --- but I think descriptions of still life can be overdone; the reader is apt to tire. I prefer to put more scenes in, presenting fresh aspects of the characters' lives, than over-elaboration of a few scenes. He thought the book a list of the main character's major copulations. He's wrong. There was much else besides copulation to depict the cordwainer's life: drinking, fighting, politics, shoemaking, trade unionism. And if Charlie Chapman (the cordwainer) was just a crude animal—was he less flesh and blood for that? Aren't many men just animals, using women to work off their sexual instincts? He overlooked the real theme of the book: Charlie born a bastard, having a stingy aunt, a miserable time as an apprentice, a tough time in London, fighting in the ring and on strike, and a life of hardness and bitterness, largely due to the disruption in his family life caused by the economic conditions of his time; all corroding his mind and souring him, his independent nature not being the sort to knuckle under and urging him to hit back hard and chance the consequences. Yes, I think Hollingworth misjudges the book; if he didn't then I didn't make a job of it; and I believe I did.

Monday 27 September. Today, I went and saw Mr [A. E.] Dove, Jack's headmaster. Apparently Jack did badly in the School Certificate, only really scraping through on the aggregate of his subjects. ... I wanted him to stop on at school; that was definite; and I wanted him to go to the university, even if I

---

[24] Leonard Hollingworth (BA, St Catharine's College, 1916) was the author of an English grammar for schools and three crime novels published in the 1930s.

have to pay. He said Jack's bad pass in the S.C. complicated matters, as he hadn't reached matriculation standard (four credits); ... [But] there's still time for him to do well. I believe he will.

As I type I can hear the piano going in the Spread Eagle playing 'All the Nice Girls Love a Sailor'. There's a lot of life up there these days; but I don't envy them a little bit. There's a lot of life round here altogether now, for the women are having a good time with the American soldiers. So good, in fact, that many of them are, or have been, in the family way; and one of them has just been arrested in Doric Street for procuring miscarriages.

October 1943

Sunday 3 October. There was an Alert last night: 1.45 a.m. till 2.45 a.m. while I was firewatching. The three of us got up, dressed and went down into the street. The night was starry and cold; searchlights up in every direction. Many of our planes were returning from a bombing raid; some had lights (red, green and yellow). There were flashes in the sky followed by half a dozen heavy crashes Oakington or Waterbeach way. We didn't know if it were bombs or gunfire. I thought very likely bombs; that, perhaps, a raider had joined our planes coming back and were on their tails as they landed. There were more explosions, this time, I should say it was gunfire; then I went back to our room and lit the gas fire and made tea. The others came in; the 'Raiders Passed' signal went soon afterwards and we went back to kip. ...

A woman round here has been had up for bringing about miscarriages. A Yank soldier bailed her out for £20. ... An American soldier tried to get a white horse to go up the little archway opposite this house on Friday afternoon: it wouldn't; so he went and got another, a brown one; that went up and slipped over on the pavement; he rolled clear and the horse was unhurt; luckily there were no children in the archway; there usually are. All this was to show off to the barmaid in the Spread Eagle. Did you ever! Then another Yank soldier came along on a little horse, Don Quixote fashion. They're a rum lot with too much cash to spend; they buy up all the English women wholesale. The way they lounge at street corners is reminiscent of another kind of lounging—of the out of work. Maybe, a lot of them were before the war.

Most **incidents** that happen in the town—stabbings, assaults—are hushed up. There's a lot go on these days we know nothing about; by 'we' I mean the general public outside eyewitnesses. …

Neil Bell sent some sultanas in return for the Ryvita and promised to send us some fish.[25]

There was an Alert every evening or night from Monday 4th to Saturday 9th October, Wednesday's occurring when Jack and Jess were in the Central cinema; a warning was flashed on the screen and the audience left.

Sunday 10 October. The Alerts during the past week have reminded us of the dreadful autumn of 1940. But so far there's been nothing doing over the town. Histon was bombed last Saturday week, the night I was firewatching and thought the crumps were bombs and not gunfire. There's a moon and maybe that's an inducement to the Germans to try reprisals for the terrible raids we are making on the Continent.

Joad has written a new book.[26] He thinks man needs a faith to believe in and argues that unless people are given a religious receptacle into which to pour their natural emotions of reverence and worship, we must expect these same emotions to be lavished on dictators. Well what's the difference in lavishing them on God instead of Hitler? Or isn't God a dictator? And Christianity has left more wars in its train than Hitler is ever likely to, or any other dictator. …

Don came home for the weekend. He popped in this morning and walking to the shop with him I soled and heeled his

---

[25] In the summer of 1942 the 'zoning' of foodstuffs was introduced. To reduce the costs of distribution retailers were permitted to draw supplies only from wholesalers within their own food zone.

[26] Joad's book mentioned here is possibly *God and Evil* (1942) or *Is Christianity True? A Correspondence between Arnold Lunn and CEMJ* (4th edition 1943).

boots in leather, having saved him a pair of soles. For the heels I used seven bits of leather, which is now very scarce.

Wednesday 13 October. There was a warning last night: 9.15 till 9.35 p.m. Today, Jess had to go under a *sub poena* as a witness in a divorce case [in the High Court]: ... While another case was on in the courtroom I was reading *John O' London's Weekly*. Suddenly I was tapped on the shoulder and the Clerk of the Court said severely that if I wanted to read I must go outside, the place was not a public reading room and my action was contempt of court. ...

 We mooned around for most of the day, waiting for the case to come off, going in restaurants for snacks and buying foodstuff to bring home. Shops were full of sweets and chocolate; they're usually empty of them in Cambridge and the month's ration of 12 ounces we waste on any rubbishy sweets that are going. We came home early in case of air raids. ...

 War news. Russia is still advancing: Italy has declared war on Germany! Churchill has declared against nationalisation of the coalmines and there's talk of compulsory call-up of labour in this industry.

Thursday 14 October. A warning last night: 8.45 till 9.00 p.m. At the assizes held in the town today, the three women had up over abortion ... were dealt with. Two got nine months, one got off. The latter had told the others what to do; she had no hand in the actual doing; and I suppose the jury decided that people need not put their heads in the fire when told. The judge said there were no mitigating circumstances. Weren't there, separated from their husbands for years and living in a neighbourhood like this? It's so easy to condemn; it would do many judges good to go to jail and find out what it is like; indeed, they should all serve six months hard labour to qualify for their jobs; then they would know just what was the sentence they were handing out. I think these women were given a raw deal by an obsolete social system that deprived them of their husbands' consortium (I think that's the legal word for it). I see little crime in getting rid of unwanted children; it was done at the women's own personal risk; apparently, a very small risk in the case of the rich: in the operation itself and in the likelihood of getting found out (class again!). And think of it from the standpoint of the children—the world they are coming into, pushed and shoved about and generally uncared for owing to the circumstances of their births. There was no separate existence; and if there was why should murder alarm the authorities when they encourage, incite and force men to murder each other in the prime of their lives for such mythical qualities as freedom and liberty. More to the point would be to send the men responsible for all the rumpus to jail.

Monday 18 October. ... I'm reading a novel 'Coin my Heart' by Hollingworth. It's in manuscript form as he hasn't so far got it published. It's good as far as I've got and I think it will see the light of day yet. I'm plodding along with 'Judas Stain'; it's about 80,000 words at present. As I've nearly twenty more years to write about John Cash's life and these 80,000 words represent about a year of it, I'll have to get a move on or I'll be bumbling along on it for ever.

There were air-raid Alerts during the night of Monday 18 October and the evenings of Tuesday and Wednesday, 19 and 20 October.

Thursday 21 October. The more I see of the Yank soldiers about here the more I think they're a race of their own and nothing like the English. There's one thing in common: the same language; nothing else. Even the Poles about here resemble us more than they do. They're a round-shouldered, flat-footed, slouching lot of men; most of them gum chewers.

There were air-raid Alerts during the evening of Friday 22 October and the evening of Saturday, 23 October.

Sunday 24 October. An Alert last night (while I was firewatching) 12.00 a.m. till 12.13 a.m. ... A lot is happening regarding the war: especially in Russia, where [Anthony] Eden (Britain) Cordell Hull (USA) and [V. M.] Molotov (Russia) are in conference and where the Russian armies are making big advances.[27] But I'm too tired to write about it and will content myself with saying that I think there will be a quick ending of the war with Germany.

---

[27] At the Moscow conference of the three foreign ministers Britain and the USA reaffirmed their commitment to invade France in the spring of 1944.

An Alert this evening: 8.22 p.m. till 9.32 p.m.

Sunday 31 October. ... Last night when I reported for firewatching, the fellow who's been with Jim Long and myself didn't turn up, having become a street leader for firewatching; and Jim Long turned up, said he was ill (he looked ill) and went home; so I went on strike on principle and returned home to bed. The local firewatching clique have had plenty of time to send another man along on our night, for they've been deliberating about switching Wilkinson over to street leader for three weeks, and I considered that I had a case against them. Only two of us did duty for 11 weeks in the summer and I knew that if one was ill, there would be difficulties; they knew it, too; and they should guard against it now the long nights are here. If they can be indifferent about it, so can I. Three's the number and three there should be.

November 1943

There were air-raid Alerts in the evenings of Monday, Wednesday, Thursday and Saturday, 1, 3, 4, and 6 November.

Sunday 7 November. Two Alerts last night while I was firewatching: 11.00 a.m. till 11.15 a.m. [and] 11.45 till 12.30 a.m.

A record week's work at the shop: £15 18*s* 6*d* worth. I should think this gave me £12 clear profit. I don't think I'd like to keep it up. Crouching over a hobiron and working fast is more exhausting than anybody might think. ...

Already, now the fear of Hitlerism is waning, the people are showing themselves out of harmony with the social system. Many asleep before the war are waking up, and beginning to realise they've been had again, having fought the war in vain. (This is the opinion of many that I talk to; not my opinion. I've felt for a long while that fighting wars was a vain sort of effort to make the world a better place to live in.)

Monday 8 November. Today, while at dinner, I received a wire [telegram] from Neil Bell which read: SOS Daily Bread Neil. This was a call for Ryvita, which I am sending him, for as it is a foodstuff that is zoned outside Devonshire, he cannot get it. It is on the points system of rationing: two points a packet (we are allowed 20 points per person a month), and as we'd run out of points through Jess [daughter] coming home at half-term I borrowed a dozen points from the next door neighbours (evacuees), and after a trot round the shops, managed to get it at the fourth one, when I sent it off, wiring him it was [on] the way. ...

Thursday 11 November. ... Poppies were sold in the street [for Remembrance Day]. I was only asked a few times to buy one. Of course, I didn't buy one. Not likely. I know better than to help those sort of charities for maimed ex-servicemen. The Government should do that.

Friday 12 November. A kiddie aged four in the street today was blowing up a used French letter, while a little girl, aged two, watched him enviously. Jess spotted him out of the window and was about to go out to him, when another woman came up and called out to his mother: 'Mrs Bates, look what your Donald's doing, blowing up one of them things the Americans use'. ...

Saturday 13 November. A letter from Neil Bell. The Ryvita took till Thursday to get to him. I must post him on a stock so that he doesn't run short. In a letter he said he'd die without it. ...

Sunday 14 November. ... Our bombing of Germany must be terrible. All day long and often all night long as well there is the roar of our bombers setting out for the Continent. ...

Thursday 18 November. This afternoon I went to the field just before the mound on [the] Harston road to be introduced to an Italian prisoner of war named Rossi. He was working there with a gang of prisoners (although the Italians are now co-belligerents these men are still prisoners) and Frank Edwards, who introduced us, was their ganger. ... Rossi is 23 and was taken prisoner at Bardia in 1941 (January). His home is in Milan and by trade he's a bookbinder. He's heard nothing from his people since May as the Germans, who occupy North Italy, do not permit correspondence. He speaks quite good English and hopes I visit him and his family in Italy after the war. He said he thought war was the outcome of government ambition and was contemptuous of the idea of men like him and me killing each other without knowing each other. I took the gang 10 lbs of Blenheim apples as a little gift and nearly 40 copies of *Lilliput* and *Men Only*, most of which I got for the purpose from Ken Craske. ...

Sunday 21 November. I'm still sending out 'The Cordwainer' and 'Tale of a Taylor' to publishers: with no luck. The former is off to Robert Hale tomorrow. ...

Tuesday 23 November. ... Mark Horner came in the shop: returned from London where he went a fortnight ago to take up a course of study promoted by some society of the blind to fit him for work as a masseur. His nerves are bad. He said he's now lost his chance and felt he's let himself down, his pride was hurt. I said I wasn't interested in his pride, only his health; and reminded him of the saying that pride went before a fall. I told him not to worry, he was 28 and healthy, he'd get a living. His answer was that he wanted a good living. I said 'So do a good many more'.

In passing, Frank Edwards said I'd argue with my own shadow!

Sunday 28 November. ... Neil Bell sent us some fish; sole and whiting; it was good. ... I didn't firewatch last night. The key was lost when I signed on and we couldn't get in the building. It was suggested that Jim Long and I broke open a small window and crawled into the place to get the key hanging up in the hall (the front door had slammed on the previous night's firewatchers when leaving the house); I said that was their job, not ours; so did Jim Long; and we came home.

December 1943

Wednesday 1 December. There was an Alert this evening from 8.07 till 8.40 p.m.

Sunday 5 December. ... The war. More raids on Berlin and a big one on Leipzig. It's terrible to read about it. I always think of the children involved. Poor little things; what an upbringing. It must engender hate. A not very happy augury for the future. ...

I went in the water this morning and felt the better for it. I never feel so fit as I do when I run over the frosted grass to go into the river naked on a winter's morning. It is an exhilarating feeling. --- ...

I'm calling this novel — the third of the series — 'The book of June.' Jess, whom it's largely about, thinks it best not to name her in the book, so I've changed her name to June (she was born in June anyway) in it. This title is in keeping with the religious or quasi-religious titles of the four and it's culled from the book of Job. So the first 'Whims of the Father' is mainly about the father, the second 'Only Begotten Son', about the son, and this one (the third) about the son's wife. The fourth (the last of the series) will be 'Judas Stain' (from which has evolved these three). What it will be like I don't know. I don't even know yet what these three are like.

Thursday 9 December. The Christmas waits are in the street playing carols. How delightful they sound. ... suddenly as I returned [from a walk] I heard the waits playing 'While Shepherds Watch Their Flock' followed by 'Once in Royal David's City'; and did they sound grand and Christmassy. I passed the band (the Salvation Army) on Brookside ... . Gradually the band has worked its way into the street and they're still playing; now it's 'Good King Wenceslas'. May peace soon be restored to us and Christmas a time of peace and goodwill.

Friday 10 December. I sent 'The Cordwainer' to Robert Hale on 22 November and as I had no acknowledgement I wrote them after a fortnight and asking if they'd received it. They sent a letter saying they had and they were sorry for the oversight, due to further call-up of staff. This morning I heard from them again saying that further reports were of an encouraging nature; in the meantime would I let them have a few autobiographical facts about myself, including when this book was written, was it a first novel, and had I written any others. ... I wrote Robert Hale as follows:

Dear Sirs,

Thank you for your letter about 'The Cordwainer'. In reply to your inquiries: I am 40 years old, married and have two children, a daughter aged 20 and a son aged 16. I am a shoe-repairer and work on my own account in a small way. My father, grandfather and brothers were all shoemakers.

I've written several other books besides 'The Cordwainer' (finished recently): their titles are: 'Tale of a Taylor' (the story of a man's sex life); 'Jim Baxter – Snob' (the tale of a shoemaker with a modern background: 1910–1939); 'Queen Street' (the story of a cul-de-sac of 25 houses). But it's only now that I feel my work is good enough to send to a publisher. ...

Well, that's that. Here's hoping!

There's a glorious full moon tonight and as I finished writing Bell the siren sounded. Shortly afterwards there was the sound of bombs crashing in the distance. The warning was from 7.15 p.m. till 8.35 p.m.

Tuesday 14 December. During the last two spells of firewatching there's been a notice on the table saying 'Water cut off'. Firewatchers with no water! I received a letter from Hale this morning asking me to submit to them for consideration: 'Tale of a Taylor', 'Jim Baxter – Snob' and 'Queen Street'. ...

Telephoning Neil Bell Jack was advised that there was a possibility of publication and that he should send the MSS in neat condition.

He told me not to get hurried, as publishers never hurried themselves; and not to sign anything if they sent it along until he's seen it, as he didn't want me to have regrets later on. ... I've written to Hale and said I'm sending off the MSS under separate cover on successive days; this is to give me the chance to get them bound. Remembering the do over 'Queen Street' with Constable, I'll keep an open mind about things; but the suspense frets me and I don't feel much in the mood for writing the last chapter of 'The Book of June'. But I must keep at it. ...

Sunday 19 December. ... Thoughts about the possibility of publication have rather flung me out of gear this week, but I'm not being too optimistic in case I'm turned down, when the disappointment will not be so great. ... Jess [daughter, home for Christmas] got A. S. Neill, *That Dreadful School* [1937] out of the public library and last night I read it through while firewatching; I didn't get much sleep, but the book was interesting. I don't agree with all he says in this and his other books (there's contradictions), but I think there's method in his madness. ...

There were Alerts on Sunday and Monday 20 and 21 December.

Thursday 23 December. ... Today, I was walking to work along Fen Causeway when two lorries carrying nine coffins (six on one and three on another) laid out in rows of three, covered in Union Jacks with wreaths on top passed me. Evidently a bomber crew off for burial. I felt shocked at the sight.

Friday 24 December. Just before 1 o'clock last night the bombers from the 'dromes round here began setting out on a big raid on Berlin. They kept roaring over ever so low; and then after going to sleep again I was suddenly awakened by a terrific explosion, the blast of which nearly sent the windows in. I guessed what it was: a bomber taking off had crashed bringing death swift and sudden to the crew; for I doubt if any of them survived that.

I left off at midday; had dinner (after a dip in the river) at the British Restaurant on Mill Road; listened to the carols broadcast from King's College, Cambridge and then a walk down the town to Bowes' bookshop. Been reading Edgar Wallace's biography by Margaret Lane [1938]; a Christmas present from [daughter] Jess. I bought her Tolstoy's *War and Peace.* I gave Jack 12*s* 6*d* to buy records; and Jess [wife] 10*s* for ear-rings (more if necessary); Jess [wife] bought me a jumper; Jack's present is to come.

Saturday 25 December. I've had the typewriter done up for £2 by a chap that comes in the shop; it's like new. ... I've spent the day eating and writing. We have a few sweets and some apples Jess stored. And for [despite] all rationing meals have been good: liver and bacon for breakfast; pork, sprouts, potatoes, plum pudding and custard for dinner (and mincepies and a cup of tea); and salmon, Christmas cake, mincepies and other titbits for tea.

Now I'm off firewatching. ---

Sunday 26 December. I returned from firewatching this morning at about 6.30. I spent most of the night reading A. S. Neill's *The Problem Teacher* [1939]; I like most of his stuff, but I don't take it all as gospel; far from it. ... Read and wrote the day away.

Wednesday 29 December. I wrote to Neil Bell tonight: 'I've just finished writing 'The Book of June' (Big Ben is striking 9 o'clock), a near shave to do it by the year end. This gives me a couple of days to get in a supply of exam books and to think about the beginning of 'Judas Stain', which I start on 1 January. Lately I've felt tumourish [Jack had a benign tumour on his back] and tiredish, but that's because I've lazed and loafed in the evenings. So I shout *"En avant"* — and feel thankful that I have 48 hours respite before doing it!'

Friday 31 December. I started writing 'Judas Stain' today, writing about 500 words. Passed most of the evening on my own reading Margaret Lane's biography of Edgar Wallace: a very unprincipled fellow according to all accounts.

1944

January 1944

Saturday 1 January. There was a terrific row in the street last night after I got to bed; Jess was up. A Londoner living in Terrace Lane wanted to fight an American who had walked into his house and put £2 down on the table. The Londoner was half-drunk and with much profanity bawled out that his wife wasn't a prostitute. At times he spoke in a pitiful maudlin manner to his pal Stan, telling him the tale how he thought the American was counting his money: 'Jist picture it Stan, us there quietlike and in 'e walks say'n he'd been told goo to number 9 (his address) an' me think'n 'e was countin' out 'is money'; then he bawled out fiercely 'You ain't gitt'n away with it Yankee, you bleedin' shithouse; I'll do yer (shades of Mrs Mop[p] a la Tommy Handley)[1] yer yeller bastard, I will'. Whining again. 'Arrest 'im Stan, arrest 'im' --- and so it went on for a long while, the Yank all the time keeping as mum as an oyster. ...

Sunday 2 January. Another fight outside last night (it was a fight this time if not the night before). Two Americans had a dust-up in the Archway over who should take two girls home; they wanted to prove who was best man. In the scrap one (if not both) of the girls had her face slapped by one of them. I was firewatching, but according to Jess there was a regular hullabaloo. What a neighbourhood!

I had a poor night firewatching. 'Boss' Benton snored his head off and kept me awake nearly all the night. On top of that a trainer plane droned over the town from the time I set out to the time I came home this morning: 6 o'clock; and in the middle of the night our bombers set out on a big raid to Berlin, returning in the early hours of this morning. The wireless re

---

[1] Mrs Mopp was a character in Tommy Handley's comedy programme *ITMA*. Her comments had ribald implications.

ports today that we lost 28 bombers. My word, the noise they make going over. ...

... I've written a couple of pages of 'Judas Stain' and read good bit of *The Common People*[2] by Cole and Postgate. ...

There were brief air-raid Alerts on 3 and 16 January.

Sunday 9 January. ... Life is very much the same: shoe-repairing, novel-writing (I've written about 7,000 words of 'Judas Stain') and now I've started examination work again. I'm in the river most days at dinnertime and trot Jim and Jock with me wherever I go.

I'm reading Margaret Lane's biography of Edgar Wallace. He strikes me as a man who had no principles at all. As for his jingoism and acceptance of society as it was (and still is) the least said the better. Apparently, she didn't think much of him as a writer. I've read very little of his stuff; and that many years ago and so I am unable to give an opinion of it. She mentions that one of the books had a sale of half a million; and in a letter to Neil Bell this morning I wondered whether a best seller was ever a really good book in view of the average man and woman being so badly educated through no fault of their own. ...

Wednesday 19 January. I sent Neil Bell some Ryvita yesterday and as Hale [the publisher] had not written sent him a wire just after breakfast this morning: DAILY BREAD DESPATCHED STOP NO NEWS FROM HALE IS IT A BAD SIGN Jack. Every morning lately I've been rather anxiously looking out for the post and at last felt I must do something; just to try to curb myself.

Neil Bell telephoned this evening round about 8.00. ... He thought the delay was a good sign and that Hale would now certainly publish 'The Cordwainer', probably two of the four and perhaps all of them as a series. ... he expected Hale to make me a handsome offer before the end of the month.

Saturday 22 January. There was an Alert last evening: 9.10 p.m. till 10.05 p.m. and the guns opened up. There was another Alert in the night: 4.45 a.m. till 5.45 a.m.

---

[2] *The Common People* was a left-wing social history of Britain since 1746, first published in 1938.

There follows an extract from a long letter, copied in the diary, which Jack wrote to Neil Bell on 22 January:

And then in walked a Salvation Army chap. Would I give a small donation?

No I wouldn't.

Why not?

Because I don't believe in the Salvation Army.

Their religious principles?

Yes.

What has that to do with their work of relieving the down-and-outs?

I was floored. True, I could have said that was the concern of the State, not mine. But that wouldn't help the down-and outs. I admitted I was in the wrong and gave him two bob [2s]. He grasped my hand and shook it. I mused. My antipathy to the Salvation Army was unreasonable. I hadn't thought deeply enough about it. The chap shaking my hand was probably a night-worker, who instead of being abed was out collecting small sums to help people worse off than himself. A better man by a lot than myself. And what were the religious beliefs of the SA to do with me? Didn't I believe in toleration? I said as much. Encouraged he said that they thought the word of Christ raised people in mind and body. I said maybe there never was a Christ. Only one contemporary historian of the time mentioned Him: one bit that might have been slipped in long afterwards. He seemed disorientated. I felt contrite. What did it matter, anyway, I added, whether he lived or not? The standards He set or that are attributed to him are good enough. He went then, seeming rather glad to go, and subdued I went back to my seat. I'd licked myself for a change. ...

A last word. It warmed the cockles of my heart to hear you call me Jack on the phone last month. You must have noticed I haven't called you Neil. Silly of me I know. It's my elementary school complex. But I'll get over it. ...

So ends the letter to Neil Bell.

Wednesday 26 January. About being tried as a CO (for that's what it is), I feel I should object to the composition of the Tribunal to start with [a meeting being expected soon]: a fat-bellied miller, a civil court judge and a local professor of history (a knight);³ three yes-men of a decadent social system; and all with one foot in the grave. Where's the worker's representative? ...

Friday 28 January. Neil Bell sent us a tin of golden syrup. ...

Saturday 29 January. There was an Alert last night at 10.30 p.m. for about an hour. ...

I've just received a bulletin called QUESTIONS FOR COs which I sent away for to the Central Board for COs. They present few difficulties to me; and many of them I can twist to the Tribunal's discomfiture. ...

Sunday 30 January. There was an Alert last night from 8.15 p.m. till 9.40 p.m. ...

February 1944

There was an air-raid Alert in the evening of 3 February and another in the small hours of 4 February.

Saturday 5 February. ... Yesterday she [Jess] and I had dinner in the British Restaurant.⁴ We do this when we have nothing at home. I've had to go to Coldham's Lane twice this week for meat for the dogs. It seems rather short. And dog biscuits are difficult to get; they have been for a long while.

Sunday 6 February. I had no sleep firewatching last night. George Benton snored his head off. As the clock had stopped in the room and none of us had watches I went for a walk in the early hours of the morning. There was a glorious moon, the weather was cold, and I walked up St Barnabas Road, along Mill Road and Queen Anne Terrace to Hyde Park Corner. The time was 3.30 a.m. I had a short talk to a war-reserve policeman who hoped the bloody war would soon be over and thought it would as we were thrashing the Germans, and then I returned along St Barnabas Road to the depot in

---

³ For the tribunal see the entry for 21 April 1944. The miller was J. Nutter of the Station Mill, Fulbourn; the justice Judge William Lawson Campbell and the historian Sir John Clapham. For the two last see notes 6–7 for 1940.

⁴ The British Restaurant, one of a State-run chain opened to provide cheap and nutritious meals in wartime, was at the corner of St Andrews Street and Petty Cury, in the Old Post Office: see note 10.

St Barnabas Road again. G.B. was still snoring heavily and I read (tried to?) Cole's *Means to Full Employment* [1943]. I came home at 5.00 and went to bed. While I was in bed there was an Alert; I haven't yet found out the time; and we got up at 9.30. I took the dogs round the 'Green' [Sheeps Green]; the river was frozen over; then I wrote Jess [daughter] and sent the *New Statesman* and *The Economist* to Don; and wrote to George Barnsley of Sheffield for some 92 rasps as my local dealer hasn't had any for months and without a good rasp shoe-repairing becomes hard work.

I'm writing and studying rather sluggishly. Things seem a bit lopsided at present. The Alert was: 6.10 a.m. till 6.30 a.m.

Tuesday 8 February. I came home from work at dinnertime today feeling that the books were back from Hale. And they were with a letter of rejection in one of them. It bowled me over and I broke down and cried. Yet, I hadn't been too hopeful all along. But the wait of 11 weeks was too long. I went upstairs to get out of the way and Jess came up and comforted me. She suggested I chucked up writing (not seriously though) and I said it would be the end of the world.

… They [the publishers] said they would probably have made me an offer for one of the books had it not been for the shortage of paper through the war (the usual excuse), very likely 'Queen Street', and thought that I might be interested in their reader's report on it. I wasn't. I know as much about 'Queen Street' as anybody can tell me. I wrote it and have read it dozens of times and know all its defects as well as its good points without anyone telling me. What I wanted to know about was 'The Cordwainer'; but there was no further word of their reader's encouraging report and why they wanted autobiographical details about me. Obviously, they were frightened off 'The Cordwainer' by the tone of the other three books and were not straightforward enough (like Michael Sadleir) to say so. I felt betrayed. I sent the letter to Neil Bell.

Thursday 10 February. Forty-one. Birthday cards from the family and a wire from Neil Bell which read MY DEAR JACK DESPITE

HALE I SEND YOU MANY HAPPY RETURNS YOU HAVE LOST THE FIRST ROUND BUT IT IS ONLY THE FIRST I AM WRITING YOU THIS MORNING NEIL.

... Jess made a plum pudding and a birthday cake. I went to the Arts Theatre with her and Jack to see a picture about Pitt the Younger. ...

Friday 11 February. Jess came home today for half-term. ... There was an Alert this evening: 8.25 p.m. till 8.40 p.m.

Sunday 13 February. Another rotten night firewatching owing to George Benton's snoring. I mooned about the streets some of the time and came home early to bed. I wrote to Neil Bell. Told him I didn't think it was lack of 'form' why my books weren't published; it wasn't how I write but what I write; and by the time I acquire 'form' in writing I'll have run dry, my writing will have no punch in it and be unreadable. ...

I'm trying to plan my next novel 'Finger in the Pie' as Neil Bell suggests. There was an Alert this evening: 8.50 till 9.40 p.m.

Monday 14 February. Don Varley was here last evening. We heard [daughter] Jess go up to bed just before 4 o'clock. ... [Jess and Don have] fallen out. [Wife] Jess and I have been very unhappy about it today and we don't feel very friendly disposed towards Don. ...

[After going to various places in Cambridge Jack went] to the public library for the address of a publisher; then to the post office to get off three of the books to different publishers; ...[then did] a bit of planning on 'Finger in the Pie'. Now for exam work and some writing of 'Judas Stain'. ... .

Thursday 17 February. ... A call from the income tax man this afternoon ... . If I didn't pay the war damage insurance on this house and 99, Shelford Road, I'd be summoned next week. Hard up I borrowed the money out of Jess's college fees and paid it.

A letter from Neil Bell this morning. Should he get Hale to send his reader's report on 'The Cordwainer', and ask in confidence if what I say and not how I say it is the stumbling block to my getting published? He said answer quickly and I wired him yes.

I went to see Maurice Dobb.[5] He was very friendly. (He's an M.A. of Cambridge and a Ph.D. of London; and he's secretary to the board of the Faculty of Economics of Cambridge University.) We had a long talk. Not only did he recommend books for the exam, but also said he'd lend me some (textbooks are now hard to get owing to the war); and had I been able to get off work during the day would have made arrangements for me to use the Marshall Library of Economics. Further, if I'll work some past papers of London University under examination conditions just before the exam, he'll go through them with me to see if he can make any suggestions. He suggested as the London School of Economics is in residence in Cambridge that I write to London University and ask to sit [the exam] here; he said it would only mean finding me a desk and they should find no difficulty is doing that.[6] He said he wasn't examining for London University any more. ...

I've written Loughborough College to try and get Jack there for a three years' course as physical instructor and games leader. ... [I] sent a lot of newspaper cuttings of his doings with my application.

Friday 18 February. Received Neil Bell's *Child of my Sorrow* from him. Determined to set everything aside except shoe-repairing and read it.

Saturday 19 February. An Alert last night: 12.35 till 1.45 a.m. ...

Sunday 20 February. Read *Child of my Sorrow* all night with my ears stuffed with cotton wool to keep out George Benton's snoring while firewatching. The cotton wool didn't work.

Monday 21 February. There was an Alert last night: 9.50 till 10.50 p.m. ... I went to the Guildhall about firewatching this

---

[5] After his Ph.D. from the London School of Economics Maurice Herbert Dobb (1900-1976) became a lecturer in economics at Cambridge in 1924, and later a Fellow of Trinity. A member of the Communist Party since 1922, he was a leading Marxist intellectual. Courteous and gentlemanly, he was very diffident, which may explain his apparent reticence when Jack talked of his failure in his degree examinations (see the diary entry for 5 August).

[6] During the war several colleges of London University were relocated to Cambridge colleges, whose resident undergraduates were themselves depleted in number.

afternoon. Managed to get changed over to Thursday nights, which is better for the weekends and rids me of George Benton's snoring. Soon, the rota system is being brought in. ...

Tuesday 22 February. I've temporarily abandoned novel writing to concentrate on exam work. Hope to polish it off this year. ...

Wednesday 23 February. There was an Alert last night: 12.02 a.m. till 1.20 a.m. There was gunfire, heavy and light guns opening up. We heard a lot of bombers going over (London was raided again) and one circling round put the wind up us. Jack came in our bed with his trousers on; I was in the middle and squashed. I felt we ought to get up, but it was cold and the bed was warm.

Thursday 24 February. Another Alert last night: 10.50 p.m. till 11.15 p.m. I didn't hear the 'All Clear'; nor my trousers falling off the bed and showering a couple of pounds worth of silver and some keys on the floor; but I was very tired last night. There was no gunfire Jess told me; but we heard today that an enemy bomber crashed Green End Road way on some allotments, just missing a number of houses. No-one was hurt, the bombs not exploding. The crew of Germans baled out in Hertfordshire.

I received a letter from the director of physical culture of Loughborough College this morning. He said the newspaper cuttings of Jack roused a good deal of enthusiasm in him; and he said he would do his best to put Jack on the way to becoming a Physical Training Instructor. He sent a prospectus and form of application, which Jack filled in and sent off this afternoon. I have written Henry Morris the local Secretary of Education [in other words, Director of Education] to ask for an interview to discuss the money side of the matter. As a last resort I shall heavily mortgage 99, Shelford Road. I am set on Jack going if they'll have him; and things look hopeful now.

Hale sent a letter with their reader's report on 'The Cordwainer'. Neil Bell had evidently faithfully carried out his task of getting them to do it. I thought the reader's report was wonderful; I've sent it to Bell, but when he returns it I will take a copy of the general opinion of the book. I wrote and thanked

Hale, saying their reader's opinion reflected all I set out to do when I started the book; that it was very gratifying, satisfying and stimulating. Would they please thank him. As the reader said the manuscript looked a bit ancient I added a postscript to the effect that it looked dog-eared as I kept all my valued belongings in a sack (typescripts included) for quick handling in case of fire through air-raids. ...

Friday 25 February. An Alert last night 10.00 p.m. till 11.00 p.m., just as I got to the place of firewatching. I watched flashes in the sky Londonwards, where there was another big raid. Again, one of the men snores; but not so badly as George Benton. ...

Tuesday 29 February. ... Robert Hale said he didn't make an offer for 'The Cordwainer' as he didn't think I'd continue writing novels; he testified to the pleasure it gave him; ... . The opinion of the reader was that the story was different from ordinary novels, that it was original and reminded him of Thomas Hardy's novel without the natural beauty found in Hardy; it was rather in the depicting of village characters—they were all so convincing. He also said I hadn't attempted a panorama of England at the time (apparently a drawback); he thought the book was very readable; ... .

To Bell Jack wrote that he had refrained from writing an historical panorama: let readers go to the history books if they wanted history. And what would my novels be like if I dragged in history—their length—my political bias? I was interested in character building. --- I hadn't got going with writing novels yet. When I got the children launched, the examination over and had shed a few war worries—then I'd start in earnest. ...

March 1944

Friday 3 March. ... This evening she [Jess, his daughter] came through on the telephone from Golcar [Yorkshire] so that we could wish her many happy returns. She said she'd received Jess's parcel in which were a birthday cake, apples, chocolate, mince pies, shortbread and a roll: an achievement on her mum's part these days. I made a special journey to Langford's to get a box and string to pack the things securely before sending. Jess also sent her £2, myself £1 not being so well off! presents being so difficult to decide on—and to get! these days. Jack sent her some powder, but it hadn't yet arrived. We got Jim to bark down the telephone his birthday greetings to her ... .

Sunday 5 March. ... The war drags on. There's much talk of the Second Front—still to be opened up. ... Of all the news, our bombing occupies first place in the papers. Twelve thousand lb bombs are now being dropped on enemy territory and Berlin is being raided day and night. ... I'm trying to get down to exam work, but have had a lot of interruptions lately. It's a wearisome job, anyway, and I can arouse no enthusiasm for it.

Sunday 12 March. ... There's all sorts of rumours going round hinting that Britain and America are about to launch an attack at the Continent. I'll believe it when it comes off. ... Lately, I've sent N.B. [Neil Bell] copies of *Peace News*. He thinks that while some of their criticism is sound much is destructive. What is their policy? Why don't they say outright what sort of world settlement they want? So I've written the editor of P.N. to ask him to ask 'Observer' (their weekly commentator) to state a case.

Tuesday 14 March. ... *From a letter written to the headmaster of the Cambridgeshire County School for Boys [A. B. Mayne], about his son Jack*:

> My daughter shortly completes her training at Avery Hill as a P.T. mistress and I feel I must do as much for him. I have a few hundred pounds saved, and as the fees at Loughborough are so high by the time he finishes his course, I shall not only be penniless, but shouldering a debt it will take a long time to repay. ...

Saturday 18 March. There was an Alert last night just before I went firewatching [and one from 10.20 p.m. till 11.30 p.m. the previous night]. I set out in all the glory of a tin hat (provided free of charge a long while ago by the Borough Council) in case of gunfire. There was none. The Alert was short: 9.25 p.m. till 9.50; ...

Sunday 19 March. ... Muller sent back 'The Cordwainer' saying they hadn't the paper to publish the book. ...

There were Alerts during the nights of Wednesday 22 March and Saturday 25 March.

 Sunday 26 March. Glorious weather. I've just been round the Fen and the Green (morning) with Jim and Jock. Besides the palms budding, the blossom — pink, white and yellow — and the daisies showed spring was here at last. ... Lately, I've felt I should describe myself as a PO, i.e. a political objector [to the war]; which is nearer the mark [than conscientious objector] in my case.

April 1944

Sunday 2 April. ... Jack's report from school was pretty bad. He seems unsettled and talks about going in the navy. Heaven forbid. ... It's not to be wondered at that the modern youth hardly knows his own mind; he's got no future; and most of them seem to fear becoming a 'Bevin Boy' (called up for the mines) more than being called up for the Services. I hope to see Jack get in Loughborough; it would ease my mind; for if he worked his future would then be assured; and I'd be very happy about it.

 Last Friday morning (31 March) we woke up to find it snowing hard. How the weather changes. Fortunately, the snow didn't settle, except on the roofs. The weather is cold and dull though and today it has rained; but after a long drought rain is badly needed. ...

Wednesday 5 April. Today, working eight hours (interrupted by customers) I did £4 3s 6d worth of work. It represents nearly 20 pairs of women's soled and heeled (the repairs were all sorts, of course) and is easily a record day's work for me. Did my back ache at the finish; and my tumour felt, as usual at such times, like a football.

Thursday 6 April. I did over £3 worth of work at the shop again today; and as I also did a lot on Monday and Tuesday the total for the four days is £13 12s 6d; which gives me about £10 net. I've worked like this to have a holiday over Easter.

Friday 7 April. Good Friday. Dull weather. I started going in the water again. The temperature was 46. ... [Among tasks, the diarist has been today] trying to read Frank Bullen's *The Cruise of the Cachalot*, which I read during the latter part of 1917.[7] I say trying to read as I've fallen asleep almost every time I've settled down to it.

Sunday 9 April. ... I've read 50 pages of Benham (I managed to do 50 pages on Good Friday)[8] ... . Sometimes, I get a bit tired of my own company, especially with only textbooks to read.

Monday 10 April. ... I've just wrapped up a couple of manuscripts to send off tomorrow. I don't like them all in one place and so I'm sending them out to avoid that rather than in hopes that they'll be accepted. ...

Thursday 13 April. The town was empty of American soldiers today. ...

Friday 14 April. There was an Alert last night: 1.40 a.m. till 2.00 a.m. I heard from London University. I can borrow books from the University library provided I get two guarantors of a certain standing. ...

Monday 17 April. An RAF officer stopped me round the 'Backs' this morning and personally thanked me on behalf of the men stationed round there for repairing their shoes so well and promptly. I've done this for nearly four years. His words made me feel guilty of helping the war effort; almost. But I square my conscience about it by regarding them as ordinary customers. It's different from taking a contract for army work. ...

Wednesday 19 April. I took an Italian-English conversation book to Frank Edwards' last night for him to hand to Claudio Rossi [an Italian prisoner of war]; then went firewatching; there was an Alert in the night: 12.50 a.m. till 1.55 a.m. I turned out; it was very cold. As I stood in the door tracer bullets streamed across the sky like golden balls appearing out of the darkness and vanishing once more into the darkness, their passage looking only a distance of a few yards (I wonder how far it really was); there was no noise; Sanderson thought it was one of

---

[7] Published in 1897, *The Cruise of the Cachalot* was an account of the cruise of a South Sea whaler from the seaman's standpoint.

[8] Frederick Charles Courtenay Benham, *Economics: A General Textbook for Students* (1938 and later editions).

our fighters chasing an enemy bomber. Soon afterwards the crash warning (something like a heavy gong) sounded from the railway station; I've heard this means the enemy bombers are within 15 miles; and then the enemy bombers could be heard approaching; at first, faintly; and then more loudly until they were roaring overhead on their way to their target; which was London according to this morning's news; a hospital was hit said the papers; when hospitals they are always mentioned; I suppose it helps to keep the hate high. ...

Don Varley came into the shop for me to mend his shoes; I repaired them. We talked while I worked. He's been for a short spell to Devonport, and was in the town for a couple of days before going to Blythe, where he's been for some while previous to going to Devonport. His ship will not be in commission till September and he thought he was safe till then. What a miserable outlook for youth these days. SAFE FOR A MONTH; and what then? ...

Thursday 20 April. Only a card from Maurice Dobb asking me to go and see him for a short talk tomorrow evening; ...

I hope he [Jack] wins a scholarship [to Loughborough]; but if he doesn't and they accept him, I'll be satisfied. I'll rake up the money. ...

Tomorrow I go before the tribunal. How do I feel? Quite calm. I mean to take the matter quietly. I'll stand a better chance by not getting ruffled. I say this knowing how hot I get about the ears over our social system; but I'll do my best to keep a tight rein on myself. ...

Friday 21 April. I went in front of the tribunal for conscientious objectors this morning at the Shire Hall at 10 o'clock. My case was the second on the list and after being sworn the chairman of the tribunal (Judge Lawson Campbell) opened the ball by asking what were my objections to war; I answered that wars led to further wars; he disagreed, saying probably that was so in the case of the last war and this, but not previously; he asked me to name any other war prior to this; I promptly answered the Franco-Prussian war, implying it led to the war of 1914–18; he said Oh, no, he didn't think so; I said Von Jugow [rightly 'von Jagow'] did (referring to his, Von Jugow's, statement that it was the system of alliances that led to the last war and that these were based on Germany's fear of France as a defeated nation) and he said Von Jugow might have done; and dropped the subject.⁹ Lawson then said that he wanted to find out exactly what pacifists thought; he agreed that pacifism was the ideal state, but it needed a long preparation for it and that was impossible with constantly recurring wars; I answered that a start had to be made; a person could only act within their limits; and I'd made a start.

There was a bit of sparring. --- Did I repair soldiers' shoes? I answered that I'd refused an army contract for shoe-repairing (Lawson Campbell turned and said to [J.] Nutter beside him that that was a good stroke of business, adding something about rates of pay that I couldn't catch), but during the last four years I had repaired hundreds of pairs of soldiers' shoes, treating them when they came in the shop as ordinary customers; I added that this seemed the sensible view to take, it was no good my preaching tolerance and practising intolerance. Nutter (a fat local miller) said that I wouldn't do work in a shoe factory engaged in army repairs then and I said Oh, no.

More sparring and I answered some questions rather quickly. Lawson Campbell smiled and said that I must not go so fast, there was plenty of time, I wasn't taking an examination in an hour and a half. There was a question about everybody being treated alike for a total war such as this; I said I didn't think we were, for economically the State used men and material so that output was at its maximum. Wasn't that right? said L.C. From the standpoint of the State, Yes, I answered, from that of the individual, perhaps No. This led to a remark by me that that was the trouble with war; its impact was unfair, falling at its heaviest on a small section of the community, the fighting men and — in this war — the bombed out. Didn't it equally affect us all? Asked L.C. No I said; it could hardly be said that a family that hadn't been bombed out suffered to the extent of one that had; or that the family of a soldier that was killed,

---

⁹ Gottlieb von Jagow (1863–1935) was German Foreign Secretary from 1913 to 1916. He published in 1919 a defence of German policy: *Ursachen und Ausbruch des Weltkrieges*.

leaving behind a widow and children, didn't suffer more than one that had gone comparatively free.

Nutter asked me what about the RAMC [Royal Army Medical Corps]. I said no, the war couldn't be prosecuted without the RAMC. L.C. didn't agree; there didn't use to be RAMCs. I said there'd have to be nowadays owing to improved education and a different outlook; L.C. still didn't agree; I was inclined to say why didn't they turn the RAMC into a fighting force then, but refrained; instead I said the casualties in a modern war made necessary a medical corps. No, said L.C. the casualties in a modern war were reduced through science to a much smaller percentage; I said percentages were no basis of reckoning; it was numbers that counted, implying that casualties nowadays were more than the size of armies in olden days. No good offering you non-combatant [status] then, said L.C. and I answered, No. L.C. then asked was I prepared to live under National Socialism. I asked did he mean the form of government that existed in Germany; he said that was the only country he knew in which it existed … . I said had this country come under National Socialism the suffering, if there were suffering, would be more evenly distributed; and the long view as well as the short view must be taken into account; for even under National Socialism things would straighten out in time and perhaps on the whole over a period of time with less suffering than that caused by constantly recurring wars.

L.C. then asked about Civil Defence. I told him I had done firewatching since its inception and business firewatching for sixteen months; I also tried to take up a course of first aid when the war started as it might be useful, going to the Old Post Office twice, but the course of instruction didn't come off.[10] … The tribunal retired for about a quarter of an hour to consider their verdicts; I was a bit anxious; their verdict in my case was that I was registered as a CO on condition that I kept in my trade as a shoe-repairer (a face-saver for them nowadays). … I was in the box about 25 minutes. …

[10] The Old Post Office was situated at the corner of St Andrew's Street and Petty Cury, next to the church of St Andrew the Great. The building has since been demolished.

This evening I went and had an hour's talk on Economics with Maurice Dobb at the Marshall Library of Economics.

Saturday 22 April. A letter from London University saying I may sit for my B.Sc. Econ. examination in Cambridge with the internal students of the London School of Economics. What a surprise. Jess [daughter] had a letter from the headmaster of Cottenham School, saying she's been appointed there as a teacher. I won just over a fiver [£5] on the day's racing. Altogether a lucky week. Before long I'll be getting a book of mine published.

A letter from Neil Bell. It had been censored, but there was nothing of importance in it. ...

There were Alerts in the small hours of Tuesday and Friday, 25 and 28 April.

Sunday 30 April. ... In a letter a few days ago Neil Bell said he'd lay ten thousand to one the Second Front comes off, and so could anybody else living on the coast between the Wash and Land's End. The newspapers talk of little else, besides our heavy air-raids on Germany and enemy-occupied territory.

RAMC tents are up on Coe Fen. I was told people in Cambridge have been asked if they could accommodate wounded soldiers in billets.

Is it all a colossal, the most colossal, bluff in military history, or is it the real thing? I ask myself and find no answer. But as everybody thinks the Second Front is imminent I still refuse to believe it.

May 1944

Sunday 7 May. ... Salute the Soldier Week has started in Cambridge.[11] These savings campaigns and their targets (Cambridge is out to raise £1,000,000) for savings are just a lie to deceive the public, to keep hate, in the form of propaganda, high. The money collected would be subscribed by the big financial institutions, anyway, and not 10 per cent represent

---

[11] Like earlier events, for example Navy Week, Salute the Soldier Week was devoted to persuading the inhabitants of a designated town to invest in National Savings. It was hoped it would boost morale as well as savings.

real savings on the part of the people (lots that save this week in the form of war savings will have the sum out and spend it next week) and that doesn't make a scrap of difference to the amount of munitions and other war material that is produced; that depends entirely on the physical capacity of the nation, which is at its peak already. *The Economist* says so bluntly. The mass of the people are quite deceived about the matter though and really believe such campaigns for savings help to shorten and win the war.

Tuesday 9 May. A glorious day and I spent the afternoon at the Old Spot at Grantchester with Jim and Jock. I read History (Waters) for the examination as I sunbathed and it was like old times.[12]

Thursday 11 May. ... As I lay among the buttercups in the afternoon I thought how grand they looked. The sight of buttercups golden in the sunshine stirs me deeply.

Monday 15 May. There was an Alert last night: 2.30 a.m. till 2.50 a.m. I heard a lot of planes go over as soon as the siren went and felt very nervous. It's odd how one is up and down over such things. Sometimes, the sound of enemy planes doesn't affect me a bit; nor does gunfire; at other times, I'm as jumpy as a kitten. But although I felt windy I didn't get up and put my shirt on although my nakedness as I lay abed urged me to do so. ...

Sunday 21 May. ... at dinnertime I thought of the Sunday 21 years ago, when we met round about 10 o'clock in the morning round the Backs. It was a delightful sunny morning, warm and pleasant; and it was so quiet there ... . This morning how different. The Backs turned into a wartime camp, men on guard. The contrast was sharp and the effect, doubtless helped by the miserable weather, very depressing.

Monday 22 May. There was an Alert last night: 3.50 a.m. till 4.15 a.m. ...

Wednesday 24 May. Jess and I went to London to celebrate our 21st wedding anniversary. ... I thought my nerves were going to be a bit rough in the train. I felt a bit odd, having a touch of

---

[12] C. M. Waters, *An Economic History of England* (1928).

my old feeling of wanting to get out of the train, but I talked to Jess and it passed off. ...

Roses were priced 5s each in a shop window near Liverpool Street; and an umbrella Jess liked the look of was £3 10s; but she wouldn't have it when she learned the price; but I regretted I wasn't better off. It's lousy taking a wife out and not having the money to buy her a present costing 70s. When I buy her anything I usually have to borrow the money off her to do so and then pay her back later.

We booked to see *The Student Prince* at the Stoll Theatre in the afternoon. Acting without experience I bought tickets for the upper circle. When I got up there only two rows from the front and a sheer drop of heaven knows how many feet, I couldn't stand it and after three quarters of an hour's mental distress, during which time the songs that were sung were quite lost on me, I told Jess I must go out. And did so. The alternative was pitching myself 'over the edge' of the low balcony down into the stalls. I can't stand heights. ...

Alas, to have very little money and be unable to do things in the grand style. And to be as highly strung as a temperamental racehorse.

Saturday 27 May. A wire from Eric yesterday said he was coming down to Cambridge today. He arrived at the shop just before 11.00 ... . We speculated about the Second Front; Eric thought Russia was waiting for us to start, thinking she's done her whack, that she'll probably make a separate peace with Germany if Britain doesn't open a Second Front. I thought perhaps our rulers would like this to happen, for it would give them the chance to negotiate peace with Germany to keep her 'on the map', preferable to them seeing her and France go 'red', a communist Europe not being very much in their line. ...

Sunday 28 May. I spent the day at the meadows with Jim and Jock. I had seven or eight dips, reading economics in between times. ... I came home, thoroughly scorched by the sun, at about 8.00 to do half of a paper on economics for Maurice Dobb to mark; and now off I go firewatching.

Monday 29 May. Whit Monday. I went to work this morning; did nearly a couple of pounds worth; and then came home and saw to the day's racing; after which I went on the river in Bert Cash's punt. Came home round about 8.00 to finish the paper on economics for Dobb. ... There was an Alert last night while firewatching: 3.05 a.m. till 3.50 a.m.

Tuesday 30 May. ... There was a terrific explosion — or rather a series of explosions — that shook my workshop this morning. These were at Chesterford, about 10 miles away, where an ammunition dump blew up. ...

June 1944

Friday 2 June. ... Jess said she heard a loud explosion in the night. It turned out to be an ammunition train that had blown up at Soham.[13] ...

Lately, a lot of trains have been taken off. Another bit of Second Front bluff? The Yanks have started a fashion — holding hands with their girl friends as they walk along. It looks odd when the officers do and salute other Americans with their other hand while doing it. Jess heard this the other day: the Americans are overpaid, over-decorated, over-sexed and over here. (Their price for a woman seems to be £3.)

Planes are always roaring overhead. We're plastering France now. ...

Footnote: what a lot of people don't know their own shoes. Well, that's my experience in the shop.

Tuesday 6 June. Firewatching last night. And the planes that went over! Mr Sanderson thought something was on the board; and he was right. I went straight to work, starting at the shop just before 6.00. ... I did 45*s* worth of repairs by half-past 9 and was clearing up to come home when I heard a wireless on the go, either that of the woman (Mrs Williams) who has the house over the shop, or one across the road. Thinking

---

[13] The first wagon of 51 in an ammunition train caught fire on 2 June 1944 as it passed through Soham station. The rest of the train was uncoupled but the first wagon exploded. Two men were killed and damage was widespread.

it was odd that news should be coming through at that hour I listened and caught the word Eisenhower and then I thought perhaps the Second Front had opened. A few moments later a chap named Austin (physically a wreck from concussion at Dunkirk) came in with a pair of boots said it had—in Normandy. I came home feeling excited. …

Jim and Jock barked greetings when I entered the house. I switched on the wireless and listened to repeated broadcasts of the invasion of France as I made myself a cup of tea and drank it with a couple of rounds of bread and jam. The slaughter it would involve kept running through my mind and I was vaguely unhappy. And there was Jim to worry about, for he's developed a knobby lump as big as a good-sized marble near the joint of his right front leg. I took him to the vet at dinner-time; … . I told her nothing matters as long as we keep him into old age. …

Maurice Dobb saw me pass along Chesterton Road from his house and came running out to find out when the exam starts. I told him Monday and although he's busy on exams for the University he fixed up to see me on Thursday afternoon. …

Wednesday 7 June. So many planes passed over the town and at such low altitude last night that it was almost impossible to sleep. …

Thursday 8 June. There was an Alert last night: 12.15 a.m. till 12.50 a.m. … I went to see Maurice Dobb at the Marshall Library. He's marked the paper I'd done and went over it with me. Upon the whole I seemed to have done pretty well with it. Three out of the five answers he passed outright; the fourth my approach was a bit roundabout and after naming the point of the question I'd wandered from it; but as I'd nailed the question he was favourably disposed to the answer, although he thought it could be better. The fifth I'd approached in wrong fashion, but he said he would give me some marks for it. He gave me some useful hints about examination technique; perhaps, the most important was to treat the questions not as though the examiner knows what you're referring to, but as a teacher explaining to a pupil. His manner seems rather guarded about it all. But I gather that he thinks external students are working in the dark all the while like moles. I'll say! ...

Saturday 10 June. Today, I paid back the £40 borrowed from the County School Careers Fund for Jess's first-year college fees. I wrote Miss [J. I.] Field, the school headmistress and thanked her. So I've squared off that bill before Jess has completed her course.

Sunday 11 June. Revised Economics all day for the exam, with intervals for walks with the dogs.

Monday 12 June. The telephone rang at dinnertime when I returned home from the Law School [where he had been taking his examination]: a wire from Neil Bell which read 'Proverbs 24.14 Neil'. I went and borrowed a Bible from a neighbour (got one at the third attempt) to decipher the message. It read 'So shall the knowledge of wisdom be unto thy soul: when thou hast found it, then there shall be a reward, and thy expectations shall not be cut off'. It was nice of him to remember the event! ...

The Exam? I wasn't much at home with the Economics; and the Banking and Currency papers; ... . And I felt off colour; ...

Tuesday 13 June. ... I woke at 5 o'clock dreaming I had missed an essential point in a question on the Gold Standard to do with changes in the price and income structure resulting from a change in the Bank Rate, to find it was only too true. Outlook black, Last year repeating itself. Felt pessimistic. Didn't look as if I would get out of bondage this year. For I felt dubious about two other of the ten questions. One I'd probably made a wrong approach; another — I wandered (a pretty sure sign I'd missed the point); which meant I'd only made a show with seven. Didn't seem worth carrying on. But determined to till I passed; or they passed me (not quite the same thing, I reckon). Got up at 6.30 and revised Modern Economic History — the morning's work.

Bought Jess a bunch of flowers at midday: sweet peas, marigolds and cornflowers [it was her birthday]. Felt seedy all day; troubled with my kidneys a bit. ...

Here's a copy of the essay, the afternoon's work. It's short, but long enough for an examiner to read through; and probably not much good; but good enough for the purpose; no good opening my mouth again this year as I did last. I've passed twice in the subject already, anyway. *The essay has not been included here.*

Wednesday 14 June. ... I revised all morning, for I had no exam on, this being the morning for the language papers, which I passed on two years ago. I felt cold and miserable and sat draped in an overcoat. Economic History (1) was the afternoon paper. I did well with it.

Thursday 15 June. Up till midnight last night. Gave Jess a bit of a hand with her books [as an insurance agent] after revision.

Economic History (2) and ditto (3) were the day's papers and I think I did very well with them. ...

Coming out of the Law School I listened to some of the LSE students of both sexes talking and giggling. They were discussing their papers. One said he'd done one and a half questions out of four, another two out of four; and another three out of five. I don't know what the subjects were, but this seemed a low average to expect a pass, even though [even if] they were marked 100 per cent on their efforts. ...

Friday 16 June. There was an Alert last night: 11.45 p.m. till 12.45 a.m. Benton, the street fire leader, knocked us up. I got up, but Jess, who now firewatches Thursday nights, was tired and refused to get out of bed. What a firewatcher! I signed the book for both of us. He went off swearing about the firewatching being all a farce.

Constitutional History was the subject today. I did very well. Luckily I didn't have to go in this afternoon, for the Oaks were run at Newmarket and I had to give up my time to the day's racing as soon as I arrived home at dinnertime. I went round to Albert Digby's with some covering bets just before 1 o'clock and he said London was getting it in the neck with rocket bombs [V1s or 'flying bombs']; the Alert was still on; and traffic was blocked between Cambridge and London on the railway.

So whatever sort of luck I have with the examination this year, I was lucky to sit in Cambridge; for had I travelled up to London every day I should have failed to arrive at South Kensington to take today's papers; and if I'd lodged in London I should have had to run the gauntlet of the bombing. ...

A letter from Loughborough. Jack didn't get a scholarship, but he passed the entrance exam, and that's all that matters. Now I must fix things up for him. Went up Long Common this afternoon with the dogs. ... Picked a couple of sprigs of a sweet-smelling [blossom] like laburnum in Newton Road coming home. ...

Sunday 18 June. Squaring up over the Derby took a long time this morning, but I managed to revise all my work for tomorrow.

Monday 19 June. Political History of the Great Powers since 1815 was the paper this morning, which finished the examination—I hope for good. As soon as I arrived home at dinnertime I started packing away books and sent back the Wolsey Hall papers for Economics.

This afternoon an income-tax man was after my blood. I gave him a couple of quid to quieten him; then I went to the Guildhall and changed the ration books for Jess. ...

Thursday 22 June. Firewatching last night. Mr Sanderson was full of gossip about the 'Doodlebugs' - the American name for the pilotless planes [V1s] – a word he obviously liked using for its newness. I went straight to work arriving just before 6.00 and the woman who lives in the shop kicked up a rumpus about my knocking.

Friday 23 June. Beginning to think about the novel I'm going to write soon. ---

Sunday 25 June. Jess and I had a walk round Midsummer Fair last night. A wartime fair, without coconuts, rock, ice cream stalls and crockery stands to name only a few of the absent items of pre-war days, it wasn't much of an attraction. We went in four side-shows: saw a large St Bernard dog, some small horses, and some imitation freaks. A man with a weighing machine guessing weights guessed ours wrong and we didn't have to pay the 3*d* he charged when guessing correctly. He guessed Jess at 9 stone 11*lbs* [*c.* 62 kilos] and she was 10 stone 7*lbs* [*c.* 66 kilos]; after feeling round my back and chest he guessed my weight as 13 stone 7*lbs* [*c.* 86 kilos] — 2 stones [*c.* 13 kilos] more than I weighed. We spent only 4*s* all told.

Monday 26 June. … An American soldier took Jim and Jock's photos this afternoon in Trumpington Street; and then mine with them. He was a pleasant chap and said he would send prints along.

Friday 30 June. There was an Alert this morning: 11.00 a.m. till about 11.10 a.m. I thought a pilotless plane was on the way and felt rather exposed in the workshop with so much glass round me; for the windows are large ones. These flying bombs as they are now called are causing merry hell in London and Southern England. The newspaper reports make ghastly reading. There were several explosions roundabout this morning, but I have no idea of what was the reason for them. People tell me there was a big bang this morning at about 4 o'clock, but I didn't hear it. A terrific explosion while we were having dinner on Wednesday is said to have been a flying bomb Duxford way.

I did a bit of cementing one day this week to stop the mice invading the kitchen, but without any effect. We've got so many they get in the piano and play it. Something will have to be done about it.

July 1944

Saturday 1 July. Jack went to see Henry Morris, the County Education Secretary this morning to discuss the possibility of help with his son's fees, though Jack senior was willing to pay himself if necessary, saying:

I was giving him the same chance as I had given my daughter. This brought up Jess's name and Morris asked me what she was doing; it then came out that she was taking up a position in the county as a teacher in September; he and his secretary (a man) then remembered her. Morris seemed pleased about that and smiled and said something about it being a family affair. The secretary then asked me the Loughborough fees and made a note of the amount, £210 per annum. Morris then said the position had changed considerably since he received

Mayne's report.[14] For two reasons. One, Jack had passed the entrance examination to Loughborough; two, the Cambridge Board of Education wanted teachers. He wouldn't promise anything, but he would bring the matter before the board at the next meeting and would do his best to obtain an award. I thanked him and said I thought Jack would justify anything they did for him (I think he will).

He then referred to my letter in which I said I hadn't answered his as I was busy revising for the B.Sc. Econ. examination of London University. ... He wanted to know what I was going to do if I passed. I told him I was a Pitman Certificated Teacher, but I hoped to establish myself as a writer. He'd remembered me when I entered the room. (I repaired his shoes time back.) He seemed generally impressed and by his manner I thought he was going to offer me a job.

As we parted he laughed and said I mustn't do too much for my children, they would never appreciate it, and would never do anything for me. I said I didn't want any appreciation from them; and I certainly didn't want them to do anything for me; I believed it was the duty of parents to set children on their feet and not expect children to provide an armchair for them in old age. He said that was a very fine outlook indeed—and the interview ended on that very pleasant note. His manner indicated that he would give me a job any time I applied for one.

Today, I started 'Finger in the Pie'.

Sunday 2 July. ... I went in the river this morning; and I did a back somersault off the top board. Must record the fact against advancing age. ... Afterthoughts on the exam. Have I mentioned that during the past eight and a half years since studying for this examination I have sat 36 whole or part days in the examination room? ...

Sunday 9 July. ... Eric Goldsmith is here for a week's holiday. He's lodging in Panton Street. The flying bombs falling in London lately have been giving people there a rough time (rough enough for Churchill to bring the matter up in Parliament) and he's glad of the rest from it.

---

[14] Mayne was the headmaster of the Cambridgeshire High School for Boys. For his report see the entry for 2 April 1944.

I've done a good week's work on the novel, which absorbs all my spare time. There was an Alert tonight while the 9 o'clock news [on the radio] was on: from about 9.10 p.m. till 9.20 a.m.

Monday 17 July. ... There was an Alert last night: 2.20 a.m. till 2.35 a.m.

Sunday 23 July. ... I had a cheery letter from Neil Bell in the week. He put at the foot of the letter (which was opened by the censor) Jack Overhill Esq., B.Sc. (Econ.), being certain that I've passed the examination, which is more than I am, as I've told him without his taking any notice. Which reminds me that Jess [daughter] and later myself went to the Law School yesterday to see if the unofficial results were published there, as it is said on a blackboard that they probably would be on 22 July, during the last day or two of the examination. They were not out. And so, not very hopefully, I wait. ...

There's another 10,000 refugees in Cambridge owing to the robot planes [V1s].

A bit of a war sensation occurred last week: some German army generals tried to bump off Hitler and he announced the fact at 1.00 a.m. the other night.[15] This is the third attempt on his life; or the third reported attempt, I should say; not quite the same thing. Is it propaganda? Or are queer things happening in Germany that will shorten the war? All we can do is wait and see. I'm going quite well with the novel. Done about 35,000 words.

Last night an English and an American soldier had a fight in Gothic Street; others stopped them. There's quarrelling and fighting outside here almost every night. This is my fire-watching night and as it is nearly 11 o'clock I must be off ---

Tuesday 25 July. ... Jack left school today. ... He brought home with his report the school magazine and his certificate for

---

[15] A group of aristocrats and senior army officers, many of them devout Christians, had been planning to assassinate or unseat Hitler since the 1930s. Naively, they made few attempts to keep their plots secret, and, as German patriots, hoped that Germany might retain some of her conquests—a desire the Allies would certainly not have granted. In July 1944 Count von Stauffenberg placed a bomb beneath a table in Hitler's conference room. It exploded, but merely wounded Hitler. The plotters were arrested and brutally executed.

winning the 50, 100 and 220 [yards] at swimming and the diving; and the school swimming and diving championship medal; … . It's been a grand year for him; he'll realise how much when he is older.

Wednesday 26 July. An Alert today: 2.20 p.m. till 2.30 p.m. I was in Fred's shop and as the machine was running didn't hear it. …

August 1944

Saturday 5 August. I've been working hard at the novel; … I've now done 50,000 words and like Johnny Walker, still going strong.[16] …

After getting a bit fretful yesterday and the day before I heard the result of the examination this morning. Jess [his wife] handed me the letter as I sat at work on the story before breakfast with the remark that it was a thin'un, meaning the thickness of the letter, in a gloomy voice which indicated failure (the letter contains the pass list if successful and that's rather bulky). She was right; I'd failed again; but although that didn't really astonish me, I was floored by the fact that I'd passed in Economics, which I was nervous about, and that I had been failed in four other subjects; three of them I had passed before (two of them twice before).

All this seemed a bit crazy on the part of London University. They failed me over the Essay (passed twice previously), over Political History of the Great Powers (passed twice previously), and English Constitutional History since 1660 (passed once previously), and the Special Subject (Economic History), the only subject I hadn't yet passed in one way or another in the final B.Sc. (Econ.) examination. Actually, the questions are not much more than duplicates of previous years' questions, and it is hard to believe that I am now worse in these subjects after extra work on them. And failed over the essay! Well, well. So now I've passed once, twice or thrice in all subjects of the exam, except in Economic History. I shall try again next year, and keep trying. That I wasn't much disturbed by

[16] A reference to the well-known advertising slogan for the Johnny Walker brand of whisky.

the result is proved by the fact that I continued with my work on the novel.

I wrote and told Neil Bell. I wonder what he'll say about it as he was so confident I'd passed. He thinks the dice are loaded against the poor but even he doesn't know how much. Frank Edwards thought it all a bit crazy, passing me in subjects one year and failing me in another and vice versa. Eric was a bit grim about it. He said the examiners were supposed to be intellectuals; apparently they had the minds of illiterates, or they'd never act in that fashion.

I met George Barlow, one of the graduates with whom I had the debate over examinations at Frank Edwards's two years ago.[17] As an honours graduate it's been very hard for him to believe the business was phoney; as Frank Edwards says — for him to think that is to disbelieve in all he stands for — but when I told him he was disgusted and said he thought it was all a swindle: a disgraceful business excluding some and cheapening it for others; and that was what was shortly going to happen with the new national drive for teachers (the idea is to turn out men with both academic and teaching qualifications in one year's training).

I rang up Maurice Dobb; … . He was rather reticent about it, but I could hear by his tone of voice that he was a little distressed about it; and I credit him with being sincere. He was ever so pleased that I had passed in Economics; he then asked me if I had allowed myself to get a little rusty in the subjects in which I'd previously passed and been failed in; I said I hadn't; I'd worked hard at all of them and hadn't spared myself. He said it was extraordinary, very extraordinary, in a subdued voice; I agreed, but not harshly, as I didn't want to give the impression that I was whining. He asked me if should take it again. I said till they passed me; and he said that my manner was positively heroic and that he admired my courage; if he could ever help me in any way I was to call and see him. Of course, he knows it's a swindle, but his position prevents him from saying so.

[17] George Barlow later became Deputy Headmaster of the Cambridgeshire High School for Boys. For the debate, see the diary entry for 7 August, 1942.

Well, so much for the B.Sc. Econ. examination for another year. Now, it's back to the novel.

Sunday 13 August. ... Bell wrote and blew me up over the examination. Said I was a fool to persist in it as obviously they have no intention of passing me. I said I was carrying on; it wasn't now just a question of a pass degree, something else may emerge from it; and although it might seem ridiculous for a Cambridge cobbler to pit himself against an institution like London University, pigmies had pulled off fights before. I said they'd dealt me terrible punishment, but their power now lacked punch, while I was still as fresh as a daisy and before I'd done I would land them one that would hurt. And I will. At this stage things are getting interesting; they keep ringing the changes a few more times so that I've sat say half-a-dozen times and passed several times in every subject without having got a degree, I'll be able to do something. Anyway, I'll have a cut. I sent off for a registration form this morning.

I'm still struggling to square my bills. It's a job. ...

Wednesday 16 August. ... An Alert this morning: 8.50 a.m. till 9.00 a.m. There was racing and I was cycling to work when the siren went; I got off my bike and looked round at the quiet of St John's Wilderness and the field opposite; the sky was a deep blue, the foliage richly green, and it seemed strange that death was passing over in the neighbourhood, for, no doubt, a doodlebug was going over. All those strange bewildering feelings associated with the siren sounding that I experienced during the early days of the war have now vanished; it's just a row now and a reminder that the war drags miserably on. ...

Saturday 19 August. An Alert today: 2.50 till 2.55 p.m.

Sunday 20 August. The weather has been glorious lately, but today it has poured with rain. ... I just plug away at the novel in my spare time and have now written 70,000 words of it, which is pretty good going.

The British and Americans in France are doing well, but it's hard to guess whether the war will end in a week or two or drag through the winter. The Russian advance seems to have slowed down a bit, probably owing to extended lines of communications. ...

Sunday 27 August. ... I bought a couple of new jackets yesterday for two guineas each [£2 2s], the first for a long while. They're what we call nowadays 'Utility' jackets, but pretty good ones and prove how cheaply good clothes could be produced for the public under government control. ...

The summer is drawing to a close and hopes of peace before the dark nights set in in earnest are high with almost everybody. Paris liberated; allied troops are only 110 miles from the German frontier (they're at Rheims); Rumania has changed sides, Germany has lost Bucharest; Bulgaria is nearly, but not quite, out of the war; Finland is angling for peace; the Russians advancing rapidly. One cannot but feel it will soon be over — in Europe, anyway. ...

I'm trying to make the most of the weather. Yesterday, Bert Cash being in Manchester, Jess and I borrowed his punt and paddled upstream to a spot just by the ladies' bathing place. There were only us and the dogs and after I'd had a swim (Jess didn't go in) we had tea. The weather was warm and we enjoyed ourselves in a quiet way. When I got home I'd won over a fiver on the day's racing, which was better than ever! ...

Wednesday 30 August. The pass list from London University about Jess's teacher's examination at Avery Hill came through this morning at dinnertime. ... Not only did she pass, but she passed well, getting a distinction in Physical Education. ...

September 1944

Friday 1 September. ... There was an Alert today while we were having dinner: 1.05 p.m. till 1.15 p.m.

Sunday 3 September. ... I'm instructing a little class of five in Life Saving at the Town Bathing Sheds. Now for the novel; I'll soon have done 100,000 words. Not bad going, but I'm three days behind schedule.

Tuesday 5 September. ... There was an Alert in the early hours of this morning; 5.20 a.m. till about 6.00. There was a heavy explosion that shook the windows soon after the siren went. The explosion and Jess saying 'Did you hear that, Jack?' woke me.

Later, I thought I heard another bang, not so loud. I thought it was a 'bug', but today somebody told me it was a German bomber that had followed some of our planes in that crashed; and that it was Steeple Morden way.

I've just sent back some books Foyles sent me 'on appro' about horseracing (for the novel I'm doing) as they were no good; I enclosed a 5s postal order to cover postage and packing although they didn't request it. …

I forgot to mention that last Sunday night Claudio Rossi, the Italian prisoner of war, telephoned me from Frank Edwards's. With other Italian prisoners he now has his liberty, and can now visit cinemas and people's houses at invitation. He was so excited he could hardly speak. Frank brought him round on his tandem and left him here. We passed the evening together and we walked some of the way back to camp with him, giving him a mac as it was raining. I told him my house was open to him at all hours.

Sunday 10 September. … Blackout restrictions are being relaxed: and Civil Defence and Home Guard; starting September 17th when one hour of the two hours Double Summer Time ends. British and American troops now front the Siegfried Line. Everybody thinks the war will soon be over, probably this month. We all eagerly await the day. Evacuees are going back to London, the fly-bomb menace apparently being over now the Pas de Calais is occupied, or nearly so, by our troops ---

Tuesday 19 September. An Alert at 4.30 a.m. lasting for six minutes.

Wednesday 20 September. An Alert at 1.40 a.m. till 2.30 a.m. … Another Alert this evening: 8.55 p.m. till 9. 35 p.m.

Thursday 21 September. A letter from Eric saying his brother-in-law Lumley had been killed by a rocket bomb [a V2] at Kew, London, and his sister buried. The bomb fell in the garden, rased the house, and his sister (in hospital) had the terrible experience of hearing her husband die. Oddly enough, when Eric was here a week or two back he told me that he stayed a weekend at his sister's; while there was a raid his brother-in-law was very restless and anxious, constantly in and out of the table shelter and tramping about the house.[18] It almost makes one believe in premonitions, although, of course, as many of those feelings don't come off as do … .

There were brief Alerts in the evening or small hours of Saturday, Sunday, and Monday, 23, 24, and 25 September.

Tuesday 26 September. There was an Alert last night just after we got to bed. It was about 10.45 pm and a chap told me today that it lasted about 20 minutes. The lamps are alight in the town tonight for the first time for five years. Much of the effect was spoiled, however, by bright moonlight. I walked up the Archway to have a look along Lensfield Road and back came memories of how we were running for the shelter in Trumpington Street just at this time of year four years ago.

Wednesday 27 September. … I've sent 'Adolescence' to Robert Hale. … About 10 days ago I sent 'The Cordwainer' to John Long, but haven't even had an acknowledgement. How publishers hold cheaply the efforts of authors.

Thursday 28 September. Jess and I went to see the film of Hemingway's book *For whom the Bell Tolls* [1940]; it was dope and showed little of the Spanish Civil War; and what little it did show was (I thought) anti-republican.

Friday 29 September. There was an Alert last night: about 4.45 a.m. till 5.30 a.m. (so I'm told); and there were a couple of crashes in the distance, one shaking the house. … Another Alert this evening: 9.20 p.m. for a quarter of an hour to 20 minutes. …

October 1944

Sunday 1 October. I wonder have I mentioned that I do work at the shop for some monks round there.[19] Some of them are

---

[18] The Morrison Shelter, provided for families lacking a garden in which an Anderson Shelter might be placed, took the form of a table beneath which people sheltered during air raids.

[19] The 'monks' were in fact friars: members of the Anglican order of St Francis founded in 1921 to minister to the unemployed 'tramping the streets'. Their mother house was at Batcombe, Cerne Abbas (Dorset) and their Cambridge base at St Francis House, Lady Margaret Road.

very interesting and one wanted me to go and have tea in their garden. They help down and outs, and the main centre is at Cerne Abbas, to which one invited me. I don't know the name of their Order, or whatever their brotherhood is called.

Maurice Dobb and Alex Wood have acted as guarantors so that I can borrow books from the library of London University. Jess [daughter] teaches history [in Cottenham] from the same book as I had 35 years ago. King Canute and the waves --- the wreck of the White Ship --- PROGRESS? The book looked as old as that, too. Poor children aren't meant to learn.

Thursday 5 October. ... Jess [daughter] and I went to hear Bertrand Russell talk on why he isn't now a pacifist. It was all rather informal and question time was free and easy. I asked three questions; Jess kept mum. Russell obviously hated Russia; spat venom at her. When somebody said they'd abolished unemployment in Russia he said so they had in Dartmoor. He disliked the authoritarian state. I said Russia was a young state, had to put down opposition, didn't he think conditions would change later. He said no, those minorities that had power never yielded it; only one man had ever done so, Charles the Fifth and he died mad. He said later in answer to another question that the Nazis could have beaten America had they beaten England; then he said in answer to another question that America would hold a communist Germany plus Russia in check and I asked if that wasn't a contradiction of his earlier statement (in words to that effect); he said no; not now America was on the lookout. Just before the end he used the remark that 'the war would be put off for a while'; I asked did this postponement of a war lessen its evils, wasn't a war in 1980 as bad for that generation as one (say) in 1960. He didn't seem to grasp my meaning and said the answer was simple, it was a war less; I said I didn't see his point, war was war at any time. He was obviously thinking of a series of wars and I of a war postponed. There were some very good questions asked; he seemed stumped at times; but then he said he wasn't trying to justify his attitude of being a CO in the last war and not in this; he was never really a pacifist; and his talk was more a confession than anything. He was witty; all there;

but as I listened to him I felt change would never take place in the present social system through men like him. It will never be done by constitutional means as he (and I) would like. ...

There were brief Alerts on Saturday evening and Monday night, 7 and 9 October.

Friday 13 October. There was an Alert last night: 12 o'clock for about a quarter of an hour. I heard a plane go over sounding something between a sewing machine and a two-stroke motor-bike and as the sound was new thought the plane was probably a doodlebug. People today tell me it was.

I went apple stealing this evening (Newton Road) and Jess and Jess going to see a play of *A Midsummer Night's Dream,* settled down to write. Then, for a short break, I went round the houses with the dogs. The siren sounded as I was in Tennis Court Road at the corner of Fitzwilliam Street. Bent on shortening my walk I turned along Fitzwilliam Street and hardly had the siren finished than up came a pilotless plane, so low that it seemed to be roaring over the rooftops. I was then opposite the house which bears a notice that Charles Darwin once lived there and going to the end of the street I looked skywards over the Museum; it was starlight; but I couldn't see the plane which put the wind up me. I walked up Trumpington Street, past the hospital; then there was a flash, but no bump, and I thought the plane had come down. Who got it? I wondered. The warning lasted from 9.45 p.m. till about 10 o'clock.

Saturday 14 October. Another Alert in the early hours of this morning: 3.30 a.m. till 4.05 a.m. Sounded like bugs [V1s] going over.

Sunday 15 October. ... Jess [wife] bought a pair of shoes yesterday: 74*s*. ...

Monday 16 October. There was an Alert last night: 10.50 p.m. till 10.55 p.m. It cut short my moralisings to Jess in bed.

Thursday 19 October. ... Robert Hale sent back 'Adolescence'. Didn't seem to like it. I was disappointed, hoping they would. ...

Jess [daughter] and I went to a PPU [Peace Pledge Union] meeting last night; there weren't many there; the discussion about compulsion in industry after the war was interesting.[20] Talking about ante-ites, Alex Wood said there were some pacifists who, in a pacifist society, would be militarists.

There's been some correspondence in the *CDN* [*Cambridge Daily News*] about the easy time Italian prisoners are having about here and Frank Edwards tells me Rossi says he walks about in shame. Rossi, a midget, is working for a farmer who makes him carry 18 stone of corn [*c.* 107 kilos], and he does it because he's afraid that if he doesn't he'll be shifted to another camp; he says his knees tremble when he carries the corn and I don't wonder.

I forgot to mention that a mass funeral was in process at the American cemetery up Madingley Road as we passed today. We counted about 30 coffins draped in flags beside the line of graves. There's thousands of American airmen buried there as shown by the rows of white crosses — a rather agonising sight, I always think, and so different from the tombstones of a quiet country churchyard; yet death is death, whether it comes violently in youth or peacefully in age. The earth from the graves is being used to raise the level of the edge of Madingley Road and how far it stretches tells its own tale.

Standing against a haystack this afternoon listening to a tractor ploughing I suddenly thought of my forebears and how I would like to read a written record of their experiences a few hundred years ago. I mentioned it to Frank; he said it would be fine; and to hear their voices on a record or see a film of them, all of which is now possible.

Monday 23 October. An Alert: 7.35 till 7.45 a.m.

From a letter to Neil Bell copied into the diary at the end of October:

> ... With regard to your daughter not liking *David Copperfield* — only a freak kid of 11 would; shows she's normal. I tried it at 14; it gave me the willies (Steerforth drowned with his arm outstretched as he rested his head on it as a boy — isn't that how it goes?) and I've never looked at the book since. I don't say *David Copperfield* isn't a better book than the book your daughter was reading; maybe; but

---

[20] The Peace Pledge Union, a pacifist body founded by Canon Dick Sheppard in 1936, claimed over 100,000 members at its height, but the number who were conscientious objectors once war started was much smaller.

not to her apparently; and she has a perfect right to her opinion. What's it matter about standards; it's the enjoyment you get out of a book that counts; … . It's one thing to judge the merits of a book from the lofty standards of LITERATURE; another to judge it from personal standards. …

Why do I like simple things? I don't know. But give me a kid's poetry book about skylarks and meadows and running streams and I'm happy; give me a poetry book full of the High Gods of Heaven and a lot more pompish [pompous?] nonsense and I shout 'baloney' and toss it aside. Few people are sincere; they don't take delight in the doing, merely in showing off. Whenever I see a dignified man I always think he's posing to the world and his bloody self. Read 40 pages of a book of Havelock Ellis's last night; he could have said it all in 40 lines.

It's the same with music. I hate jive; it jars; and I don't like symphony music; I'm not musically minded enough to understand either. I like ballads. Why do I like them? Again I don't know. But I'm thrilled right through when I hear a song like *Roses of Picardy* sung as I like to hear it sung. …

November 1944

Thursday 2 November. Don Varley came into the shop today looking very fit and well. He's on a corvette, about 250' long; had 28 days at sea without touching land; sunk a sub[marine], 400' below them; the explosion made them think they'd been torpedoed; found human flesh afterwards and knew they'd had a kill; … .

Saturday 4 November. An Alert this evening from about 7.45 pm till about 8.00 p.m. … I gave 15*s* 8*d* for a ream of paper at Heffer's today and had to beg for it as well as pay for it as they wouldn't part till I said I wanted it for a manuscript. …

Sunday 5 November. … I asked an old college tutor who comes in the shop if he could name some modern books on economic history; he said it was outside his province (he coaches in history, but a different branch, I suppose) and he would ask his son; later he stopped me in the town and said there were no really modern books on the subject later than Fay and Lipson, but one was being written, but it wouldn't be out before I took my exam.

Tuesday 7 November. I went to see the Leather Controller of this district this morning about my leather quota. I'm not getting anything like the amount I'm supposed to. He seemed an efficient sort and we talked for nearly an hour. I might now get my quota; perhaps, a bit more. ...

Friday 10 November. There's been a lot of 'to-do' about 'rag' by students in the town on Guy Fawkes Day. It was a bit unexpected. They had a bonfire on Market Hill, turned over cars, smashed bus windows, fought policemen, etc, and the affair got into the London dailies. The *Daily Herald* ran a leader about it, expressing contempt, and the *Cambridge Daily News* has been full of letters for and against the raggers. How intolerant the working class has shown itself. One bright spark suggested the students should be publicly birched! And we fight Hitler! Letters from 'Ex-Sergeant', 'British Working Man' etc were nauseating. So was the pious nonsense about men dying for them (the students) on the many battle fronts. As Frank Edwards says 'Few of those men would lend me a quid; I'm sure they wouldn't die for me!' Of course, conscription is the test; give the fighting men the chance to come home! What an odd world it is. All this fuss over a few young men doing a little damage during high spirits, when most of the youth of the world is being trained to smash anybody and anything on the other side, which after all is the human race. The students' replies in the paper were dignified and sensible on the whole.

In the evening of Sunday 5 November several hundred undergraduates gathered in Cambridge market place – a student 'rag' on Guy Fawkes day being a Cambridge tradition. Two 'buses were stopped and their windows broken. Petrol was siphoned from cars; bonfires were started in Market Square and several cars were damaged by fire. A constable was struck on the jaw. 'Proctors were on the Square, but had little effect in the excited mob. One who tried to calm down a section of the crowd from the Victoria cinema steps was unable to make himself heard.' (Cambridge Daily News, 6 November 1944). In the five days from 6 to 10 November many letters were published in the paper from civilians, servicemen, dons and students complaining of the nuisance, the damage, and the waste of petrol brought across the Atlantic at risk of torpedoes – the guilty being highly privileged young men. 'Disgusted East Anglian' asked if 'nothing can be done to stamp out the bitter contempt with which the Cambridge undergraduates treat the laws of this country? Had it been a lot of poor uneducated youths amusing themselves in such fashion ... they would have been taken to gaol, and there would have been no bail for them either.' (CDN, 8 November.) *Mrs D. V. Walker wrote from 1 Rose Crescent: 'It was a singularly inappropriate moment to have chosen for an outbreak of ragging. Mr Churchill has this week drawn our attention to the seriousness of the fighting on the German borders ...'* (CDN, 6 November.) *Lieutenant David Holbrook of the Royal Armoured Corps thought that the 'mass hysteria and hooliganism' ... reminded one 'of those who joined the S.S., Hitler's children'.* (CDN, 7 November.) *There were calls for the guilty to be taken into the army, or put in the glasshouse, or publicly birched.*

Jack Overhill's much more liberal and tolerant spirit is quite at odds with the dislike of privilege which the diary usually reveals. Many letters to the newspaper shared his attitude: what was shown on Guy Fawkes night was merely youthful high spirits natural amid the hardships of war; only a minority of students had been involved, and they would soon be dying in battle. Two ex-students called Ingrams declared that the rag had relieved the tedium of the Cambridge policemen's lives, and J. M. Williams, an undergraduate of Trinity Hall, thought 'it would be crime if an attempt were made to turn undergraduates into dignified gentlemen'. (CDN, 8 November.)

Saturday 11 November. There was an Alert in the early hours of the morning: round about 2 o'clock I'm told, lasting for five or ten minutes. Poppy Day; i.e. Armistice Day. I didn't buy a poppy; never have done. ...

Sunday 12 November. A lot of talk in the paper about the new German weapon, V2. This has turned out to be rocket bombs fired from the Continent. They go 60 or 70 miles in the stratosphere and travel faster than sound. Is this invention the forerunner of rockets fired at the moon? Very likely.

Monday 13 November. An Alert this evening at 6.25 p.m. for five or ten minutes. ... I bought two secondhand overcoats for £2 and 35s.

Tuesday 14 November. ... An Alert this evening: 7.10 p.m. for about a quarter of an hour. ...

From a letter of 16 November to Neil Bell, copied into the diary:

> ... A greengrocer charged me a bob [1*s*] for a cabbage the other day; they were 1*d* when I was a kid and did the shopping. ... I've got out 55 pages of the manuscript [in fact, typescript] of 'Finger in the Pie'. I want to write a novel – 'The Miller of Trumpington'. It's beginning to nag at my thoughts to and from work (and while I'm at work), but I'd better finish the one I'm on and get out at least three of the 'Whims of the Father' books first. ..

Friday 17 November. An Alert this evening at about 7.30 p.m. for a few minutes.

December 1944

Sunday 3 December. ... The Home Guard stood down today and there's been parades all over the country. I saw them march by up the top of the archway as I sat in this room. ... I'm working (slaving is nearer the mark) to finish the novel by Christmas. Have got out 129 pages of the fresh manuscript. ...

Sunday 10 December. An Alert this evening: 6.50 till 7.10 p.m. I heard the plane (a bug) go over while I was in Trumpington Street. The explosion came some minutes later when I was in the house.

Tuesday 12 December. There was an Alert this evening at about 7.30 p.m. till 8.00 p.m. Heard a bug go over and an explosion. There was apparently a couple of them last Sunday night and they fell between St Neots and Bedford. ...

Sunday 17 December. There was a terrific explosion the other night; we didn't know what it was; perhaps, a V2. There's protest all over the country over our war with the Greeks. Churchill's sabre-rattling has raised a lot of indignation.

Monday 18 December. There were two Alerts last night. The first was from 3.50 a.m. till 4.50 a.m. Jack, unused to the rocket bombs (the siren never goes in Loughborough [where he was at college], he says) came down into our bed. I said rocket bombs; I should have said flying bombs (doodlebugs), although I've been told one or two rocket bombs have fallen in Cambridgeshire; but can't swear to the truth of it. We heard what sounded like bugs going over and an explosion or two in the distance. Jack didn't like the sound of them as they drew near and (like all of us) said 'Keep going' (how selfish!). I tried to cheer us all up by saying 'It's one of ours—lovely E-e-e-english bomber'. Ridiculous, of course, for a man of my age!

The 'All Clear' sounded and Jack went back to his own bed. Then the siren sounded again. I don't know what time, but Jess heard it was just after 6.00 a.m. Neither do I know how long the warning lasted. Jack kept in his own bed that time, being too tired to turn out. It's odd how a new weapon of attack affects one. I felt as nervous as Jack when I heard the first V1 go over, but they affect me less now. And yet all the while there was no difference between them and the ordinary bombing planes. … They just drop down on us and that's precisely what the bombs from a bomber do.

Wednesday 20 December. One of Jack's pals named Mitcham, now 18, is trying to get into the Fleet Air Arm as a pilot. And he gave my name as a reference! This was a teaser and stumped me for a while. But I finally decided I must give the reference. The purpose for which it was used was no concern of mine. And it was his wish. One question I had to answer was whether he held or expressed views tending to subvert the constitution. The others were: The time I'd known him. How. Disposition. Character. Habits. Games. Alcohol. Financial embarrassment, etc.

Saturday 23 December. … He [Jack] bought me Frink's *Morbid Fears and Compulsions* [1921] in Bowes as a Christmas present. Jess [daughter] bought me Shaw's latest book [*Everybody's*] *Political What's What* [1944]. … This afternoon I went down the town with the Jesses: bought [daughter] Jess Walter de la Mare's *Collected Rhymes and Verses;* bought Jess [wife] a scarf. (I gave Jack a quid [£1] to buy his own present.) …

Monday 25 December. … Been on the novel all day. Plenty of grub this Christmas: pork, a leg of lamb, a fat chicken and a rabbit. Jess made a fine plum pudding and a fine cake. We had an orange each, a few dates, some muscatels and almond nuts. And lemonade. Pretty good going for the fifth Christmas of the war. ... I've nearly finished the book; another day or two. ...

Wednesday 27 December. Back to the grindstone today, for I made a start at the shop, and not entirely without that Christmas feeling. Last night it froze sharp: the river temperature was 32 degrees today when I went in, and the air 26 degrees. The journeys to and from the shop were picturesque, the frost on the trees making it seem like fairyland. ...

Sunday 31 December. I came to a full stop with the novel on Thursday; found the last chapter was no good at all because of some minor changes I made in the two preceding chapters. I rewrote the chapter, finishing last night. Today I have retyped it — 10 pages — and feel very satisfied with it. I think the ending is now a better one. So now 'Finger in the Pie' is finished. It's taken six months to the day, as I started on 1 July. But it's been a good six months' work and a good effort, chance whether the book is ever published. It's not only a novel, but a chronological record of horseracing and a history of bookmaking and betting changes during the last 40 years.

I forgot to mention that people were glum over Christmas as the Germans under von Rundstedt on the Western Front pushed us back into Belgium and France, seeming to have caught us napping.[21] It will probably lengthen the war, even if it doesn't affect the ultimate decision of it.

The Russians are battling round Budapest and will probably get to Berlin first. The fighting in Greece continues, although Churchill flew there, met the leaders of the opposing sides and talked things over with them.[22] The Greeks (I mean the

---

[21] The German attack through the almost impenetrable Ardennes forest achieved complete surprise. It aimed to split the Allied armies in two and recapture Antwerp, their main supply port. After initial success the German army was defeated by early January, losing nearly all their tanks and aircraft.

[22] During the German and Italian occupation of Greece in 1941–44 the guerrilla resistance was dominated by Communists and republicans, while the monarchist government in exile wished to restore King George II. When the Germans withdrew in October 1944 the monarchist leaders returned, forming an uneasy government with the Communists. A Communist rising in December was bitterly fought, not least by British troops. Churchill, obsessed by the need to keep Communist influence out of the

Left-wingers) mistrust him and are not being hoodwinked. ... I've been in the water almost every day, but cold though the weather has been I didn't believe it when I saw the custodian at the 'Sheds' had put down the river temperature as 28 degrees!

Mitcham, Jack's pal, has been accepted for the Fleet Air Arm as an air-gunner—I'm sorry to say. ...

Mediterranean, flew to Athens on Christmas Eve to attempt conciliation. A ceasefire was patched up in January 1945, but civil war broke out between the opposing factions in 1946, lasting until 1949 when the Communists were defeated.

1945

January 1945

Monday 1 January. Jess, Jack and I sat up last night and saw the old year out. We let the fire go out and went to bed cold. Jack said he'd like to do it, he never had, and I was busy reading through the novel looking for typing errors and didn't mind sitting up, but I think it was an effort on Jess's part. Jess [daughter] went to bed. Trust her!

An old lady came in the shop and explained the loud bangs we constantly hear round about (bombs, or our own planes blowing up) as due to tree-falling [tree-felling?]. What big trees they are! But she added that she didn't believe it—not altogether.

Wednesday 3 January. I finished the corrections last night and after sitting contentedly over the fire browsing about the book and then reading a few of de la Mare's verses, I went to bed. It was midnight. This morning I took the book to the binder's and wrote Neil Bell saying I'd be sending it on in a day or two—on the wings of a prayer!

Two Alerts this evening. The first at 7.00 lasted about a quarter of an hour. The crash of the explosion rattled the windows. About a quarter of an hour later—roughly 7.30 p.m.—the siren went again. This warning lasted more than an hour. The bug [doodlebug] went over at about half-past eight. I heard it and went out. There was a crowd outside. It was low and roaring in the sky like a huge sewing-machine. It was heading St Neots way and an explosion occurred about 10 minutes afterwards. Jack and Jess [daughter] have gone to a dance with Alan King at the Guildhall.

Sunday 21 January. … The manager of the Regal cinema in the town stopped me one morning on Parker's Piece and after asking me if Jock was my dog asked me if I would parade Jock at the Regal when another picture of Lassie, the collie dog, is shown there to help with a hospital collection. I agreed.

On January 9th there was about three inches of snow. We've had snow on and off since and the weather has been wintry. ... On January 10th Neil Bell wired me that the novel was fine. ... He wrote Michael Joseph about the book and they now have it under consideration. On January 13th there was an Alert for about 20 minutes at 6.30 a.m. We heard nothing.

Lately, I've thought about a novel about a carrier. I shall call it 'Bob Carter — Carrier' or 'The Fen Tiger'. I shall have to delay writing it as I've started retyping 'Sins of the Father' and I must increase my examination work. Russia has started a big offensive and there's a chance she'll soon knock out Germany and end the war with her. ...

Wednesday 24 January. The cold is like a blanket. There's a little snow on the ground, frozen hard, and this morning the chart in the bathing sheds stood at 20 air, 32 water (the water temperature has been 32 for some while), ... The Russians are advancing all along the line (to use the phrase of the last war) and now have a bridgehead across the Oder, the last German defence line before Berlin. ...

Sunday 28 January. According to the papers the weather during the past few days has been the coldest for 50 years. ... when we awoke this morning there was a thickish layer of snow on the ground. The frost however has been intense and has wrapped round one like a cold blanket. Mark Horner called round this morning at 12.00 and we went in the river. Had to smash the ice with a duckboard. A little blizzard raged on the way home. At night abed our noses are like icicles. ... A split thumb quick, which has been painful while at work and abed, hasn't helped to raise my flagging spirits. ... As for exam work — Yah!

February 1945

Sunday 4 February. ... Today, I heard a naval officer say to a woman as I passed that a lot of intellectual sergeants were getting about. --- Jess tells me that she saw a little boy aged about five out of Gothic Street pass the front window yesterday; he had no hat, no coat, no socks; another little boy ran up to him and said 'I mustn't come with you, must I, you've got chicken pox'; the other agreed; and they walked along together.

Sunday 11 February. The Russians are over the Oder, the last natural defence before Berlin in the East. ... We made a terrible raid on Berlin last Saturday. The casualties must have been awful. The war cannot end too soon to end the suffering. ...

Claudio Rossi came round with another Italian this evening. He's now a male nurse at the POW camp on Hauxton Road and was taking the other fellow to Addenbrooke's Hospital. I tried to play the piano this evening and couldn't play at all. And after all my years of practice in my 20s. ...

Sunday 18 February. I found a diamond ear-ring last week and returned it to the police station. The lady it belonged to is sending me a reward! Half a crown [2s 6d], I bet. ...

Sunday 25 February. To my surprise the lady to whom the diamond ear-ring belonged sent me £3. It's against my principles to take rewards for finding things; just benefiting out of somebody else's bad luck is no good; but I kept the money, being hard up just now, very hard up, indeed. But I resolved after giving Jack a quid [£1] for luck that when the tide turned I would send Addenbrooke's Hospital £3 to balance the matter. ...

March 1945

Sunday 4 March. ... Jess was 21 yesterday. Jess [wife] made a slap-up plum pudding for [despite] all wartime rationing; and a very fine birthday cake. I had a walk round the town with the Js in the afternoon. Ordered a volume of Keats as a present for Jess. Jess [wife] tried to buy her a ring. We went into one shop and asked the price of a ring we liked the look of; it was £54. We nearly collapsed and then laughed so much over the price that the assistant (an elderly woman) laughed as well. Jess drew a blank at another shop, but the jeweller said he'd be having some rings in of the sort she wanted. And that's the way it is in wartime.

The war drags on with the final blows from East and West still to be delivered. Germany fights on heroically. And to remind us that the war isn't over for all the partly lit streets and adjustments that are being made in preparation for peace there was a raid by piloted planes on this country last night — the first time for nine months the announcer said on the wireless today. I heard the Alert and 'Raiders Passed' signals and upon inquiry today was told the siren sounded at 12.30 a.m. but I don't know how long the warning lasted. A few minutes ago the siren went again; that was at 8.05 p.m. and the Alert is still on. I hoped all that was over, but nothing is over until the ball stops rolling. And that may be soon. …

Monday 5 March. The warning last night lasted about an hour; and the previous one lasted (so I was told today) about an hour and a half.

The novel came back from [Michael] Joseph today. … There was only a rejection slip with it, which, in view of the circumstances, seemed rather odd. … He [Neil Bell, on the telephone] said the rejection didn't mean a thing these days owing to the paper shortage, but the rejection slip was a bit dirty and he asked if he could write M. J. to find out why he hadn't published the book. I said yes he could with pleasure. He also said not one new writer in a hundred is getting published at present …, but the war would soon be over and then things will be different … . He said send the book to Hale. …

Tuesday 6 March. I sent the book to Robert Hale today. I mentioned in my letter a few of the nice things Neil Bell said about it. …

Thursday 8 March. I went with the Js to see a film called *Frenchman's Creek*. It was in technicolour and that was beautiful. But the story based on a novel by a famous authoress [Daphne du Maurier] was the usual romantic nonsense. People were queuing up to see the film and I thought how could I expect my novels to be published when such escapist stuff is the vogue. My stuff is too realistic, too lifelike; or so it seems.

From a letter to Neil Bell copied in the diary:
   … Claudio Rossi, the Italian POW now speaks very good English. The other day while at Frank Edwards's he watched Frank's

eleven-year-old daughter Molly do her homework. She couldn't think of a word. He said 'Appropriately will do very well there, Molly'. She said, 'Yes, so it will. How do you spell it, Claudio?' And the other day he entered Frank's house with the remark: 'Mr Frank, some fellow called out "Whacheer Tich" as I was coming along. What did he mean?' When Frank told him he kept repeating 'Whacheer Tich'! …

Sunday 11 March. Michael Joseph wrote to me and to Neil Bell, who sent me M. J.'s letter. M. J. thought FITP ['Finger in the Pie'] a remarkable and distinguished achievement and that he didn't publish the book because it didn't fit his list and because he didn't have the paper. … I don't take a scrap of notice of such nonsense. He'd have found the paper had he wanted. …

Sunday 18 March. There were two Alerts last night. The first between 9.00 p.m. and 10.00 p.m. A chap told me today piloted planes came over. The other was in the middle of the night: 2.00 a.m., and lasted 25 minutes. The same chap told me it was a doodlebug and that it went Ely way. …

Nowadays there's always the heavy roar of planes going over. It is such a part of the world nowadays that it often passes unnoticed; something like a ticking clock in a quiet room isn't noticed; and as one suddenly becomes aware of the ticking of the clock so does one become aware of that dull roar overhead and think what it means — just devastation and death --- racial suicide. ---

Tuesday 20 March. Don Varley came in with Jess [Jack's daughter] last night. Jess [wife] shook hands with him. He seemed a bit self-conscious. …

There's talk of allowances being given to children, starting at the second child … . The amount is 5s a week. But it's to be subject to income tax deduction and parents will get from 2s 8d to 3s 4d a child. This is the funniest thing out, I reckon. Even the people of this country aren't so silly that they don't know the difference between say 3s and 5 bob [5s]. Or, is that how the Government rates their intelligence? Failing that Officialdom is itself up the pole.

Wednesday 21 March. There was an Alert last night at 9.00 p.m. lasting for about an hour. ...

Friday 23 March. The RAF camp round the Backs has gone to Quy. They cleared out today, leaving the place looking like a deserted village (I must be thinking of Goldsmith's poem!) I well remember their coming; it was during June 1940; such a long time ago now. At first, there were just a few men in a small tent; ... . One of the men told me today that he was one of the first to come and he would be one of the last to leave; I said he could have had a worse billet and he agreed. He told me that even when it was known they were clearing out a stove was put in one of the huts; he said the taxpayers' money must be spent on something.

Saturday 24 March. There was an Alert early this morning: 3.45 a.m. It lasted only about a quarter of an hour. We heard a crash in the distance and thought it was a 'bug'. There was another Alert at 7.15 a.m. for about 10 minutes. We heard another crash and again thought it was a 'bug'. ...

Thursday 29 March. There was an Alert this morning for about three minutes at 9.00 a.m. The newspapers give the impression that the end of the war is imminent. ...

Friday 30 March. Good Friday. I worked this morning at the shop and I am now trying to finish the novel off over Easter.

Saturday 31 March. ... Claudio Rossi came round this afternoon and stayed for tea and most of the evening. Jess [his wife] and I had an argument when he was here ... ; it was about poetry versus novels. Of course, I championed the novel; not that I really dislike poetry; I just like to pretend I do to Jess, especially when she tells me it shouldn't even be read to oneself, but aloud. ---

April 1945

From a letter to Neil Bell dated 1 April and copied into the diary:
> ... While on the subject of what I can no longer do—I can't play the piano at all. I tried the other evening. Not to be wondered at. I've written seven novels and a bit during the last five years in my **spare time**, to say nothing of an inter and three finals for the B.Sc.

Econ. I'll not mention the other odds and ends, not least among them being a father and a CO.

Thursday 5 April. The novel came back from Hale today; I wasn't surprised. I wrote and told Neil Bell and asked if he'd put me on to Pollinger, his agent. I'm fed up with hawking my books; if an agent can't market them, then I don't think I'll be able to. Hale mentioned what his reader said about 'Finger in the Pie'. It was so naïve as to be almost funny. I said so to NB, adding that I now regarded all publishers as lying humbugs. I do. And have done so for a long while.

Sunday 8 April. 'Whims of the Father' is now completed. ... Now I must get on with my examination work in earnest. I'd sooner relax a bit, but there --- .

Friday 13 April. Startling news this morning: first that Roosevelt the American President had died suddenly; and then that Jess's sister's husband was dying. ...

Saturday 14 April. Neil Bell has told me that he has doubts about Pollinger handling my books; he's so full up, having about 100 authors on his books, that he'd probably refuse GBS. He's suggested that I tried somebody named Cecil Hunt and I've written him. ...

[During the promised victory celebrations] I shall work. Victory? There can be no victory in war; only death and devastation. Peace? Who can believe it with the Jap war still on our hands and the final showdown between Capitalism and Communism to come. Besides, I don't like being told when I'm to make merry.

Sunday 22 April. ... I spend all my spare time now revising for the examination in June. It's a boring job and keeps my mind at a low level. ... The papers are full of German atrocity stories, which seem to be substantially true. Nobody can defend that sort of thing, but some of those who now shout the loudest were those that praised Hitler and company the most over the way they rid their country of trade unions and other forces that were the only real bulwarks against it; ... . I'm wondering just what will happen to the high lights of the Nazi party. Will they be let off by fine-spun legal pretexts? Very likely. ...

The blackout ends tomorrow and full street lighting starts in July. ...

Monday 30 April. I sent the following letter to Neil Bell this morning, making a copy of it as an afterthought. *An extract from the letter follows*:

> ... Treating the book [Bell's novel *The Handsome Langleys*] as a textbook I learned much that I wanted to know. This was largely to do with topics of conversation. I think now that I shall be able to **build** books. And in future I shall certainly always plan them, which I have never yet done.

May 1945

Tuesday 1 May. The allies (actually, I think it was the Americans) and the Russians linked up last week. ... When I walked to work this morning in bitterly cold weather ... bombers were roaring over; yet for all that the Backs seemed rather tranquil and there was a peaceful sort of air about everything. Of course, this was merely my imagination; my mind was playing tricks with me; but peace after nearly six years of war is something to think about and apt to cause illusions.

Grey hairs have been coming in Jess's hair for several years; and now they are coming in mine. Not many yet, but they are coming and I can already visualise myself a grey-haired man, whether old or not. Alas! But time is not to be denied, nor is age. ...

Wednesday 2 May. [Daughter] Jess came into our bedroom this morning and said that it was given out on the 7 o'clock news that Hitler according to the German radio was dead and that the new Fuehrer was Dittmar. ... Anyway, Hitler was dead and Doenitz (Jess got hold of the wrong name) was henceforth the big noise in Germany and he'd ordered his people to fight on.[1] ...

---

[1] Karl Doenitz (1891–1980): commander-in-chief of the U-boat fleet from 1935 to January 1943, and of the German navy from then until April 1945. Before Hitler committed suicide he nominated Doenitz as his successor. He ruled Germany as President until 22 May 1945, when the Allies arrested him. Found guilty of war crimes at the Nuremberg trials he was imprisoned for ten years.

Tonight's news is that the German army has unconditionally surrendered in Italy and Western Austria. So perhaps (a news flash has just come through on the wireless: the Russians have captured Berlin; it's about 10.15 p.m. Jess and I both felt excited when the woman announcer said a news flash was coming through. A man announcer then gave out the item — and what an important item! of news), so perhaps the Germans don't intend to fight on.

The Civil Defence starts being disbanded from today (I think) and arrangements are being made for evacuees to return to London during the next month or six weeks. And there's to be no more air-raid warnings, the system being discontinued today at midday. ...

Friday 4 May. ... The Js are at the theatre and as I sat at supper a news flash came through on the wireless at 8.50, repeating one given 20 minutes earlier, which I didn't hear being out with Jim and Jock for a stroll round Gresham Road — a place I rather like because I used to amble along there when a boy reading 'bloods' about Dick Turpin; and there's some french windows to a house on the corner where I could picture Dick Turpin riding in and out on his nag Black Bess. Well, to come to that news flash: it said that the Germans had unconditionally surrendered in Denmark, Holland and North-West Germany; so it looks as if the war in Europe will soon be over and peace declared.

Now I'll bore myself with some examination work till about 11.00, when it will be bedtime. But first an afterthought. I went to the pictures tonight and I saw the film of the atrocities in the German concentration camps. The scenes were indeed awful, but undoubtedly they were made the most of, for the dead wouldn't be lying about as they were shown. It wouldn't have been healthy for the German guards and warders.[2]

[2] The film was of Bergen–Belsen concentration camp, liberated by the British 11th armoured division on 15 April. Evidence does not support Jack's sceptical comment. The camp was very overcrowded and ravaged by starvation and typhus. Five or six hundred inmates were dying each day. In March the guards had abandoned the burial of the dead, and corpses were placed in the piles found and filmed by British soldiers: Ben Shephard, *After Daybreak: The Liberation of Belsen*, 1945 (2005).

Sunday 6 May. ... The war isn't over yet, but it is nearly, and everybody is keyed up and awaiting the end. There is much talk of V-day and celebrations, which must be restrained owing to the war with the Japanese; particularly in Cambridge as so many Cambs men were taken prisoner by the Japs at the fall of Singapore just over three years ago. There's only Norway and another pocket or two holding out (rather I should say the Germans in Norway); when they surrender it will all be over; but the peace will present some pretty problems. All isn't well with Britain and Russia in San Francisco, where there's a peace conference being held, over the Poles. Goodness knows what will happen unless the leaders of the different nations can found a lasting peace. Future wars don't bear thinking about. ...

London University have advised me that I can again sit with the LSE in Cambridge for the examination in June; which is a relief ... .

Monday 7 May. It was stated on the wireless last evening that the end of the war in Europe would be declared in a day or two; ... . This dramatisation of the impending event reminded me of the baloney that was put over the wireless when King George the Fifth died and when Edward VIII abdicated. ... At 8 o'clock I went along to the little shop farther up the street and I was told there that according to a news flash on the wireless V-Day would be tomorrow, [and that] Churchill would speak on the radio at 3.00 in the afternoon. This was stated at 9 o'clock on the wireless, the announcer adding that the king would speak at 9.00 tomorrow night and that tomorrow and the next day would be public holidays. I then had a stroll round the houses with Jim and Jock; some flags were out, mainly in the poorer streets. When the pubs turned out at 10.00 a little crowd formed at the top of Gothic Street and tried to get up a sing-song; it was a row; and now it's petered out after about half an hour and there's quiet in the street. ...

Tuesday 8 May. This is V-E (Victory in Europe) Day. I biked to work this morning, posting off a *CDN* to Jack on the way; I did seven pairs of repairs in the shop and left off at 10.30 to come home and see to the racing, for it was One Thousand

Guineas day at Newmarket. The bells rang while I was at work and as I came home; there were plenty of people about; and the day was delightfully warm, although not very sunny. The streets were decorated with flags, but the attitude of the people struck me as very sober. I won nearly £4 on the racing after a good deal of mathematical juggling; in between times I listened to the radio; the Jesses went on the river at 2.30 and at 3.00 I heard Churchill speak on the wireless; he ended by saying 'Advance Britannia. Long live the cause of freedom. God Save the King.' And then the buglers of the Scots Guards sounded the cease fire and the end of the war. I worked out the bets, cooked the dogs' dinners and went for a swim; then I came home and had my tea. Fred and Liz [his brother and sister-in-law] then came in and as soon as they'd gone Jack rang through from Loughborough for a short talk as it was V-Day. I told him two of his pals, George Harvey and Bob Rowe, came round this afternoon to see if he'd come home. I then had a stroll on Parker's Piece with the dogs and read some economic history, which I'd read on and off all day in preparation for the examination; I walked some way down St Andrews Street; there were crowds about, but there was nothing happening and I came home with the dogs—to go out again to the pictures; I saw the film *A Song to Remember* at the Regal; it was about Chopin and the piano-playing (and the film itself) were beautiful; I thoroughly enjoyed it; and (may I add) I was inspirited by the story. I believe there's been a torchlight procession through the town tonight and a bonfire on Midsummer Common; but I've seen nothing of these things. I've just had a walk round the houses with Jock: a small bonfire burns on the Plant'un; it would disgrace schoolboys; and as I mooched along searchlights were giving the victory sign in the sky. While I write the people in Gothic Street are having a sing-song; they have a piano in the street. Altogether it's not been an excitable day. And as it's half-past eleven I think I'll get to bed.

Wednesday 9 May. V-E Day plus one (as it's called). ... I went in the water at teatime and met a young man named Dennis Boles ..., a flight-sergeant in the RAF. We met him years ago before he volunteered for the air force through the Cashes. ... He's crashed in a bomber six months ago and had both his legs broken; the pilot was killed; and two of the gunners; he's a navigator. ... [Afterwards] Jess and I then had a walk. There was a searchlight display on Parker's Piece and crowds of people about, especially round a contraption playing music of a sort. We then walked to Christ's Pieces, where the bandstand was lit up and couples were dancing to a panatrope, or something similar, for there was no band.[3] Home we came to be regaled with music from Gothic Street: piano and singing. We saw a few little bonfires in the streets. Morals, judging from appearances, are at a very low ebb; but that's only to be expected. So ends the victory celebrations. And as the Catholic [church] has just struck a quarter past twelve I'll get to bed.

Thursday 24 May. It's 11 o'clock at night and as I type the 'wolf-wagons' are going by; this is the name for the American army lorries which bring the American soldiers into the town from just outside, and, I believe, the name has something to do with the lorries being used for carting town girls to and from the American camps for dances.

Empire Day; and 22nd anniversary of my wedding day. I sent Jess a greetings card and bought her a pink nightdress (for which six coupons—mine!—were given) as a present. ...

Neil Bell read 'Whims of the Father' and wrote me lengthily about it. Apparently, there was nothing good about it at all. ... He once said I was never to take notice of anything he said in his letters; and perhaps that's the best thing to do, although it cuts both ways and makes all his past praise of no value. He also told me to go my own way and take no notice of anybody, so I'll take refuge in that. ...

Peace in Europe has brought its troubles, but that was only to be expected. I'll not enumerate them, they'll all be in the history books. And so to bed.

Sunday 3 June. Neil Bell writes that he isn't well. He has an ulcerated stomach and has to take care of himself. ... Which might account for the odd letters he wrote me about 'Whims

---

[3] A panatrope was an early form of electrical record-player, consisting of a pickup, an amplifier and a loudspeaker.

A tea to celebrate VE day in Hobart Road, May 1945

Children gathered outside St Andrew's church hall, Chesterton, to celebrate VJ day, August 1945. Tea followed the taking of the photograph.

of the Father'. ... he thinks he's booked for the high jump before long. All going well I hope to go and see him shortly; just get the examination [London External B.Sc.] over.

I've just posted a letter to the *News of the World* offering them 'Finger in the Pie' for publication in serial form. ...

Last Friday Charlie Driver and myself examined nearly a score of adults of both sexes, VAD [Voluntary Aid Detachment] and Red Cross workers, for the Royal Life Saving Society resuscitation badge; there's another score to examine tomorrow night. Some of them were a bit weak over the physiology, but as their practical work was good we passed them; for that's what counts. It was a change for me to be the examiner not the examined.

The other day I rang up the RSPCA inspector and told him there was a pony on Coe Fen wearing a halter with two ropes trailing on the ground under its front feet, which sometimes had it over and certainly made life difficult for it. He's been and seen it and I'm glad to say that it now has a different halter with only a few inches of rope hanging from it. Why do the owners of horses act in such a manner? Is it callousness, cruelty, indifference or just plain thoughtlessness?

Tomorrow I'm seeing Maurice Dobb, who has promised to clear up a number of economic questions for me. I'll be glad when the examination is over. I want a rest; and I mean to have one; albeit, I'm already thinking of another book—*The Miller of Trumpington* based on Chaucer's poem.[4] I believe I could make a job of it.

The Js are at the Red Lion, Grantchester. They confess they're getting tired of their Sunday jaunt there for tea, the tea being a poor one for 1s 6d.

---

[4] This was Jack's last novel to be published, by the Staples Press in 1953. An historical novel, it is not concerned with the proletarian matters characterising his other fictions, and it has an action-packed narrative. It is perhaps among the best of Jack's 26 fictions.

July 1945

Sunday 1 July.

In this entry of 2,500 words, Jack described the four weeks when the diary had been neglected:

I shut up the shop on Thursday the 7th June for a final revision for the [B.Sc.] examination, which began in Monday the 11th. ... On Friday [8 June] there was racing and the Oaks was run at Newmarket; I lost; ... . Jack also came home on that day to register as a conscientious objector the day following. ... On Saturday the Derby was run at Newmarket; I was very busy, but I won on the day and clearing off the Friday's loss showed a profit on the two days' racing of about £14, which was worth working for. ... In the evening [9 June] Gothic Street held its VE Day celebrations. Those responsible made a good job of it, giving the children and old people an excellent tea for wartime. The Chief Constable and his wife were present. The street was decorated with flags and streamers, there were games for the women and children, there was music in the shape of wireless and a piano; and there was a large crowd to participate and watch. I dodged in and out of the house at odd times to see how things were progressing. The street was floodlit when it was dark; there was a striptease act by a man (it was quite funny) and dancing.

On Monday 11 June Jack began his fourth attempt at the Final examinations for the B.Sc. Econ., on this occasion sitting in the Law School with candidates from the London School of Economics in the Senate House. He wrote:

I adopted fresh tactics throughout the examination, quoting the names of authorities and the books for everything I said. ... [For example] Question 2 — to do with financing the present war — I wrote about our gold holding going to America when the war started (quoting reports in the papers the previous day) our foreign investments, savings, borrowings, Bank borrowings, including Treasury Deposit Receipts, and Lend-Lease (ie payments in kind instead of money) with a reference to the growing National Debt; ... . That afternoon [Tuesday 12 June] I took the English Essay; I had tried to place it, and managed it, for there was one dealing with Problems of Suburbanisation, and I had read up the Barlow, Scott and Uthwatt Reports. I managed to keep my rough copy, although I was only two or three rows from the front where the vigilator sat, and I have typed it out and included it with this diary. ...

I started back at work at the shop on the day following the end of the examination, that is, the Tuesday [19 June]. Customers were waiting for me on the doorstep and that morning I took in 50 or 60 pairs of repairs. It was a busy week all round, for in addition to being rushed at the shop there were three days racing; and with Jess away [on holiday] I had to see after myself pretty well, ... It was a week when I ate scrappy meals of bread and cheese (or marg[erine]) washed down with tea or cocoa; and ate them standing, answering the telephone over the racing and the door over the shop repairing in between bites. ... Altogether it was one of the rottenest fortnights I've ever lived. The past week at the shop was the best I've had; I did £16 14s of work I should think I earned between £12 and £13 net; which is good for a one-man band without any machinery. ...

Yesterday [Sunday 31 June, or perhaps Saturday 30 June] I took Jess into partnership with the racing. From now on it's share and share alike with it; and I'm reducing covering to a minimum; and hoping to cut it out altogether. We won £9 on the day. I hope our £25 capital continues to increase while I pay my way with work at the shop.

I've seen our tenant at 99 Shelford Road and asked them to get out by the end of October. I hope they do so without any trouble. It's not easy to get tenants out of furnished houses nowadays if they get awkward; and we all want to go back. This house is too cramped, and the neighbourhood is too slummy. Besides, 99 Shelford Road is our home.

Frank Edwards suggests (because Midsummer Fair has come and gone) that I ought to stand up in a sideshow at the fairs as an example of failure! There can be few men about who've written a dozen unpublished books and sat four times for a final degree, he says, and if necessary he'll do the shouting. ...

By the bye, I passed Maurice Dobb round the Backs last week. He asked how I got on in the exam. I told him I thought I had done very well, but I thought that before and it had proved wrong. He said he hoped I had better luck this year. And in a way that suggested my name was coming out of a hat. Still, there's a lottery touch about the B.Sc. Econ. examination; or so it seems to me. ...

And I'd like to add that I only went to the fair on one night, the last night, which was last Tuesday [26 June]. I went with Jess [wife] and Jess [daughter]; and I spent 2s 3d. Everything is a bigger swindle than ever at the Fair nowadays. There's little thought about entertaining the public, and not only overcharging, but adding to it mean attempts at cheating over change. Many people have told me over this. Soon the Fair people will kill the goose that lays the golden egg. Were these the reasons that there were so few people there on Tuesday evening? ... We all had a sixpenny go at a main attraction that consisted of a couple of cockerels spun round to send a lighted indicator over the names of a number of towns (I mean imitation cockerels, of course); the person that held the ticket of the name of the town was the winner. There were 90 towns, which represented winnings of 45s; the prizes were worth from 5s to 10s (e.g. saucepans); and as the whole affair didn't take a minute it must have been a gold-mine for the proprietors. ...

I'm already thinking of another novel: a period novel round about 1730; but I'm not tackling it yet. [This was *The Miller of Trumpington*] ...

So concludes Jack's backward glance at June 1945.

Tuesday 3 July. ... I'm reading Dickens's *Great Expectations*; I liked it at first, but not now; it's Victorianish; and for all his detailed descriptions of people and things they are so vague and shadowy as to appear unreal. It was my intention to read all his works, but I don't think I shall be able to. So much of the book is about such trivial things that they're hardly worth writing about; they bore me. There's no depth in the book and it gives me the feeling that Dickens had no knowledge outside the ordinary affairs of very ordinary men and women; but maybe that was all to do with the time in which he lived; writers can't say what they like now; and they certainly couldn't then.

The General Election is in full swing; ... .
From a letter to Neil Bell dated 4 July:

... What I have in mind is to write the book about *The Miller of Trumpington*, which will be the title. ... I decided to make it a novel about the eighteenth century, a time which, for some reason, is in my blood. It's not important whether it's 1730 or 1780, but it'll certainly be eighteenth century. The story will move between Trumpington, Cambridge and London; it'll be a roistering sort of book; ... . For, boys! Can I paint that picture! I'm ploughing through the whole century. My 'Miller' will mix with rogues, vagabonds, cut-throats, highwaymen, thieves; ... . I'll lie about everything as heartily as any novelist ever lied; ... . It'll be nothing, for example, for my Miller to meet Dick Turpin in the flesh 33 years after Turpin was hanged at Tyburn on the grounds that Turpin wasn't hanged at all. What care I about facts? History is all a lie, anyway.

I've just written and asked London University library if they can send me the Newgate Calendar ... and any other books dealing with the life of the time. And any you can name or send will be greatly appreciated. Because I'm going to know my stuff before I start; ... .

Before I've finished I'll take the shine out of these ruddy publishers that keep turning their noses up at me. I'm not done with yet. As for writing 500 words a day — 5,000 is nearer the mark; for that's the only way I can write. If I wrote 500 and thought about it and dwelt on it you'd say I was hopeless; and I should be. When I write I'm full of vim; I punch and punch and punch — at the typewriter. ...

Thursday 5 July. General Election Day. Coming down Pound Hill I saw a man enter the school to vote; and I was suddenly thrilled at the sight; it seemed grand and a fine way of framing a government. There's nothing wrong with the democratic system of government; only the present abuses associated with it; if they're removed — and they can be — it'll want a lot of beating; for it's the nearest approach to Man's right to rule himself. Jess and I polled at Russell Street school this afternoon; ... .

A middle-aged woman I meet round the Backs, who makes a fuss of the dogs, walked along with me today and as she was returning from the polling booth she told me she had been to vote and asked me whether I was interested in politics. I said yes, adding that I was politically interested as my father used to get me to read the newspaper to him. I told her he was a staunch radical and she asked did I follow his line of thought or strike out on my own. I said I was theoretically a communist; and she said she was glad I was only a theoretical communist; I said I couldn't be anything else as I was living under Capitalism and that I thought Socialism was the only hope for mankind. We talked a bit; it was easy to guess she was a Tory; and then she asked if I studied Economics; I said yes. Had I anything to do with the London School of Economics; I said I'd just sat for the fourth time for the B.Sc. Economics degree as an external student. She then said she greatly admired me for it as she was on the administrative staff of the LSE and she understood a London external degree was very, very hard. Which, I thought, was all rather odd.

Friday 6 July. ... Today, the woman opposite told Jess her husband didn't vote as he only received a notice from Tuffnell, the Tory candidate, and he wasn't voting for him. He thought the notices sent out by the different party candidates gave him authority to vote and as he didn't receive one from Symonds, the Labour candidate, he couldn't vote for him. It's incredible to think electors can be so ignorant. ...

Watching Jess preparing dinner today and doing half a dozen things at once I thought what a lot of learning and skill there is in being a trained housewife, able to do things expeditiously and well. It takes the shine out of many so-called arts and crafts.

Sunday 15 July. ... The *News of the World* contains an article today entitled 'Russian hands stretch out—for what?'; it's by Richard Wyndham; and it's a good example of the stuff that's now appearing in the Tory press. Apparently, the people of this country are not to be blinded by all that Russia has done during the last few years against aggression, but are to be wideawake to the fact that she is penetrating into other countries, Iran, for example, and doing in Turkey, the Balkans and the Middle East all that Hitler was bent on doing in *Mein Kampf.* [If] our Tory bosses are crazy enough to involve us in a war with Russia, [and] chance whether we could ever win it (we couldn't); in fact, the *News of the World* must check Russia and a lot more nonsense. Is the present time merely a prelude to another war? If so heaven help us as we only managed to scrape through this by the skin of our teeth and the devil's own luck. Maybe, the common people will exercise common sense, however.

Friday 20 July. ... Mr Murfitt came in the shop the other day with his daughter; she was down in the dumps because she had failed a Social Science examination under (I believe) the London School of Economics; she failed a couple of years ago in the Higher School Certificate Examination and judging from her manner I should say this second failure has had a bad psychological effect upon her. I tried to cheer her up by relating a few of my own failures; and I urged her to try again, saying I should if I failed the B.Sc. Econ. again, when her father chimed in with the remark 'Good old Jack'; and he added that she should have a good talk with me as it would do her good! ...

Wednesday 25 July. ... I examined six members of the Granta Swimming Club at the Leys School bath this evening for certificates and bronze medallions of the Royal Life Saving Society. They all did their work well. In examining pupils I concentrate on their ability to rescue a drowning person, pick up an object from the bottom of the bath (or river) and readiness and ableness in applying artificial respiration. Capability is what counts with me rather than a rigid regard for detail.

Thursday 26 July. ... Last night before going to bed just after 11 o'clock I walked a little way up Trumpington Road with Jock. I saw two married women, whose husbands are in the army, [and] who live in this neighbourhood, walking along with two American soldiers. They were waisting one another, the heads of the women pillowing on the men's chests, and were obviously heading for a secluded spot ... . I returned home to bed and just after midnight these two women and the mother-in-law of one of them parked themselves outside our window to exchange confidences in rather loud tones. They often do this and we hear snatches of the conversation, which is all to do with their virtuous repulsion of the men they go out with. To get more detail I got up and came down to take a verbatim shorthand report of their talk, but unfortunately I couldn't hear them so plainly downstairs as upstairs. ...

The General Election has resulted in a sweeping victory for Labour with many prominent Tories ousted. I was prepared almost for anything, but hardly Labour getting a strong working majority. I couldn't credit the British people with so much common sense. ... Even the borough and county have returned Labour members. This means I'll need to rant less; which reminds me that Frank Edwards pointed at my seat in the shop the other day and said 'When you're dead and people come and look at the place where you worked they'll say "That's where he sat and fumed and swore" '.

August 1945

Thursday 2 August. ... When I came home today it was to find the result of the examination had come; I had failed again—in History and the English Essay. Jess [wife] had opened the letter. I've got no comments to make about my fourth failure; I've said pretty well all I have to say long ago. I shall sit again next year and for as many years as it is necessary to pass. But how boring and how stultifying. I must boil my preparation next year down to a final revision of about a month.

This afternoon the Jesses, myself and the dogs went picnicking at Paradise, borrowing Bert Cash's canoe. The weather was sunny and hot (eventful this year) and I got suntanned; but mainly on my back as I usually sit with my back to the sun; a habit formed through reading outdoors. I had three dives in the river; swims were short as the [water] temperature was only 56 degrees. ... I made notes all the afternoon from Bayne Powell's *English Country Life in the Eighteenth Century* for my next book *The Miller of Trumpington,* which I hope shortly to write.

The Americans were today given the Freedom of Cambridge (whatever that is), something many people think they have had for a long time; in fact, ever since they arrived in the town. In consequence there was dancing on Parker's Piece this evening and a display of fireworks. The crowd was a big one and the fireworks pretty good. The 'Piece' was floodlit near the Hobbs Pavilion. A feature of the fireworks display was the parachutes that descended from some of the exploding crackers; Jess [wife] wanted one as a souvenir, but she didn't get one.

Friday 3 August. My examination failure had its usual stimulating effect as I was up at half-past six this morning when I went for a walk with the dogs on Parker's Piece, reading up about the eighteenth century in the *Encyclopedia of Modern Knowledge.* ...

 I left off [swimming] just after 4.00 and went to the bathing sheds, where I met Dennis Boles, whose father was a German and who lived in Germany under the Weimar Republic as a boy. Knowing the Jesses were at Paradise we went to see them, swimming part of the way and walking the rest. We found them there and talked a while before returning. He is 23 and thinks he is shortly to go to Japan with the RAF. ... He thinks education in comparison with Germany in this country is backward. I agreed. Not without reason. For could anything be more senseless than London University's method of not revealing details to candidates; for example, there's three papers under the heading Economics, namely Economics, Banking and Currency, and World Economic History; if a candidate fails in Economics he might have failed in one, two or three of the papers; and he is not told which so that he can concentrate on the particular section or sections in which he has failed. No, he must get down to it and swot up on what he has probably passed in already without knowing it. There seems to be a low form of cunning about all this; it's as though London University are playing a game, saying 'we've failed you, but we are not telling you how or why'. Obviously the intention is not to educate, but to obstruct; and if that's the way education is organised in Britain the country will be in a backward state once Russia (and Germany) get going again.

 Today, I resumed French, Spanish and Italian reading. I cannot let examination work interfere any longer with my desire to read in these languages.

Saturday 4 August. ... I saw Maurice Dobb in the town; he asked if the examination result was through; I told him; he murmured 'that's bad, oh, that's bad' and hurried off; presumably to avoid discussing the matter; although I hadn't the least inclination to do so.

Sunday 5 August. ... My mind is full of *The Miller of Trumpington* novel; it's taking shape and will (I think) be a good book when it's written.

Evening. A nice day beside the river at Paradise, ... I whiled away the time swimming and reading; and messed about a bit with Jack. And trying to float I found that at long last I could float. Immediately, I started thinking about having a cut at the RLSS [Royal Life Saving Society] diploma, the examination for which is suspended for the duration of the war.

Monday 6 August. ... I didn't like the tone of last week's *Economist*; it was patronising and contemptuous to[wards] the new Labour government. The paper is supposed to be impartial. How soon it's showed its sting.

Tuesday 7 August. ... Later I rode all over Cambridge to try and get fish and chips and failed; I reckon I biked about seven miles going as far as Barnwell Bridge in one direction and over Mill Road in the other.

An Italian prisoner of war came in the shop for some rivets; I gave him what he wanted; then we had a talk; he was 25 and had been in the army for 5¼ years; he said the war had lasted too long and that such men as Hitler and Mussolini were all right for war but no good for peace; it was five years of his life wasted; and a change was needed [to stop] workers of different nations fighting one another. He spoke very good English. ...

A new atomic bomb has been dropped on Japan by the Americans. Apparently, Britain shared in the discovery. The newspapers and wireless talk of nothing else. Old Mr Cash said in the shop that a lot of the work on it was probably done in Cambridge; I thought so — at the Cavendish laboratory where Lord Rutherford was trying to split the atom years ago. I added that if such was the case it was a good job the experimenters didn't make any serious mistakes.

Wednesday 8 August. The wonders of this new discovery, the atomic bomb, are all the news. It means that before many years nobody will need to work, will live on the fat of the land, take afternoon trips to Borneo, weekend trips to Mars and much more of a similar sort—according to the newspapers. More likely it will mean sending us underground ten miles instead of ten feet in the next war—or worse; bursting up the planet.

I was out with the dogs this afternoon and a boy stroking Jock said 'What a fine rug he'd make'; he then wanted old Jock to give him a ride. I told him not unkindly not to get on Jock's back as he wouldn't wear that (he wouldn't). And I was struck by both observations of the boy. There he was a ten-year-old kid assuming superiority to a fine animal like Jock; he just took it for granted; which was more than I did.

Startling news at 9.00 this morning on the radio: Russia declares war on Japan from tomorrow. I wondered if the new atomic bomb was the reason. Anyway, it should help to speed up the war in the Pacific.

Friday 10 August. A gloriously fine day after the rain. And glorious news as well, for just after 1.00 as I was seeing to the racing a chap came into the room and said 'So the war's over' in a casual sort of way, which immediately led to Jack switching on the radio. At the tail end of the news it was announced that the Japanese had accepted unconditional surrender with reservations about the Mikado retaining complete sovereignty over Japan. There has been little excitement locally; people are taking the news very matter-of-fact; waiting, I suppose, for confirmation of it before celebrating. So far (10.00 p.m.) this hasn't come through; but I, in common with many, feel that it will and that at long last the war is really over.

Just after 9.00 tonight Jack and I walked as far as the University Arms and came up Regent Street; there were few people about and all was quiet.

All the comments I've heard about the atomic bomb are unfavourable. Nobody seems to be impressed with the possibilities of the benefits likely to be derived from the discoveries relating to it; only what will happen if there's another world war.

Sunday 12 August. At last I [and son Jack] set out for Brixham to see Neil Bell. ... We caught the 6.50 train to Liverpool Street, getting a carriage to ourselves. ... All the cafés and restaurants were closed in the neighbourhood of Liverpool Street and so we went on to Paddington, getting there at 9.30. We queued up (the queue was about 15 deep and fairly long) for the train to Devon; our wait lasted about an hour and a quarter and I fetched tea and biscuits from the refreshment room, queuing up there for nearly half an hour, there being only two men round an urn to deal with the crush. A policeman rather insultingly showed me the way to a lavatory; and the Salvation Army came on to the platform and played (not sacred music) to hearten us and revive our drooping spirits; then we were in the train and bound for Devon. It was a long tiring journey as we didn't get a seat and stood and sat in the corridor until the last few miles of the journey with everybody falling over us going to and from the lavatory. ...

[At Brixham] Neil Bell and his family were waiting to greet us. As he came up the steps and shook hands he said 'You're the son' and then seeing Jack behind me said 'No, but there isn't much difference between you'. A little man he was very much as I had pictured him, but for all his lined face was more like the earlier photos of himself than the one Douglas Glass took of him last year. ...

Jack and his son also met Neil's wife and their three children, and their pets — a sheepdog, a cat, and a canary - and learned that Bell's real name was Stephen Southwold, and that he suffered from a duodenal ulcer. The two families enjoyed three days exploring Brixham and the coast, swimming, and discussing books and writing. Bell told Jack about H. G. Wells's libidinousness: 'I was surprised and wondered how such noble thoughts (and many of H. G. W.'s thoughts are indeed noble) could come from such an ignoble fellow ... [for his actions show] a lamentable lack of a sense of responsibility'. Bell suggested that Jack should write a book on swimming — 'not a textbook, but something embodying all my experiences to do with it', and he suggested the title 'Swimming for Fun' — suggestions that Jack was soon to follow. However, 'Swimming for Fun' was never published. A typescript is in the Cambridgeshire Collection of the County Library.

Tuesday 14 August. ... After supper we talked beside the fire till 12.30. At midnight N.B. switched on the wireless and we heard the announcer say that after Big Ben had sounded the Prime Minister, Mr Attlee, would make an important announcement. We knew what was coming and at long last heard Attlee declare that the Japanese had accepted the surrender terms and the war was over. Attlee's phrasing sounded an imitation of Churchill's and his 'God Save the King' drew a contemptuous grunt from N.B. I thought it was odd that I should hear the end of the war in Neil Bell's house and said so; I added that he had greatly heartened me during the war and I had a lot to thank him for; he said he had a lot to thank me for as well, for the Ryvita I had sent him had kept him alive; Mrs Bell said that when Ryvita was zoned they had written all their friends, but none had responded by sending any; and yet I who they didn't know personally, had done so. I told them how I managed to scramble up the points for the Ryvita: a bit of a job. I noticed a bonfire across the bay as I went upstairs to bed and at my call they went out to have a look.

Thursday 16 August. ... A taxi hired by N.B. took us to the station and we left Churston round about 11.30 a.m. The train seemed one of only first-class coaches and so we got in one; when the woman ticket-collector came round and looked at our tickets she demanded another 10*s* 7*d* each; I refused to pay and there was a little altercation about there being third-class carriages; apparently there were and we hadn't looked far enough as she led us along the corridor to one of them; but we got good seats all the same. We arrived at Paddington at about 4.30 p.m. ... We waited three quarters of an hour at Liverpool Street and then caught an express train home; it left at 5.50 and didn't even stop at Bishop's Stortford; we reached Cambridge at 7.20. ... [Returning to Saxon Street from the river Jack's wife] Jess said it seemed as if we'd been away six months. ... Jess and I had a short walk to Brooklands Avenue with the dogs; then she went to the V-J celebrations on Parker's Piece with [daughter] Jess. I wasn't tempted to go being too tired and after making a start by writing about 500 words of 'Swimming for fun' I went to bed. My holiday—the first since I went to Aunt Emma at Haverhill in 1913—was over.

Saturday 18 August. ... [A short while ago my nephew Roland] deserted from the army. He knocked around for a while and then he was captured in London. There were several charges against him: desertion, stealing a bicycle, stealing an identity card from his sister, resisting arrest and something else. Charged before the local court he was bound over in his own recognisance for the sum of £5 and now awaits (I suppose) a court martial. Tough luck on a boy of 18.

Last evening I heard Jess arguing with her mother; ... . The argument was to do with the consideration the Americans show to women; [daughter] Jess said it wasn't consideration at all, but just a form of cunning to get what they wanted. --- She thought women should stop wanting men to act the part of cavaliers now they wanted the same rates of pay and to be on terms of equality. ---

Monday 20 August. ... Murfitt and his daughter came in the shop this afternoon; when I told him about my examination failure he said 'Fancy! The little pups they let through; and they fail you, who could turn them inside out in the subjects. ... He said why didn't I write London University and ask them if there was any need to keep taking subjects I'd passed in two or three times. I said what was the good. But maybe I will write.

From a letter to London University dated 21 August and copied in the diary:

> Ten years ago at the age of 32 I started working for a London University degree, sitting for the Special Entrance Examination in December 1936. [As] a married man with two children there were difficulties from the beginning and these difficulties were increased with the war, when owing to necessity I returned to my trade as a shoe-repairer. I am a one-man business doing nearly 100 pairs of repairs a week without machinery and that shoe-repairing has been very essential work during the war was made plain by a statement in *The Economist* last year that the waiting list for repairs all over the country was from five weeks to three months. Apart from the war I have been compelled to work hard at my job to pay the fees for my children's education. ...

Two days ago I re-registered for the B.Sc. Economics examination for the fifth time, my record for which is as follows:

Economics	Passed twice
English Essay	Passed twice
French translation	Passed
Italian translation	Passed
English Constitutional History since 1660	Passed twice
Political History of the Great Powers since 1815	Passed three times
Modern Economic History	Failed four times

For years I have worked hard to pass this examination, getting up early, going to bed late and utilising every spare moment; and helped, no doubt, by the bad psychological effect of a tumour I have developed in the small of my back I am now feeling the strain of my 42 years and overwork. I am wondering, in the circumstances, if you will permit me to take Modern Economic History alone next year. This would avoid the stultifying effects of studying subjects in which I have passed two and three times. And another year's concentrated study of Modern Economic History would perhaps see me through the examination and give me the opportunity further to improve my education. ...

Thursday 23 August. There was a row in Gothic Street towards midnight. The people at the corner threw a couple of pails of water over a group of revellers that were having a sing-song after turning out of the pubs. That was indeed rousing a hornets' nest. The language of some of the women was vile. Eventually, the police were telephoned and one came round to find out what all the trouble was about. ...

Friday 24 August. I asked Neil Bell when Jack and I were there if he would try and get the two Jesses holiday accommodation in Brixham. He said he would and managed it and tomorrow they are off to Brixham for a week. ... The Prime Minister talks of the serious financial position which the country is in; for the USA have abruptly stopped Lend-Lease; obviously, the action is aimed at the Labour Government in Britain; according to last week's *Economist* it is openly said in America that they are not financing the British experiment in socialism. It remains to be seen what happens.

Saturday 25 August. ... This evening I rang Neil Bell to see if they'd arrived all right; he hadn't seen them yet, but he thought they had as he sent a taxi to the station to meet them and he would have been informed if they hadn't arrived.

Sunday 26 August. … Neil Bell telephoned me this evening and then handed Jess the line. She and Jess didn't leave London till 12.00, arriving at Churston at 6.00. She said the weather had been grand. …

I found a weight card in my pocket, got when I weighed myself at Brixham. I weigh 10 stone 10½ lbs — DRESSED *[c.* 68 kilos]. I must be like a lathe; and yet I don't look particularly thin. On this card it says 'You are of a generous disposition, and it pays you handsomely'. …

Monday 27 August. … I had dinner at the café near the shop; a slice of brisket, chips, two rolls and a cup of tea for 1s 6d; which is cheap for these days, a fellow telling me that a friend of his on holiday at the seaside being [was] charged 5s extra for a morning cup of tea.

September 1945

Saturday 1 September. The two Jesses arrived home this evening. …

Monday 3 September. The weather this evening was sunny and similar to the day the war broke out six years ago. I thought of it as I went along the Backs and felt the past six years were well behind us, although six years of life had gone with it.

Seeing three Germans sitting rather forlornly in a lorry outside the shop today while the driver was in a café, I went and bought them nine buttered rolls with tomatoes in them. The Jerries were very grateful when I handed them over. I hear they don't get anything like enough to eat. … Attlee spoke at 9.00 p.m. An appeal to the soldiers not to demob. [demobilise] themselves.

Monday 10 September. … I've written nearly 30,000 words of 'Swimming for Fun'. …

Sunday 16 September. … The bookmaking is going badly. … Yesterday Jess [daughter] saw an American soldier trying to get a lift in a car; the car didn't stop and he shouted after it;

Jess laughed and he then shouted at her, saying among things she couldn't hear that but for Lend-Lease she wouldn't eat!

Last week Frank Edwards cut my hair. I noticed he'd had the heavy supports against air-raids taken out of his kitchen. This struck me forcibly as a sign that the war had ended and I said 'Peace and Prosperity'. ...

Cambridge had 424 Alerts and a few false alarms during the war. (Is my tally correct? I mean in this diary; for these are the official figures.) Thirty people were killed and seventy hurt by the bombing; 51 houses demolished; 1271 damaged [within Cambridge itself] 1600 h.e. [high explosive] bombs, 7 mines, 10,000 incendiaries, five fly bombs and one rocket were dropped in the county [the entire county, including Cambridge itself] and only three people killed and twenty-three injured [in the county outside Cambridge]. It's almost unbelievable.[5]

Sunday 23 September. I measured Jack's height this morning as soon as he got up, for it is then we're at our tallest. He was 6 feet and 3¾ inches. He believed I was getting shorter, but measuring me he found I was still 6 feet and ¾ of an inch. ...

Thursday 27 September. I finished writing 'Swimming for Fun' today. It's about 50,000 words in length and has only taken six weeks. Easily the quickest book I have written, and as [daughter] Jess says the book is the development of a sentiment.

October 1945

Sunday 14 October. The Sommervilles have ended their tenancy of 99 Shelford Road, which means that we're going back. Last night Jess and I went and had a look over the house; it was in pretty good condition. But it didn't seem like home;

---

[5] Jack copies these figures accurately from the *Cambridge Daily News*, but as presented there they are slightly misleading. The figures for bombs and the like are for the geographical county, including Cambridge, that for incendiary bombs is an estimate which may be exaggerated. The casualty figures cited in the phrase at the end of the paragraph are for the area of the county outside the city. Michael Bowyer's definitive study *Air Raid! The Enemy Offensive against East Anglia 1939–45* (1986), p. 330, states that 39 people were killed in Cambridge and 71 injured. Colchester, Ipswich and Lowestoft each suffered greater casualties in both categories.

not yet. We had a look down the garden and what astonished us most was the size of the trees. The cherry tree in particular was huge. It all gave me a curious feeling of time having slipped by. ...

Thursday 18 October. ... I was up late Tuesday night sticking in photos [in 'Swimming for Fun'] with Jess's help. Yesterday I took it to the bookbinders; they made an excellent job of the binding in full cloth for 10s 6d, for I got the book back from them today, when I sent it to Neil Bell.

Sunday 21 October. Went to Shelford Road with the two Jesses this afternoon. I whitewashed the pantry. We all had a bath before coming home, hurrying to beat lighting-up time at 5.30. The evenings seem to draw in quickly now we've gone back to Greenwich time.

Tuesday 23 October. An unexpected telephone call from Jack from Loughborough this morning to say that he is to go before the tribunal for conscientious objectors next Monday in Nottingham. The news was rather startling and I told him to keep his pecker up; I would be there with him. ...

  Blast these bloody wars that cause parents and children so much mental anguish. It's about time the Labour Government abolished conscription. But they're handling things rather timidly. A little step towards socialism is done by a hearty bolstering up of capitalism; and with an apologetic air that makes one wonder about the success of a gradual changeover like that which is being attempted.

On Monday 29 October Jack was in Nottingham, at the hearing of his son's application to be excused military service by a tribunal for conscientious objectors, described by the diarist as 'three rather uncouth men and a decidedly snotty little judge who was old and rather deaf'. Jack jun. spoke, and Jack spoke to support him, admitting that he had influenced him but that his son's beliefs were his own, freely arrived at. Jack jun. was registered for non-combatant service.

November 1945

Friday 9 November. I've heard from London University about the letter I wrote them... . They say all I need take is the subjects I failed in this year; viz., Essay and Part 2 Modern Economic History, as they had credited me with the rest of the papers. I'm given till 1948 to pass in these; i.e. three attempts if necessary. It was pleasing to learn I had only failed in one of the three Modern Economic History papers. I'm now wondering if I've passed in every subject in this examination, for it's on the cards I passed Part 2 Modern Economic History in one of my previous three attempts at the examination; for I've passed the essay twice.

Sunday 11 November. Neil Bell came through on the telephone just before 10.00 p.m. … He then spoke about 'Swimming for Fun'. They'd all read the book and had thoroughly enjoyed it; he had sent it to Robert Hale and he was certain Hale would publish it. He had written to Hale in eulogistic terms about the book; … I was going to be all right this time. He'd told Hale to write him first and as soon as he received confirmation of acceptance he would wire me. …

From a letter to Neil Bell dated 12 November:
> … Racing. My wife and I were glad when the season ended. We didn't get anything out of it, but have the nucleus of a business again. I think things will change when conditions are normal. Hope so, anyway. Although I don't like this way of earning money. It gets more repugnant to me every year. It's so damned silly and conflicts with my beliefs about the social system. I only do it *in extremis*. That's my only excuse; but as things are it's a pretty sound excuse.

Sunday 18 November. Frank Edwards took the bed linen and some other stuff in his car to the house this morning and we moved in. Back again at 99 Shelford Road after six years! We had dinner at Saxon Street and the two Jesses cycled here. I walked with Jim and Jock. I felt strange as I looked round the front room of the house at Saxon Street before I left. How glad I was to be going. I should often be there in the future, as we intend keeping the place on as an office for bookmaking, but it would no longer be home, thank goodness.

Sunday 25 November. … ['Swimming for Fun':] the book was returned by Hale yesterday. Same old take—no paper; and he didn't think it would greatly interest the public. What a sell!

I telephoned N.B. and told him the news. He was astonished and said he'd write me. ...

December 1945

Sunday 2 December. ... I sent 'Swimming for Fun' to Cecil Hunt [his literary agent]. He wrote and said he hoped to do something with it, although the paper position was still bad and would be for months. He complimented me on the appearance of the book and said it was a pleasure to have a workmanlike manuscript to offer to a publisher.

Need I record that I don't know which way to turn to pay my way. After all, I'm always hard up.

Sunday 9 December. ... I walked into the town this morning with Jock and went in the water. The river was frozen over and the temperature only 32 in and 26 out. I beat the carpet this afternoon; it needed it!

Monday 10 December. I sent 'The Cordwainer' and 'Tale of a Taylor' to Cecil Hunt. My hands are cracked, in an awful state, especially the index finger of the right hand, which I use when putting in rivets at work.

Tuesday 11 December. Claudio Rossi has just taken an examination in English. An Italian padre, an officer, sat beside him. He asked Rossi how many 'c's' in occasion. Rossi waited his chance and when the examiner's back was turned held up two fingers. Frank Edwards told him it was a sin, which Rossi denied. Frank asked him whom he confessed to. Rossi said the padre! Frank asked him whom the padre confessed to!

Thursday 13 December. Jess and I went to see the film *The Son of Lassie*. It was nothing as good as *Lassie Come Home*. Some time back the manager of the Regal stopped me on Parker's Piece and asked me if I would let Jock parade at the cinema during the showing of the film; I said yes; but heard nothing from him; maybe, he's not there now; ... .

Friday 14 December. Jess and I went to see *Rebecca* [from Daphne du Maurier's novel] at the Arts Theatre. It was a mediocre play acted rather badly. I felt the 4s each for admission gross overcharging.

Saturday 15 December. Jess tells us she's going to marry Dennis Boles; and pretty quickly.

Sunday 16 December. There's much hullabaloo over the loan America has made us. The *Observer* thinks well of it, but *The Economist* and *New Statesman* can't be dismal enough about it. Apparently, Britain can only pay back in goods and America must encourage an import surplus, which means increasing wages in America to absorb this surplus; something Big Business in Yankeeland has no intention of doing; in fact, is bent on doing just the opposite by reducing wages.

Friday 21 December. All had Christmas dinner at the British Restaurant. A fine meal. I got a double helping!

Sunday 23 December. ... Went to the County Folk Museum to see Lambeth the curator for local colour for my next novel *The Miller of Trumpington*; he hadn't any; suggested I called on Dudley Ward, the literary executor of Rupert Brooke, who lives at Grantchester;[6] I went this evening to the Old Vicarage, but there was nobody at home.

Tuesday 25 December. Intent on bathing at Byron's Pool this morning I went there with Jim and Jock although it rained and had a dip. ...

Wednesday 26 December. Xmas present: book tokens from Neil Bell (a guinea) [£1 1s] and [daughter] Jess (half a guinea); a book *Cashel Byron's Profession* from [wife] Jess. The latter isn't bad, but it dates and is rather pompously written.[7]

Thursday 27 December. Jess and Dennis married at the Shirehall at 9.45 a.m. Jess nervous, but not so much; Dennis turned up all smiles; met his mother for the first time. I witnessed the marriage with her; asked if I could sign with my own pen; the female assistant to the registrar said yes if I dipped it in the bottle of ink on the table; obviously, a prevention against the

---

[6] Brooke and Ward had been close friends since their Cambridge days. Ward had been an undergraduate and then a Fellow of St John's; after periods as a journalist and a civil servant he had become a banker. He lived at the Old Vicarage, Grantchester.

[7] A novel (1886) by George Bernard Shaw.

marriage being invalid, which I suppose it would be if there was only one witness, and that could conceivably happen if a disappearing sort of ink was used by one of the two witnesses. Jess and Dennis went straight off to the Lake District for their honeymoon. ... I intended going to work, but considered the day was eventful enough to take a holiday. I'm daunted at the prospect of being a grandfather in a year or so. Ain't old enough.

Saturday 29 December. Gloomy thoughts about my financial position, which is bad. Been putting the photo album up to date. The next job is this journal, the first score of pages of which I intend to retype as they have no margins, when I shall have it bound. Then for *The Miller of Trumpington.* ...

Sunday 30 December. ... [For tea]: two rounds of bread and dripping, a round of bread and marmalade, a piece of Xmas cake, two or three buns, a jam tart and two large cups of tea; after tea we had an orange each; then I wrote Michael Sadleir about 'Finger in the Pie' and wrapped up the book, which I had bound last week, ready to send to him. ...

The year is nearly ended. And I've realised none of my ambitions and am no richer. The number of words I've written is fewer than I've done for years; only 'Swimming for Fun' to my credit; and that's very short; and what I've typed in this journal, except for letters, mostly to Neil Bell. But what I've done is clear in mind: retyped 'Whims of the Father' from January to March; from then till June I worked for the B.Sc. Econ. again; a short rest and then from August to October I wrote 'Swimming for Fun'; from October till the present I've worked on this house, saving myself with Jess's help about 100 pounds, which has been worth while, for there's no place like home. Actually, I've had a very hard year, for there's been the shoe-repairing and horse-racing as well; and Jess had had a hard year's work as well. Really, I've realised an ambition, for one of them was to keep Jess till she married and I did it. ...

I type with my feet cocked over the fire, the machine on my lap; Jess alternately reads the newspapers and snoozes beside me, while the dogs snooze on the floor — with full bellies as I've just given them their dinners of meat and meal.

Jess Overhill with her daughter Jess, January 1946

Monday 31 December. ... I start a fresh programme tomorrow: first of all I retype the first twenty pages of this journal preparatory to having it bound; this will take ten days or a fortnight; then for *The Miller of Trumpington*. In addition I start reading history for the exam in June, and the five volumes of the *Encyclopedia of Modern Knowledge*. And so another year ends. ---

Epilogue

In 1945 Jack, aged 43, had as many years still to live. He returned to bookmaking, was at last awarded his London external degree, and taught in Cambridge Technical College and several village colleges. He remained, in his son's words, 'a man of the Left'. His contentiousness remained for some decades, as his daughter-in-law Jill remembers. It was no doubt fed by the continued failure to get his novels published, the prize which had eluded many efforts. About 1958 he finished his autobiography, 'No Mother Love'. The publishers to whom he sent it declined to take it, though one was willing to publish 'the most important parts'. Jack is said to have refused with a typical comment: 'It was all important to me'.[1]

Yet Jack made a new departure. As the need to study left him he gained the time to reflect, while his academic success gave the self-confidence to write about his childhood and youth — which in retrospect had obsessed him — in a more succinct and relaxed way. In the 1960s and later he made more than fifty broadcasts, mostly no more than fifteen minutes in length and often revisiting his early life. Akin to them were ten two-page articles written for the *East Anglian Magazine* in the 1970s. A typical one is 'Sing All Ye Merry', a documentary, detached and light in tone, about Christmas as a holiday from the frugal lives of Jack and his two brothers in Gothic Street in 1910, told in deft detail concerning real people and places.[2] The three boys sing carols outside the house of the Reverend J. C. Conybeare in Union Road, and he

---

[1] So I have been informed by Mr A .B. Evans, at one time Head of History at Netherhall School, Cambridge.
[2] *East Anglian Magazine*, December 1974.

gives them sixpence. 'A tanner to share! It was the luck of a lifetime', and it was spent on 'juicy chips' from a shop in Russell Street. Their father, E.T.O., bought a cask of beer from Dale's brewery in Gwydir Street, and Nap and Perce, aged fifteen and nine, got drunk while E.T.O. was out.

Jack's longest broadcast was a masterpiece and his finest single work: 'A Regular Snob', given on the Third Programme on 28 January 1967 and several times repeated. 'A Regular Snob' is about Jack's childhood with his father in Gothic and Saxon Streets. The broadcast, delivered without a script and lasting sixty minutes, was slimmed down from the ninety minutes taped by the BBC in the studio. It seems perfectly structured with not a redundant word, which is a tribute not only to Jack but also to the BBC's adroit and unobtrusive editorial gifts. In the unofficial recordings that fortunately circulate, Jack's grave and measured bass voice draws the listener in to tales of a distant and unfamiliar world, the life of the poor in Cambridge a century ago. 'A Regular Snob' became famous overnight, and was much praised by critics in newspapers, among whom we might mention Anne Duchene writing in the *Guardian*. Jack's was one of the first authentic working-class voices to be heard on the radio, certainly at the length of 'A Regular Snob', and the programme was made amidst the fascination with social and proletarian history in the new universities, notably at Warwick. It was published in a collection edited by Michael Marland, *The Experience of Work* (1973).

At Christmas 1985 occurred the death of Jack's wife Jess, to whom he owed so many patient years, and the brief time remaining to Jack was as we might expect, melancholy and regretful. He died in 1989.[3]

[3] Mr Tony Cowley, an old friend of Jack, described his last years to me when I talked to him on 3 December 2006.

Index

Admiral Graf Spee, German pocket battleship 15
Africa 88, 149, 193, 199, 217, 220, 222
air raids and warnings 1, 3, 26, 28, 29, 30, 32–33, 34, 37, 38, 39–40, 41, 44, 46, 47, 48, 49, 50, 51, 53, 54, 55, 57, 58, 59, 60, 63, 65, 67, 69, 71, 72, 73, 75, 76, 77, 78, 80–82, 83, 84–85, 86, 87, 88, 89–91, 92, 93, 94, 96, 97, 98–99, 100, 101, 103, 104, 106, 107, 110, 111, 112, 113, 114, 115, 117, 118, 120, 121, 122, 123, 131, 139, 149, 159, 160, 165, 166, 167, 168, 169, 170, 172, 173, 175, 177, 178, 179, 181, 182, 184, 188, 197, 201, 202, 203, 211, 214, 217, 218, 219, 220, 221, 222, 225, 226, 228, 229, 233, 236, 237, 238, 240–241, 242, 243, 244, 245, 246, 248, 250, 251, 254, 256, 257, 258, 259–260, 261, 262, 263, 264–265, 268, 269, 271, 272, 274, 276, 278, 279, 281, 282, 283, 284, 286, 287, 288, 290, 291–292, 295, 296, 298, 299, 300, 324
Allen, Mr --- 119
Allies 182, 238, 240, 278, 302
American Freeman, newspaper 228
Americans 175, 177, 190, 199, 200, 208, 233, 240, 247, 253, 271, 281, 302, 315, 317, 321
Amos, Maurice
  The English Constitution 190
Anderson, Sir John 209
Armistice Day 128, 290
ARP wardens 29, 30, 40, 57, 58, 78, 87, 151
Askey, Arthur 127, 165
Astor, Nancy, Viscountess Astor 169, 185
Atlantic Ocean 15, 57, 102, 112, 150, 289
ATS (Auxiliary Territorial Service) girls 160, 221
Attlee, Clement, MP, 63 112, 320, 323
Augsburg 152
Australia 93, 140, 196
Austria 303
Austrians 148, 216
Avery Hill Training College, London and Yorks. 154, 170, 185, 262, 282
'Baedeker raids' 152
Bahamas 216
Baird, John Logie 65
Balkans 15, 94, 96, 313
Baltic 15
Band, Joan 233
Band of Hope 56, 189, 214
Barbusse, Henri 31
Bardia 159, 247
Barlow, George 280
Barnsley, George, of Sheffield 257

Barton (Cambs.) 183
Basham, Mr — 97
bathing sheds 119
Bath (Som.) 152
Baxter, Beverley, MP 18, 22, 25, 26, 31, 61, 64, 229, 230, 231, 250
Bayne Powell, Rosamond
  English Country Life in the Eighteenth Century 315
Beaverbrook, William Maxwell Aitken, 1st Lord Beaverbrook 134, 207
Bebee, Mr — 120
Bedford 113, 117, 124, 182, 291
Belfast 98
Belgium 23, 23, 24
Bell, Neil (Stephen Southwold) 3, 5, 14, 17, 18, 25, 26, 30, 31, 33, 34, 52, 53, 66, 69, 86, 88, 91, 102, 124, 134, 139, 141, 142, 144, 145, 146, 147, 153, 170, 172, 174, 175, 180, 188, 196, 197, 198, 199, 208, 209, 210, 211, 212, 213, 220, 224, 228, 230, 232, 234, 235, 236, 239, 240, 243, 246, 247, 248, 250, 252, 254, 255, 256, 257, 258, 259, 260, 262, 268, 273, 278, 280, 287, 291, 295, 298, 299, 300, 301, 302, 306, 312, 319, 320, 322, 323, 329
  novels
    Abbot's Heel, The 3
    Child of my Sorrow 259
    Cover his Face 212, 213
    Handsome Langleys, The 302
    Lord of life 52, 53
    Not a Sparrow Falls 14

Peek's Progress 180, 188
Seventh Bowl, The 66
Son of Richard Carden 30
So Perish the Roses 31, 33
Tower of Darkness 141, 188
True Story of my Father 66
Truth about my Father, The 66
'Root of all evil, The' (short story) 199, 220
Benghazi 88, 89, 140
Benham, Frederic Charles Courtenay, economist 264
Bennett, Joe 103
Benton, George, firewatcher 253, 257, 258, 259, 260, 261, 274
Berlin 103, 202, 237, 248, 251, 253, 262, 293, 296, 297, 303
Best, Gerald 184
Beveridge Report 195, 207
Bevin, Ernest 24, 48, 85, 88, 235, 263
Birmingham (Warcs.) 60, 90, 160, 161
Bishop's Stortford (Herts.) 320
Bismarck, The, German battleship 101, 102, 116, 213
Bizerta 220
Blenheim bombers 37
Blitz 73
Blyth, shipyard (Northumb.) 265
Board of Trade 191, 219
Bofors guns 152, 168, 181
Boles, Dennis, flight-sergeant, RAF 305, 316, 328–29
Boris, king of Bulgaria 237
Borneo 318
Boyd, Martin 213, 214
Boy Scouts 186
Brading, Peter 184
Brains Trust 122, 200

Bren guns 67
Brest 143
Bristol 60
British Broadcasting Corporation 123, 149, 154
British Empire 15, 86, 149, 192, 216
British Summer Time 91, 103–04, 111
British views of the war 4, 8, 13, 55, 180
Brixham (Devon) 319, 322, 323
Brooke, Rupert 177, 329
Brown, Edward O., mayor 113
Buchan, John
  Thirty-nine Steps, The 145
Bucharest 282
Buckinghamshire 1
Buckley (Flints.) 1
Budapest 293
Bulgaria 237, 282
Bullen, Frank
  Cruise of the Cachalot, The 264
Burkitt, Cyril 4
Cambridge
  Addenbrooke's Hospital 27, 29, 73, 98, 133, 187, 297
  Arts Theatre 258, 327
  Backs, The 12, 29, 59, 62, 64, 73, 91, 98, 151, 161, 175, 264, 269, 300, 310, 312, 323
  Barnabas Road 9, 205, 223, 256, 257
    Devonshire Motor Works 205
  Barnwell Bridge 317
  Barrow Road 50, 62
  Barton Road 32, 67
  Bateman Street 227
  Boot's 18, 66, 134
  Borough Council 23

Bowes & Bowes bookshop 76, 213, 251, 292
British Restaurant 256, 328
Brooklands Avenue 37, 84, 100, 123, 135, 137, 194, 320
Brookside 33, 41, 59, 36, 43, 62
Burleigh Street 7
Cambridge and County High School for Boys 58, 107, 186
Cambridge and County High School for Girls 64, 126, 178
  Careers Fund 273
Cam-Tax garage 73
Castle End 8
cattle market 81
Cavendish Avenue 82
Cavendish Road 78
Central cinema 133, 150
Chalmers Road 166
Cherry Hinton Road 81
Coe Fen 29, 64, 76, 93, 101, 109, 121, 139, 152, 160, 162, 203, 209, 226, 263, 268, 308
Coldham's Common 212
Coldham's Lane 98, 256
County Hall 10
Cross Keys public house 114
Devonshire Motor Works 205, 223
Doric Street 189, 242
Downing Archway 119
Eastern Omnibus Company 81
Fen Causeway 139, 251
Fitzroy Street 77
Fitzwilliam Street 55, 286
Folk Museum 126, 328
Friends' Meeting House, Jesus Lane 129

335

Cambridge (cont'd)
  General Post Office 23
  Gothic Street 29, 31, 47, 52, 31, 33, 49, 55, 71, 80, 106
  Great Eastern Street 115
  Green End Road 260
  Gresham Road 303
  Greyhound, The, public house in Coldham's Lane 63, 64, 65, 67, 78, 89, 90, 136
  Guildhall 7, 87, 116, 148, 259, 275, 295
  Hauxton Road 297
  Hills Road 78, 81, 82, 83, 91, 94, 98, 131, 217
    bridge 26, 78, 131
  Hobson's Brook 41, 87, 100
  Homerton College 98
  Huntingdon Road 12, 120
  Hyde Park Corner 84, 256
  Jesus Green 234
  King's Parade 167
  Langford's leather shop, Fitzroy Street 43, 57, 261
  Lensfield Road 29, 31, 119, 160
  Leys School, The 64, 98, 314
  Little Rose Inn 52
  Long Common 62, 100, 125, 135, 275
  Lyons tea rooms 66, 111, 134, 150, 185
  Madingley Road 12, 287
  Market Hill 289
  Market Place/Square 62, 84, 289
  Marks and Spencer's 66, 111, 134, 135
  Marshall's aerodrome 41, 67, 76, 160, 223, 268, 272
  Midland Bank 118
  Midsummer Common 8, 102, 212, 305
  Midsummer Fair 229, 275, 310, 311
  Mill Road 76, 113, 175, 190, 218, 251, 256, 317
    British Restaurant 251
    Broadway 218
  Milton Road 218
  Newmarket Road 52, 77
  Newnham 32, 34, 81
    Newnham School 187
  Paradise 41, 43, 159, 184, 315, 316, 317
  Paradise Corner 38
  Newton Road 275, 286
  Northern Hotel 184
  Panton Street 53, 86, 165, 189, 277
  Parker's Piece 40, 67, 72, 73, 110, 120, 122, 152, 160, 165, 168, 179, 181, 232, 295, 305, 306, 315, 316, 320, 327
    Hobbs' Pavilion 316
  Pemberton Terrace 38, 58, 189
  Pembroke College 52
  Perne Road 78
  Perse School for Girls 54, 98, 314
  Perse School for Boys 73
  Petty Cury 66, 256, 267
  Pickerel Inn 30
  Pike and Eel public house 237
  Pound Hill 312
  public library 10, 144, 156, 207, 250, 258
  Regal Cinema 123, 131, 295, 305, 327
  Regent Street 318
  Roman Catholic church 65, 73, 81, 86, 96, 107, 110, 165, 217
  Round Church 167

Russell Street 54, 211, 312
Sainsbury's store 94, 111
St Andrew's Street 107, 256, 267, 305
St Barnabas' Road 9, 256, 257
St John's Wilderness 151, 281
St Paul's church
  evening classes 147
St Paul's School 208
St Peter's Terrace 40
Saxon Street 4, 23, 59
Scroope Terrace 78, 114, 120
Senate House 309
Sheep's Green 22, 64, 72, 101, 103, 109, 119, 135, 161, 162, 199, 257, 263
Shelley Terrace 34
Shire Hall 265, 328
Short Common 59, 77, 125
Silver Street 204
Snob's Stream 161
Spread Eagle, The, public house 5, 48, 58, 114, 242
Stourbridge Common 174
Technical College 331
Tenison Avenue 46
Tenison Road 45
Tennis Court Road 286
Terrace Lane 253
Thompson's Lane 167
Trumpington Road 52, 115, 140, 314
Trumpington Street 33, 40, 52, 54, 55, 58, 73, 77, 81, 100, 152, 286
Union Road 33
University Arms hotel 318
Vicarage Terrace 27
Victoria Bridge 234
Victoria Cinema 14, 39, 115, 165, 289
Wellington Street 85

Westminster College 198
Woolworth's 135, 181
Cambridge AFS [Auxiliary Fire Service] 90
Cambridge Anti-War Council 93, 95, 120
Cambridge Daily News 90, 92, 121, 141, 181, 199, 238, 287, 289, 290, 304, 324
Cambridge Permanent Benefit Building Society 126
Cambridge University 240
  Botanical Gardens 139
  Cavendish laboratory 317
  Downing College grounds 174
  Emmanuel College 93, 172
  Faculty of Economics 259
    Marshall Library 259, 268, 272
  Faculty of Law 273, 274
  Fenner's cricket field 45
  Fitzwilliam Museum 209
  Girton College 148
  King's College 29, 91, 251
    Chapel 43
  Library 207
  Museum of Archaeology and Ethnology, now of Archaeology and Anthropology 125
  Officers' Training Corps (CUOTC) 30
  Proctors 289
  Senate House 227
  Trinity College 182
  Trinity Hall 93, 95, 290
  Union Society 167
Cambridge(shire) Board of Education 277
Cameronian Regiment 52
Canada 24, 61, 82, 83
Canadians 177

Canterbury 155, 182
capitalists 8
Cardiff 69, 221
Casablanca 205
Cash, Bert 3, 4, 7, 24, 38, 41, 66, 101, 116, 148, 160, 173, 187, 271, 282, 315
Cash, John 206
Cash, Mrs, wife of Bert 62
Cash, Mr, senior 317
Cash, Tom 184, 206
Cash family 32, 41, 43, 66, 159, 181, 306
Castle, Mr --- 133
Catania 235
'Cato', Beaverbrook journalists
 Guilty Men 134
Caucasus 181
Cerne Abbas (Dorset 284, 285
Chamberlain, Neville, Prime Minister 24, 148, 216
Chandler, A. B., headmaster of Russell Street school 45, 126, 147
Chaplin, Charlie
 Great Dictator, The 78
Chatto and Windus, publishers 229
Chaucer, Geoffrey 230, 308
Chelmsford (Essex) 221
Cherry Hinton (Cambs.) 38
Chesterford [Great?] (Essex) 271
Chesterton (Cambs.) 85, 96, 113, 119, 120, 151, 272
 Pye's factory 119
China 217
Chivers' jam factory, Histon (Cambs.) 92, 166, 179, 181
Chopin, Frederic 305
Christmas at the Old Town Hall (radio programme) 135

Churchill, Winston 24, 25, 26, 27, 28, 29, 42, 45, 64, 67, 77, 83, 94, 99, 103, 105, 110, 112, 113, 136, 140, 142, 153, 161, 177, 186, 192, 194, 205, 210, 213, 214, 216, 222, 244, 293
Churston (Devon) 320, 323
Civil Defence 88, 189, 267, 283, 303
Clapham, Professor John Harold (Sir) 35–36
Clee, Ted, custodian of bathing sheds 119
Colbert, Claudette 196
Cole, G. D. H.
 Common people, The 254
 Intelligent Man's Guide through World Chaos 141
 Means to Full Employment 257
Cologne 155
Communism 46, 113, 130, 154, 202, 301
Communist Party 8, 9, 120, 132
conscientious objectors 23, 28, 32, 34–36, 37, 46, 48, 52, 54, 60, 63, 73, 74–75, 87, 88, 113, 116–117, 124, 134, 163, 171, 186, 196, 238, 287
 Appellate Tribunal 186
 Central Board of 87
 Eastern Area Tribunal 196
Conservative Party 146
Constable & Co. Ltd, publishers 25, 26, 31, 102, 144, 213, 250
Cooper, Charles Henry, *Annals of Cambridge* 125
Cornforth, Maurice 120
Coton (Cambs.) 55
Cottenham (Cambs.) 3, 4, 5, 109, 111, 218, 268, 285

Coventry (Warcs.) 57, 59, 60, 90
Coward, Noel 123, 205
Craske, Charlie 16, 78, 97, 166
Craske, Ken 166, 248
Craske family 65
Crete 102, 103
Cripps, Stafford 24, 82, 141, 145, 151, 194
Cummings, Arthur John 148
Czechs 216
Daily Herald, The 56, 64, 102, 116, 179, 194, 196, 289
Daily Mirror, The 24, 148, 149
Daily Telegraph, The 148, 212
Daily Worker, The 75, 76, 148, 183, 185, 186, 207
Darlan, François 199
Darwin, Charles Robert 239, 286
Debden aerodrome (Essex) 25
Defence of the Realm Act 132
Defence Regulations 75, 146
de la Mare, Walter
  Collected Rhymes and Verses 292, 295
Denmark 23, 35, 303
Dent, J[oseph] M[elaby] & Sons, publishers 214
Derby, the, horse-race 309
Devon 66, 319
Devonport naval base (Devon) 265
Dickens, Charles
  Christmas Carol, A 135
  David Copperfield 287
  Great Expectations 311
  Pickwick Papers 202
Dieppe 177, 178, 186, 188
Digby, Albert 103, 274
District Manpower Board 214, 219
Ditton (Cambs.) 25, 51, 117
Dobb, Maurice Herbert, economist 259, 265, 268, 270, 271, 272, 280, 285, 308, 310, 317
Doenitz, Karl 302
Donetz, river 214
Doodlebugs (V1 bombs) 275, 276, 278, 283, 286, 291, 292, 295, 299, 300
Dornier, German aeroplane 84
Double Summer Time 283
Dove, A. E., headmaster 241
Dover 143
Doyle, Arthur Conan, Sir
  The Hound of the Baskervilles 72
Drigo, Riccardo
  Les Millions d'Arlequin 224
Driver, Charlie 308
Duff Cooper, Alfred, 1st Viscount Norwich 51
du Maurier, Daphne
  Frenchman's creek (film) 298
  Rebecca (film) 327
Dunkirk 62, 164, 166, 200, 208, 213, 217, 218, 272
Dutch 182
Duxford (Cambs.) 27, 29, 52, 54, 60, 67, 114, 276
East Anglia 90, 120, 324
Economist, The 144, 156, 207, 269, 317, 328
Eddy, Nelson 123
Eden, Anthony, MP 245
Edinburgh 173
Edwards, Frank 10, 14, 17, 25, 26, 28, 30, 32, 34, 34–36, 37, 42, 43, 52, 54, 55, 58, 60, 61, 66, 72, 73, 74–75, 75, 91, 94, 101, 105, 113, 116, 117, 124, 128, 146, 153, 154, 156, 161, 162, 163, 170, 171, 172, 177, 180, 183, 184, 185, 186,

Edwards, Frank (cont'd) 188, 189, 191, 192, 201, 202, 211, 218, 247, 248, 264, 280, 283, 287, 289, 298, 310, 315, 324, 326, 327
Edwards, Molly, daughter of Frank 55, 299
Edwards, Mrs 43, 63
Edwards, Mrs Joan 10, 54, 55, 58, 117, 124
Edwards, family 42
Edward VII, King 190
Edward VIII, King 304
Egypt 140, 159, 163, 190, 191, 192, 193
Eighth Army 190, 193, 214
Eisenhower, Dwight David 272
Electric Light Co. 128
Elizabeth, Queen, wife of George VI, 14, 82, 250
Ellis, Havelock 92, 288
  Morals, Manners and Men 92
Elvin, H. Lionel 92, 95
Ely (Cambs.) 117, 299
Emergency Powers Act 17
Empire 15, 86, 93, 149, 153, 182, 192, 216, 306
Encyclopedia of Modern Knowledge 316, 331
Engelbrecht, Helmut Carol
  Merchants of death, The 67, 190
Essen 155
Estonia 51
evacuees 1, 6, 17, 24, 44, 47, 48, 51, 109, 114, 127, 194, 208, 247, 283, 303
Everyman's Library 135
fascism 8, 149, 196, 211, 214, 215, 216
Fay, C. R.
  Great Britain from Adam Smith to the Present Day: An Economic and Social Survey 288
Field, Miss J. I., headmistress of the Cambridgeshire County Girls School 273
Finland 15, 17, 23, 25, 127, 282
Finucane, Paddy 165
firewatching 178, 187, 195
Fleet Air Arm 292, 294
Ford, Eric 30
Fowler, Henry Watson
  Modern English Usage 196
Fowlmere (Cambs.) 46
France 23, 24, 26, 28, 52, 61, 64, 99, 108, 149, 151, 177, 195, 222, 245, 270, 271, 272, 281, 293
  Devil's/Delville Wood 186
Franco, Francesco 31, 265
Frink, Horace Westlake
  Morbid Fears and Compulsions 292
Fudge, William Kingston, publisher with the Mitre Press 18
Fulbourn (Cambs.) 84, 88, 256
Gandhi, Mohandas Karamchand 175
Gem, The, comic 98
General Election 312, 315
George V, King 304
George VI, King 304
German nationalism 7
Germans 1, 9, 14, 16, 69, 71, 83, 92, 93, 105, 107, 111, 122, 123, 128, 130, 140, 141, 148, 152, 154, 155, 161, 174, 177, 178, 182, 188, 192, 194, 198, 202, 205, 216, 221, 232, 235, 240, 243, 247, 256, 260, 293, 324

Ghost Train, The (film) 127
Gigli, Beniamino 224
Gigney, --- 109
Glass, Douglas, photographer 319
Golcar (Yorks.) 261
Goldsmith, Eric 15, 21, 42, 74, 115, 116, 160, 169, 184, 224, 225, 236, 270, 277, 280, 283
Goldsmith, Oliver
   Deserted village, The 300
Gone With the Wind (film) 191
Gould, Rupert C. 200
Granta Swimming Club 41, 109, 314
Grantchester (Cambs.) 1, 25, 32, 33, 37, 81, 105, 107, 119, 151, 153, 160, 167, 168, 173, 177, 182, 183, 202, 219, 220, 222, 269, 308, 328
   Byron's Pool 32, 151, 328
   Green Man Inn 153
   Meadows 1, 3, 32, 37, 81, 153, 221, 222
   Old Vicarage 328
   Red Lion Inn 105, 183, 202, 219, 308
Great Eversden (Cambs.) 214
Great Yarmouth (Norf.) 90
Greece 88, 93, 103, 237, 293
Greenland 101
Green, Mrs A. J., wife of the licensee of the Cross Keys 52
Guy Fawkes Day 289
Haddenham (Cambs.) 218
Haldane, John Burdon Sanderson 148, 239
Hale, Robert, publishers 248, 249, 254, 257, 258, 260, 261, 284, 286, 298, 301, 326

Hamburg 59, 235
Handley, Tommy, broadcaster 124, 253
Hanighan, Frank Cleary
   Merchants of Death, The 67
Hansard (Parliamentary debates) 212
Hardwick (Cambs.) 124, 189
Hardy, Thomas 261
Harker, Gordon 133
Harston (Cambs.) 46, 155, 201
Harvey, George 305
Haslingfield (Cambs.) 46, 176
Haverhill, Suffolk 16, 42, 97, 238, 321
   Woolpack public house 97
Hawaii 131
'Haw-Haw, Lord' (William Joyce) 14, 51, 62, 77, 123
Hawtrey, Ralph George, *Currency and Credit* 106
Hayek, Friedrich August 226, 228
Heidelberg 46, 97
Heligoland 143
Hemingway, Ernest: *For Whom the Bell Tolls* (film) 284
Hess, Rudolf 99, 100, 103, 105
Hewart, Gordon, first Viscount Hewart 163, 164
   New Despotism, The 163
Higher School Certificate 110, 181, 182, 240, 314
Hiner, Bill (Bill Adams in 'Queen Street') 43, 45, 47, 49
Histon (Cambs.) 6, 77, 109, 120, 166, 181, 218, 243
Hitler, Adolf 1, 46, 64, 78, 86, 93, 95, 99, 100, 105, 121, 130, 131, 132, 133, 148, 163, 185, 198, 199, 205,

341

Hitler, Adolf (cont'd)
   210, 213, 243, 278, 289,
   290, 301, 302, 313, 317
 Mein Kampf 313
HMS *Ark Royal* 128
HMS *Hood* 101, 102
HMS *Jervis Bay* 57
HMS *Prince of Wales* 133
HMS *Rawalpindi* 15
HMS *Repulse* 133
HMS *Royal Oak* 9
Holbrook, David, Lieutenant 290
Holland 23, 24
Hollingworth, Leonard, schoolmaster and writer 241, 245
 'Coin my Heart' 245
Home Front 3, 5, 6, 10, 21, 22, 26, 29, 30, 32, 38, 40, 42, 43, 44, 47, 48, 54, 58–59, 59, 61, 62, 63, 64, 72, 74, 75, 76, 78, 83, 84, 85, 87, 91, 95, 96, 97, 100, 107, 111, 114, 115, 118, 119, 121, 122, 127, 128, 131, 135, 139, 141, 143, 144, 146, 147, 148, 150, 151, 152, 155, 160, 162, 166, 168, 169, 170, 175, 176, 179, 180, 182, 183, 184, 186, 188–189, 190, 191, 193, 195, 197, 198, 200, 201, 204, 209, 212, 217–218, 219, 221, 224, 233, 239–240, 242–243, 245, 247, 251, 253, 256, 264, 268, 271–272, 274–275, 277, 278, 283–284, 287, 289–290, 291, 295, 297, 299, 300, 302, 303, 304, 305, 306, 309, 312, 313, 315, 315–316, 317, 318, 320, 321, 322, 323–24
Home Guard 24, 41, 62, 127, 131, 135, 139, 160, 170, 196, 206, 234, 283, 291
Home Secretary 148, 183
Hong Kong 135
Hore Belisha, Leslie 71
Horner, Mark 192, 205, 218, 248, 296
Horsefield, John Keith
 The Real Cost of the War 150
Horseheath (Cambs.) 42
House of Commons 94
Howard, Sidney 133
How Green Was my Valley (film) 184
Huddersfield (Yorks.) 202, 240
Hughes, Roland 228, 236
Hull, Cordell 245
Humphreys/Humphries, Mr 23, 83, 95, 118, 120, 144
Hunt, Cecil, literary agent 301, 327
Huntingdon 12, 84, 120, 124, 201
Hurricane aircraft 65. 119
Huxley, Thomas 239
identity cards 7
Independent Labour Party 62
India 97, 151, 175, 178, 188, 194, 216
Ingrams, --- 290
In Which We Serve (film) 205
Ipswich (Sfk) 90, 325
Iran 313
Ireland 196
Italians 88, 103, 235, 238, 247
Italy 72, 194, 222, 234, 237, 238, 240, 244, 247, 303
ITMA (*It's That Man Again*), radio programme 124, 201, 253

Jacobs, William Wymark 114
Japan 128, 131, 133, 151, 316, 317, 318
Japanese 133, 135, 140, 142, 151, 188, 304, 318, 320
Jews 86
Joad, Dr C. E. M. 122, 198, 200, 229, 243
  Guide to Modern Thought 198
Jock the newspaperman 30, 31, 40, 53
John O' London's Weekly 172, 173, 244
Joseph, Michael, publisher 146, 148, 296, 298, 299
Joyce, James
  Ulysses 230
Junkers 88 , 167
Kain, Cobber 28
Keats, John 297
Keith, Roberts Porter <?> 239
Kennedy, Joseph 56
Kent, George Duke of 179
Kerch 154
Ketelbey, Caroline Doris Mabel
  History of Modern Times, A 227
Keynes, John Maynard 145, 213, 226
Kharkov 154
Kidman, Dunlop 27, 164, 217
Kiel 152
King, Alan 295
King's Royal Rifles 94, 96
Kirkwood, David, MP 62
Labour Exchange 6, 7, 87, 92, 149, 170
Labour Leader, The 95
Labour Party 196, 216
Lake District 330
Lamb, Charles 31, 34, 167
Lambeth, R. C., curator of the Folk Museum 126, 328

Land's End (Cornwall) 268
Lane, Margaret, biographer of Edgar Wallace 251, 252, 254
Lassie, canine film star 295, 327
Lassie come home (film) 327
Latvia 51
Laval, Pierre 151
Lavender, Jack 108
Lawrence, David Herbert, author 34
Lawson Campbell, William, Judge 34, 35, 36, 256, 265, 266, 266–67
League of Nations 15
Lease and Lend Bill 113
Leather Controller 289
Leigh, A. C. 41
Leipzig 248
Leningrad 116, 203
Leopold, King of the Belgiums 24
Letchworth (Herts.) 197
Libya 140, 161, 214
Lilliput (magazine) 248
Linton (Cambs.) 33, 60
Lipson, Ephraim 203, 205, 207, 288
  Economic History of England, An 205
Lithuania 51
Liverpool 60, 61, 74, 164, 226, 270
Lloyd George, David, MP 64
Local Defence Volunteers 30
London 14, 16, 18, 41, 60, 63, 21, 43, 63, 65, 71, 73, 74, 75, 82, 86, 87, 95, 99, 101, 120, 121, 122, 148, 151, 155, 156, 159, 172, 173, 183, 195, 202, 203, 204, 221, 222, 226, 227, 228, 236,

London (cont'd)
   241, 248, 259, 260, 268,
   269, 274, 275, 276, 277,
   279, 281, 282, 283, 289,
   323
  Aerated Bread Company café
   74
  Aldgate 74
  Billingsgate 74
  Charing Cross Road 74
  Cheapside 74
  Docks 16
  Downing Street 167
  East Finchley 1
  East Ham 203
  Ebury House 74
  Endsleigh Street 87
  Fleet Street 74
  Foyle's bookshop 74, 283
  Gower Street 21
  Hyde Park 224
  John Lewis's store 74
  Liverpool Street station 74,
   224, 226, 270, 319, 320
  Ludgate Circus 74
  Marshall Street baths 183
  Minories 74
  Muswell Hill 1
  Paddington station 319, 320
  Royal Exchange 74
  St Paul's cathedral 74
  Selfridge's 121, 155, 183
  Serpentine, lake 224
  South Kensington 21, 155,
   171, 225, 226, 227, 274
  Stoll Theatre 270
  Strand, the 74
  Streatham Hill 21
  Tottenham Court Road 21
  Tower of London 74, 141, 188
  Victoria Station 21, 74
  Windmill theatre 223
  YMCA central hostel 21, 224,
   225
 London Appellate Tribunal 73
 London University 33, 66, 95,
   172, 173, 215, 226, 236,
   259, 264, 268, 277, 279,
   281, 282, 285, 304, 308,
   316, 321, 325
  B.Sc. Economics 215, 224,
   313, 321
  Examination Halls 157, 171
  Library 312
  London School of Economics
   228, 259, 268, 304, 309,
   313, 314
 London, Jack 7, 53
  Scarlet Plague 53
 Long, Jim 231, 246, 248
 Long, John, publisher 284
 Longstanton (Cambs.) 114
 Lordsbridge (Cambs.) 166
 Loughborough College 259,
   260, 262, 263, 265, 275,
   276, 277, 291, 305
 Lubeck 152
 Lucas, Silas (rightly Elias) 125
 Ludman, Mrs 37, 40
 Luton (Beds.) 219
 MacCarthy, Desmond 229
 Macdonald, Jeanette 123
 MacDonald, Malcolm, MP 82
 MacDonald, Ramsay, MP 82, 95
 Macmillan, Lord : *Report on
   Finance and Industry* 213
 Madingley (Cambs.) 182
 Maginot Line 23, 24, 29
 Magnet, The, comic 98
 Man Loaded With Mischief,
   Cambridge Inn sign 125
 Mareth Line 214
 Marlborough, John Churchill,
   1st Duke of 178

Mars 318
Marshall, the Rev. Bernard 33
Marxist theory 15
Maxton, James, MP 62
Mayne, A. B., headmaster of the Cambridgeshire County School for Boys 262, 277
McGovern, John, MP 62
Mediterranean Sea 89
Meldreth (Cambs.) 49
Men Only (magazine) 248
Merseyside 89, 98
Messerschmidt aircraft 44
Meyer, C. B. 7
Middle East 240, 313
Midlands 84, 164
Milan 247
Milton (Cambs.) 218
Ministry of Health 91
Ministry of Labour 96, 183, 214
Mitcham, ---, friend of Jack junior 292
Molotov, Vyacheslav Mikhailovich 245
Mons 9
Montagu, Ivor *Traitor Class* 67
Moore, Mrs 66
Morris, --- 3, 4
Morris, Henry, Director of Education for Cambridgeshire 260, 276
Morrison, Herbert 194
Moscow 24, 25, 116, 123
Moth aircraft 124
Mrs Miniver (film) 200
Muir, Ramsay 31
  How Britain is Governed 163, 164
Muller, Frederick, publisher 262
Murfitt, Mr and Miss 314, 321
Murfitt, Mr, farmer near Royston 196

Mussolini, Benito 205, 234, 238, 317
Napoleon 6, 178
Nassau 216
Nathan, Harry Louis, 1st Baron Nathan 154
National Fire Service 218
National Government 28
National Register 7
National Service 89, 196, 198, 202, 213, 235, 244
National Socialism 267
Nazism 113, 154
neighbours 31, 52, 91, 105, 106, 114, 127, 179, 221, 228, 244, 247, 253, 296, 314–315, 322
Neill, Alexander Sutherland, psychologist and educationalist 56, 250, 251
  Problem Teacher, The 251
  That Dreadful School 250
Newcastle-upon-Tyne 90
Newgate Calendar, The 312
Newmarket (Sfk) 77, 90, 114, 219, 274, 305, 309
News of the World, The 71, 308, 313, 314
New Statesman, The 257, 328
Newton (Cambs.) 46
New Zealand 24, 133
Normandy 272
Norman, Montague Collet 199
North Africa 88, 193, 199, 220, 222
Norway 23, 101, 304
Norwich (Norf.) 152
Nuremberg 100, 199, 237, 302
Nutter, J. 256, 266, 267
Oakington (Cambs.) 98, 104, 110, 111, 114, 115, 168, 242
Oaks, the, horse-race 274, 309

345

Observer, The 328
Oder, river 296, 297
Odessa 116
Once a crook (film) 133
One of our aircraft is missing (film) 182
Orel 235
Orwell (Cambs.) 183
Ottawa 136
Ouse, river 180
Overhill, Albert, nephew of the diarist 9, 85
Overhill, Bill, nephew of the diarist 23
Overhill, Charles, uncle of the diarist 97
Overhill, Eliza, mother of the diarist 85, 86, 98
Overhill, Ellington Thomas (E.T.O.), father of the diarist 9, 16, 18, 47, 85, 90, 96, 97, 98, 103, 192
Overhill, Fred, brother of the diarist 7, 16, 17, 18, 25, 26, 54, 57, 63, 67, 78, 83, 89, 90, 97, 137, 151, 170, 192, 196, 198, 279, 305
  his daughter 90
Overhill, Fred, son of the diarist's brother Fred 17, 192, 196, 198
Overhill, Henry ('Nap'), brother of the diarist 47
Overhill, Henry, nephew of the diarist 9, 189
  Olive, his wife 189
Overhill, Jack
  arguments 10, 123, 129, 170–171, 172–173, 183, 248, 285, 287–288, 289, 300
  as a radical 8, 15, 31, 46, 48, 127, 208, 209, 211, 221, 227, 238–239, 244, 265–267, 312–313, 313, 315, 317
  attitudes to Britain 7, 67, 77, 83–82, 88, 92, 94, 103, 108, 125, 130, 131–133, 142–141, 149, 178, 183, 188, 192, 192–200, 194, 195, 197, 209, 210, 255–256, 313, 316, 325, 328
  bookmaking 3, 6, 12, 27, 42, 44, 53, 66, 72, 92, 100, 103, 217, 225, 268, 271, 274, 275, 282, 304, 305, 309, 310, 324, 327, 329, 331
  compassion 28, 41, 142, 164, 179, 186–185, 231, 323
  conscientious objector (CO) 6, 9, 10, 13, 16, 17, 29, 87, 92, 93, 95, 96, 118, 124, 149–148, 170, 183, 191, 192, 198, 204, 205, 206, 209–210, 215–216, 236, 238–237, 247, 255–256, 263, 264, 265–267, 285, 286–287, 290, 292, 301, 325
  diary 14, 147, 188, 201, 329, 330
  dogs 5, 8, 10, 12, 29, 32, 48, 49, 58, 61, 62, 64, 72, 83, 87, 93, 100, 108, 119, 123, 124, 125, 128, 135, 137, 138, 139, 140, 150, 152, 153, 170, 194, 197, 204, 209, 210, 212, 219, 221, 227, 233, 237, 254, 256, 257, 262, 263, 269, 270, 272, 273, 275, 276, 282, 286, 295, 304, 305, 315, 316, 318, 320, 326, 327, 328, 329
  dreams 137, 162, 232, 238
  examinations 21, 22, 170, 170–171, 172–173, 180,

186, 204, 206, 209, 221, 224, 225, 226, 227, 228, 232, 234, 235, 236, 272, 272-273, 273, 273-275, 275, 277, 278, 279, 281, 304, 308, 309-311, 313, 314, 315, 316, 317, 321-322, 325-326, 329
farming 3, 4, 5, 6
firewatching 69, 78, 83, 88, 89, 98, 99, 118, 120, 139, 177, 181, 189, 204, 205, 207, 208, 210, 213, 217, 218, 219, 223, 231, 239, 240, 242, 243, 246, 248, 250, 251, 253, 256, 259, 261, 262, 264, 270, 271, 274, 275, 278
health 90, 123, 175, 200, 206, 234, 235, 252, 263, 273, 323, 328
houses 4, 5, 6, 7, 9, 12, 13, 14, 23, 65, 118, 125, 129-130, 154, 161, 203, 204, 258, 260, 276, 310, 325, 326, 327, 330
job searches 16
money 4, 5, 7, 12, 16, 25, 27, 29, 31, 32, 46, 60, 62, 64, 72, 82, 102, 103, 106, 123, 127, 162, 166, 258, 270, 275, 281, 297, 327, 329
morality 220, 297
national service 87, 214, 219, 237
neuroses 17, 109, 119, 124, 156, 165, 269, 270
novels
 'Adolescence' 100, 284, 286
 'Big Bastard, The', AKA 'The Chancer', AKA , 'The Cordwainer' 87, 98, 104

'Bob Carter — Carrier' or 'The Fen Tiger' 296
'Book of June. The' 249, 252
'Chancer, The', previously 'The Big Bastard', AKA 'The Cordwainer' 104
'Children Can't be Told' 206
Cordwainer, The, previously 'The Big Bastard', then 'The Chancer' 111, 122, 125, 134, 139, 145, 146, 148, 170, 229, 231, 241, 248, 249, 250, 254, 257, 258, 260, 261, 262, 284, 327
'Finger in the Pie' 258, 277, 291, 293, 299, 301, 308
'He Couldn't Leave the Pretty Girls Alone' 209, 229
'Jim Baxter — Snob' 18, 21, 22, 25, 26, 54
'Judas Stain' AKA 'Stain of Judas' 229, 235, 237, 245, 249, 252, 254, 258
'Kiss of Judas, The', AKA 'Sins of the Father' 197, 206
Miller of Trumpington, The 291, 308, 311, 312, 315, 317, 328, 329, 330
'No Bed of Roses' 87, 116
'Only Begotten Son' 235, 249
'Prisoner in the Pie' 191
'Queen Street' 173
Romantic Youth 18
'Sins of the Father' AKA 'Kiss of Judas' 206, 296
'Square Peg' 231, 235
'Stain of Judas' AKA 'Judas Stain' 206
'Tale of a Taylor' 88, 102, 218, 248, 250, 327

Overhill, Jack, novels (cont'd)
   'Tormented Flesh' 69
   'Whims of the Father' 161,
      206, 249, 291, 301, 306, 329
  Pitman Certificated Teacher
     277
  public spiritedness 282, 308,
     314
  reading 8, 17, 53, 72, 111, 114,
     141, 150, 160, 181, 184,
     208, 209, 212, 237, 240,
     250, 251, 254, 259, 264,
     295, 311, 315, 316, 317
  reminiscences 6, 13, 47, 109,
     121, 147, 151, 161–162,
     165, 174, 184, 189, 208,
     224, 269, 284, 323
  shoe repairs 6, 7, 9, 10, 12, 13,
     21, 22, 28, 37, 48, 49, 50,
     54–55, 58, 64, 83, 87, 96,
     98, 101, 108, 116, 121, 127,
     129, 138, 139, 140, 141,
     143, 144, 145, 146, 147,
     151, 152, 153, 154, 156,
     161, 162, 165, 168, 169,
     176, 178, 179, 180, 181,
     182, 184, 185, 188, 189,
     190, 191, 192, 198, 204,
     205, 207, 208, 212, 214–
     215, 220, 222, 227, 230,
     231, 232, 233, 237, 241,
     243, 246, 249, 251, 253,
     254, 257, 259, 261, 263,
     265, 266, 271, 275, 277,
     278, 283, 284, 285, 289,
     293, 296, 299, 300, 301,
     310, 319, 321, 329, 329
  social diffidence 255
  study 1, 10, 12, 13, 17, 25, 26,
     28, 33, 40, 50, 55, 66, 69,
     72, 74, 76, 77, 87, 95, 106,
     108, 118, 119, 121, 126,
     127, 129, 135, 136, 137,
     138, 141, 143, 144, 145,
     149, 151, 153, 154, 155,
     156–158, 159, 161, 172–
     173, 176, 189, 203, 207,
     212, 213, 214, 218, 219,
     222, 223, 224, 225, 226,
     227, 252, 254, 257, 258,
     259, 260, 264, 265, 269,
     270, 271, 273, 274, 275,
     285, 288, 296, 300, 301,
     303, 305, 309, 316, 330, 331
  swimming 12, 21, 25, 32, 38,
     41, 64, 72, 92, 105, 107,
     108, 109, 114, 119, 126,
     128, 138, 153, 159, 164,
     176, 180, 181, 183, 199,
     200, 204, 207, 218, 221,
     222, 228, 231, 234, 249,
     251, 254, 263, 270, 277,
     282, 293, 296, 305, 315,
     316, 317, 319, 327, 328
  'Swimming for Fun' (book)
     319, 321, 323, 324, 325,
     326, 327, 329
  views on religion 115, 228,
     231, 238–239, 243, 255
  views on the war 1, 7, 9, 12,
     14, 15, 17, 23–24, 26–27,
     28, 29, 30, 31, 41, 42,
     46–47, 52, 58, 61, 67, 73,
     84, 86, 88, 92, 93, 99, 103,
     105, 107, 110, 112–113,
     116, 118, 120, 123, 127,
     128, 131–133, 138, 140,
     141, 145, 146, 149, 151,
     153, 154, 159, 161, 166,
     167, 168, 169, 175, 177,
     178, 185, 186, 187, 192,
     193, 194, 195, 197, 199,
     205, 208, 211, 212, 213,
     214, 215, 217, 220, 222,

233, 234, 245, 246, 247,
248, 262, 268, 268-269,
270, 299, 301, 303
writing 12, 18, 21, 22, 25,
26, 28, 31, 33, 39, 43, 44,
47, 48, 49, 50, 53, 54, 55,
60, 63, 64, 69, 71, 75, 77,
84, 86, 88, 98, 101, 102,
104, 105, 108, 111, 116,
118, 121, 122, 124, 125,
126, 127, 128, 129, 133,
134, 137, 138, 139, 144,
145, 146, 148, 149, 159,
160, 163, 170, 176, 177,
180, 181, 182, 184, 185,
186, 189, 191, 192, 194,
197, 198, 204, 206, 207,
208-209, 211, 212, 214,
229, 229-231, 231, 233,
234, 235-236, 237, 239,
240, 241, 245, 248, 249,
249-250, 252, 254, 257,
258, 260-261, 262, 264,
275, 277, 278, 279, 280,
281, 282, 283, 284, 286,
291, 292, 293, 295, 298,
299, 300-301, 306, 308,
311, 312, 315, 317, 321,
324, 325, 326, 327, 328,
329, 330, 331
Overhill, Jack, son of the diarist
1, 4, 7, 9, 10, 13, 22, 25,
26, 28, 30, 32, 33, 38, 45,
49, 51, 52, 53, 55, 56, 58,
59, 60, 63, 65, 66, 71, 72,
74, 75, 77, 80-81, 82, 89,
93, 98, 105, 107, 114, 115,
117, 118, 119, 122, 123,
127, 130, 134, 135, 136,
137, 139, 141, 145, 150,
156, 164, 165, 166, 170,
179, 182, 184, 185, 187,
189, 191, 196, 197, 199,
204, 207, 208, 209, 210,
213, 214, 216, 219, 220,
224, 225, 226, 232, 233,
234, 235, 236, 237, 240,
241, 251, 258, 259, 260,
262, 263, 265, 275, 277,
278-279, 291-292, 295,
297, 305, 309, 317, 318,
319, 322, 324, 325
Overhill, Jess, daughter of the
diarist 3, 26, 28, 30, 31,
32, 43, 45, 50, 53, 58, 59,
60, 64, 65, 66, 71, 72, 74,
80-81, 83, 93, 96, 100, 101,
102, 110, 111, 126, 127,
128, 135, 137, 138, 139,
140, 148, 150, 151, 153,
154, 159, 165, 166, 170,
176, 178, 181, 182, 184,
185, 190, 198, 199, 202,
210, 213, 217, 218, 219,
232, 233, 235, 238, 240,
247, 250, 251, 257, 258,
261-262, 262, 268, 273,
276, 282, 285, 286, 292,
295, 297, 298, 299, 302,
303, 305, 308, 315, 316,
321, 322, 323-324, 326,
329, 329
Overhill, Jess, wife of the diarist
1, 4, 5, 8, 10, 12, 13, 14, 18,
26, 27, 28, 31, 32, 33, 37,
38, 43, 45, 48, 49, 50, 51,
52, 53, 58, 59, 60, 61, 62,
63, 64, 65, 66, 71, 73, 74,
77, 80-81, 84, 85, 86, 90,
91, 93, 94, 95, 96, 98, 100,
102, 103, 106, 107, 108,
109, 110, 111, 112, 114,
117, 118, 119, 121, 123,
124, 125, 126, 127, 134,

Overhill, Jess, wife of the diarist (cont'd) 135, 137, 140, 141, 142, 144, 145, 148, 149, 150, 151, 153, 155, 156, 157, 158, 159, 161, 162, 164, 165, 166, 167, 168, 175, 182, 184, 185, 187, 188, 189, 190, 191, 193, 195, 196, 199, 200, 201, 203, 204, 205, 207, 208, 210, 212, 215, 219, 222, 225, 226, 229, 232, 233, 234, 235, 236, 237, 238, 239, 244, 249, 251, 253, 256, 257, 258, 260, 262, 269, 270, 271, 273, 274, 275, 279, 282, 284, 286, 292, 295, 296, 297, 298, 299, 300, 302, 303, 305, 306, 308, 310, 313, 315, 316, 320, 321, 322, 323, 324, 325, 326, 327, 329, 330
   Gladys, sister of 6, 85, 111
her brother in law 301
Overhill?, John (surname unknown), nephew of the diarist 200
Overhill, Liz, wife of Fred, brother of the diarist 305
Overhill, Mabel, sister of the diarist 85
Overhill, Percy, brother of the diarist 47, 109, 165
Overhill?, Roland, (surname unknown), nephew of the diarist 228, 236, 322
Overhill, Tom, brother of the diarist 27, 63, 123
Oxford 13, 74, 82, 94, 154, 161, 163, 164, 195
Pacific 140, 175, 190, 318

Palme Dutt, Rajani
   World Politics 1918–1938 132
Parliament 82, 83, 93, 103, 146, 154, 158, 159, 163, 186, 277
Partridge, Jean 233
Pas de Calais 283
Paul, Harry 116, 117, 124
Pavlov, Ivan 239
Peace News 17, 46, 192, 207, 213, 262
Peace Pledge Union 286, 287
Pearn, Pollinger and Higham, literary agents 301
Penguin New Writing 111
People's Convention 108
Pepys, Samuel, *Diary* 160, 181
Pioneer Corps 74
Pitt, William, the younger 258
Poland 92
Poles 216, 245, 304
Ponsonby, Arthur, 1st Baron Ponsonby 216
Portsmouth 90
Postgate, Raymond
   Common People, The 254
Potton (Beds) 49
prices, rationing and shortages 7, 9, 25, 48, 51, 56, 61–62, 63, 64, 66, 69, 72, 74, 77, 84, 85, 89, 90, 91, 94, 95, 98, 101, 102, 103, 104, 106, 107, 108, 110, 111, 112, 113, 114, 115, 116, 118, 121, 125, 127, 128, 130, 134, 137, 138, 139, 140, 143, 146, 147, 150, 153, 154, 155, 159, 164, 166, 169, 177, 179, 181, 183, 185, 189, 190, 195, 201, 202, 205, 207, 213, 219, 222–223, 229, 239, 244, 246, 247, 251, 256, 275,

282, 286, 288, 289, 290, 291, 297, 308, 317, 323
Prudential Insurance Co. 155, 187
public assistance 7
Quick, Peter 229, 230, 231, 236
Quy (Cambs.) 300
Rampton (Cambs.) 111
Ramsey (Hunts.) 188
Ramsgate (Kent) 188
Raven, Charles, Regius Professor of Divinity 128, 129
Reader (or Reeder), Mary 125
Red Army 209
Red Cross 308
Remarque, Erich Maria
   All Quiet on the Western Front 134
Reynolds' News 15, 91
Robeson, Paul 51
Robinson, Joan, economist 207
Robinson, P. R., headmaster of Trumpington school 151
Rodwell, Miss, gym teacher 166
Rogers, Thorold
   Six Centuries of Work and Wages 213
Roget, Peter Mark, John Lewis and Samuel Romilly
   Thesaurus of English Words and Phrases 135, 197
Romania 282
Rommel, Erwin 88, 140, 159, 193
Roosevelt, Frank Delano 67, 112, 113, 122, 205, 301
Roses of Picardy (song) 288
Rossi, Claudio, Italian prisoner of war 247, 264, 283, 287, 297, 298, 300, 32
Rostock 152

Rostov 130
Rowe, Bill, communist 148
Rowe, Bob 305
Royal Air Force 37, 41, 52, 59, 62, 63, 71, 77, 91, 98, 109, 133, 152, 158, 177, 179, 182, 205, 209, 214, 264, 300, 305, 316
Royal Air Force Volunteer Reserve 164
Royal Army Medical Corps 132, 267, 268
Royal Life Saving Society 308, 314, 317
Royal Observer Corps 81
RSPCA (Royal Society for the Protection of Animals) 308
Russell, Bertrand 285
Russia 23, 8, 15, 17, 25, 46, 51, 53, 71, 75, 82, 84, 100, 104, 105, 110, 113, 116, 118, 119, 120, 123, 127, 128, 130, 138, 141, 153, 163, 175, 185, 193, 194, 197, 208, 211, 214, 217, 226, 232, 237, 240, 244, 245, 270, 285, 304, 313, 314, 316, 318
Russians 107, 116, 127, 130, 154, 161, 169, 188, 194, 195, 202, 205, 208, 214, 282, 293, 296, 297, 302, 303
Rutherford, Ernest, Lord 317
Rutherford, Mark, pseud. (William Hale White)
   Autobiography 208, 209
Ryder, Jack 202
Ryvita 243, 246, 247, 254, 320
Sadleir, Michael 33, 88, 98, 102, 139, 144, 223, 229, 230, 257, 329

Sadleir, Michael, novels
  Fanny by Gaslight 33
  Privilege 223
Saffron Walden (Essex) 25, 42
St Nazaire 150
St Neots (Hunts.) 180
St Pierre, Bernardin de
  Paul et Virginie 72
Sale, Alan and Mrs 179
Salerno 240
Salute the Soldier Week 268
Salvation Army 249, 255, 319
Sanderson, Mr 264, 271, 275
Saturday Social, The, journal 149
Sayers, Richard Sidney
  Modern Banking 213
Schacht, Hjalmar 199
Scotland 100, 179
Scotsmen 48
Scots Guards 305
Sebastopol 159, 161
Second Front 116, 120, 149, 167, 186, 207, 212, 222, 233, 262, 268, 270, 271, 272
Serbia 89
Shakespeare, William 83, 230
  A Midsummer Night's Dream 286
  King Lear 83
Shaw, George Bernard 301
  Cashel Byron's Profession 328
  Everybody's Political What's What 292
  Major Barbara 115
Sheffield 64, 83, 257
Shelford (Cambs.) 3
Shelley, Percy Bysshe 213
Sicily 232, 234, 235
Siegfried Line 1, 61, 283
Sindall, Miss, deliverer of *Peace News* 213
Singapore 133, 135, 141, 142, 143, 304

Smithy Fen (Cambs.) 4, 111
Smolensk 214
Snelson, Ken 187
Soham (Cambs.) 271
Solomon Islands 175, 190
Sommerville family, tenants at Shelford Road 324
Song to remember, A (film) 305
Son of Lassie, The (film) 327
Son of Tarzan (film) 18
Southampton 60
Spanish Civil War 46, 284
Spitfire aircraft 27, 38, 41, 44, 167, 217
SS *Athenia* 15, 16
Stalingrad 181, 185, 186, 188, 190, 194, 205, 214, 224
Stalin, Joseph 25, 148, 185, 205
Stapledon, Olaf
  Last and First Men 8
Star, The, newspaper 223
Steeple Morden (Cambs.) 283
Steinbeck, John
  Of Mice and Men (film of novel) 39
Stirling bombers 104, 168
Stone, Irving
  Sailor on Horseback 14
Student Prince, The, operetta 270
Sunday Dispatch, The 59
Swaffer, Hannen 196
Symonds, Arthur L., Labour MP for Cambridge 313
Temple, William, Archbishop of Canterbury 182
Thinkers' Library 92
Third Reich 99, 128
Those Kids from Town (film) 208
Tobruk 159
Toulon 195

Tressell, Robert,
  The Ragged Trousered Philanthropists 46
Trumpington (Cambs.) 107, 312
  Shelford Road 3, 4, 6, 9, 12, 13, 14, 65, 116, 118, 154, 203, 258, 310, 325, 326
  School 151
Tuffnell, Richard, Tory MP for Cambridge 313
Tunis 220
Tunisia 205, 214
Turkey 313
Turpin, Dick 303, 312
U-boats 9, 57, 58
United States of America 46, 61, 64, 71, 113, 128, 131, 161, 217, 220, 222, 262, 285, 309, 323, 32
Varley, Don 138, 182, 186, 189, 190, 195, 197, 202, 203, 206, 207, 208, 209, 211, 212, 223, 227, 228, 233, 235, 238, 240, 243, 257, 258, 265, 288, 299
V-Day 304, 305
V-E (Victory in Europe) Day 304, 305, 309
V-J celebrations 320
Voltaire 18
Voluntary Aid Detachment (VAD) 308
von Jagow, Gottlieb 265, 266
von Rundstedt, [Karl Rudolf] Gerd 293
Wales 1
Walker, Kenneth
  Physiology of Sex 55
Wallace, Edgar 145, 251, 252, 254
  biography by Margaret Lane 251, 252

The Flying Fifty-five 145
War Agricultural Committee 231
war, course of the 1, 15, 23, 23–24, 37, 46, 57, 61, 71, 85, 88, 89, 93, 96, 97, 101, 102, 104, 105, 112, 113, 121, 122, 128, 130, 131, 140, 141, 142, 143, 149, 150, 152, 153, 154, 155, 159, 161, 163, 175, 177, 178, 181, 185, 186, 188, 190, 191, 193, 194, 195, 202, 205, 214, 218, 220, 221, 222, 224, 228, 231, 232, 234, 235, 237, 238, 240, 244, 245, 253, 262, 271–272, 278, 281, 282, 283, 288, 290, 293, 296, 297, 298, 300, 302, 302–303, 303, 304, 317, 318, 320, 323
Ward, Dudley 328
Warship Week 131
Wash, the 268
Waterbeach (Cambs.) 77, 84, 98, 122, 131, 242
Waters, C. M.
  An Economic History of England 269
Watson, Jerry, schoolmaster 208
Webb, Billy 30
Webb, Mr ---, window-cleaner 119
Week, The 75
Weimar Republic 316
Wells, Herbert George 5, 14, 17, 18, 32, 45, 46, 71, 86, 176, 195, 319
  Outline of History 5
  Fate of Homo Sapiens 45, 4
  Science of Life, The 176

White, William Hale, see Rutherford, Mark 208
Wilburton (Cambs.) 218
Wilkinson, ---, firewatcher 246
Williams, J. M. 290
Williams, Mrs 34, 271
Williams, Ronnie 39
Williamson, Henry
 Beautiful Years, The 198, 203
 Dandelion Days 203
 Dream of Fair Women, The 216
 Flax of dream, The 203
Wolsey Hall, correspondence college, Oxford 66, 172, 173, 226, 228, 235, 275
Women's Voluntary Service 187
Wonfer, Cecil 186, 301
Wonfer, Mrs, mother of Cecil 185
Wood, Dr Alex 92, 93, 95, 129, 163, 285, 287
Woolton, Lord, Minister for Food 87
Workers' Educational Association 172
World News and Views, journal 148
Wyndham, Richard 313
York 152
Ziegfeld Girl (film) 131
Zilliacus, Konni, MP 24
 Why we are Losing the Peace (or *Between Two Wars*) 24
Zola, Emile 18